HRD in Small Organisations

Small organisations are of growing importance as a source of employment opportunities, and yet HRD in small organisations is a neglected field of study. This book aims to redress this deficiency, providing a comprehensive and contemporary review of research into the practice of HRD in small organisations.

The book is divided into three sections for easier reference. The focus of part one is on the context of HRD research in small organisations, the contextual characteristics of small organisations and the implications of these for the design and conduct of research into HRD practices. Chapters in part two report the results of research that inform an understanding of approaches to HRD, including recent ones such as those based on developments in information and communications technology. The third part is concerned with HRD methods as they are applied and practised, and examines constructs such as mentoring and coaching.

All of the chapters are based on recent or current research. There is, however, diversity in the methodological assumptions informing the structure of the research - resulting in a reflection of the eclectic nature of HRD research and writing.

HRD in Small Organisations will be of essential interest to students, academics and policy advisers within the fields of HRD and HRM.

Jim Stewart is Professor of Human Resource Development at Nottingham Business School. An active researcher and writer for many years, Jim is the single or joint author of many articles and books in the HRD field, including three others in this series, and is UK Editor of *Human Resource Development International*.

Graham Beaver is Professor of Corporate Strategy and Business Development at Nottingham Business School and is responsible for much of the academic research on business growth and strategic management, particularly as it affects small and emerging enterprises in the economy. He is a founding Editorial Board member of the journal, *Small Business and Enterprise Development* and the Editor of the International Management Journal, *Strategic Change*.

Routledge Studies in Human Resource Development

Edited by Monica Lee
Lancaster University, UK

HRD theory is changing rapidly. Recent advances in theory and practice, how we conceive of organisations and of the world of knowledge, have led to the need to reinterpret the field. This series aims to reflect and foster the development of HRD as an emergent discipline.

Encompassing a range of different international, organisational, methodological and theoretical perspectives, the series promotes theoretical controversy and reflective practice.

1 Policy Matters
Flexible learning and organizational change
Edited by Viktor Jakupec and Robin Usher

2 Science Fiction and Organization
Edited by Warren Smith, Matthew Higgins, Martin Parker and Geoff Lightfoot

3 HRD and Learning Organisations in Europe
Challenges for professionals
Edited by Saskia Tjepkema, Jim Stewart, Sally Sambrook, Martin Mulder, Hilde ter Horst and Jaap Scheerens

4 Interpreting the Maternal Organisation
Edited by Heather Höpfl and Monika Kostera

5 Work Process Knowledge
Edited by Nick Boreham, Renan Samurçay and Martin Fischer

6 HRD in a Complex World
Edited by Monica Lee

7 HRD in Small Organisations
Research and practice
Edited by Jim Stewart and Graham Beaver

8 New Frontiers in Human Resource Development
Edited by Jean Woodall, Monica Lee and Jim Stewart

9 Human Resources, Care-Giving, Career Progression and Gender
A gender neutral glass ceiling
Beulah S. Coyne, Edward J. Coyne, Sr. and Monica Lee

Also published in the series in paperback:

Action Research in Organisations
Jean McNiff, accompanied by Jack Whitehead

Understanding Human Resource Development
A research-based approach
Edited by Jim Stewart, Jim McGoldrick and Sandra Watson

HRD in Small Organisations

Research and practice

**Edited by Jim Stewart and
Graham Beaver**

 Routledge
Taylor & Francis Group

LONDON AND NEW YORK

First published 2004
by Routledge
2 Park Square, Milton Park, Abingdon, Oxon, OX14 4RN

Simultaneously published in the USA and Canada
by Routledge
270 Madison Avenue, New York, NY 10016

Transferred to Digital Printing 2004

Routledge is an imprint of the Taylor & Francis Group

© 2004 Editorial matter and selection, Jim Stewart and Graham Beaver;
individual chapters, the contributors

Typeset in Baskerville by
BOOK NOW Ltd
Printed and bound in Great Britain by
Antony Rowe Ltd, Chippenham, Wiltshire

British Library Cataloguing in Publication Data
A catalogue record for this book is available from the British Library

Library of Congress Cataloging in Publication Data
A catalog record for this book has been requested

ISBN 0-415-29960-8

Contents

Figures

Tables

Contributors

Jim Stewart leads the HRD group of academics at Nottingham Business School and is joint course leader of the school's highly successful Doctorate in Business Administration. An active researcher and writer for many years, Jim is the single or joint author of many articles and books in the HRD field, including three others in this series. He holds three national roles with the CIPD, is UK editor of *Human Resource Development International*, reviews editor of the *International Journal of Training and Development* and also Chair of the University Forum for HRD. Jim was co-award holder, with Professors Jean Woodall and Monica Lee, of the ESRC Research Seminar Series on human resource development.

Graham Beaver is responsible for much of the academic research on business growth and strategic management at Nottingham Business School, particularly as it affects small and emerging enterprises in the economy. He is a founding editorial board member of the journal, *Small Business and Enterprise Development* (and reviews editor from 1996- 9) and the editor of the international management journal, *Strategic Change*, now in its twelfth year of publication. Graham is a Fellow of the Centre for SMEs at Warwick Business School and a Visiting Lecturer to Warwick, Cranfield, Sheffield and Brunel University Business Schools. He has recently been appointed Adjunct Professor to the School of Management, Queensland University of Technology, Brisbane, Australia.

David Devins is a Principal Research Fellow at the Policy Research Institute (PRI), Leeds Metropolitan University. Following a number of years working in the private sector, David joined the PRI where he has researched a variety of issues associated with small and medium sized enterprises and contributed to the development of policy and practice at the local and national level. His current research interests lie in researching the small firm learning context and wider workforce development activities and business support.

Elaine Eades is Programme Director of the BA (Human Resource Management) at the University of Liverpool Management School. A Fellow of the Chartered Institute of Personnel and Development, she was Lead Academic for the first HR-based Teaching Company Scheme Project in the UK, sited in the small manufacturing company which is the subject of the case study in this text. She has been involved in a range of HR consultancy and management development activities with small companies across a variety of sectors.

Thomas N. Garavan is a lecturer with the Department of Personnel and Employment Relations at the University of Limerick, Ireland. Thomas lectures in training and development, human resource development and vocational training and education. His research interests include training design, 360-degree feedback processes, management development processes, stakeholder approaches to training management and management development centre processes. He is the editor of the *Journal of European Industrial Training* and associate editor of *Human Resource Development International*. He is co-author of *Training and Development in Ireland: Context, Policy and Practice* and *The Irish Safety and Health Handbook*.

Jeff Gold is Principal Lecturer in the School of Economics and Human Resource Management at Leeds Business School. He is a founding member of the school's HRD unit, which specialises in research, consultancy and training relating to various themes in Organisation and Strategic Learning. Jeff's recent projects include the creation of strategic learning partnerships with a number of private sector organisations. He has also acted as an adviser to the Professions Working Group of the Council for Excellence in Management and Leadership. Jeff is the co-author with John Bratton of *Human Resource Management: Theory and Practice*, now in its third edition.

Claire Gubbins is a doctoral candidate at the University of Limerick and is researching the career outcomes of HRD professionals using a social capital perspective. She lectures in the areas of human resource development, human resource management and organisational behaviour at the University of Limerick. Claire is a graduate member of the Chartered Institute of Personnel and Development. She is co-author of the second edition of *Training and Development in Ireland: Context, Policy and Practice*, a leading textbook in the field of training and human resource management in Ireland.

John Hamblett is a Senior Lecturer at Leeds Metropolitan University Business School. His research interests concern the relationship between developments in the regulation of social relations in the workplace and lifelong learning.

Rosemary Hill is an independent HR consultant and researcher specialising in individual and organisation development across a wide range of industry sectors. Her PhD research explored human resource development in small organisations. Rosemary is currently working on a number of strategic HR projects within central UK government and the Civil Service. Rosemary is a Visiting Fellow in the department of HRM at the Nottingham Business School and an associate lecturer with the Liverpool Business School at Liverpool John Moores University.

Rick Holden is Principal Lecturer and Head of the Human Resource Development Unit at Leeds Metropolitan University. Before moving to Leeds, Rick was a personnel and training officer with Cadbury Schweppes plc and a lecturer at Newcastle College of Arts and Technology. His research interests include workplace learning and the SME graduate labour market. He is editor of the MCB Emerald Journal *Education and Training*.

Gill Homan is a Senior Lecturer in HRM specialising in the areas of reward systems, development and organisational learning. Recent research has included two ESF funded projects into the management development needs of owner-managers in SMEs, while current research involves SME responses to equality and pay. As Chair of the Manchester Branch of the CIPD 2001- 3, Gill has been heavily involved in the establishment of a number of SME development networks.

Kate Hutchings is a Senior Lecturer in the School of Management, Queensland University of Technology, Australia and holds a PhD from the University of Queensland. She specialises in international HRM and cross-cultural manage-ment. Kate held a prior appointment at the University of Queensland, has taught short courses in Malaysia and China, and has had visiting appointments at Rutgers University, USA, and Copenhagen Business School, Denmark. She is active in four professional associations and is a reviewer for three international journals in Australia and Europe. She is currently undertaking research on networking in Australian organisations in China and knowledge sharing in China and Russia.

Paul Iles is Head of the Centre for Leadership and Organisational Change and Professor of Strategic HRM at Teesside Business School. A chartered psychologist, associate Fellow of the British Psychological Society and Fellow of the CIPD, Paul has published extensively on management assessment and development, HRD, career development, organisational learning and develop-ment, knowledge management, diversity and international HRM. He is currently working on knowledge management, leadership and organisational change in the North East of England and in China and on international joint ventures and alliances. In recent years he has been a visiting professor at the Universities of Paris, Mauritius and Bautou, China, and is an associate editor of *Organisational Transformation and Social Change* as well as being on the editorial advisory board of the *Journal of Managerial Psychology*.

Jonathan Lean is a Senior Lecturer in Strategic Management at the University of Plymouth Business School and also MBA Programme Director. His PhD research examined training and business support provision for micro-firms in peripheral areas. He has published in the areas of small business management and training/support provision and policy.

Alma McCarthy is a Lecturer in the Department of Management in the Faculty of Commerce at the National University of Ireland at Galway. She lectures in human resource management, organisational behaviour and human resource development. Her areas of research interest include 360-degree feedback processes, work- life balance, management development, development centre processes and appraisal and performance management systems.

Juliet McMahon is a lecturer at the University of Limerick, Ireland. Her main research interest is in the area of small enterprise. She was a founder member of the Small Firms Research Unit at the university and completed a PhD exploring employment relations in small Irish Enterprises. Current interests include employee voice and management of conflict in small enterprises.

David Megginson is at Sheffield Hallam University where he is Professor of HRD. He is co-Chair (with Sir John Whitmore) of the European Mentoring and Coaching Council. David is co-author of *Mentoring Executives and Directors, Cultivating Self-development, Mentoring in Action, Human Resource Development, Line Manager as Developer, Developing the Developers Report, Organisational Learning in Surveying Organisations* and *Self-development: A Facilitator's Guide.* He is series editor of Kogan Page's Fast-track MBA series. David consults with voluntary and public bodies (including the Public Service Leaders' Scheme, Addenbrookes Hospital and Kings, Guys and Thomas's Hospital Trust) and a number of blue chip companies. His current research and writing interests include continuous professional development of managers and professionals.

Clare Rigg is Lecturer in Public Leadership and Organisation Change at the School of Public Policy at the University of Birmingham. Following a number of years in local urban regeneration she worked at the University of Central England Business School in management development. Her research is into the inter-relations between individual learning and organisational development.

Eugene Sadler-Smith is Professor of Human Resource Development at the University of Plymouth Business School. His research is concerned with human resource development in a range of contexts but with a particular consideration for employees in smaller firms and the use of technology-based learning methods. In addition to mainstream HRD research, Eugene has long-standing interest in managers' thinking and learning styles. Before becoming an academic in 1994 he was a training manager in a large public utility organisation.

Sally Sambrook studied and worked at Nottingham Business School for eight years before joining the University of Wales Bangor in 1999, retaining links with Nottingham as a Visiting Research Fellow. Sally was appointed as Project Manager in the Centre for Learning Development on a research project exploring the quality of computer-based learning materials. After two years as Lecturer in HRM, she joined the School of Nursing, where she teaches research methods on the BSc and MSc degree programmes. Prior to her academic career, Sally trained as a nurse and became involved in training other nurses and in general personnel management. Consequently, her research interests include studying HRD within the health service. In addition, Sally researches the changing role of HRD professionals, managers and learners and explores the factors influencing learning in work. Sally has published numerous journal articles, edited texts and book chapters on HRD.

Sue Shaw is Head of Postgraduate Programmes at Manchester Metropolitan

University Business School. She entered academic life after a number of years working as an HR practitioner in manufacturing and wholesaling. She is actively engaged with the Chartered Institute of Personnel and Development and serves on its national Membership and Education Committee. She is currently researching aspects of people performance and her other research interests extend to HR careers and women in management.

Vikki Smith is a Development Adviser at the Learning and Skills Development Agency. She works within the Support for Success programme, funded by the Learning and Skills Council, which aims to support providers across the post-16 sector to improve quality and learner outcomes. The particular focus of her work is the management of a series of action research projects, whereby providers introduce a new dimension to their provision with a view to improving learner retention and achievement.

Paul Stokes is a Senior Lecturer in OB/HRM within the School of Business and Finance at Sheffield Hallam University. He is an experienced researcher and consultant within the Mentoring and Coaching Research Group as well being the Route Leader for the MSc in Mentoring and Coaching degree. His publications and research interests are focused on knowledge management, organisational learning and counselling within mentoring. Paul is the co-ordinator for the Voluntary Sector Mentoring Network at the university.

Scott Taylor is a Lecturer in Organizational Behaviour in the International Management and Organization Group at Birmingham Business School, University of Birmingham. He studied people management in smaller companies for his doctorate at Manchester Metropolitan University. Scott is currently researching Investors in People, spirituality at work and corporate university initiatives. Recent publications on these topics can be found in *Journal of Management Studies, Journal of Management Education* and *Organization*.

Richard Thorpe is Professor of Management at Manchester Metropolitan Business School. Following a number of years working in manufacturing industry, Richard joined the Pay and Reward Centre at Strathclyde University Business School researching into payment systems. Later at Glasgow University, he changed his research focus to small and medium sized firm growth and development taking part in the ESRC evolution of business knowledge initiative, leading a project that focuses on examining small firms as activity systems.

Denise Thursfield is a Senior Lecturer at Leeds Metropolitan University Business School. Her research interests are in the areas of skills and the relationship between work and learning. More recently her research has focused on developing an historical dimension to the study of work and learning through analysis of Independent Working Class Education in the early twentieth century.

Kiran Trehan is Head of Department of Management and Human Resourcing at the University of Central England, where she undertakes research, teaching and consultancy with a variety of public and private sector organisations in the area of human resource and organisational development. More recently, her research interests have been in the area of small business development, with a particular focus in HRD. Her fields of interest include critical approaches to HRD, management learning and power and emotions in organisational development. Her current research interests include critical thinking in HRD and critical reflection with particular reference to power, knowledge and control.

Alison Wilson has been actively involved in managing research projects, focusing on small businesses, for Manchester Metropolitan University Business School since 1999. Alison is currently managing an ERDF project directed at building managerial capability in small firms. Research interests include management development in the small business sector and equal opportunities. She is a member of the Small Firms Enterprise Development Initiative Research Advisory Group.

Maurice Yolles is an Associate Professor at Liverpool Business School and a Fellow of the Richardson Institute for conflict studies at Lancaster University. He has considerable experience in management systems, information management and managerial cybernetics and has published widely in the field. He is the editor of the *International Journal of Organizational Transformation and Social Change* and the director of the Centre for Creating Coherent Change and Knowledge. Maurice has been involved in a number of international projects in change management.

Acknowledgements

We would like to acknowledge the contribution of a number of individuals and organisations. First, the ESRC for its financial support for the original seminar, 'HRD in Small Organisations'. Second, Professors Jean Woodall and Monica Lee, the joint holders with Jim Stewart of the ESRC award, for their encouragement to produce this book. Third, the staff of Routledge, especially Joe Whiting and Annabel Watson, for their patience and understanding. Our contributors deserve our acknowledgement and thanks for offering their work to the project. Debbie Wojtulewicz provided much needed and appreciated secretarial and technological expertise. Finally, thanks to our partners and families for their continuing patience and support.

Professor Jim Stewart
Professor Graham Beaver
Nottingham Business School

1 Researching and practising HRD in small organisations

Jim Stewart and Graham Beaver

Introduction

This book arose out of the ESRC funded Research Seminar Series on 'HRD: the emerging theoretical agenda and empirical research'. The series itself was an initiative of the University Forum for HRD. The Forum had identified the practice of HRD in small organisations as both an underdeveloped and growing field of research and so one of the award holders of the ESRC grant and co-editor of this volume, Jim Stewart, organised a seminar on the subject. The papers presented at the seminar form the core of the book and are joined by additional contributions from leading researchers in the field, drawn from membership of the UFHRD.

In common with the other volumes in the Studies in HRD Series, the overall purpose of the book is to advance knowledge and understanding of the concept of HRD and its professional practice. Debate on the meaning of the concept continues to be vigorous (see McGoldrick *et al.* 2002) and so this volume does not impose or even reflect a single or unified definition. Neither does it reflect a single research paradigm. All of the chapters are based on recent or current research. However, there is diversity in the methodological assumptions informing the design of that research. The contributions therefore reflect the eclectic nature of HRD research and writing signalled and celebrated by McGoldrick *et al.* (2002). What is distinctive and important about the contributions is the common and unifying focus on small organisations. The latter term is a deliberate choice. The more commonly used term small and medium enterprises (SMEs) was rejected for three reasons. First, that term implies and is associated with organisations operating for profit in industrial and commercial sectors of the economy. By definition, this excludes the public and voluntary sectors, although it is recognised and acknowledged that the latter is likely to be most significant in terms of organisation size as a defining characteristic. The factor of size though is the second reason for rejecting the term SME. Various official agencies such as the European Commission and ministries of national governments provide and operate different definitions of SME based on numbers employed. This variety is reflected in the contributions to this volume. Our position as editors has been to accept the variety of definitions applied by the contributions. Finally, our view is that the term SME tends to emphasise and support the assumption of scaled down versions of large or larger organisations. In contrast, the term *small organisations* reinforces the concept of 'smallness' as being the important, if not defining, characteristic which has significance for the nature of HRD practice in that context.

We also consider the importance and significance of the context of small organisations to be self-evident. Small organisations are of growing influence as a source of employment opportunities (see Stewart and Knowles 1999, 2000; European Commission 2001). This of course has implications for all aspects of organising and managing. Given though the current policy emphasis on learning and development as a factor in achieving success, however defined or measured, it is arguable that HRD research is of particular importance. As Rosemary Hill (Chapter 2 in this volume) argues, HRD in small organisations is historically, a neglected field of study. This volume is a contribution to remedying that situation.

Aims

The overall purpose of the book then is to provide a comprehensive and contemporary review of research into the practice of HRD in small organisations. Following from this overall purpose are two main aims. First, to describe and disseminate the results of a wide range of research on HRD in small organisations. Achievement of this aim will in turn support learning and teaching of HRD. The second aim is to provide examples of HRD research projects in small organisations. The intention of this second aim is to stimulate, support and inform future research.

A number of subsidiary aims flow from the two main aims. The first of these is to describe and analyse the context of research and practice of HRD in small organisations. As already indicated, no single definition of 'small' is imposed. However, a consistent theme of the chapters is that 'smallness' implies certain characteristics that differentiate and define the context of small organisations. The book as a whole aims to identify and examine those characteristics. The second subsidiary aim is to critically examine and analyse a variety of approaches to HRD, which are developed and adopted in response to contextual characteristics of small organisations. As with other terms and concepts, the book does not adopt a singular or consistent understanding of the term 'critical' and certainly not the limiting understanding associated with 'critical theory'. Contributors adopt and apply their own understanding, including that of critical theory in some cases. What is common though is an attempt to question what is arguably the dominant paradigm of analysing HRD approaches in small organisations as scaled down versions of those adopted in large organisations.

This varied critical style is reflected in a third subsidiary aim, which is to describe and analyse a range of HRD methods as they are applied and practised in the context of small organisations. A final objective is to provide a useful resource to all of those with an interest in the practice of HRD in small organisations.

Readership

The last objective gives some indication of our intended readership. The book, and its constituent contributions, can be considered to fall into the publishing category of research monograph. That signals that the content will be of relevance and interest to academic researchers and policy advisers and makers. We would include in that category those researching and studying HRD as students. In particular, the book is intended to support those working at doctoral level, and those on specialist master's programmes in HRD and HRM. In addition, those on more generalist master's programmes such as MBAs studying specialist HRD or HRM electives are an intended and expected readership. The particular focus of small organisations suggests another category of potential readers. The study of the management of small organisations is an established subject in its own right. We argued earlier that HRD is of particular significance and importance in that study. Therefore, academics and students working in the field of small organisations are also part of our intended readership. The study of HRD and small organisations are both increasingly a feature of undergraduate programmes. Final year undergraduates electing to study such modules are a further category of readers.

A final point needs to be made about intended and potential readership. We described 'research monograph' as a publishing category that, in that context, is defined in opposition to 'textbook'. The latter is intended to signal a book intended to support what is now referred to as learning and teaching. In our view, such distinctions are not helpful and this book is certainly intended by us to provide the support traditionally associated with textbooks.

Structure and organisation

The overall structure of the book reflects its main and subsidiary aims. For that reason, the individual chapters are grouped into three parts. Part I contains four chapters. What these chapters have in common is a focus on the *context* of HRD research in small organisations. Both of these components are examined; that is the contextual characteristics of small organisations and the implications of these for the design and conduct of research into HRD practices. Following this context setting, Part II contains five chapters which report the results of research that informs understanding of *approaches* to HRD. These approaches include a number which are either directly connected to, or are indirectly associated with, initiatives taken under the vocational and educational training (VET) policy of the UK government. Such initiatives form a long history of government interventions that have attempted to support the survival and success of small organisations. Other chapters in this part examine recent approaches such as those based on developments in information and communications technology. Part III is concerned with HRD *methods*. The distinction between approaches and methods is somewhat arbitrary. A sense of scale and scope is applied here so that constructs such as mentoring and coaching are defined as methods. The overall logic then reflects that sense of scale and scope as we begin with context and move into approaches before completing the book with chapters focusing on methods.

Individual chapters adopt a similar structure and a common content, which may include the following items:

- objectives
- theoretical context
- research context
- findings/results
- interpretation
- conclusions and learning points.

The commonality of content is intended to support the identification and synthesis of emerging themes. We do not attempt to do this ourselves since leaving that task to our readers supports the use of the book as a resource to support learning and teaching. In addition, our reading of the contributions suggests scope for much argument and debate on what those emerging themes might be and so we do not wish to close off that debate by providing what might be seen as a definitive interpretation.

While the organisation of the contributions into the three-part structure has what we believe to be a defensible logic, the book does not have to be read as a single narrative. Specific chapters or parts can be read independently depending on particular and personal interests. Thus, the book can be seen and used as a resource to be used as and when necessary or desired.

Bibliography

European Commission (2001) *Employment in Europe 2001: Recent trends and prospects*, Luxemburg: EC.

McGoldrick, J., Stewart, J. and Watson, S. (2002) 'Postscript: the future of HRD research', in J. Stewart, J. McGoldrick and S. Watson (eds) *Understanding HRD: A research-based approach*, London: Routledge.

Stewart, J. and Knowles, V. (1999) 'The changing nature of graduate careers', *Career Development International*, 4, 7: 370- 83.

Stewart, J. and Knowles, V. (2000) 'Graduate recruitment and selection: implications for HE, graduates and small business recruiters', *Career Development International*, 5, 2: 65- 80.

Part I

The context of HRD in small organisations

INTRODUCTION

This part contains four chapters which examine various aspects of the context of HRD research and practice in small organisations. Chapter 2, by Rosemary Hill, presents an argument which seeks to explain why HRD research has neglected the field of small organisations. The argument in part rests on the premise that HRD needs to be understood in a different way if its practice in small organisations is, in turn, to be understood. A related premise is that large firm logic is inappropriate to the small organisation context. Based on these and other premises, Hill provides a particularised and contextualised way of understanding HRD in small organisations which, she argues, will inform and support future research.

Chapter 3 by Scott Taylor, Sue Shaw and Richard Thorpe can be said to support Hill's thesis. Drawing on research in four small organisations, the chapter demonstrates the important influence of 'situated' social practices on learning and development. In doing so, the chapter also questions and challenges more traditional and established ways of accounting for HRD practices in small organisations. These traditional and established approaches are, arguably, weaker because of their reliance on a logic which is more appropriate to large(r) organisations. The challenge to those approaches is continued in Chapter 4 where Clare Rigg and Kiran Trehan apply a discourse analysis and critical learning perspective to provide novel understandings of HRD practice in small organisations. In common with Hill, this leads them to question current and dominant definitions of HRD. It also leads, as with Hill and with Taylor, Shaw and Thorpe, to an argued shift in the approach to and focus of research when examining HRD in small organisations. And according to the research reported in the chapters, this call results from new understandings of the context of small organisations.

Chapter 5 by Graham Beaver and Kate Hutchings widens the debate to set HRD in the context of HRM and all aspects of people management in small organisations. The chapter lends some support to Hill's argument that the study of HRD, as with that of HRM, in small organisations is a neglected field. It also though takes a less critical and challenging approach to the application of concepts and approaches more commonly associated with large(r) organsiations. Thus, it acts as a reminder that such dichotomies may be less valid and useful than some of the earlier chapters might suggest.

The overall message of this part of the book might be summarised as something like this:

- Research into HRD in small organisations is a neglected field of study.
- The social context of small organisations differs in significant ways to that of large(r) organisations.
- Given the above different concepts, or at least different understandings of established concepts such as HRD, are required to research and analyse learning and development practice and processes in the social context of small organisations.
- Along with different conceptual understandings, different approaches to and methods of research can also be of more utility.

- There is though still a place for the traditional and established approaches to researching HRD in small organisations.

This brief introduction and summary suggests some lines of thought for readers to follow when reading the chapters in this opening part of the book. The chapters themselves though provide a wealth of detail and insight which will no doubt suggest additional themes.

2 Why HRD in small organisations may have become a neglected field of study

Rosemary Hill

Objectives

The main purpose of the chapter is to explore possible reasons why human resource development in small organisations may have become a neglected field of study. It proposes a theoretical model to explain this current context, and draws upon case-study research to support and illustrate the validity of the model. The main argument advanced is that the mistaken application of 'large-organisation logic' to HRD in small organisations is fundamental to the problem of its neglect as a field of study. The explanatory model introduced in the chapter aims specifically to show how the application of large-organisation logic in small organisations causes barriers at various stages of HRD research.

This tenet is underpinned by a further argument based upon what appears to be a predominant theme in the literature about HRD in small organisations. There is a substantial amount of evidence to suggest that small organisations do not have the HRD expertise, infrastructure and general resource more usually enjoyed by larger ones (see for example, Hill 2001; Hill and Stewart 1999; Matlay 2001; Westhead and Storey 1996, 1997; Wognum and Bartlett 2001). At first appraisal, this may indicate that HRD in small organisations is characterised by conditions of absence and deficiency. The author, however, questions the notion that small organisations do not 'do' HRD - that is HRD founded and conceptualised in conventional, large-organisational logic and models. For on the basis that many small organisations do survive - in the United Kingdom, for instance, 99 per cent of businesses have fewer than fifty employees (Department for Education and Employment (DfEE) 2000) - it is not unreasonable to think that they must be doing something right. Furthermore, if we believe the vast amount of academic and practitioner literature about the value of HRD and learning to organisational capability and performance (see, for example, Shelton 2001), then some of what small organisations do right could, arguably, be construed as 'developmental'.

The next section discusses in more detail what is known about HRD in small organisations and proposes an alternate conceptualisation. This is followed by an explanation of the research context and design, to include its logic and methodology. Findings about the HRD approaches in three small case-study organisations are then advanced, leading to a concluding theory of why HRD in small organisations may have become a neglected field of study. The chapter closes with a summary of key learning points about researching HRD in small organisations. Some further areas for research are also suggested.

Theoretical context

What is known about HRD in SMEs?

Harrison (1997) suggests that most of the literature about managing and developing people in small organisations derives from observations in larger organisations. Lane (1994) too questions the relevance of conventional training and development (T&D) approaches in SMEs and what is understood about HRD in small organisations. He writes:

> Understanding how SMEs approach training and generating models of effective practice from within SMEs themselves would be a worthwhile endeavour. Too much emphasis in the past has perhaps been placed on external experts telling entrepreneurs what to think and what to do. Companies do vary in their vision, with some aiming for rapid growth and others for steady growth or niche markets. These differences may very well be reflected in different training policies. We need to understand the extent to which such ideas are part of a company's philosophies.
>
> (Lane 1994: 21)

This highlights the individualistic nature of small organisations and a need for organisational perspectives and activities, including HRD, to reflect this. Vickerstaff and Parker (1995: 60) report that 'Case-study-based work has revealed a high degree of unplanned, reactive and informal training activity in small firms, where there is typically unlikely to be a dedicated personnel manager or training officer'. Other literature (for example, Cosh *et al.* 1998; DfEE 1997a; Gibb 1997; Harrison 1997; Joyce *et al.* 1995; Lane 1994; Metcalf *et al.* 1994; Storey 1994; Storey and Westhead 1997; Westhead and Storey 1997) supports this and its sibling argument, that in many small organisations training does not take place at all. Moreover, where training does occur in small organisations, not only is it more likely to be reactive and informal but also it tends to be short term and almost exclusively directed at the solution of immediate work-related problems rather than the development of people. Such factors suggest that T&D in small organisations is predominantly job-skill related, delivered on the job as part of the job, and is seen not so much as '" proper" training' but instead regarded as 'part of everyday life' (Joyce *et al.* 1995: 19). These arguments also suggest that the dynamics of HRD in small organisations are notably different from those in larger enterprises.

Metcalf *et al.* (1994) discuss training in the context of staff retention and morale and the anxiety felt by some firms about the poaching of trained staff; Storey (1994) comments upon the strategy adopted by small firms of poaching trained labour and then moulding it to their requirements. Harrison (1997) makes a link between

informal training, tacit skills and the poaching of trained labour in small organisations. In claiming that crucial, tacit skills are particularly vulnerable in small
organisations, she offers, perhaps, a rationale for small organisations *not* to train and
develop their workforce. She writes:

> Once a skill becomes explicit, and systematically based training can be provided
> for it, then the skill becomes mobile and can be poached or copied by other
> organisations. Loss of valuable tacit skills represents a loss of strategic assets.
>
> (Harrison 1997: 57)

Table 2.1 summarises factors typically cited in the literature as triggers and motivators and barriers to HRD in small organisations. The summary is an amalgam of
views from the authors referenced previously. Certain factors in Table 2.1 appear in
both columns - a presence of such seen as triggers and motivators and an absence

Table 2.1 Determinants of HRD in small organisations

Triggers and motivators	*Barriers*
Strategy: training can reflect organisation's vision and strategy.	Inability to demonstrate clear link between T&D and performance in small organisations.
Growth: rapid growth or objectives for growth necessitate staff recruitment and/or acquisition of new skills.	Owner-managers fear poaching of trained staff and skills.
Innovation: the organisation is an innovator and strives to operate within niche markets.	Employees not interested in training as they do not want more training to do their jobs better, or there is no promotion anyway if they do improve.
Link to business performance: training can be shown to reap business improvements and costs of training are balanced against bottom-line return on performance.	Training rated as irrelevant or unimportant to the business with no apparent company benefits. Entrepreneurs have no real desire for training.
Owner-manager perspectives: owner-manager has a positive experience of or outlook towards T&D; and/or is aware of/has experience of HRD issues; and/or is well educated/trained/qualified personally.	Lack of internal HRD awareness/expertise to include lack of training analysis and planning skills. Cost of training both in terms of real cost and time away from the job.
Culture: the organisational or management culture is related to training.	Owner-managers ignorant of the benefits of training.
Recruitment difficulties: where recruitment of skilled labour is constrained by market conditions.	Owner-managers themselves are not well educated and/or have no formal qualifications.
Technology: there is new technology in the firm.	Owner-managers more concerned with short-term survival issues than T&D issues.
Firm size: larger organisations incur lower unit costs in training staff.	Due to the diverse nature and limited numbers on training courses, the cost of supplying training to small firms is higher.

Table 2.1 Continued

Triggers and motivators	Barriers
Industry sector: formal workplace training more likely in manufacturing than service sector firms.	
Nature of training: training is made relevant to the small organisation's diverse needs and delivered on site in flexible form; training is located in practice; company employees with particular expertise conduct training sessions.	It is more difficult to supply training to a variety of small organisations who might be at varying stages of development. Promotion is less likely in small organisations than larger ones - this is particularly relevant to managers.
Change initiatives: training is more likely when the firm is undertaking change programmes such as customer care, ISO 9000, Investors in People, NVQs, performance-related.	Next job for an employee or manager in a small organisation is likely to be in another small organisation rather than internally.
Expectations: there is a workforce expectation and desire for betterment.	Management training in particular provides a long-term, rather than short-term, benefit to the organisation.
External help: training is more likely where 'good' external help is available (e.g. appropriate small-firm consultancy)	Training material is irrelevant/not geared to the needs of the particular needs of the small organisation. Supply and/or quality of the training provision is not good.
Rationale for training: training is undertaken to ensure that the job is done 'in our way'.	Lack of suitable information on training.

Source: Hill (2001).

regarded as 'barriers'. For example, where T&D can be shown to reap business improvements this is a potential trigger or motivator, whereas an inability to demonstrate any link is considered a barrier. From the data in Table 2.1 it appears that fundamentally, small organisations implement HRD as they see necessary for survival, growth and the accomplishment of business objectives. There is, however, a perception in the literature (for instance, Storey and Westhead 1997) that HRD does not happen in small organisations due to an ignorance of the benefits. But what are the benefits of HRD to a small organisation? Who sets the criteria for such benefits - the small organisations or those who provide the T&D? It is likely that owner-managers of small organisations see HRD as a means to an end rather than as an end in itself, and view the availability of external provision not so much as a compelling reason to train but more as help when and how appropriate. Small organisations may informally and intuitively analyse their T&D needs anyway, instinctively focusing upon business aims and improved performance. This reinforces earlier views that HRD activities in small organisations may not be seen as 'proper training' but as part of everyday life, with 'the job' unwittingly deployed as both a facilitator and a focus of learning.

An alternate conceptualisation of HRD in small organisations

The foregoing indicates that conventional conceptualisations of HRD may not be appropriate for small organisations, and an alternate conceptualisation is developed here. It is based in a fundamental proposition that learning is (or should be) the focus of HRD. In advising that learning is the focus of HRD and that learning occurs naturally among human beings, Stewart (1992: 26) positions HRD as 'essentially an intervention in the natural learning process of organisations and individuals'. In a small organisation in particular, where the owner-manager may believe that learning is organic within the job, it is possible that the job itself might implicitly become an HRD intervention. The owner-manager of a small organisation may, however, be more familiar and comfortable with T&D than HRD and be more inclined to reject formal training programmes and employee development structures in favour of informal training and natural learning processes. Use of the terms 'T&D' and 'HRD' in the chapter reflect that position: that is, they are used to mean the same. This recognises the possibility that HRD is more likely to be perceived and talked about (Sambrook 2000) in a small organisation as T&D. It also recognises a potential difficulty in trying to label and explore a phenomenon (HRD in small organisations) that apparently does not exist. It is further argued here that the nomenclature of HRD may be of secondary importance to what HRD, as labelled in a particular context, might achieve. In this sense, HRD is positioned as a processor, or an intervention in a small organisation's natural learning processes arising from naturally occurring organisational situations. This concurs with an earlier suggestion that, in a small organisation, the job itself may serve to become an HRD intervention.

Together, these arguments suggest that small-organisation HRD/learning occurs not just on the job, but *through* the job, whereby work becomes a processor of learning. Thinking of HRD as an organic component embedded within a small organisation's infrastructure and normal routines seems a more useful conceptualisation than its usual manifestation in more conventional frameworks and activities, such as off-the-job training and formal manager development programmes. Figure 2.1 suggests how the 'HRD' relationship between 'small organisation infrastructure and normal routines' and a 'small organisation's natural learning processes' may prohibit the evolution of a conventional notion and language of small-organisation HRD - a view that could explain why small organisations appear not to 'do' HRD. Put another way, 'HRD' occurring through the job as part of normal work and problem-solving routines is not consciously thought of as HRD, and as a result is likely to be spoken about by owner-managers in terms of 'business as usual' and not HRD.

As also indicated in Figure 2.1, new knowledge generated will typically be tacit - predominantly intuitive, subjective and automatically deployed in the subsequent enactment of on-the-job skills and behaviours (Harrison 1997; Nonaka 1996).

Research context

The theory and explanatory model developed in the chapter originate in the author's doctoral research into HRD in small organisations in the North West of England. Although it was not a specific aim of the study to evolve such a theory (the

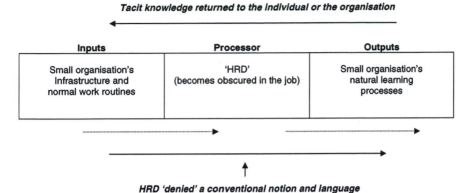

Figure 2.1 HRD in a small organisation.

research problem essentially concerned the poor take up of UK national HRD programmes in small organisations), findings also seemed to furnish a rationale as to why HRD in small organisations may have become a neglected field of study.

A logic for researching HRD in small organisations

The research design reflects the 'positive logic' about HRD in small organisations alluded to in the previous section. That is, while acknowledging views about small organisations not 'doing' HRD in a conventional sense, research methods and questions were formulated on the basis that small organisations *do* 'do' HRD, but that it is difficult to find as HRD policies and activities are embedded within organisational infrastructures and operational routines. The research, therefore, sought HRD not exclusively within traditional frameworks (formal training courses and induction programmes, for instance) - that by and large were not there to be found anyway - but within phenomena such as organisational changes, markets, competitive strategies, evolution and growth, leadership influences, and inclinations towards innovation and creativity.

Methodology

The primary research strategy was to collect data intermittently by means of a multiple-case study (Yin 1994) from October 1996 to June 1998, with a follow-up visit made during the first half of 1999. The three organisations used for casework were accessed by means of a preliminary survey conducted from January to June 1996, comprising a postal questionnaire of 350 local small organisations and a series of face-to-face interviews. As well as access to the cases, the survey was used to gain an initial understanding of some of the problems, views and experiences of the owner-managers in a wide range of small organisations in the area.

The three case-study organisations are shown in Table 2.2. From impressions

Table 2.2 The three case-study organisations

Organisation	Details	Approx. nos. employees (at time of selection)	'Special' organisational function/phenomenon
Case 1	Light engineering, design and build of machines for mainly the automotive industry. Trading as a limited company from a single site. International trade.	19(*small enterprise*)*	Design innovation
Case 2	Install/maintain security and telecommunications systems. Trading as a PLC from several UK sites. National trade.	70(*medium enterprise*)*	Evolution and growth
Case 3	Youth and community projects in the voluntary sector. Operating as a registered charity from a single site. Serving the local community only.	6(*very small/micro enterprise*)*	Leadership

Source: Hill (2001).

Note
* 'Small', 'medium' and 'micro' defined according to the European Commission's definition of small and medium sized enterprises.

gained in the survey, the organisations had advantages of a contrasting and complementary mix of management styles, organisational structures and cultures, markets and ambitions. Case 1 (design and build engineering) provided an opportunity to study the effect of design innovation on the way it viewed HRD. As an organisation at a crossroads with regard to its market direction and growth, Case 2 (security and telecommunications) demonstrated an interesting blend of trade and service aspects and, therefore, evolving HRD needs. In complete contrast, Case 3 (youth and community projects) operated locally as a registered charity in the voluntary sector. This organisation experienced not only rapid growth through its involvement as a supplier to the UK government's welfare-to-work programme, the New Deal (DfEE 1997b), but also three changes in leadership over the period of research contact. As indicated in Table 2.2, and in keeping with the research logic explained earlier, a particular organisational function/phenomenon in each case - that seemed *especially* typical of, and critical to, each case - was focused upon during empirical investigations. It was from within these 'special' functions/phenomena (design innovation in Case 1; evolution and growth in Case 2; leadership in Case 3) that the HRD approaches adopted by the three cases, together with a rationale for these approaches, became discernible for observation and description.

Analysis and evaluation of main findings

Table 2.3 summarises findings about the cases' HRD approaches, factors influencing these approaches, leadership styles and patterns of evolution and growth.

Table 2.3 Summary of main findings in the cases

	Case 1 (design and build engineering)	Case 2 (security and telecommunications)	Case 3 (youth and community projects)
HRD approach	Within the limits of individual capability and responsibility against the background of the product.	Ad hoc, or developed to a 'reasonable sufficiency' to instil/retain customer confidence, balanced against a need to limit legal liability and disruptions to work.	Focused upon developing the organisation. T&D is eclectic but gradually becoming more integrated. Delivery is creative, resourceful and opportunistic, reliant upon external funding.
Factors influencing HRD approach adopted	Shaped by traditional engineering values and needs located in rather entrenched owner-manager perspectives. Case 1's stated HRD needs were more aspirational than operational. No internal HRD expertise to enable development of alternative HRD perspectives.	Reflects the MD's views of T&D as 'lost time' and a work disruption. HRD focus is on engineers as both MD and sales and technical directors are former engineers. No internal HRD expertise to enable development of alternative HRD perspectives.	Reflects the industry it serves, and a need to develop more formal processes to satisfy external scrutiny. Although restricted by funding, this approach has evolved over time under the influences of three different leaders, all of whom have some HRD experience and acumen.
Leadership style	*Managing director:* involved, technically practical and hands-on, sociable, relaxed, highly visible.	*Managing director:* aloof and autocratic. Not visible, but would like to be so - up to a point.	*Development manager, current leader no. 3:* eclectic, busy, pace-setting, commanding, controlling. Involved, but would like to be less so.
Evolution and growth	Driven by a pride in product and design innovation and a need to establish new overseas markets. Rapid growth.	Driven by a need to change market perceptions to match its new trading status (from limited company to PLC) and integrate suite of products. Moving to a 'one-stop-shop'. Rapid growth.	Driven by a need to become a supplier to a potential 'competitor' *(New Deal)* and participate in other important national programmes. Rapid and eclectic growth.

Each case is then discussed separately, followed by a cross-case summary of conclusions about these findings.

Case 1 (design and build engineering)

Case 1's informal HRD approach mirrored a set of core beliefs and values surrounding an espoused reputation and capability for innovative product design. The following two comments from the technical and financial managers respectively sum up Case 1's HRD approach: 'everything is done against the background of the product'; and 'working within the limits of individual capability'. While organisation development emerged from extensive activities directed at the improvement of design, build and test processes, individuals were mainly held responsible for their own development and, to a great extent, for their own performance. The development of individuals was uncomplicated: employees came to the organisation already qualified to do the job and received little formal T&D thereafter, apart from any reactive training and what might be learned naturally through the job. For example, the financial manager said that his personal development was mostly down to his own motivation and commitment; both he and the technical manager indicated that performance appraisal in Case 1 was by default, the latter saying:

> Performance appraisal is by error, being pulled up for doing something wrong. I don't believe in individual performance appraisal. Each person has a role within an overall company performance. The appraisal of collective contribution is more important than individual appraisal, who is to say that one person has contributed more than another has. Contribution is more meaningfully appraised by default.
>
> (Technical manager, Case 1)

On the basis that individuals were qualified craft workers, and that collective contribution was assessed in terms of product/project compliance and financial return, then Case 1's philosophy of performance appraisal by default may have been contextually effective. However, while shop floor skills requirements seemed adequately served, the overall HRD approach may not have been sufficiently supportive of the levels of creativity and competitiveness that Case 1 aspired to. There was nothing to show that performance and development of the management team was assessed nor understood; they worked on and learned from projects and product development independently as individuals. Given the status afforded Case 1's design capability, this indicates a serious deficit in its learning system (Tushman and Nadler 1996).

Case 1's commercial environment and the backgrounds and perspectives of the managing director (MD) and the technical manager were seen as primary influences in shaping the organisation's HRD approach. An engineering environment had influenced Case 1, and had also shaped the experience and expertise of its owner-managers. This meant that HRD was bound by *engineering* tasks and work arrangements, and had to be specific to an engineering environment. The MD and the technical manager recognised that more formal ways of sharing individual knowledge and learning were perhaps required, but had neither the time nor the expertise to do this. So, they relied upon traditional ways, as that was what formative professional experiences had taught them worked best. In short, Case 1 was a knowledgeable and knowledge-hungry organisation that didn't know, and had inadequate ways of knowing, what it knew.

Case 2 (security and telecommunications)

Case 2's sales and marketing director used the term 'ad hoc' many times to describe HRD in his organisation, an approach that is, perhaps, best reflected in the views of the MD: 'Training is important but people's employment terms and conditions are more important. Training has never been developed in [Case 2] as it's lost time. Training is a balance between the costs of running a competitive business' (MD, Case 2).

Paradoxically, the MD was nervous about an untrained workforce claiming that 'the business liability is greater with them'. So, HRD as 'lost time' was balanced against a need to retain customer confidence and limit legal liability resulting from the possibility of negligent field practices. Although Case 2 reduced employee numbers, it experienced rapid evolution and growth in products and markets. There was an imperative to mould market perceptions of Case 2 from a single-product, family business to a multi-product PLC. The unexpected loss of a major contract prompted the introduction of a staff appraisal process through which the MD sought information about himself, his organisation and his employees - openly inviting individuals to comment not only about themselves but also about colleagues. Unfortunate, too, was the fact that information was gleaned from employees without reciprocity, as individual T&D requirements were discussed and then subsequently ignored. The appraisal process, even though neither fully developed nor understood - and questionably ethical (Stewart 1998) - was perceived by both management and staff as a turning point in Case 2's history - a phenomenon alluded to by one employee as them having come out from under a cloud.

Even though the sales and marketing director stated on several occasions, that growth had a significant impact on HRD and that 'Utopia would be to have an engineer knowledgeable of all divisions of the business', not much was done about this in terms of cross-skills development. The sales and marketing director also explained that cross-skills training would be to a 'reasonable level', that he wanted engineers who could 'within reason, create customer confidence', because they needed people working five days a week without interruptions for training, and that the HRD fall-out of change 'had not yet crystallised, but tends to focus on the engineering side'. An overall picture emerges of HRD as a cost, with fears about the liability of an untrained workforce rationalised against the unacceptability of a known variable - the disruption to work through T&D. Although the sales and marketing director eventually indicated that his view had moved from HRD as a 'nice to have' to a 'need to have', he still had to convince executive colleagues, especially the MD. As Case 2 had realised record turnover and profits that year, the sales and marketing director was finding this challenging: and given Case 2's performance (ostensibly without developing individuals to the more advanced and integrated skills level required), *some* of what it had done could have been 'developmental'.

Case 3 (youth and community projects)

The voluntary sector in general features in the UK government's plans for promoting lifelong learning and social responsibility, and tackling unemployment and social exclusion (DfEE 1998). As a supplier to the 'options' phase of the *New Deal* (DfEE 1997b), Case 3 had to develop more formalised HRD processes such as induction and personal development planning for New Deal participants to prescribed DfEE standards, which over time, were gradually extended to all Case 3 employees and volunteers. If the voluntary sector shaped Case 3, then it also shaped Case 3's HRD. The development manager (DM) - Case 3's then leader - described HRD as 'necessary and forward thinking'. Perceiving HRD in a broad context by highlighting the pastoral care of employees and shortcomings in employee benefits, she also said, 'We believe in looking after our workforce and our individual employees at the same time. It partly compensates for low wages and uncertain conditions of employment'.

The T&D of individuals was mainly externally funded and provided. Internal development activities were aimed at the improvement of organisational structures, systems and processes, encouraged by a need to satisfy external pressures, such as the *New Deal* and another crucial (to Case 3) government programme, *Millennium Volunteers* (DfEE 1999). Overall, the approach to HRD was creative and resourceful, but fragmented and opportunistic. Having gone some way to secure Case 3's infrastructure, the DM seemed ready to attend to the development of individuals through coaching, feedback and the cultivation of more formally managed learning processes. Time showed, however, that the DM's somewhat eclectic and pacesetting style was not able to accommodate these people development processes.

Cross-case summary of conclusions about findings

The three HRD approaches are individualistic, each one a reflection of the organisation's operating environment and leadership influences. Three differing leadership styles emerge, each trying to bring about organisational change in his or her own way. All three are technically experienced in their respective fields. All appear to exert significant influence over their respective organisations. Each leadership style echoes a combination of industry perspectives, personal capabilities (including the extent of HRD expertise) and personal preferences - the MD in Case 1 through a highly involved and visible shop floor presence, the MD of Case 2 by temporarily stepping out of his solipsism to glean knowledge from employees, and Case 3's development manager setting the manner and pace for change and then 'pulling from the front'. Globally, the data in Table 2.3 suggest pace and movement. All cases are chasing new markets, a commonality perceived as the main driver of change in each. It is also interesting to note here that while matters of leadership and evolution and growth were selected for special consideration in Cases 3 and 2 respectively, it became apparent that one construct could not be studied without automatically drawing in the other. Good insights into Case 2's evolution and growth were achieved through an analysis of its leadership, while in Case 3, leadership perspectives were also well meshed with the organisation's evolution and growth. Furthermore, design innovation - the special research focus in Case 1 - was central to that organisation's leadership tenet and its pattern of evolution and growth.

It seems that, in each case, HRD is concentrated upon developing the organisation to meet the particular demands of its operating environment and circumstances: engineering and product development needs in Case 1; to a reasonable sufficiency and balance in Case 2; and attention to issues concerning both society and enterprise in Case 3. It also seems that the cases directed HRD effort at organisational level first, and at individual level second - or, in Cases 1 and 2, hardly at all. However, there were differing rationales in each case for developing organisation over individuals. Case 1 preferred to employ qualified craftsmen and saw individual development as the responsibility of individuals; Case 2's MD felt that T&D was lost time; and the DM in Case 3 recognised a need for personal intervention in the development of employees, but saw the augmentation of formality and work projects as more pressing and immediate priorities.

In conclusion, development in the three cases gravitated naturally towards current, critical organisational issues, and towards organisational requirements before those of individuals: their T&D was a secondary or a non-existent consideration. Findings do, therefore, seem to support the alternate conceptualisation of HRD advanced earlier in the chapter. That is, it may be more appropriate to position HRD in a small organisation as an organic component embedded within its infrastructure and normal routines - in particular, those that embrace *current, critical issues.*

Interpretation

HRD in small organisations presents a paradox of simplicity and abstruseness. The HRD approaches adopted in the cases studied were individualistic, informal reflections of industry norms and expectations and owner-manager perspectives, in turn having been shaped by life and industry experiences and capabilities. A corollary to this is that HRD seems more naturally directed at the development of organisational knowledge and capability than at the T&D of individuals. Since learning seems typified by tacit knowledge and skills, the extent of 'HRD' enacted becomes obscured, misunderstood and underestimated. This makes small organisation HRD significantly different from conventional notions of HRD. As well as being central to understanding the problem of whether or not small organisations 'do' HRD, these conclusions also underpin the theory advanced here of why HRD in small organisations may have become a neglected field of study. Figure 2.2 illustrates this theory at three levels: entry level, empirical level and theory-building level. Each level represents a research stage.

Entry level

Problems of access to organisations for research purposes (Easterby-Smith *et al.* 1993) are likely to be greater in a small organisational context. As small organisations tend to be independent and individualistic - and inwardly focused upon current,

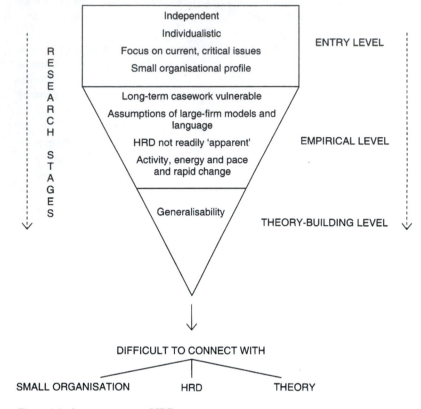

Figure 2.2 A theory of why HRD in small organisations may have become a neglected field
of study.

critical issues - owner-managers are unlikely to offer research access unless there is
something in it for *them*. In short, connecting with small organisations is difficult if
you haven't got much to offer. As it seems that (conventional) HRD is not high on a
typical small organisation's agenda, then HRD research from an owner-manager's
perspective probably constitutes 'not having much to offer'. But feelings of 'what's in
it for me?' can extend to a researcher too. For, given a typical profile, small
organisations may not have much to offer a researcher in terms of HRD content,
organisational structures and facilities, financial reward, or commitment to a long-
term programme of work. It seems that these factors could represent significant
barriers at research entry level.

Empirical level

The chapter has shown that the *context* for researching HRD in small organisations is
important. That is, exploring HRD within a small organisation's infrastructure,
routines and critical issues. As case studies are thought better than surveys for

investigating organisational context (Yin 1994), long-term casework would seem more conducive to researching HRD in small organisations than surveys. However, the susceptibility for case studies (Easterby-Smith *et al.* 1993) and small organisations (Storey 1994) to fail, renders research longevity within them highly vulnerable too. By way of illustration, Case 1 (design and build engineering) went into receivership in late 1998, fortunately (for the research) after the bulk of the fieldwork had been completed. This occurrence, say twelve months earlier, would have had a seriously debilitating effect on the programme of work. Sadly too, Case 3 (youth and community projects) followed a similar path in mid-2001; Case 2 (security and telecommunications) sold out to a large multinational competitor during 2000. The 'three out of three' scenario depicted here clearly illustrates the degree of vulnerability of small organisations to a variety of both internal and external pressures. It also hints at how readily research access in a small organisation could also be summarily withdrawn due to organisational failure, or as a reaction to pressures of work, sudden and rapidly changing circumstances, or quite simply an owner-manager's whim. Research access could also be subject to continual disruption through frequent last-minute postponements of scheduled visits. This last situation was certainly typical of the research featured in the chapter.

As it seems that historically most of what is known about HRD in small organisations derives from large organisations (Harrison 1997), there is a danger of assuming large-organisational HRD models in small-organisational settings. The language of the small organisation (and, therefore, the language of small-organisational HRD) is grounded in activity, energy, pace, sudden change and having to find ways out of problems rather than planning for them to happen: a phenomenon succinctly expressed by Case 1's technical manager as 'being in it'. The language of conventional HRD tends to be more elegantly articulated within formal frameworks, models and interventions, and does not connect well with the language of small organisations, or the HRD approaches developed more instinctively by organisations. Happily, though there is a growing body of knowledge about HRD in small organisations now emerging from both research and organisation development activities conducted specifically in small organisations (see for example the work of Birch 1998; Matlay 2001; Sadler-Smith *et al.* 1999; Sadler-Smith *et al.* 2000; Smits *et al.* 2001; Wognum and Bartlett 2001).

In summary, problems at the empirical level seem to fall broadly into two categories: those concerned with sustaining research access, and those concerned with difficulties in connecting with HRD in a 'recognisable' form. It is possible that these factors may significantly impact upon the prospect of empirical investigations failing to satisfy a set of preordained research aims and objectives.

Theory-building level

What constitutes a small organisation? There could be a world of difference between one employing five people and another employing forty-five. According to most quantitative definitions (see, for example, Trades Union Congress (TUC) 1997), both would be categorised as 'small'. Small organisations may be found in a wide and varied range of familiar (engineering, and security and telecommunications, for example) and less usual (such as youth and community projects) industry sectors. Small organisations are also well represented by a myriad of diverse entrepreneurial enterprises, typically run by sole traders. There is a major implication for post-empirical theory building in all of this. Because of the vast miscellany and idio-syncrasies within the so-called small and medium sized sector, matters of external validity - the capability of a study's findings for generalisation (Yin 1994) - to the wider population of 'small organisations' can inhibit the evolution of credibly validated theory.

Conclusions

Researching HRD in small organisations is problematic. While such problems may not be exclusive to small organisations, it is argued that they are substantially intensified by small organisational tendencies towards unpredictable, eclectic and idiosyncratic perceptions and behaviours. The biggest issue is perceived as one of 'connection'. As indicated in Figure 2.2, it is difficult to connect with

- small organisations themselves at entry level
- HRD in any recognisable form at empirical level
- valid theories about HRD in small organisations at theory-building level.

So, what needs to be done? While it is not the purpose of the chapter to respond to this inquiry in any detail, some ideas based upon experiences gained in the research are offered here as key learning points for further reflection and action.

Learning points

Problems regarding research access may be eased with some hard evidence of how a more purposively managed HRD approach could complement a small organisa-tion's *own* approach. As the author was invited by all three cases to offer feedback and suggestions for improvement, it was evident that the owner-managers were receptive to help that acknowledged and built upon existing organisational processes and capabilities - provided it incurred minimum intrusion upon time and resources. For example, a simple learning log to help Case 1's apprentice record his develop-ment, a single-page proforma to support Case 2's appraisal process and a facilitated session aimed at clarifying roles and responsibilities in Case 3 were suggested and implemented.

Potential problems at empirical level can be helped by means of a robust, yet flexible, research design constructed within a 'positive logic' as outlined earlier in the chapter. Small organisations do not relate well to planned research schedules, systematic data collection and formal reporting. Although extremely willing to share their views and experiences, owner-managers do not tolerate what they perceive as interference rather than help. They like to tell, and be listened to. So, once access is agreed, it seems sensible to invest sufficient time and energy getting to know the small organisation and its owner-managers prior to starting data collection. Adequate contingency built into the research programme to cater for sudden changes in circumstances and schedules is also essential.

As an integral part of doing research, matters of validity and theory development may, inevitably, remain challenging. An axiom that, perhaps, serves as a reminder about the importance of attention to the development of robust, yet creative, research designs. However, if as portrayed in the chapter, small organisations are so individualistic, how practical is it to generalise a study's results beyond its research population? This embraces a further question about how we define and use the terms 'small organisation' and 'SME': broadly as labels to distinguish them from large enterprises, or more narrowly to a set of specific quantitative and/or qualitative criteria? In sum, perhaps, the notion of researching HRD under the banners of 'small organisation' or 'SME', is too broadly based without a clear understanding of what is meant by the terms within a particular piece of research.

A further thought relates to the ongoing debate about the merits and demerits of defining HRD (ESRC Research Seminar 2000). Views advanced in the chapter raise significant issues about the philosophical, conceptual and practical basis of HRD and its relevance to small organisations, and also about HRD research processes in small organisations. Fundamental to that agenda is the matter of HRD definition. From the research discussed in the chapter, emerges a belief that offering a universal definition of HRD could be detrimental to the prospect of furthering long-term research opportunities into HRD approaches in small organisations. Given the arguments presented, how realistic or sensible is it to apply a generic definition of HRD within a small organisational context? In conclusion, the author chooses to position, rather than define, HRD in a small organisation as an indefinable processor of naturally occurring organisational learning and development processes.

Finally, in terms of suggestions for further research, there seems a need to accelerate both the quantity and quality of HRD research in small organisations, and to ensure that appropriate mechanisms for the continued dissemination of HRD research practices in SMEs are in place. As owner-managers may see 'bottom-line' consequence (whatever 'bottom line' means in a particular context) as *the* most critical issue that HRD has to connect with, more investigations into the impact of HRD on small organisational capability and performance is recommended as an important area for further research. From an owner-manager's perspective, such an agenda might be sufficiently appealing for him or her to commit and stay 'connected' to a piece of research.

Bibliography

Birch, D. (1998) 'HR and understanding small and medium-sized enterprises', *Human Resource Development International*, 1, 4: 443- 50.

Cosh, A., Duncan, J. and Hughes, A. (1998) *Investment in Training and Small Firm Growth and Survival: An empirical analysis for the UK 1987–95*, DfEE Research Report RR36, London: DfEE.

DfEE (1997a) *TECs and Small Firms Training: Lessons from skills for small businesses*, DfEE Research Report RR27, London: DfEE.

DfEE (1997b) *Design of the New Deal for 18–24 Year Olds*, London: DfEE.

DfEE (1998) *Blunkett Sets Out Importance of Youth Volunteering for Healthy Communities*, News Bulletin 315/98, 18 June 1998.

DfEE (1999) *Fast Track Millennium Volunteer Projects Get Go-Ahead*, News Bulletin 463/99, 22 October 1999.

DfEE (2000) *Small Firms Set for Healthy Future*, Skills and Enterprise Executive Issue 4/2000, SEN Publication, London, DfEE.

Easterby-Smith, M., Thorpe, R. and Lowe, A. (1993) *Management Research: An introduction*, London: Sage.

ESRC Research Seminar (2000) *Defining HRD: The debate so far*, Kingston Business School, Kingston University, UK, 5 October 2000.

Gibb, A. A. (1997) 'Small firms' training and competitiveness: building upon the small business as a learning organization', *International Small Business Journal*, 15, 3: 13-29.

Harrison, R. (1997) *Employee Development*, London: Institute of Personnel and Development (IPD).

Hill, R. (2001) 'Human resource development in small and medium-sized enterprises: barriers to national HRD', unpublished PhD thesis, Nottingham Trent University.

Hill, R. and Stewart, J. (1999) 'Human resource development in small organisations', *Human Resource Development International*, 2, 2: 103-23.

Joyce, P., McNulty, T. and Woods, A. (1995) 'Workforce training: are small firms different?', *Journal of European and Industrial Training*, 19, 5: 19-25.

Lane, A. D. (ed.) (1994) *Issues in People Management No. 8: People Management in Small and Medium Enterprises*, London: IPD.

Matlay, H. (2001) 'Training in family and non-family owned small businesses: an empirical overview', in conference proceedings *Exploring the Frontiers of Small Business 24th ISBA National Small Firms Policy and Research Conference*, Hinckley, 14-15 November 2001, vol. 1, pp. 1039-57.

Metcalf, H., Walling, A. and Fogarty, M. (1994) *Individual Commitment to Learning, Employers' Attitudes*, Sheffield: Employment Department, Research Strategy Branch.

Nonaka, I. (1996) 'The knowledge creating company', in K. Starkey (ed.) *How Organizations Learn*, London: International Thomson Business Press.

Sadler-Smith, E., Down, S. and Field, J. (1999) 'Adding value to HRD: evaluation, Investors in People and small firm training', *Human Resource Development International*, 2, 4: 369-90.

Sadler-Smith, E., Gardiner, P., Badger, B., Chaston, I. and Stubberffield, J. (2000) 'Using collaborative learning to develop small firms', *Human Resource Development International*, 3, 3: 285-306.

Sambrook, S. (2000) 'Talking of HRD', *Human Resource Development International*, 3, 2: 159-78.

Shelton, R. (2001) 'Helping a small business owner to share knowledge', *Human Resource Development International*, 4, 4: 429-50.

Smits, T., Wognum, I. and Pye, J. (2001) 'SME Network Learning', in supplement to conference proceedings Second Conference on HRD Research and Practice Across Europe 2001, *Perspectives on Learning in the Workplace*, 26-7 January 2001, University of Twente, Enschede, The Netherlands, pp. 137-40.

Stewart, J. (1992) 'Towards a model of HRD', *Training and Development*, October: 26-9.

Stewart, J. (1998) 'Invervention and assessment: the ethics of HRD', *Human Resource Development International*, 1, 1: 9-12.

Storey, D. J. (1994) *Understanding the Small Business Sector*, London: Routledge.

Storey, D. J. and Westhead, P. (1997) 'Management training in small firms - a case of market failure?', *Human Resource Management*, 7, 2: 61-71.

Trades Union Congress (TUC) (1997) *The Small Firms Myth*, London: Economic and Social Affairs Department, TUC.

Tushman, M. and Nadler, D. (1996) 'Organizing for innovation', in K. Starkey (ed.) *How Organizations Learn*, London: International Thomson Business Press.

Vickerstaff, S. and Parker, K. T. (1995) 'Helping small firms: the contribution of TECs and LECs', *International Small Business Journal*, 13, 4: 56- 72.

Westhead, P. and Storey, D. J. (1996) 'Management training and small firm performance: why is the link so weak?', *International Small Business Journal*, 14, 4: 13- 24.

Westhead, P. and Storey, D. J. (1997) *Training Provision and the Development of Small and Medium-sized Enterprises*, DfEE Research Report 26, London: DfEE.

Wognum, I. and Bartlett, K. (2001) 'An examination in response to strategic learning needs in SMEs', in supplement to conference proceedings Second Conference on HRD Research and Practice Across Europe 2001, *Perspectives on Learning in the Workplace*, 26- 7 January 2001, University of Twente, Enschede, The Netherlands, pp. 133- 6.

Yin, R. K. (1994) *Case Study Research Design and Methods*, 2nd edn, Newbury Park, CA: Sage.

3 Neither market failure nor customer ignorance

The organisational limitations of employee training and development

Scott Taylor, Sue Shaw and Richard Thorpe

Introduction

Employee training and development are important aspects of human resource management activity. However, managers in smaller organisations cite training and development as the most problematic aspect of people management, especially during periods of expansion. We suggest that training and development practices in smaller organisations are characterised by 'lacks'. First, managers in small companies are seen as resistant to the provision of training opportunities through a lack of time, money or market knowledge. Second, we examine the argument that suitable training and development are not provided for employees in small companies, as suppliers have concentrated on larger, wealthier organisations. We propose that these images of managers in small companies and training suppliers generate a picture of the management of small companies which neglects the internal organisational processes of negotiation in requesting and granting training. Recognition of this dynamic, we suggest, may help to understand the perceived failure of training and development initiatives in smaller organisations. Thus, low levels of formal training and development in smaller organisations may be neither market failure nor customer ignorance.

Next, we outline the training and development processes which employees and managers undergo in four small companies. More than sixty interviews from four case studies, two from manufacturing and two from the service sector, are analysed. We focus in particular on the experiences of two training managers, one from a manufacturing company and the other from a service provider. From this, we identify three key issues in the negotiation of training and development. First, the competence of managers to gauge what training is needed; second, the problematic linkage of training and skills levels to pay; and third, the acquisition of recognised credentials for employees, in addition to informally acquired job competence.

We then return to the issues raised in the introduction, and in particular the argument that low levels of training take-up in smaller companies are the result of either ignorance of training opportunities or the failure of the market to provide appropriate content. We question both of these propositions, and suggest that internal organisational dynamics play a key role in the facilitation of training and development in smaller companies.

Training as investment: employee development to improve performance

> Everybody can see what everybody else is doing - everybody understands why they're doing it, just by listening, and so training is first class without having any kind of structure at all. It really is just learn from other people. There's an energy thing there as well, because . . . people pick it up at the same pace - well, they do or they don't, but if they don't then you can clearly see it.
>
> (Owner-manager, *Bodywork*)

If recruitment and selection can be seen as the first people management task underpinning the entry of a new employee into an organisation, training and development can be seen as the second. Vital to making the new recruit a useful member of the company, training and development has been found to be the area of human resource management (HRM) that generates most difficulties in small organisations, particularly during periods of expansion (Greening *et al.* 1996). It is also the area of people management about which least is known (Pettigrew *et al.* 1990).

This chapter presents data relating to processes of training and development collected during a study of people management in smaller organisations in 1998 and 1999 (Taylor 2001), drawing on more than sixty interviews with owner-managers, managers and employees. The analysis takes the approach that owner-managers, managers and training providers are not 'authoritative interpreters' (Bittner 1965: 149) of managerial initiatives in use, and investigates the situated processes of training and development. This involves taking employees' understandings and perceptions as a means of understanding organisational practices in context (Scott *et al.* 1989), in part to access the inevitable conflict over resources in the organisations studied (Scase 1995), and in part to locate training and development within wider organisational processes (Curran *et al.* 1997). Through this, we seek to provide an account of the lived experience of individuals that offers an alternative perspective to those based on self-administered questionnaires completed by managers, the research method that has been pre-eminent in investigations of managerial practices in smaller organisations (Curran *et al.* 1997).

Investigating human resource development in organisations involves an assessment of the aims, means and base of workplace training. There is substantial evidence that the level of formal, structured training (defined as the range of content provided by an external organisation or individual) varies linearly in relation to the number of employees (Storey and Westhead 1997). It is similarly acknowledged that the level of formal training is influenced by other factors, such as organisational maturity, firm ownership, levels of innovation, fear of losing valuable members of staff to more highly paid jobs or more prestigious organisations (Stanworth *et al.* 1992), the structure of the organisations (Marshall *et al.* 1995) and rate of growth and union activity (Storey and Westhead 1997); yet size (in terms of number of employees) remains a prominent dynamic.

However, the processes of training and development in smaller organisations have been neglected in favour of the analysis of owner-managers' learning processes (Down 1999), driven by the 'grail-like' search (Goss 1991) for identifiable and transferable entrepreneurial traits (Caird 1993; Chell *et al.* 1991) or capacities (Gibb 2000). Even the nature of the managerial task in smaller organisations has been lost in the rush to analyse entrepreneurial activities, and investigations into the skills, behaviour and attributes of the owner-manager (Gibb 1999). However, the publicity accorded to this tightly defined notion of 'the entrepreneur' can be contrasted with the relative lack of emphasis on two groups: non-owning managers in smaller organisations, and organisations that are not specifically 'entrepreneurial' (as defined or perceived). Organisations that are neither small, high-growth and entrepreneurial, nor large, prestigious and multinational are relatively neglected, as are their managers (Bresnen and Fowler 1996).

The low levels of formal training and personnel development in British companies have been considered problematic since business education was highlighted as important to the performance of national economies (Handy 1987; Constable and McCormick 1987). The resourcing and promotion of structural initiatives such as the Management Charter Initiative (MCI), Investors in People (IiP) and Training and Enterprise Councils (TECs), and the introduction of Learning and Skills Councils, have helped to define this time as the Learning Age. Combined with this, the increasing emphasis on workplace learning and the growth of management education, in particular since the late 1970s, represent prima facie evidence that levels of business training are increasing (Facteau *et al.* 1995). Undergraduate and postgraduate students on courses with 'management' or 'business' in the titles now form the second largest student body of any discipline in British universities; more than 30,000 people are currently registered for MBAs alone. The impact of this industry may have affected the small firm less than the large organisation; smaller organisations have shown marked reluctance to become involved in training and management development (Arthur and Hendry 1990; Kitching and Blackburn 1999; Storey and Westhead 1997). It is often argued that this 'failure' of smaller organisations, arguably manifest in low levels of IiP take-up (Ram 2000), is hindering the growth of the firms concerned and therefore the international competitiveness of 'UK plc' (Curran *et al.* 1997).

Increasing participation in management and employee development in smaller firms has therefore become a matter of government policy, with public funding for research into small firms to raise their status (ESRC 1994), multiple structural supports targeted at small firms (Hutchinson *et al.* 1996), and highly specific course design and delivery, again often paid for from the public purse (Creagh *et al.* 2000; Storey and Westhead 1997). There is therefore strong structural and practical evidence to suggest that small firms have not been 'excluded' or ignored in the provision of training for the sector - indeed, quite the opposite. The plethora of different courses and advisory bodies may even be counter-productive (Durham University Business School (DUBS) 1990). Indeed, it has been argued that managers in smaller organisations see such initiatives as supply-led, rather than demand-led, resulting in scepticism as to the appropriacy of the content (Vinten 2000). In this respect, calls for qualitative improvement in provision, and good practice in delivery and course design, seem more apposite than more structural innovations (Gibb 1983, 1987, 1999, 2000). However, this may be possible only through, first, the increased use of conceptual and analytical research rather than reportage, and second, the acknowledgement that smaller organisations need to be defined by more than simply the number of employees (Curran and Stanworth 1979; Johnson and Tilley 1999).

In addition, many training and development initiatives are sold on the basis that performance benefits will ensue. Benefits are conceptualised according to norms of performance based on the 'logic of accounting' (Gowler and Legge 1983). However, evidence from the United Kingdom (Storey and Westhead 1997) and North America (Baldwin *et al.* 1994) on the correlation of levels of employee training and business performance indicates that for such claims to be used as the basis of encouraging smaller organisations into learning is at best misleading. In a reflection of the wider debate over HRM practices and organisational performance, studies often fail to prove causal or even correlative links, and rely on the 'feelings' of managers that performance is improved by training initiatives (Smallbone *et al.* 1993; Marshall *et al.* 1995). It is an article of faith that development improves organisational performance; proof has simply yet to be found. This is reflected in a current debate within HRD as to whether organisational performance or learning should be the focus of promotion.

Following Hill and Stewart (2000), we use the terms 'training and development' and 'HRD' interchangeably throughout this chapter, taking the actions of training and personnel development as the operational aspects of the wider philosophy of HRD. Linking training and development to organisational performance is the central *raison d'être* of the state-supported IiP initiative. However, we suggest that concentrating too much on whether training pays will not enhance our understanding of the nature and meaning of working and managing in smaller organisations, through which informed and relevant developmental courses can be constructed (Gibb 1997a). Research may need to frame our understanding of training and developing people in smaller organisations through taking more account of the social organisation of work. Equally, we accept that the 'psychological contract' perspective, concentrating on the individual level and excluding wider structural conditions, also provides a thin analysis. It is therefore important to maintain a twin focus on the individual and on the structural conditions of training provision.

Thus, we do not approach employee development or training as a variable to be tested in the search for performance-improving 'panaceas' (Gill and Whittle 1992). Nor do we take a sample of organisations that are exceptional in any way beyond being unique human and organisational contexts for the 'social drama of work' (Watson 1980: 44). Above all, we do not seek to assess the managers and case study organisations in relation to a set of aspirational norms of best practice in training and development. Rather, this chapter attempts to understand and analyse the practices of employee training and development as perceived by both managers and those managed, and to investigate local and often seemingly commonsense understandings of how managers and employees are developed.

Research context

The data on which this chapter is based were collected through interviews, observation and documents. Each of the four companies involved employs fewer than fifty people. Diamondcom, Zincpipe and Bodywork are owned by the founders, while Gearbox is the British production and assembly site of a European parent. Diamondcom and Bodywork provide services to larger companies; Zincpipe and Gearbox manufacture tools and components for the chemical and motor industries respectively. All four companies have been trading for more than ten years.

This research sought to provide data and analysis relevant to the management of people in smaller organisations, with the key defining aspect being the number of employees. In this, we would argue that ownership is of secondary importance, as is the sector in which the company trades. We sought to focus on the dynamics of managing a relatively small number of people as we were investigating personnel structures, in particular the presence or absence of the techniques and philosophies associated with HRM. Informal, semi-structured interviews conducted with employees, line managers, functional managers and owner-managers were transcribed by one of the authors, to encourage the emergence of early analytical themes and familiarity with the data. In addition, any documents available in the organisations relating to personnel and HRM issues were analysed, and time was spent in the companies shadowing various people or hanging around in work and social areas. Through these various data collection strategies, we were able to gather information on HRD structures, employees' perception of training and development interventions and structures, and managerial strategies for people development.

We suggest that these multiple strategies provide us with an opportunity to analyse the conduct of HRD in these four companies to a depth that is rare in small firms research. The multiple perspectives of all of those individuals involved in training and development enable a rich and complex picture of practice to be drawn, complementing analyses that rely on self-administered questionnaires or interviews with owner-managers. In particular, the key role of the constraints within the companies could not have been explored in such depth without spending time with and around employees and managers from all levels.

In summary, we would emphasise two aspects of this research. First, it allows for the analysis of the HRD processes in action, as well as taking into account historical practices conditioning current approaches. Second, it provides an account of HRD to complement quantitative analyses of, for example, skills levels, to enable appreciation of the micro-political and social issues involved in developing people in smaller organisations.

Data analysis and interpretation

Employee induction: 'this is where you sit . . .'

> The first thing that happens . . . they have an induction, by Mary usually, [to] show them round the building, health and safety, usual stuff, and [they're] given a starter pack . . . after that, it depends on the individual.
>
> (Owner-manager, Bodywork)

For most employees, the first day at work in a new job and a new organisation is likely to be stressful. At Bodywork, Diamondcom, Zincpipe and Gearbox, this anxiety is reduced somewhat by the methods of recruitment, as many new employees are recruited from the local community through friends and relatives already working at the companies. Nonetheless, the first day of paid employment with the company forms their initial experience of many of the procedures and processes. This is particularly the case with training, in the form of induction and initial job training.

The induction process was presented by many as taking place in an atmosphere of some disorganisation:

> The guy who would have trained me up wasn't here, he was in Scotland. So it was like, 'This is all the work that needs doing which is left, because he's gone - off you go!' So I just sort of made it up as I went along and went with it. He came back from Scotland after a few months, so he sort of like showed me what to do, but the first time I was just dropped in it . . . [I] just picked it up and ran with it.
>
> (Manager, Zincpipe)

> When I joined in January, one of the ladies . . . was off with a broken leg, the other one left shortly after in February, so for four months until Linda came back I was literally thrown in at the deep end, and it was more a case of just treading water rather than making huge profits . . . then the lady with the broken leg came back, and we recruited [someone else].
>
> (Employee, Bodywork)

> I did a few hours' induction on the first day, and that was it. It wasn't much more - the induction was mainly around, one, the computer system, secondly, the QA procedure. You know, what's expected of you - you don't just put your bum on a seat, there's a certain way of doing it and you have to meet certain standards in doing it. My training was around that, and then you're thrown in at the deep end . . . you were expected to watch and listen to the other[s] . . . as to how they go about doing the job.
>
> (Employee, Bodywork)

The obvious benefits of this kind of induction and initial training are that it is cheap and superficially labour-saving. A director of Bodywork outlined the ways in which new employees could pick up the norms to which they were expected to work:

> Everybody can see what everybody else is doing - everybody understands why they're doing it, just by listening, and so training is first class without having any kind of structure at all. It really is just: learn from other people. There's an energy thing there as well, because . . . people pick it up at the same pace - well, they do or they don't, but if they don't then you can clearly see it.
>
> (Owner-manager, Bodywork)

In this, the induction and initial training can serve as a strong and structured introduction to the 'way things are done around here' (Kunda 1992), as well as allowing the employee to grasp rapidly at least the scope of the skills needed to perform the job task.

These methods of induction and initial training are highly embedded in the spatial organisation of the company. Being able to watch and learn from others is reliant on working within sight and earshot of colleagues with experience of the job; being able to grasp rapidly the way in which the company operates relies on a lack of formalised systems and rules, and on the basic job task being relatively easy to present. In addition, the care taken to gather extra-functional information during the recruitment and selection process at the four companies (Taylor 2001), and being able to assess quickly and effectively 'what they've brought to the party, to then look at what they need to do to achieve . . . what we want from them' (Owner-manager, Bodywork), helps to support the ad-hoc means of induction and training.

However, the characterisation by the owner-manager at Bodywork of the induction and initial training as 'first class' in content and conduct was not shared by all of his employees, or those at other case study companies. It was seen as particularly problematic by those given responsibility for a new recruit. 'Watching and learning', to achieve any learning, involves being watched and taught, something for which incumbent employees often had little time or patience:

> You're looking at two to three months' training to get into the swing of the job, so until they can get into the swing of it, you can't leave them alone . . . they don't even work overtime . . . you're just getting held back all the time. I know it's not their fault, you've got to train them, but you get that busy, you get behind with your work, so you've got to like stay to get it out.
>
> (Employee, Zincpipe)

> You can't just bring people and tell them, 'There's a job' . . . They brought [a] lad in, he's with me now . . . I'm trying to teach him . . . he's very slow and he's never had any experience on the tools we're using.
>
> (Employee, Zincpipe)

These comments indicate considerable personal frustration at being 'landed' with someone to train, with the trainers falling behind in their own work, and perhaps being forced into doing overtime. This was particularly evident at Zincpipe and Gearbox, the two manufacturing firms, where shop floor employees presented the manufacturing processes as highly specialised and therefore requiring long periods of in-company training. From this, we would suggest that the 'cost of training' could be seen as including both lost time through the interruption of productive work and resentment at being asked to do something nominally beyond contract.

In-house training: continuing learning from colleagues

In our case study companies, then, in induction processes and initial job training, responsibility falls primarily on the new individual and immediate colleagues. This was extended to the processes of ongoing development in the workplace, where 'need-to-know' and 'know-who' combined to generate the know-how to perform job tasks (Gibb 1997b):

If we have a problem computer-wise, we go to Wayne, and he teaches us. There's not a scheme of training and development. Wayne's very good; if I'm ever stuck on something Wayne can generally answer the question. But it's just a case of 'if you don't know, ask', rather than set training.

(Employee, Gearbox)

Nobody actually sat me down and said, 'It's this and this'; it was just picking things up really and learning from the lads on the shop floor . . . I said, 'Oh, that looks good', so I had a go. They said, 'Here, have a go', so I had a go . . . I just stick my nose in and have a go, just asking questions, really.

(Employee, Zincpipe)

It's very difficult to actually take time out to train somebody, so you've got to sort of manage it fairly closely . . . and it's really time with us. You've got to just watch it being done, and learn from it.

(Employee, Bodywork)

Many of the employees in the four companies saw this system of training as having advantages and disadvantages. Once again, the informal system could perhaps function effectively in a very small organisation with little time pressure, but in a slightly larger organisation with production pressures it brought significant difficulties for those responsible for training:

With it only being nine people here [when I started] . . . there was nothing at the college at the time, there was no day-release. It was all down to experience, it was all hands-on, through the hours you put in . . . but you put in the hours and you're finding more out, because when we were only nine people here . . . when one person struggled in one job, you'd all rush in and help - if you were struggling in your job, they'd all come in and help, and by doing that you all find out - whereas all that's gone now, you're all separated into separate divisions, you're all on timesheets, whereas at one time, you didn't have timesheets - not specific timesheets. It was like - what you'd done that day, any complications and what was it and how did you get round it. None of that now - it's more the time sheet rules, and everybody's thinking, 'Oh, I've got to get this out, and I haven't got time to help him', so they're not learning the same as what the other people, the older members of the company have done . . . There's only a few of us that have a wide variety of the knowledge in the shop. It won't get passed [on as much] in a regime [like this] as where somebody else will come and learn everything in the shop, because it can't run that way now . . . People tend to come in and stay on that product . . . but it won't get passed on as fast either, 'cause we had to do it, 'cause there was only a small team we actually had to do it.

(Employee, Zincpipe)

Last week I had one semi-skilled lad and two trainees. I was actually building, and then in dispatch spraying, and dispatching as well - I was doing everything last week. Now I can't keep my eye on the lads, on the trainees . . . I'm organising work to be done, I'm trying to train young lads, [and] I'm trying to train some of the older lads because it's a new range that's come in . . . I'm trying to show them . . . and I'm overseeing the test and the dispatch and the spraying . . . It's hard, and like I say I'm organising the whole work thing . . . It's sad really . . . on the shop floor, we have trainees and the training facilities are absolutely nil. I'm the [NVQ] assessor, and I just haven't got five minutes to spare . . . and they [the trainees] just don't get the time that they deserve, and it's sad. These young trainees, they aren't having the time spent with them that they should be. It's a case of, 'Here's some tools, do this, do that, do that', and that's it, I'm off again. They're asking other lads who are building, 'Is it right, that? Am I doing it right?' At the end of the day, they're working on their own . . . it's wrong, they should be shown correct . . . [all] because of the demand for getting stuff out of the door. There's just no time with having such a small workforce.

(Supervisor, Gearbox)

It is often suggested that smaller organisations do not train staff formally because of lack of money and time. At Gearbox, however, the lack of time, partly generated through expecting people to perform multiple roles, can be seen to hinder even the informal training that was required for shop floor employees to perform job tasks. This was reinforced by a shop steward there:

They got the shop floor supervisor, who works on the benches . . . now Mick is wholehearted, he's a very generous type of person, and they said, 'You're going to be sorting out the training.' They sent him to college on a course, he went on a two-day course, he got a certificate. Now he's supposed to sort out the training. But the problem is, we're such a small workforce, they go to Mick and say, 'Now listen - we're very busy tonight. We want this out, this out, this out, this out, this out, this out, this out . . . ' And it all . . . what about the training? 'We're going to [have] Friday mornings for doing training, we're not going to do anything Friday morning. Friday morning will be for training. We'll get the lads in here, we'll sort everything out' - and it just never happens. They talk it very well - if you go in and say to them, 'Listen', they'll sit and listen and say, 'Yes, yes', but they don't do anything . . . and they expect like loyalty in return.

(Employee and shop steward, Gearbox)

In this, the position of the shop floor training supervisor can be seen to be so complex that it is unsurprising that training is the first thing to drop during busy periods. Given production demands, in which there is an expectation of material contribution from the supervisor, directing training becomes the last thing on the list to accomplish. This dynamic was also present at Zincpipe:

They keep saying, 'We're going to train you on this, we're going to train you on that', but it never materialises, anything like that. Time and time again, 'We're going to move you to do this, move you to do that . . . ' and then when we got busy, people had to go back on their old jobs, so it was stopped again.

(Employee, Zincpipe)

[I've had] basic training on the switchboard and then just basic training on dispatch . . . I came back from holidays last year, didn't even take my coat off, and I sat there, and he [the manager] said, 'Right, how do you fancy dispatching?' Just like that, so there's no getting into the system slowly or . . . I think it was because of the business situation. All of a sudden it just got so busy at that time, and I don't think Trisha could do two jobs at once, so they decided to appoint me to do the dispatching, and they got someone else to do reception.

(Employee, Zincpipe)

However, the training manager at Bodywork (who was not expected to contribute to the 'productive' side of the organisation) emphasised individual managerial and employee choice in deciding where to place training on the priority list. She also indicated that, while there was no pressure to 'get products out the door' in a literal sense, as at Gearbox and Zincpipe, customers retained absolute priority:

The thing is, because of the work we do here, it's a case of making time to do the training at times, because you've got to respond straight away to clients who come on the phone. You can't put that to one side and concentrate on training - training, really, it's there for people if they want it, but some people, they just want to get on with the work . . . and they put training at the back of their priorities, really. I think it's really because of the way the business works . . . I have a moan at them at times, and it's great now that we're all on email, because I can just keep sending emails all the time to them until they answer [laughs] . . . You can tell them, you can advise them, but other than that it's down to that person, and whether it's of benefit to them.

(Manager, Bodywork)

The approach to training at the four organisations may perhaps be best summarised in the words of one of the owner-managers at Diamondcom, which express succinctly the lack of formal managerial responsibility felt for the basic and ongoing development of employees (Knights and McCabe 1998): 'I believe in getting people on the bike and shoving them off'.

However, the idea of freedom to engage in personal development in these workplaces was complex. Many employees related how they were not particularly interested in training, once a basic level of competence had been achieved, particularly in the administrative sections of the organisations:

We have ongoing training processes, mainly for the works . . . Trevor does come with these leaflets that we get, 'Would you like to come on a training course?' and things like that, and he wouldn't object if we wanted to, but I really don't want to!

(Employee, Gearbox)

Elizabeth, training manager, Bodywork

Elizabeth started work for the company as a typist, but the owner-manager knew her from when they both worked for another company. He knew that Elizabeth had ambitions to go beyond the administrative role she was stuck in, and that she was interested in training and development. When Elizabeth was taken on at Bodywork, she negotiated training as part of her job role, and then became the company's first training manager. In the eighteen months after Elizabeth joined Bodywork, the company doubled in size from twenty-five to almost fifty employees. So many new members meant that training and development became key to retaining staff, and making sure that they knew what was expected of them. Training manager was suddenly a full-time job.

Most of the training at Bodywork is internal, and is often delivered through self-study courses. Employees borrow books, videos and cassettes, and sometimes go on work placements to other companies. If there is something that Bodywork can't do internally, then employees can be sent on short courses externally – this is especially the case for management training. The main difficulty for Elizabeth is making the time to organise the training, and then persuading employees that they can find the time to do the training she has sorted out for them. Bodywork is a company driven by its clients, so people find it difficult to set aside time through the day to concentrate on training. They also work such long and intensive hours that the evenings and weekends are difficult to use for more work-related activities. Training goes to the bottom of the priority list, because of the way the business works. Elizabeth deals with this by 'having a moan' at people, and bombards laggards with emails reminding them of their training duties. Ultimately, though, she takes the approach that you can advise people and put some pressure on them, but it's down to that person in the end. They most often decide on training when it's of obvious benefit to them, and this is often based on whether they want to change jobs – within the company or into another organisation.

The owner-manager is seen as 'easy-going' on training. Employees go to him in the first instance, as the budget holder, and request training; he then sees Elizabeth and they sit down together and decide whether there's a business case for the expenditure, in line with the IiP procedures they follow. IiP helps with the decision-making process, and also on the paperwork more generally, as Elizabeth has to keep everything up to date. However, whether training can be linked to company performance is another question altogether. The owner-manager does want to see bottom line benefits from training, while Elizabeth sees it as more of an investment to make recruitment and retention easier. No one really knows the answer to this in Bodywork, but they do know that if they don't train then they will lose people quickly, and that they won't be able to do their jobs as well in the time they have there. The budget is 'open', in as much as there is no formal limit on the amount of training that can be done over a certain period.

The people that I've been working with don't want career paths, they just want the job that they've got . . . in my department, people just want the jobs that they've got.

(Owner-manager, Bodywork)

At Diamondcom, the reluctance to become involved in training for career development was related to the more substantial rewards to be had 'on the shop floor' for a salesman, and the lack of 'places to go' within the organisation even if the skills were acquired:

At the end of the day, if I want to be a manager or make the money, I will always plump for making money as opposed to being a senior manager that's walking round looking in cupboards and stuff like that [laughs]. I'd rather do that [sales] any day of the week. I can't sit in all day and go through papers. I just lose the edge, and just end up getting up bored with it.

(Employee, Diamondcom)

They do promote internally . . . but like, my position, I don't think I can get any higher than I am, which is why I left before . . . unless they create a position for me, which I don't think - may do, may not.

(Employee, Diamondcom)

In this, the complex organisational dynamics of size, reward and training come together. Another employee at Gearbox described the constraints of working in a smaller organisation, with a lack of vertical complexity and specialisation, and so space to move (Daft 1986):

There isn't a lot of movement, really . . . There was a job last year when a gentleman left, he went to another company, and the job became vacant . . . That could have been a place that I could have gone to, but it wasn't a lot different from what I'm doing . . . That would have been more than a move to the side rather than upwards. Other than that, other than going for something completely different, sales or something like that, being contract manager [laughs] . . . or go back down on the benches [laughs] . . . I'd like to have a go but I don't think they'd let me, the unions. I did like the assembly side of it, I did enjoy doing that, but I saw this moving upstairs as a good move, out of the overalls, out of the oil and dirt, and stuff. Wages improved a bit, so it was a good opportunity.

(Employee, Gearbox)

The financially negative implications of becoming a manager for one, contrasted with the financial and social move from 'the benches' to an office post, also hint at the complex interconnections between skills, payment levels, and social status. In combination with the lack of formal training on the shop floors of Zincpipe and Gearbox, this formed an area in which employee dissatisfaction was strongly manifest.

Skills for money: the value of paper

Zincpipe and Gearbox operate differentiated payment systems for hourly paid employees, based on categorisation into unskilled, semi-skilled and skilled (Gearbox), and Grade 1 and Grade 2 (Zincpipe). Wage levels are negotiated collectively for hourly paid employees, and individually for managerial staff. At Bodywork, employees were either paid a basic wage, with monthly and annual bonuses according to individual and departmental performance, or salaried. At Diamondcom, wages were fixed, and individually negotiated, with the standard exception of those in sales, who worked on commission.

Payment systems are often key areas of conflict in organisations (Pettigrew 1985), yet most analyses see them as operational and structural, rather than cultural, with the 'social soil' being neglected in favour of the performative claims of payment systems (Bell 1999). At Gearbox, training was closely linked to payment, but this conflicted with the 'flexible' working practices of the shop floor, as a shop steward outlined:

> What these two young lads have done is they've picked the job up, and other people have come in on skilled money [but] they [the lads] are on semi-skilled money. They can do the job . . . that these skilled men can't do, but they [management] won't pay them the skilled money . . . they hadn't had the [training], so we said, 'Well, let's do the training, let's sort the training out and get the formal thing done'. They've been told for years, 'We will sort you out'. One of the two lads just turned 30, and he was told at 18 he would be [trained], in a few years' time . . . He can do the job but they won't pay him the money. I feel sad for him, because I feel like they've been led up the garden path a bit.
>
> (Employee and shop steward, Gearbox)

Methods of learning through asking and experience, while often regarded fondly at Zincpipe, were also seen as disadvantageous to employees:

> We've never had any specific thing to say, 'You can teach this, you can do that.' It'd be nice to have that, because . . . it's something to go in your CV. If I ever left here, all I've got on my CV is plastics fabricator . . . whereas with my plumbing I've got City and Guilds . . . It'd be nice to have something like that here.
>
> (Employee, Zincpipe)

> If you had formal training, you'd have something there to prove yes, I have done it. If there's ever another take-over, I've done it, it's there, black and white. Every time there's a take-over it's just going by [word of] mouth, and what they've heard from management before . . . [and] if you don't hit it off with your last management, that management could tell them anything, and you're fighting it all the time.
>
> (Employee, Zincpipe)

The training manager at Bodywork, however, saw this dynamic as part of a negotiation of demands and needs, balancing the good of the employee and the cost to the organisation:

> [The owner-manager] is really quite easygoing . . . I think if someone goes to him, or they come to me, and say, 'I want training in this', we will sit down and think, 'Does this person really need it, or is it going to make any difference to the company?' . . . I think really it's best if we can do internal training, 'cause I mean the time and it's more convenient for them, but people want training from outside.

Development of the individual as an independent instrument of labour power, transferable to other organisations, has often been argued to be a source of owner-manager resistance to formal employee training in smaller organisations (Hill and Stewart 2000). One employee at Gearbox found an alternative to gaining formal qualifications and progressing within the workplace, perhaps indicating one danger of not facilitating training and employee progression:

> In this particular environment, where you're doing the same thing day in, day out, it's a variation on a similar theme . . . It does tend to get a little bit tedious and boring . . . I just took on being a shop steward as something different, and it has proved a lot different, to be honest . . . I enjoy doing it. It's a battle. I can see what's going on here [on the shop floor], so with that objective in mind I can go up there and at least put my views across the table . . . We just don't seem to get anywhere [laughs].
>
> (Employee and shop steward, Gearbox)

In this, the development of the employee through union activity could be seen as replacing training and development through his job. Although the constraints are many in small organisations, it may be that by denying people the space, time and freedom to train formally, they will ultimately take opportunities elsewhere, inside or outside the company.

Flexible working practices are combined with flexible payment at Gearbox, although this also led to difficulties on the shop floor:

> They have this flexibility. Now John works in the stores, and he gets paid skilled money . . . At certain times when things get a bit busy, they'll say to John, 'Come off the stores and come on the benches and build these units' . . . Now he can't do these units, because obviously he's just a storeman, so he'll ask these semi-skilled lads how to do the job. Now they're telling somebody how to do the job who's getting paid more money than them. And what'll happen sometimes is the storeman may go on holiday for a few weeks . . . so they say to the semi-skilled lad on the bench, I want you to go work in the stores . . . They'll pay him skilled money while he's working in the stores, for three weeks. He works in the stores, he's been in the stores for a week, there's a bit of pressure on the benches, the works manager will come to him and say, 'Go on the benches' . . . and they'll

Alex, shop floor supervisor and training manager, Gearbox

Alex joined Gearbox when the company where he served his time began to have problems and lay people off. He had a friend working at Gearbox who told him that there were some vacancies coming up, so Alex applied for a job as a fitter and got it. He sees his current job as relatively secure, even in slack periods, and enjoyed coming to work until recently, when it 'began to get a bit of a chore'. Gearbox is a subsidiary of a large European company with a high degree of financial and operational autonomy. For twenty years, it was managed by an 'old school' MD; recently, he retired, with the result that a new management team came in and changed many of the traditional practices, including training and development.

The previous management encouraged an informality on the shop floor which allowed older employees to train newer members as work was being done. The 'older fellows showed the younger lads the ropes', and this led to a workforce which passed on large amounts of tacit knowledge and grew together as a community. The respect between shop floor employees for specific areas of expertise was high. This was in a context of low pressure to 'get things out the door'; as long as the work got done more or less within the timescales of the customers, then everything was fine.

However, the new managerial approach, in part driven by ISO certification, focuses more on the written constraints and procedures of work than before. Now, managers with little background understanding of the nature of the work done on the shop floor try to manage through invoking customer pressure and demand. Individual and company performance are both appraised largely on compliance with schedules and quality standards. Alex sees this as a major difficulty. Previously, the work schedules coming from upstairs were seen as reliable – managers had the expertise to spot errors before they got to the manufacturing area, senior employees could question orders if they didn't feel right, and there was a lot of co-operation between individuals to make sure that the products were to the required standard.

Now, however, job cards frequently come on to the shop floor without having been assessed by production specialists, and employees don't have the experience or back-up to be able to assess them on the manufacturing floor. There are still many trainees in Gearbox, but Alex doesn't have the time to put programmes together for them or make sure that they go through the NVQ system, as he is almost always too busy dealing with manufacturing errors and bottlenecks. Alex often finds himself building, spraying, dispatching – trying to cover the entire manufacturing process. Trainees don't have the time spent with them that they deserve, most often being shown the tools and being told to get on with it. People are leaving, to go to other companies with more structured training programmes or to go back to college to get more formal qualifications – 'fed up of getting roastings', as Alex puts it.

send him back to the benches and they say, 'I'll pay you skilled money because you're supposed to be in the stores for three weeks', and he's working next to a lad who's getting less money than him for doing the same job . . . They can't understand the problems they create by doing that, and when you go and try to explain to them that it's creating a problem, it's creating a problem of morale . . . it's affecting production because it's flipping counterproductive, and [they say,] 'I can't see what the problem is.' The problem's there - anybody with any logic and sense can see the problem that is there.

(Employee and shop steward, Gearbox)

Decisions as to whether to pay for a job task, a set of skills or an individual cause further difficulties at Zincpipe. A management buy-out, which took place shortly before the period of the research, enabled the payment system, which was seen as problematic, to be changed:

[They are] trying to sort the wages out. There was a massive gap between the Grade 1 and then the Grade 2 workers . . . They tried to narrow it. It was basically the people who'd been here the longest who had the most skills, and what's happened now is they've brought in a payment-for-skills programme . . . The lad next door, he's brand new, they only started him two weeks ago, he's on the start rate, then you have an intermediate . . . and then once you've got two skills you go up another grade, three skills gets you a bit more - we're only talking like 2, 3 per cent but it's a little incentive and you go up and up and up . . .

(Employee, Zincpipe)

However, another employee pointed out the inherent flaw of this system, particularly if used to motivate staff or encourage ongoing career development:

We've now got it so that you can learn more - the more you know the more you get. The only trouble is myself, and a few other lads, Nigel and Chris . . . we're on top money, so what's our goal? We've got to the top of the ladder now . . . so then you've got the problem where your top workers [are] thinking, 'Christ, I'm only worth twenty quid . . . more than him, so you tend to feel a bit grieved, but . . .'

(Employee, Zincpipe)

At Zincpipe, the key dynamic in introducing the new payment system and job grading was the shop floor workers' perception of the new production manager. He had joined Zincpipe only a few months previously, recruited by the operations manager from their previous employer. A shop floor employee explained how this could affect employee acceptance of the shop manager and the procedures:

So, all he [the shop manager] actually did were come round with a sheet of jobs and say, 'Can you do this?' 'Yes.' 'OK - can you do this?' And that's it . . . Now, that, to me, is no way to treat somebody's skills, on a piece of paper, but that's

> what happened . . . I mean, we had one lad here who was down here [in the stores] for two weeks, while I was on holiday . . . [he] put down on his sheet that he's a trained storeman . . . didn't have a bloody clue, just signed the stuff off the back of the wagon . . . If you've ever done any of this job, you know damn well it's . . . At last count, we've got about 600 lines, and it'd take you a fortnight just to know where they are, never mind what they are . . . so he's picked it up in a fortnight, that's not bad going.
>
> (Employee, Zincpipe)

The reduction of a job to a piece of paper outlining the skills, and the implied conversion of hard-won skills to a 'corporate currency of variable status and value' (Scarbrough 1996: 37), was related to a perceived loss of individuality at Zincpipe:

> Everything's individual. There are times when you think they're trying to run it as though every part is, you know, run it like a conveyor belt system, but they'll never do it because there's too much individuality about it. So, it's a very skilled job basically, you know - you can't just get anybody in and expect them to do it. It's took me thirteen year now and I still say I don't know everything. You've got to learn it within time.
>
> (Employee, Zincpipe)

Interpretations and conclusions: the responsible employer?

This chapter seeks to provide an analysis of the processes of HRD in four smaller organisations, rather than the more usual account of how to achieve growth through the development of management skills (Marshall *et al.* 1995). Our aim here has been to develop an understanding of 'how the inherent incompleteness and elasticity of any rule-set work on any given occasion of its use' (Boden 1994: 204). The interplay between the structure of training and the actor in training and development is manifest in the uses of a high-profile business improvement initiative relating to training and personnel development, Investors in People. Bodywork had, at the time of the research, just been awarded IiP for the second time; Diamondcom had committed to achieving the standard; Zincpipe had been assessed (and failed); only Gearbox was not involved in any way. However, the difference between achieving the IiP standard and providing investment for the people in the organisation in terms of buying either external or internal training was, for one of the owner-managers of Bodywork, part of the game of achieving standards on their own terms (i.e. those of a smaller organisation):

> When we did the quality thing, it was a case of, 'Right, let's do ISO 9000, that's great, let's look at what we do - it's an opportunity to look at how the business was working from an analytical point of view and to see whether or not we were wasting our time' . . . Part of ISO 9000 was to keep proper training records - we said, 'Yep, that's dead easy because nobody gets any training, so keeping records is really not an issue!'

As well as revealing a wariness towards external organisational or managerial rules (Gunnigle and Brady 1984), this comment indicates the concentration on the structural aspects of such initiatives as ISO certification and IiP. The structural change and conformity to norms involved in the achievement of these 'badges' gives little indication as to whether cultural change is taking place (Bell *et al.* 2001).

The induction training at the four organisations studied was found to be highly opportunistic, with much of the responsibility being placed on the new employees (who were expected to watch and learn), and existing employees (who were expected to watch and teach). This may have served to bring the new employee into the organisation in a cultural sense, with values and norms being transmitted at the same time as functional information, perhaps in the expectation that 'unity of circumstances' would result in 'unity of conduct' (Bauman 1997). Further, we argued that the systems of ongoing personnel development followed this template of individualised responsibility. This may be compared to practices in large Far Eastern organisations, as outlined in Rohlen (1974) and Fruin (1983). They both report highly structured training and development, oriented towards producing subjects with strong adherence to group norms (Kondo 1990). According to Rohlen, 'company training is designed to foster self-reliant people harnessed to the work of the organisation' (1974: 211). This was perhaps more evident, and more evidently problematic, due to the more technically complex low-level jobs, at Zincpipe and Gearbox. In addition, employees at those two organisations saw a lack of formal qualifications as highly problematic internally and externally - internally in relation to payment levels based on skills measured through paper qualifications, and externally if they wished to transfer skills to another organisation. They also saw the increasing time pressures of production as squeezing the slow, careful training necessary to bring new employees through. Finally, at Gearbox, a shop steward presented the lack of formal training or possibilities for individual progress in the organisation as key to his decision to become enthusiastically involved in the trade union, perhaps using the management of 'his' members (Collinson 1992) as a proxy for development in his work role.

These issues, and those raised in the introductory review, raise questions as to the nature and means of HRD in smaller organisations. The relative lack of engagement of managers in smaller organisations with formal management education and employee development is, as noted at the outset, increasingly taken as a prominent dynamic in business failure. However, the analysis of this chapter, concentrating on training and personnel development as embedded within the four organisations studied, leads us to question whether and why employees and managers would participate in formal development given the demands it makes on the organisation and the individual. The socially embedded nature of the learning and learning needs in these organisations would seem to indicate that the range of barriers to convincing small organisations that it would be of benefit to participate in training either employees or managers is wider than simply structural or operational.

It may be argued that those doing two, three or even four jobs at once, such as the shop floor supervisor at Gearbox, will not find the space or time to achieve learning and development for themselves or for others, no matter what the structural, extra-organisational incentive or encouragement. Further, it may be that employees require structural protection against the informal obstructions to training and development common to smaller organisations. Thus, the resistance of owners of small companies to legislation (Bendix 1963; North *et al.* 1997; Scase and Goffee 1982) - which often succeeds, due in part to the efforts of powerful employers' federations (Westrip 1982) - may be a further barrier to positively affecting employment practices such as training and development in these organisations. It may be that the intrusion of abstract systems of training would undermine pre-existing 'local forms of control' (Giddens 1991), a further disincentive for owner-managers to institute 'freedom' in personal development. The training and development practices found at Diamondcom, Bodywork, Zincpipe and Gearbox contain much that is admirable in rational terms: they are cheap, fast, efficient, multipurpose and effective. However, a number of observations indicate the costs of not formally training and developing employees and managers: the possible effects on those unable to swim in the deep waters of watching and learning by doing; the effects on those employees without formal qualifications to transfer in the event of redundancy or dismissal; the (possibly unconscious) reproduction of orthodox and discriminatory power relations by managers and owner-managers through informal practices (Grey 1996); and, above all, the productive inefficiency of training whose demands on employees hinder customer service. Although the four organisations in this study are evidently 'managing to survive' (Ram 1994) in terms of their training and development systems, they may not be managing to survive in the longer term (Kerr and McDougall 1999), or in a way that will bring change and improvement to the organisations.

Ultimately, then, this chapter seeks to suggest that formalising training and development practices may enable individuals and their skills to become included in a society that supports a notion of expertise as structurally legitimised (Kondo 1990). Smaller organisations and institutional support for small firms may be failing employees in this respect (Kets de Vries 1991), with the organisations and their employees remaining socially and culturally excluded (Kondo 1990). In seeking to address this problem, it is necessary to avoid the danger of the structure and institution becoming more ceremonial and mythical (Meyer and Rowan 1991), or rule-bound, as has arguably been the case with IiP (Bell *et al.* 2001). Yet it seems evident that employees in smaller organisations do need some form of institutional support in training and development, for as long as the affiliations and loyalties they bring to the workplace extend beyond those espoused by management (Van Maanen and Kunda 1989).

Learning points

- Managers within smaller organisations perceive training and development as the most problematic aspect of people management.
- The level of formal structured training provision is influenced by a range of factors including organisation size.
- Government policy and public funding have sought to encourage research into

training needs within and delivery of training to smaller organisations although initiatives such as IiP have tended to concentrate largely on structural aspects.

- Focus to date has been on manager development and its role in achieving organisational growth.
- A number of barriers relating to the individual employee and the owner/manager operate against the provision of training and development.
- Formalising training and development practices is not only important to the prosperity of small firms but is also a means of legitimising an individual's skills and expertise.

Bibliography

Arthur, M. and Hendry, C. (1990) 'Human resource management and the emergent strategy of small to medium sized business units', *International Journal of Human Resource Management*, 1, 3: 233- 50.

Baldwin, J., Chandler, W., Le, C. and Papaililadis, T. (1994) *Strategies for Success: A profile of growing small and medium-sized entreprises (GSMEs) in Canada*, Ottawa: Statistics Canada.

Bauman, Z. (1997) *Postmodernity and its Discontents*, Cambridge: Polity Press.

Bell, E. (1999) 'A cultural analysis of payment-systems-in-use in three chemical companies', unpublished doctoral thesis, Manchester Metropolitan University.

Bell, E., Taylor, S. and Thorpe, R. (2001) 'Investors in People and the standardisation of professional knowledge in personnel management', *Management Learning*, 32, 2: 210- 19.

Bendix, R. (1963) *Work and Authority in Industry*, New York: Harper and Row.

Bittner, E. (1965) 'The concept of organisation', *Social Research*, 32: 239- 55.

Boden, R. (1994) *The Business of Talk: Organisations in action*, Cambridge: Polity Press.

Bresnen, M. and Fowler, C. (1996) 'Professionalisation and British management practice: case evidence from medium-sized firms in two industrial sectors', *Journal of Management Studies*, 33, 2: 159- 82.

Caird, S. (1993) 'What do psychological tests suggest about entrepreneurs?', *Journal of Managerial Psychology*, 8, 6: 11- 20.

Chell, E., Haworth, J. and Brearley, S. (1991) *The Entrepreneurial Personality*, London: Routledge.

Collinson, D. (1992) *Managing the Shop floor: Subjectivity, masculinity and workplace culture*, Berlin: de Gruyter.

Constable, R. and McCormick, R. (1987) *The Making of British Managers: A report of the BIM and CBI into management training and development*, London: British Institute of Management.

Creagh, M., Barrow, C. and Morrow, T. (2000) *Building Business: Management training for small firms*, Bedford: Cranfield School of Management.

Curran, J. and Stanworth, J. (1979) 'Self-selection and the small firm worker: a critique and an alternative view', *Sociology*, 13, 3: 427- 44.

Curran, J., Blackburn, R., Kitching, J. and North, J. (1997) 'Small firms and workforce training: some results, analysis and policy implications from a national survey', in M. Ram, D. Deakins and D. Smallbone (eds) *Small Firms: Enterprising futures*, London: Paul Chapman.

Daft, R. (1986) *Organisational Theory and Design*, St Paul, MN: West.

Down, S. (1999) 'Owner-manager learning in small firms', *Journal of Small Business and Enterprise Development*, 6, 3: 267- 80.

Durham University Business School (DUBS) (1990) *Small Business Management Training*

Experience in the United Kingdom 1970–1990, a report prepared by Durham University Business School for the Department of Employment, Durham: DUBS.

ESRC (1994) *Small Firms Research Initiative*, Swindon: ESRC.

Facteau, J., Dubbins, G., Russell, J., Ladd, R. and Kudisch, J. (1995) 'The influence of general perceptions of the training environment on pretraining motivation and perceived training transfer', *Journal of Management*, 21, 1: 1-25.

Fruin, W. (1983) *Kikkoman: Company, Clan and Community*, Cambridge, MA: Harvard University Press.

Gibb, A. (1983) 'The small business challenge to management education', *Journal of European Industrial Training*, 7, 5 (whole issue).

Gibb, A. (1987) 'Enterprise culture: its meaning and implications for education and training', *Journal of European Industrial Training*, 11, 2 (whole issue).

Gibb, A. (1997a) 'Small firms' training and competitiveness: building upon the small business as a learning organisation', *International Small Business Journal*, 15, 3: 13-29.

Gibb, A. (1997b) 'Policy research and small business: from know what to know how', in M. Ram, D. Deakins and D. Smallbone (eds) *Small Firms: Enterprising futures*, London: Paul Chapman.

Gibb, A. (1999) 'Can we build "effective" entrepreneurship through management development?', *Journal of General Management*, 24, 4: 1-21.

Gibb, A. (2000) 'Corporate restructuring and entrepreneurship: what can large organisations learn from small?', *Enterprise and Innovation Management Studies*, 1, 1: 19-35.

Giddens, A. (1991) *Modernity and Self-identity*, Cambridge: Polity Press.

Gill, J. and Whittle, S. (1992) 'Management by panacea: accounting for transience', *Journal of Management Studies*, 30, 2: 281-95.

Goss, D. (1991) *Small Business and Society*, London: Routledge.

Gowler, D. and Legge, K. (1983) 'The meaning of management and the management of meaning: a view from social anthropology', in M. Earl (ed.) *Perspectives on Management: A multidisciplinary analysis*, Oxford: Oxford University Press.

Greening, D., Barringer, B. and Macy, G. (1996) 'A qualitative study of managerial challenges facing small business expansion', *Journal of Business Venturing*, 11: 233-56.

Grey, C. (1996) 'Towards a critique of managerialism: the contribution of Simone Weil', *Journal of Management Studies*, 33, 5: 591-611.

Gunnigle, P. and Brady, T. (1984) 'The management of industrial relations in the small firm', *Employee Relations*, 6, 5: 21-4.

Handy, C. (1987) *The Making of Managers*, London: NEDO.

Hill, R. and Stewart, J. (2000) 'Human resource development in small organizations', *Journal of European Industrial Training*, 24, 2/3/4: 105-17.

Hutchinson, J., Foley, P. and Oztel, H. (1996) 'From clutter to collaboration: business links and the rationalisation of business support', *Regional Studies*, 516-22.

Johnson, D. and Tilley, F. (1999) 'HEI and SME linkages: recommendations for the future', *International Small Business Journal*, 17, 4: 66-81.

Kerr, A. and McDougall, M. (1999) 'The small business of developing people', *International Small Business Journal*, 17, 2: 65-74.

Kets de Vries, M. (1991) 'Whatever happened to the philosopher-king? The leader's addiction to power', *Journal of Management Studies*, 28, 4: 339-51.

Kitching, J. and Blackburn, R. (1999) 'Management training and networking in small and medium-sized enterprises in three European regions: implications for business support', *Environment and Planning C: Government and Policy*, 17: 621-35.

Knights, D. and McCabe, D. (1998) 'What happens when the phone goes wild? Staff, stress and spaces for escape in a BPR telephone banking work regime', *Journal of Management Studies*, 35, 2: 163- 94.

Kondo, D. (1990) *Crafting Selves: Power, gender, and discourses of identity in a Japanese workplace*, Chicago: University of Chicago Press.

Kunda, G. (1992) *Engineering Culture*, Philadelphia, PA: Temple University Press.

Marshall, J., Alderman, N., Wong, C. and Thwaites, A. (1995) 'The impact of management training and development on small and medium enterprises', *International Small Business Journal*, 13, 4: 73- 90.

Meyer, J. and Rowan, B. (1991) 'Formal structure as myth and ceremony', in W. Powell and P. DiMaggio (eds) *The New Institutionalism in Organisational Analysis*, Chicago: University of Chicago Press.

North, J., Blackburn, R. and Curran, J. (1997) 'Reading small businesses? Delivering advice and support to small businesses through trade bodies', in M. Ram, D. Deakins and D. Smallbone (eds) *Small Firms: Enterprising futures*, London: Paul Chapman.

Pettigrew, A. (1985) *The Awakening Giant: Continuity and change at ICI*, Oxford: Blackwell.

Pettigrew, A., Arthur, M. and Hendry, C. (1990) *Training and Human Resource Management in Small to Medium Sized Enterprises: A critical review of the literature and a model for future research*, Sheffield: Training Agency.

Ram, M. (1994) *Managing to Survive: Working lives in small firms*, Oxford: Blackwell.

Ram, M. (2000) 'Investors in People in small firms', *Personnel Review*, 29, 1: 69- 91.

Rohlen, T. (1974) *For Harmony and Strength: Japanese white-collar organisation in anthropological perspective*, Berkeley, CA: University of California Press.

Scarbrough, H. (1996) 'Understanding and managing expertise', in H. Scarbrough (ed.) *The Management of Expertise*, London: Macmillan.

Scase, R. (1995) 'Employment relations in small firms', in P. Edwards (ed.) *Industrial Relations in Britain*, Oxford: Blackwell.

Scase, R. and Goffee, R. (1982) *The Entrepreneurial Middle Class*, London: Croom Helm.

Scott, M., Roberts, I., Holroyd, G. and Sawbridge, G. (1989) *Management and Industrial Relations in Small Firms*, Department of Employment Research Paper 70, London: Department of Employment.

Smallbone, D., North, D. and Leigh, R. (1993) 'The use of external assistance by mature SMEs in the UK: some policy implications', *Enterpreneurship and Regional Development*, 5: 279- 95.

Stanworth, J., Purdy, D. and Kirby, D. (1992) *The Management of Success in 'Growth Corridor' Small Firms*, London: Small Business Research Trust.

Storey, D. and Westhead, P. (1997) 'Management training and small firm performance: why is the link so weak?', *International Small Business Journal*, 14, 4: 13- 24.

Taylor, S. (2001) 'Managing people in smaller organizations', unpublished PhD thesis, Manchester Metropolitan University.

Van Maanen, J. and Kunda, G. (1989) 'Real feelings: emotional expression and organizational culture', in L. Cummings and B. Staw (eds) *Research in Organisational Behavior*, vol. 11, London: JAI Press.

Vinten, G. (2000) 'Training in small and medium-sized enterprises', *Industrial and Commercial Training*, 32, 1: 9- 14.

Watson, T. (1980) *Sociology, Work and Industry*, London: Routledge and Kegan Paul.

Westrip, A. (1982) 'Effects of employment legislation on small firms', in D. Watkins, J. Stanworth and A. Westrip (eds) *Stimulating Small Firms*, Aldershot: Gower.

4 Now you see it now you don't

Comparing traditional and discourse readings of HRD in small organisations

Clare Rigg and Kiran Trehan

Objectives

Research into human resource development within SMEs has been dominated by representationalist perspectives of organisation, by narrow definitions of HRD as training and by quantitative research methods. There have been more recent exhortations to advance the understanding of SME HRD through qualitative and longitudinal methods but, as a consequence of limited theorising on HRD, there has also been a lack of clarity over what might be researched. Within the small firms literature, intensive studies of the workplace are comparatively rare, yet, as Curran *et al.* (1996) argue, snapshot approaches based on survey evidence have frequently been used to formulate views on HRD activities. How then can research be encouraged that involves in-depth scrutiny of HRD within SMEs and small organisations more generally?

This chapter will argue for the potential offered to researching, understanding and practising HRD in small organisations, of taking a learning view of HRD and a discourse perspective on organisation and learning. The arguments are demonstrated through comparing a traditional and a discourse interpretation of research material collected ethnographically in three small companies.

We aim to contribute to a research approach which we believe will deepen understanding of HRD in small organisations by combining three strands that have not generally been integrated: ideas from recent debates on what HRD comprises, perspectives on learning, and a discourse perspective on organisation. Our argument is that this integration offers new insights for fruitful research into and practice of HRD in small organisations.

In summary the objectives for this chapter are to:

- explore the value of a discourse perspective in understanding HRD activity within small organisations;
- compare traditional and discursive readings of HRD.

The chapter is structured as follows: the next section introduces the three case study companies, providing brief details on their size, business and engagement with formal HRD activity. This is followed by an outline of the theoretical context, which explores literature on HRD in small organisations, and draws from current debates on how HRD might be theorised, before offering a discourse perspective on organisation and learning. Following explanation of the research context, this conceptual framework is applied to demonstrate contrasting interpretations of the three companies' HRD offered by a discursive reading compared with a traditional reading.

Introducing the companies

The three companies are Metal Tubes, Feeding the Stars and Radical ReDesign. All company and personal names are pseudonyms.

Company 1: Metal Tubes

Metal Tubes was founded in the early 1990s by two men, friends who used to work together, and now has ten direct employees. Their business is to project manage the design and installation of air-conditioning systems. The business is successful and steadily growing. Company members' engagement in formal HRD is summarised below:

- Fifty per cent of staff have engineering degrees.
- Both directors did Diploma in Management Studies (DMS) and MSc during the first three to four years of Metal Tubes.
- One has begun a Doctorate in Business Administration (DBA).
- Two project staff have begun DMS.
- One trainee is sponsored on a part-time degree.
- Two Modern Apprentices are employed and sponsored in training.

Company 2: Feeding the Stars

Feeding the Stars was started in the late 1980s, providing mobile accommodation, food, shopping and servicing for film sets on location around Britain. The founder was a woman who had worked for several years in the television industry. There are now ten to fifteen employees, varying month by month with assignment. Company members' engagement in formal HRD is as follows:

- The owner-manager completed a DMS in 1999.
- No others are formally training, although the owner-manager is encouraging two of the staff to also begin a DMS.
- No other post-school qualifications have been taken apart from HGV licences.

Company 3: Radical ReDesign

Radical ReDesign was created as a design agency in the early 1990s by the current managing director. It is successful and growing, with thirty employees currently.

Their business is now defined as 'designing the customer brand experience', deploying graphic design, interior design and architecture to help clients rebrand themselves. Formal HRD activity is as follows:

• Over 80 per cent of staff have professional/graduate qualifications in graphic design, interior designer, architecture and marketing.
• Two account managers have recently done the Chartered Institute of Marketing's postgraduate Diploma in Marketing.
• Short (one-day) formal courses are annually used.

In summary, if a traditional HRD reading of the companies is made, defining HRD as training, measured quantitatively by number of training days or spend per head per annum, Metal Tubes would be hailed as a high HRD investor. Radical ReDesign would be described as having a very highly qualified workforce and as having moderate HRD activity. Of Feeding the Stars it would be said that there is currently no training going on, and the workforce is not highly skilled, although the owner-manager is relatively unusual among entrepreneurs in having a formal management qualification. However, through exploring discourse perspectives on organising, managing and learning, this chapter will show that a quite different reading of the cases is possible.

Theoretical context

One of the key arguments of this section is that while theorising of HRD has recently taken great strides, published empirical research into HRD in general, and specific-ally about small organisations remains dominated by narrow definitions of HRD, poor theorising and methods confined to measurement of the easily measurable.

HRD research in SMEs: 'Small firms don't train, do they?'

The prevailing wisdom on HRD in small firms is epitomised by the statement that SMEs do not spend equivalent on training compared to medium and large companies,[1] and rarely have a staff member with a dedicated HRD or training role (Westhead and Storey 1997; Hill and Stewart 1999; Hill 2001). Ergo their HRD is inferior, disorganised, if not non-existent. Academic and policy-orientated consul-tancy research into SME HRD activity have, until recently, predominantly been through quantitative survey, using such measures of HRD activity as the training expenditure or number of days training per head (e.g. Hitt 1998; Sadler-Smith *et al.* 1999; Training 1998; Welch 1996; Westhead and Storey 1997), or the take-up rates of NVQs or other SME provision (Further Education Funding Council (FEFC) 1994; as critiqued by Jennings *et al.* 1996; Matlay and Hyland 1997).

Some studies have taken a broad definition of HRD, for example, Jennings *et al.* (1996) refer to training and organisation development, when discussing HRD in small firms; Hill and Stewart (1999: 108) define HRD as 'an intricate web of issues and activities'. However, most frame HRD as training and development, in the traditional ASK (attitudes, skills and knowledge) style. For example the definition within the UK Investors in People is 'any activity that develops skills and/or knowledge and/or behaviour . . . including formal courses, on-the-job, shadowing, mentoring, coaching etc.' (Investors in People UK 1996: 271).

Pettigrew *et al.* (1990) argued, on the basis of a comprehensive overview of existing research on training and HRD in small businesses, that there was a notable paucity of research on training and related issues, such as organisational learning and human resource development. They went on to highlight that the literature is distinguished by a lack of specialised research that ascertains the importance or otherwise of human resource issues to small business strategies. Hendry *et al.* (1991: 2) add to the debate by highlighting that in the growing field of small business research 'the human resource dimension, including the training of employees, has largely been neglected'.

Storey and Westhead (1997), in their review of research on training and HRD argue that they were unable to consistently document methodologically well-conducted research, which produced reliable results that could be generalised across the whole sector. Matlay (1996) adds to the debate by pointing out that most of the research conducted in this area appears to be quantitative, and longitudinal research appears to be absent in the area of training and human resource development. Consequently, very few data exist in this arena.

However, despite the above, it is becoming somewhat commonplace to point out the importance of HRD within small business development. Ram *et al.* (2000) argue that academic commentary (Hendry *et al.* 1995) and the crowded platform of enterprise support initiatives (Matlay 2000; Storey 1994) are testimony to the coupling of training and small business performance. The importance of HRD to the delivery of organisational goals has not diminished. Yet, despite the hype of HRD activity, Keep (1989) and Storey (1994) argue that training remains a cost rather than an investment and that it is haphazardly undertaken, with limited systematic planning and with no indication that it forms part of a rigorous HRD approach and strategy. The growing body of research within the SME sector consistently shows a gap between academic rhetoric and small business practices in relation to HRD. Training and development issues in SME's remain paradoxical and primarily driven by the market positioning of the firm, the prevailing economic conditions and the shortage of relevant training at affordable prices (see Matlay 1999; Matlay and Hyland 1997).

There are voices critical of the assumption that the barometer of HRD activity in SME's is expenditure on training. For example, Curran *et al.* (1996), critique the focus on vocational training and quantitative research methods, and broaden the field, presenting a typology of training that incorporates informal and off-the-job sources, such as trade fairs and networking. Nevertheless, this still constrains HRD to training activities. Anderson and Skinner (1999: 236) have argued: 'Previous studies of small firms . . . have tended to take a quantitative, cross-sectional approach . . . [which] cannot fully incorporate the complexity of management and organisation development processes'. Vickerstaff and Parker (1995: 60) make a similar argument, arguing the benefit of qualitative research: 'case study based work has revealed a high degree of unplanned and informal training activity in small firms'.

On not defining HRD

Lee (2001) argues for non-definition - drawing from Chia's (1996) ontology of becoming as justification. She says: 'instead, I suggest we seek to establish, in a moral and inclusive way, what we would like HRD to *become*, in the knowledge that it will never *be*, but that we might thus influence its *becoming*' (Lee 2001: 338, original emphases).

There is much to find appealing in her argument, however, we want to argue that non-definition has different consequences for theoretical discussions than for empirical research. We suggest that much HRD research has suffered by being predicated on an assumption that HRD is training, and that therefore, if you want to know about HRD in organisations, you research training activity, be it formal or informal. While we do not propose imposition of a definition of HRD for universal use, we believe it is essential to engage in debates as to what comprises HRD if HRD research is to be deepened and enriched.

We are arguing that impoverished research results from underdeveloped theory. Jim McGoldrick *et al.* (2001a) make the converse argument concerning the impact of impoverished research on theory: 'The process of defining HRD is *frustrated* by the apparent lack of boundaries and parameters, and *elusiveness* created through the lack of depth of empirical evidence for some conceptual aspects of HRD' (McGoldrick *et al.* 2001a: 344, original emphases). They go on to say that 'empirical elusiveness derives from an *inability to show* that HRD has a substantive presence in organisations' (McGoldrick *et al.* 2001a: 349, original emphases).

Concluding the benefits of their holographic metaphor they say: 'it emphasizes the analytical significance of mutually involved processes of social and discursive construction . . . [and] provides interesting methodological questions concerning empirical research' (McGoldrick *et al.* 2001a: 352).

It is to this space that we hope this chapter will contribute, drawing from research undertaken by one of the authors (Clare Rigg) that took a discourse perspective into management learning and practice.

Theorising HRD

Debates on how to define HRD or whether to define it at all have produced some great discussions (e.g. Lee 2001; McGoldrick *et al.* 2001a). One of the exciting developments is the broadening of HRD beyond a focus on training to encompass learning. For example, McGoldrick *et al.* propose a holographic metaphor to understand HRD as: '"the fluid, multifaceted, integrated social artefacts" which are the "continuing outcome" of contextualized learning. HRD then serves as *collective noun* for the various concepts, theories and methods devised to manage and control learning' (McGoldrick *et al.* 2001a: 351, original emphases).

Summing up authors' perspectives in their edited collection, they conclude:

> HRD has a central focus on and concern with learning . . . Therefore we can
> conclude that HRD will be increasingly concerned with facilitating the learning

of individuals, teams and organizations through the design, structuring and organization of work itself.

(McGoldrick *et al.* 2001b: 396)

It is not that in the past there have not been voices calling for recognition of learning within HRD. Marsick and Watkins (1990) are perhaps most notable, drawing attention over ten years ago to informal and incidental sources of learning: 'Informal learning . . . can be planned, but includes learning that is not designed or expected. Incidental learning, by definition, includes the unexpected' (Marsick and Watkins 1990: 215).

Not only does this perspective collapse any boundary between work and rest-of-life, in that experiences outside work can provoke learning about work, but also they acknowledged learning as a collective, not simply an individual process: 'In the process of seeking answers to collective problems, other people learn along with the person initiating the action' (Marsick and Watkins 1990: 217).

Other writers who present a perspective on HRD as integral to organisation processes, include Walton, who talks of human development as part of the fabric of an organisation (cited by Kessels 2001: 387), and says: 'At one level, everyone in a learning organisation is an HRD practitioner . . . [we] all take responsibility for supporting our own learning and that of others. We become part of a network of self-supporting and other-supporting learning communities' (Walton 1999: 407).

Kessels talks of HRD as a 'corporate curriculum' - 'the "rich landscape" of the work environment that invites you to explore, meet others and develop' (Kessels 2001: 388). Such processual views of organising will be elaborated on later.

What we felt was lacking in almost all writing on HRD as learning, was any articulation as to what constituted learning, and consequently how learning might be researched. The next section proposes that if we move away from the representationalist assumptions of organisations on which most HRD research has been predicated, a discourse perspective on organisation provides a framework for researching microprocesses of learning through researching organisation discourses.

Small organisations: what is an 'organisation'?

Most HRD research has been dominated by what Robert Chia describes as *'representationalist thinking'* (1996: vii), the attempt to capture and describe an external reality. Examples of such thinking are illustrated by what Gareth Morgan (1990) describes as functionalist conceptions of organisations, where they are presented as rational systems (Simon 1957), natural systems (Barnard 1938; Parsons 1951) or as open systems: 'coalitions of shifting interest groups that develop goals by negotiation; the structure of the coalition, its activities and its outcomes are strongly influenced by environmental factors' (Scott 1987: 23). Such views are by no means confined to pre-1960 writing. Implicit within more recent books, with titles such as *Organizations and Technical Change* (Preece 1995), is a systems model of organisations.

Functionalist perspectives, as described by Morgan (1990), include Taylorism, human relations, Theory X and Y, structure and technology (e.g. March and Simon 1958), systems theory (e.g. Parsons 1951; Blau 1965; Lawrence and Lorsch 1967), all aim to understand organisations so as to control, predict and search for efficiency. Reed (1992) categorises these as social systems perspectives, in which an organisation is defined by its structure rather than through the individual members. Reification is also evident in language commonly found in management writing, such as 'its history, its corporate culture, societal characteristics, levels of unionisation' (Wilson and Rosenfeld 1990: 4). Although they also say 'at its broadest, the term organization can refer to any collective social arrangement [with] purposive nature' (1990: 6), Wilson and Rosenfeld still conceive of an organisation as some 'thing' more than the collection of individuals, in that they maintain an organisation will normally survive 'beyond the tenure of its present constitutive individuals' (1990: 7).

In contrast with structural perspectives is a more processual perspective of organisations, a view that Mike Reed terms 'negotiated orders', in which an organisation is conceived as 'the temporary product of interactional processes' (1992: 84). Here there is still some sense of reification, even though there is a stronger sense that an organisation cannot exist without people. Considering how interactions might be informed, Morgan offers the view of an organisation as the product of people's unconscious minds, what he terms a 'radical humanist' perspective: 'Organizations . . . are rich in symbolic significance, and many organizational events and activities are to be understood as manifestations of deep psychic processes.' (See also, for example, Pondy *et al.* 1983; White and McSwain 1983.)

Moving further into the realm of organisations as being constructed, rather than structural, Morgan articulates an interpretive perspective of organisations in which an organisation is a

> Socially constructed web of symbolic relationships that are continuously negotiated, renegotiated, affirmed or changed . . . The world of organization is seen and understood as a realm of activity characterised by particular forms of myth-making that expresses significant networks of rules or models of action and gives form to contextually based systems of meaning.
>
> (Morgan 1990: 19)

Reed (1992: 105) terms this view as a 'symbolic construction' of an organisation, a 'processual cultural artefact' in which the focus of organising is through collective meaning making (epitomised for example by Pfeffer 1981; Pettigrew 1985).

Within these latter perspectives, ideas of collective meaning and the role of symbols and myths in meaning-making are fundamental. However, other authors differentiate between individual and shared meaning-making. Ideas of organisations as *interactions* have been developed to differentiate between an organisation as an individual conception and as a shared framework. Denise Fletcher differentiates between a social constructionist perspective, where an organisation is a 'shared system of intelligibility' (1997: 78), and a constructivist perspective, which sees the organisation as in the mind of the individual, reduced as she says to the 'cognitive processing of the individual' (1997: 76).

The idea of organisation combining shared meanings, yet having some sense of realism is found in conceptions such as Clegg and Hardy's, in which they are

> Sites of *situated social action* more or less open both to explicitly organized and formal disciplinary knowledges such as marketing, production, and so on, and also to conversational practices embedded in the broad social fabric, such as gender, ethnic and other culturally defined social relations.
>
> (Clegg and Hardy 1999: 3)

This notion that an organisation is more than just the people is also articulated by Czarniaskwa, in her conception of 'an institutionalised action-net . . . interconnecting acts of organizing' (1998: 26). She suggests an organisation is a community of meaning rather than a community of life (or people), a view echoed by Paul DiMaggio's patterns of shared meaning (cited in Nohria and Eccles 1992).

Fletcher draws on the idea of network, suggesting an organisation is 'a network of interactively shared meanings' (1997: 94), where a network is: 'the social relations in which every individual is embedded' (1997: 49). She says 'Organisations [are] constituted by a mix of social relational processes which are continuously being aligned and negotiated as organisational members attempt to achieve their daily work tasks and personal goals' (1997: 4). She also sees an organisation as more than the members, in that she suggests: 'collective meanings become institutionalised within the organisation through social relational patterns and the development of a common language' (Fletcher 1997: 94).

A discourse perspective on organising

The role of talk is also fundamental to a discourse perspective of organisations. Grant *et al.* (1998: 12) argue: '"organization" can be seen as a continuous process of social accomplishment which, in both senses of the term is *articulated* by and through the deployment of discursive resources.' They maintain discourse is essential to 'constructing, situating, facilitating and communicating the diverse cultural, institutional, political and socio-economic parameters of "organizational being"' (1998: 12). For Mumby and Clair 'discourse is the principal means by which organization members create a coherent social reality that frames their sense of who they are' (1997: 181).

Discourse has been variously defined. At the simplest level it refers to spoken dialogue (Sinclair and Coulthard 1975), although commonly the term is used to encompass written as well as spoken text (e.g. Gilbert and Mulkay 1984; Potter and Wetherell 1987). With the recognition that 'texts' can be multi-semiotic, discourse has been widened by some to encompass music and art, for example Fairclough (1995). Others define discourse more broadly, as discursive practices: not only language, but also ideas and philosophies (Van Dijk 1997). If discourse is understood in this way, discursive practices 'do not just describe things, they *do* things' (Potter and Wetherell 1987: 6), i.e. talk is intended to shape practices. Tony Watson (2000: 563) refers to discourse as 'a piece of language in action'. However, this is not to suggest that organisations are no more than language, or are simply figments of social imagination, without material being. We will be drawing from network views of organisation, their ideas of action, the role of language, and the notion of dynamic processes that reinforce, yet can change an organisation. We will draw on the view of discourse as discursive practices that shape action, defining an organisation as a network of shared meanings which are created, perpetuated and modified through discursive practices.

Sambrook and Stewart's (1998) distinction between discourse as noun and as verb is helpful in clarifying the research focus. The distinction is employed in the following way: discourse is understood as a coherent, but not watertight, system of meanings which encompasses language, ideas and philosophies. Discourse as noun is the content of a particular discourse - the discursive resources or particular ideas or words which have no inevitable meaning, but are interconnected together to give a discourse its logic and apparent coherence. So the concepts power, control or performance have different meanings within technicist and critical management discourses.

Discourse as verb are the practices deployed to express dominant values, beliefs and ideas - the discursive practices or acts which convey meaning (Van Dijk 1997). For Foucault (1969) discursive practices '*position* us in relations of power' (cited by Ian Parker 1992: 6), or as Ian Parker defines it, they are an act or practice which 'reproduces the material basis of the institution' (Parker 1992: 17). Discursive practices encompass a range of communicative acts,[2] both verbal and non-verbal, including stories, narratives, rituals such as making the tea or the format of meetings, rhetoric, language games such as names, conversations, sense-making, signs and architecture - the physical organisation of space and bodies. Fairclough (1995) describes these as forms of textual production and interpretation (cited in Grant *et al.* 1998: 3).

The distinction between discursive practice and discursive resource has methodological implications, in that a focus on resources is a focus on the content, while inclusion of discursive practices is to recognise that the processes of communication (or textual production) shape our sense of the world as much as the content of any communication. As Grant argues, 'Everyday attitudes and behaviour, along with our perceptions of what we believe to be reality, are shaped and influenced by the discursive practices and interactions we engage in and are exposed or subjected to' (Grant *et al.* 1998: 2).

Fundamental to the meaning-making engaged in by people at work is language: 'using words everyday to make sense of what they are doing and to persuade others' (Watson 1994: 585). Jill Woodilla also emphasises the role of talk: 'Socially constructed meaning is created in language-based interactions with "conversation" as the most common taken-for-granted practice' (1998: 31). She further argues that discourses can be used to exert power, for example, through controlling meanings, and to challenge power, as some differences of interpretation get suppressed by a dominant discourse. Her views also illustrate the potential for marginalisation and silencing of some voices, which cannot contribute to meaning-making.

Some authors, exploring relations between talk and action, caution against implying a simple linear link between new talk, new meaning, different thinking, new action. For example, Hardy *et al.* (1998: 69) ask 'exactly *how* do shared understandings, created by conversational narratives and interaction lead to action?' They suggest that any action that emerges from particular conversational activity and content is mediated by an individual's identity, skills and emotions.

In summary, concepts of discourse, discursive practice and discursive resource are fundamental to the conceptualisation of managing and organising. Following on from this we ask the question, to what extent is a process of learning to engage with new discourse?

Learning

When a learning perspective on HRD is adopted, this opens up greater recognition that development is ongoing through informal, continuous processes, what Hendry (1994) describes as learning through rather than on the job. Anderson and Skinner (1999: 241) suggest 'Indeed, as the process of business development occurs, those involved will be constantly developing, largely through informal, often unplanned, training and experience as part of their normal job'. However, as identified above, these mystical processes of 'learning' are rarely articulated.

Learning is one of those concepts used in much literature as if it was self-evident what it means. Yet within the literature on management and organisational learning there is rarely an explicit discussion of what it means to say someone is learning, or has learnt. There is much focus on how we might learn, but a definition of learning is usually implicit. Arguably, this might reflect how little is really understood about learning processes, in terms of neurology, emotion and consciousness, rather than the cognitive and development psychology which dominate discussion on learning.

For example, for Casey (1983: 39) learning is about 'doing things differently'. Harri-Augsten and Thomas (1991: 47) suggest: 'learning is better thought of as a change within the person. It appears as a new or improved way of thinking or feeling about something or of perceiving it or doing it'. Their definition seems to collapse several categories together, as does Revans's thesis that

> true learning consists mainly in the reorganization, or reinterpretation, of what is already known - does call for the learners to understand what may be preventing them from using more fruitfully that to which they already might have access, if only they knew also how to secure that access.
>
> (Revans 1980: 289)

Griffin's questions to learners produced an interesting list of forty learning processes which they named, including making meaning; creating knowledge; expanding alertness; releasing creativity; creating energy; being aware of self as a learner; validating oneself; unlearning; questioning assumptions and ideas; reframing with new assumptions; changing the past (Griffin 1987: 216).

Within the adult learning literature, some writers try to distinguish between different learning processes to present a dichotomy of learning, differentiating between an external view of learning, where a person adds on new knowledge, or an internal view, where a person is deeply changed (for example, Rogers 1983; Freire 1972; Argyris and Schön 1996). What these share is a view that there are different levels of learning, one at which the self is untouched, another at which it is affected, producing changes in values or perspectives. Other writers conceive of levels of learning, but along a spectrum, rather than as a dichotomy. For example Bateson (1973) outlined four levels of learning:

- Level 0, where there is no learning, response is habitual, without regard to context, and responses to feedback is poor.
- Level I at which there is error correction, through trial and error responses to new contexts.
- At Level II there is an ability to recognise and inhabit different contexts; to be able to take different perspectives, but still to hold one worldview.
- At Level III a person has an ability to step outside their previous worldview, has an awareness of their own subjectivity, has gained control over habitual ways and can take responsibility for making changes.

This perspective on learning connects with what people think they are doing when they are learning, almost what they will allow themselves to learn. Belenky *et al.* (1986) encapsulate this idea when they talk of women having five stages of development (or learning) they can move through:

1   *Silence:* women experience themselves as having no voice and being subject to external authority.
2   *Received knowledge:* they believe that they are capable of receiving and reproducing knowledge, but not creating it.
3   *Subjective knowledge:* knowledge is seen as personal, private and subjectively known.
4   *Procedural knowledge:* where they apply objective procedures for obtaining and communicating knowledge.
5   *Constructed knowledge:* where the learner comes to view knowledge as contextual and themselves as potential creators of knowledge, through both subjective and objective strategies.

What this suggests is that individuals' learning is connected to their relationship with themselves and their world, in particular their sense of control over and contribution to it. It also implies an interplay between cognition and emotions in learning, (as strongly argued, for example, by Vince 1996; Trehan and Rigg, in preparation).

The significance of this discussion is that we want to argue that there is a relationship between Bateson's and Belenky's views of learning and a discourse perspective, in the sense that learning can provide new discursive resources and contribute to new discursive practices - put simply, new ways of thinking about, talking about and doing work.

Summary of theoretical context

In summary, the conceptual framework for this study draws on a definition of discourse as comprising language, ideas and philosophies. Individual ideas and language are discursive resources coalesced together with apparent coherence, and communicated through discursive practices that shape meaning and action, which do not just describe things, but do things. Organisation is defined as a network of shared meanings which are created, perpetuated and modified through discursive practices, but in so doing the idea of network is used not as a reification but as a dynamic process.

We have argued that although recent theorising on HRD has broadened to encompass learning and to see HRD as integral to organising processes, most HRD research and in this context most research on HRD in small organisations remains dominated by HRD defined as training activities and by a reification of organisations in which they are conceived as 'things', particularly structures. This frames the possibilities for research narrowly, encouraging a quantitative approach, only measuring the easily measurable 'things' like expenditure, training days and qualifications.

We also argue that, although a number of people have been advocating qualitative and longitudinal research for some time, there has frequently been no clarity as to what to research. However, if HRD is framed as learning, the research focus shifts to processes through which individuals learn and to organisational processes which promote learning. If a discourse perspective is taken where 'organisations' are conceived as 'networks of shared meaning which are created, perpetuated and modified through discursive practices', research can focus on the 'social relationship processes', the language used, the discursive resources and practices deployed.

Research context

The conceptual framework for this research was based on the concept of discourse deployed in three ways, first, within a network perspective on organisations, with 'talk' seen as essential both to the conception of organisation; second, to the process of managing; third, learning is presented as an encounter with new discourse. In taking an organisation discourse perspective on the concepts of organisation and managing, talk and language are entwined with action. Management practice is therefore open to research through studying the talk/action in use, the 'network of action' or in other words, the discursive practices of a particular organisation and the language or discursive resources managers use. This focus lends itself to ethnography because of the possibilities to collect accounts, to observe actions and processes and to explore the feelings, thoughts and meanings people attribute to situations, as they happen. In particular this study used 'Microethnography [which] zeroes in on *particular* settings drawing on the ways that a cultural ethos is reflected in microcosm in selected aspects of every day life' (Wolcott 1995: 102).

The form of micro-ethnography employed was shadowing of key managers interacting with other people in the course of their work, combined with semi-structured ethnographic or narrative interviews of them and their colleagues.

Czarniawska (1998: 28) describes her use of shadowing as allowing 'me to move with them and to move from one point in an action net to another because I am after not individual experience but a collective construction'. In this study the aim of the shadowing was to observe key collective events, such as particular kinds of meetings, which could constitute Wolcott's cultural ethos in microcosm. This was combined with two other ethnographic methods, narrative interviews and ethnographic interviews. In narrative interviews, using Czarniaswska's definition of 'chronological relations of events that occurred under a specified period of time' (1998: 28), I explicitly asked for stories, for example, of organisation members' early impressions when they joined the company; for accounts of funny and difficult incidents. Ethnographic interviews (Spradley 1979) were defined as generalised, of the moment, not necessarily collecting stories. An example would be taking the opportunity at a tea-break in the middle of a meeting, as we waited for the kettle to boil, of asking someone what they meant, felt or thought about a particular aspect of the meeting.

This combination of methods offered the possibility of taking an ethnographic approach, with its benefits of depth, while not being an ethnography in the sense of studying one organisation through long-term immersion as a participant observer.

In the three case study companies three core managers were shadowed, accompanying them throughout a day at their workplace, observing them interacting with their work colleagues, interviewing them and several of their colleagues, talking to people opportunistically, observing organisation members going about their work as a non-participant observer. In total eleven people were interviewed. The resultant research material was a mixture of tape recordings, which became transcribed texts; notes and documents such as compliments slips, and project records from the key meeting and logos. The material therefore combined research notes and verbatim records of language used in various interactions, and accounts of discursive practices employed.

Findings

The research material was analysed with the aid of two key readings: Parker's (1992) framework for discourse analysis and Weick's (1995) concept of sense-making. While Parker's steps were not followed to the letter, they provided a sorting category for analysing actions within particular settings, for instance with questions such as in Step 2, 'What are the connotations evoked to me?'; in Step 5, 'What's the relationship between the text author and the addressee - what "role" are they being put in to receive the message?' or in Step 6, 'What right has the addressee to speak - what can they say?' The value in Weick's sense-making was his guidance to consider authoring, identity construction and what he calls ongoing reality-making through retrospective sense-making.

This chapter presents just a small part of the research analysis, discussed in terms of learning.

HRD in the case study companies: comparing a traditional with a discourse reading

In this section the three companies are revisited and a comparative picture presented of their HRD activity from a traditional and a discourse reading of HRD.

Company 1: Metal Tubes'

Metal Tubes

Ten people.
Nine years old.
Project manage the design and instalment of air-conditioning systems.
Successful, growing.
Fifty per cent of staff have engineering degrees.
Company set up by two friends who used to work together in a large company.
Both directors did Diploma in Management Studies (DMS) and MSc during the first three to four years of Metal Tubes.
One had begun a Doctorate in Business Administration (DBA).
Two project staff begun DMS.
One trainee is sponsored on a part-time degree.
Two Modern Apprentices.

Key members interviewed
Sam: director
Bethany: project design and sales manager
John: project manager
Andy: project manager

In Metal Tubes there is a strong ethos that improvement comes from learning, which can be formal, but also everyday. Much of this is done collectively, socially, through reviews that enable reflection and questioning of experience, as well as systematically researching some areas (e.g. project management literature) to share with all staff. Formal, course-based learning is encouraged to be brought into the company, through practice, and explicitly, not simply to affect the individual's knowledge and qualification.

One form is through a project review stage built into the project management steps applied to every piece of work. Another is the way in which Sam and others have researched and presented ideas in their monthly communications forum on quality management, risk management and project management. At this forum, which is attended by all staff, except the apprentices, each project manager reviews their progress, problems and achievements. Others question them on what they've done and why. They can be asked to come to the next meeting having researched into a particular area. For example, one project manager had recently prepared a presentation on planning; one director and another project manager were reading up on project management, preparing a workshop for the other staff. The forum is also a place for 'bringing issues with other people to the table', for giving and receiving feedback. One interviewee said: 'there is no blame factor whatsoever, the only thing that [the directors] do ask is that if the job hasn't gone particularly well, that you learn from it and show that you are learning. The only time that they would not be happy is if you did not learn from your mistake.'

The directors said that all they talked about in the early years was the DMS, and how they were building the company with ideas from their course learning. From the perspective of other staff 'they decided that, you know, they had got this knowledge, let's start bringing it into the company so . . . like the communication meeting . . . the role clarification.'

A standard item on the communications forum agenda is 'training and development' when each person's current or future training and development is discussed. A fundamental principle is that individuals learn, formally on courses, from their work experiences, and from research into theory and practice outside a course context. However, there is also an expectation that this individual learning is systematically shared with others so that all members can learn. So much of the source of new practice comes in this way. As Sam said:

> We find that individuals tend to learn themselves but don't pass that learning on to others and to the wider organisation, and to change the systems that we use, so we have put certain things into play from the projects that Don and I did to try to enable this company to do that, and we go through a cycle of doing it better and doing it not so good.

In the two ensuing accounts Sam was explaining how aspects of how they organise evolved from his Diploma in Management and his MSc course:

> Yes, we have what we would call a - well we have a communications forum which was designed from my DMS paper, funnily enough, that was one of the outputs of my paper. I mean it's a meeting really but we do it in a certain way, for instance we have a workout, what we call workout at the end of the meeting, where everybody sort of gets stuck in and tells everybody what they think of everybody. Usually it's bad but sometimes it can be good as well, because we do try to do the good and the bad, and that is one way of sharing information.
>
> Well this thing about continuous improvement . . . I mean in our business a few years ago it was called total quality management and that was part of continuous improvement, and then from the DMS point of view, and certainly the Action Research MSc point of view, that is very much something you are doing in action research, you are finding out a piece of information, applying it, checking it out and then going back to the literature or your peers or some other area to find out some more information and gradually rack it up how you improve the company, so the two things are very similar. You can overlay action research on to the sort of company that we wanted to be, that was a

company that knew very little to start with but wanted to improve ourselves through the methods that we were getting from the DMS and MSc.

He went on to outline other forms of review they employ, designed to improve their practice:

> On this job we are going to have a peer review as well, so we will do it, we will get to certain milestones on the project and we will stop and we have organised different agendas for different types of review, but one of them is called peer review, and that is when people, the other people in the company, will come into the meeting room, will present how far we have got so far, and we will ask for their inputs into the project, but also we will be telling them what we have done and why we have done it in the way that we have, so that they can go away with some learning from that.
>
> Risk management is another one that we are doing just now . . . I have gone to the books, done the risk management reading, now I am going to present at the next communications forum, but also I have given them copies of the various chapters that I think . . . I have read and summarised most of them, to other people so we can have a proactive meeting on risk management. So I will do fifteen minutes on it, saying this is what I have read, this is what I think, this is what a risk register is, you have read the stuff, so what do you think and how can we then simplify it as much as possible . . . and then we will – people will go away with some understanding of risk management and some forms and some – or I will go away with their thinking on what I have done, plus what they have read, and we will have a new process in place.

This story illustrates both the use of 'external expertise' to gain ideas, but also a collaborative way of evolving a process of working.

Bethany echoed the use of projects as a source of learning, as well as drawing from literature:

> We are working on a new project now, in Torbay, and it's a very prestigious project for us at the moment. Sam is going to be the design manager and he has kind of picked his team for the project, and basically Sam and I are doing the design work together and we are kind of reading lots of books about project management and getting loads of ideas and just doing things in a far more effective manner than we did on Cardiff, so I suppose the learning from Cardiff has really helped me on this project for Torbay, it's good.

These accounts illustrate 'big' sources of developments in practice. However, the communications forum, a discursive practice directly modelled on Sam's management course, also illustrated how a small exchange was used as a discursive practice to bring about new actions from members. On one project there was a significant unexpected cost. As the project manager circulated his cost sheets, there was general laughter and banter on the contra charge item. It referred to carbon filled vats, which

Sam had costed on the basis of simply filling up with carbon, a complete misinterpretation of what was involved which had resulted in a significant under-quote. Sam: 'This is another example of something special or different that should go on the risk register. We didn't have one then'.

In this interaction Sam's discursive act was to use his mistake as a parable of learning for them all, to reinforce his earlier directive on using a risk register.

In conventional training terms HRD would be visible within the company through their formal courses. However, taking a discursive approach to HRD the level of development is higher, and reaches far beyond formal courses.

Company Two: Feeding the Stars

Feeding the Stars

Ten to fifteen people, varying month by month with assignment.
Thirteen years old.
Provides mobile accommodation, food, shopping and servicing for film sets
    on location around Britain.
Owner-manager completed a DMS in 1999.
No others are formally training, although the owner-manager is encouraging
    two of the staff to also begin a DMS.
There are no post-school qualifications apart from HGV licences besides the
    owner-manager's DMS.

Key members interviewed
Dale: owner-manager
Jim: mechanic
Grant: assistant manager/site manager

Dale described how she brought her course learning into the workplace:

Dale: each week was - I was on a learning curve and that was it, every week, and
        not only did I teach myself - I was learning, my husband was learning as well,
        . . . so each week I used to come in and practice, practice on them . . . I put
        everything into practice and they all used to know . . .

        so I sat down next to Jim [the mechanic] and I was talking to him as I used
        to. Every Wednesday he used to say 'How did you get on?' and I just said 'I
        can't get my head round this', and he was coming out with stuff that he didn't
        realise he knew, you know . . . and he was really giving me loads of
        information. I said to him 'Do you realise?' He said, 'I'm thick I'm only a
        mechanic' and I said 'No you're not'. And he was actually feeding on it.

        So I tried to give them what I have learned now, to be better supervisors
        and managers and we are looking for courses to send them on . . .

CR: how can you see that?

Dale: Well they're a lot more understanding now. They'll come in here saying 'I'm not taking him, he's bloody useless, I don't know why he's here.' I say 'Sit down and talk about it' . . . they all do that now . . . they do the same with their lads.

Some of the micro-processes which promote learning are small examples of reflective practice; for example, Jim, the mechanic relates how

> now we make notes and Dale [the owner-manager] wants to put everything in a book and I put everything in a book and it just corresponds. I mean like last night, I was round the house last night and we had a half-hour talk and we sorted it out, so communication I think is the main thing, which I think we lacked before.

Jim's role is to service the company's vehicles, including their generators, of which there can be six in different locations around the country at any one time. Although he visits the locations, and resolves many problems directly himself, he is based at the company's premises and also works by talking the site staff through problems, i.e. by helping them develop the capability to resolve their own problems: 'I'll get, oh Jim I forgot to tell you this, this and this and I just talk them through it. Most of them are very good lads and you can talk them through a problem and they can do it'.

These are examples of informal processes, discursive practices, which opportunistically develop people. However, Dale has also formally introduced what she sees as a key idea from her course experience. Communication meetings are held involving all the team, albeit erratically because of the staff being away on location for two to three months at a time, particularly in the summer. The purpose of these was described as being to air problems; to share feelings about work; to be open and clear the air; to exchange experiences of working. The model for these is the action learning set which Dale engaged in during her DMS.

Company Three 'Radical ReDesign'

Radical ReDesign

Employs around thirty people.
Over ten years old.
Turnover growing.
Created as a design agency originally.
On the company compliments slip, their business is now described as: 'designing the customer brand experience'.
Over 80 per cent staff have professional/graduate qualifications in graphic design, interior designers, architecture and marketing.
Two managers have recently done or are doing the Chartered Institute of Marketing's postgraduate Diploma in Marketing at their own request.
Short (one-day) formal courses are used.

> *Key members interviewed*
> Rick: brand consultant
> Rowan: marketing director
> Catriona: account manager
> Andy: account manager

In Radical ReDesign, learning is not a dominant discursive resource of the company, and neither formal nor informal learning interactions are part of the discursive practices deployed to develop new ways of working. A few individuals have attended formal courses, but they initiate this themselves, and whether their learning affects their practice is incidental. There is no training and development agenda item within regular meetings and there is no developmental appraisal system. Rick, the brand consultant, has completed the Chartered Institute of Marketing's postgraduate Diploma in Marketing. Rowan, the marketing director, has a degree, but no postgraduate management education; Catriona is also studying the same postgraduate Diploma in Marketing.

Rick was enthusiastic about his course learning and has drawn from his diploma to organise seminars for his colleagues, with the aim of sharing his newly formed ideas on brands and the role of design. He said his Diploma in Marketing gave him both a business language that helped him talk to clients and a new language of thought that gave him a different way of thinking about graphic design, and of enacting his role, in other words new discursive practices. As a result of his course learning he has redefined his role from account manager to brand consultant and in parallel he said he had redefined the company business from one of producing graphic design products, to one of providing consultancy in creating a customer experience, to help clients rebrand themselves.

From other people's stories and my observations it could also be argued that the dominant discourse of this company is implicitly one of non-learning. For example, in several of Catriona's comments she suggested a climate of fear that stifled exchange and described her perception of how people conceal their mistakes, and become adept at managing appearances within the weekly sales meeting, which is supposed to be the main site where managers exchange progress reports on their projects:

> if you can blag it in the meetings, you can get away with it anyway. If you can just say 'Yep, done that. Two grand, no problem.' You could be lying. It's all about attitude, it's not about a reality, it's not about honesty. By any means. I don't think it is anyway 'cause I think there's a lot of lies that go around in that atmosphere as well. Because you have to defend yourself, 'cause you're in a forum, public debate in front of your colleagues. So, if you have to blag it a bit, then you probably will. And I have done in the past.

She said:

I think it's the nature of the meeting. I don't feel that we pull together as a team anyway. Which I've said countless times, that we need to have more meetings where we sit and say, look, this is what we've been doing this week on the accounts. So it's more . . . it's less about sales and more about the opportunities that might, it should be more about the opportunities that might be in the account. So I might say, or Louise might say oh I did something, blah blah blah with my client, have you thought about doing that with yours? Oh no I haven't, maybe I'll ask them about that.

In her view Rowan's persona stifles talk, to the detriment of exchanging experiences of each other's projects, or of bringing about more or different working practices:

Catriona said:

> If I was working in combination with somebody, or with a *team* then it would be very different, you'd have to share, it would be more female. And I think, I can't say for sure, but I think more would be got out of me, I don't know exactly how, but it would be a more honest interaction. And maybe I would, well I would work differently, I'd work with other people . . .
>
> we never ever sit down together, apart from that Monday morning meeting, we never sit down as a *team* of people, running accounts, and say 'What's happening on yours?' So I've got no idea what Adrian does, and I don't really know what Louise does. We chat occasionally, but it's not a relaxed atmosphere downstairs either. Because everybody needs to be seen to be working because of that driving person there.

The suggestion here is of an organisation discourse that neither encompasses discursive resources of sharing or continual learning and improvement nor promotes discursive practices of exchange or collaborative problem-solving. This picture can also be drawn from Rowan's own words. First, he is impatient to see changes in the company, and impelled by a sense of urgency. If he could he said he'd close the company down and restart it, as a way of achieving the changed ways of working he'd like to see. Then, he said: 'I'd change it today'. A second insight comes from a discussion we had on organisation development. We talked through types of possible interventions, which are designed to involve people, to generate ideas from them, to work with 'hearts and minds'. His response, made without irony, was 'You mean, pretend to ask them what they think?'

Interpretation

Now you see 'it', now you don't

If a traditional HRD reading of the companies were made, defining HRD as training, measured quantitatively by number of training days or spend per head per annum, Metal Tubes would be hailed as a high HRD investor. Radical ReDesign could be described as having a very highly qualified workforce and as having moderate HRD activity. Of Feeding the Stars it would be said that there is currently no training going on, and the workforce is not highly skilled, although the owner-manager is relatively unusual among entrepreneurs in having a formal management qualification.

A contrasting picture is presented if the cases are interpreted from a discourse perspective. Metal Tubes emerges as a company in which learning and improvement are integral discursive resources. Learning was perhaps the most frequently used word by all those I interviewed, through both formal, and on-the-job means. It seemed a discursive resource that was integral to their accounts of the company.

Several processes within Feeding the Stars are discursive practices that promote learning, through conversations that share the owner-manager's formal course learning, and through the communications meetings. A discursive reading of this company's HRD presents a picture of more extensive HRD activity than a traditional reading.

The organisation discourse of Radical ReDesign neither encompasses discursive resources of sharing or continual learning and improvement nor promotes discursive practices of exchange or collaborative problem-solving. A discourse reading of the company as presented here suggests a company with a dominant discourse of non-learning - a worse picture than conventional measures would suggest.

Learning and practice

The case studies illustrate one approach to HRD in small organisations, through which the engagement of one or two influential individuals in formal learning, has been fed back into the company, through changed language and practices, in effect producing new management discourse. Taking a discourse perspective reveals processes of learning and development that go well beyond the individual who did a course; that affect other staff both individually and collectively in their working practices, even encompassing processes which facilitate 'unlearning' (Anderson and Skinner 1999). With all three focal managers it is possible to say that their course-acquired language had become a language of action in their managing and organising. In other words they had been provided with new discursive resources.

Conclusion

There has been much interest recently in whether HRD benefits companies' bottom line. This debate seems dead-end, while it is dominated by definitions of HRD as training and research methods that measure training spend and qualification levels. One observation from the three case companies in this chapter is that these methods fail to detect patterns of organising, or relations between individual learning and organising. The case studies illustrate how a processual and discursive view of HRD, enables the possibility of seeing a different picture of HRD in SMEs. If a processual view of organisation is taken, seeing 'them' as networks of interaction that are created and sustained by discursive practices, and HRD is understood, both as interconnected with learning, and as discursive action, this opens up possibilities for future research methods and research questions, see Figure 4.1.

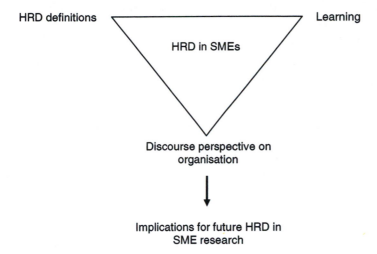

Figure 4.1 A discourse perspective on HRD and learning in SMEs.

Learning points

- HRD can be the engagement of one or two influential individuals in formal learning, that gets fed back into the company, through changed language and practices, in effect producing new management discourse. Processes of learning and development then go well beyond the individual who did a course, affecting other staff both individually and collectively in their working practices.
- Formal HRD investment can be undermined by organisation processes that block learning, so measuring organisations' formal HRD activity alone can give a highly distorted perspective on their HRD.
- To enhance understanding of HRD within SMEs, if not more generally, a discourse perspective on organisation and on HRD, indicates a need for research methods that enable the study of HRD in action - the micro-processes of development. Taking a discursive view of HRD is therefore to research how it is done, and talked about; how development occurs in the course of talking and working.

Notes

1 We use the European Commission's definitions of small: 0- 49 employees; medium: 50-249; large: 250+ (Commission of the European Communities Recommendation of 3 April 1996).
2 Discursive act and discursive practice will be used interchangeably.

Bibliography

Anderson, V. and Skinner, D. (1999) 'Organizational learning in practice: how do small businesses learn to operate internationally?', *Human Resource Development International*, 2, 3: 235- 58.

Argyris, C. and Schön, D. (1996) *Organizational Learning II: Theory, Method, and Practice*, Wokingham: Addison-Wesley.

Barnard, C. (1938) *The Functions of the Executive*, Cambridge, MA: Harvard University Press.

Bateson, G. (1973) *Steps towards an Ecology of the Mind*, London: Paladin.

Belenky, M. F., Clinchy, B. M., Golderger, N. R. and Tarube, R. (1986) *Women's Ways of Knowing: The Development of Self, Voice and Mind*, New York: Basic Books.

Bennett, R. J. and Robson, P. J. (1999) 'The use of external business advice by SMEs in Britain', *Entrepreneurship and Regional Development*, 11: 155- 80.

Blau, P. M. (1965) 'The comparative study of organizations', *Industrial and Labour Relations Review*, 28: 323- 38.

Casey, D. (1983) 'Where action learning fits in', in M. Pedler (ed.) *Action Learning in Practice*, London: Gower.

Chia, R. (1996) *Organizational Analysis as Deconstructive Practice*, Berlin and New York: De Gruyter.

Clegg, S. R. and Hardy, C. (eds) (1999) *Studying Organizations*, London: Sage.

Curran, J., Blackburn, R. A., Kitching, J. and North, J. (1996) *Establishing Small Firms Training Practices, Needs, Difficulties and Use of Industry Training Organisations*, London: HMSO.

Curran, J., Blackburn, R., Kirtching, J. and North, J. (1997) 'Small firms and workforce training: some results, analysis and policy implications from a national survey', in M. Ram, D. Deakins and D. Smallbone (eds) *Small Firms: Enterprising Futures*, London: Paul Chapman.

Czarniawska, B. (1998) *A Narrative Approach to Organization Studies*, Qualitative Research Methods Series 43, London: Sage.

DiMaggio, P. J. and Powell, W. (eds) (1991) *The New Institutionalism in Organizational Analysis*, Chicago: University of Chicago Press.

ENSR (1997) *The European Observatory for SMEs – Fifth Annual Report*, European Network for SME Research, Zoetermeer: EIM Small Business Research and Consultancy.

Fairclough, N. (1995) *Critical Discourse Analysis*, London: Longman.

Fletcher, D. (1997) 'Organisational networking, strategic change and the family business', unpublished PhD thesis, Nottingham Trent University, UK.

Foucault, M. (1969) *The Archaeology of Knowledge and the Discourse on Language*, translated from the French by A. M. Sheridan Smith, New York: Pantheon (1982).

Freire, P. (1972) *Pedagogy of the Oppressed*, Harmondsworth: Penguin.

Further Education Funding Council (FEFC) (1994) *NVQs in the Further Education Sector in England*, Coventry: FEFC.

Gerhardi, S., Nicolini, D. and Odella, F. (1998) 'Towards a social understanding of how people learn in organizations', *Management Learning*, 29, 3: 273- 97.

Gibb, A. (1999) 'Entrepreneurship and small business management: can we afford to neglect them in the twenty-first century business school?', *British Journal of Management*, 7, 4: 309- 22.

Gilbert, G. N. and Mulkay, M. (1984) *Opening Pandora's Box: A sociological analysis of scientists' discourse*, Cambridge: Cambridge University Press.

Grant, D., Keenoy, T. and Oswick, C. (eds) (1998) *Discourse and Organization*, London: Sage.

Griffin, V. (1987) 'Naming the processes', in D. Boud and V. Griffin, *Appreciating Adults Learning: From the learners' perspective*, London: Kogan Page.

Hardy, C. L., Thomas, B. and Phillips, N. (1998) 'Talk and action: conversations and narrative in interorganizational collaboration', in D. Grant, T. Keenoy and C. Oswick (eds) *Discourse and Organization*, London: Sage.

Harri-Augsten, S. and Thomas, L. (1991) *Learning Conversations*, London: Routledge.

Hassard, J. and Pym, D. (eds) (1990) *The Theory and Philosophy of Organizations*, London: Routledge.

Hendry, C. (1994) *Human Resource Strategies for International Growth*, London: Routledge.

Hendry, C., Jones, A., Arthur, M. and Pettigrew, C. (1991) *Human Resource Development in Small to Medium Sized Enterprises*, Employment Department Research Paper 88, Sheffield: Employment Department.

Hendry, C., Arthur, M. and Jones, A. (1995) *Strategy through People: Adaptation and learning in the small-medium enterprise*, London: Routledge.

Hill, R. (2001) 'Researching HRD in small organization', in J. McGoldrick, J. Stewart and S. Watson (eds) *Understanding Human Resource Development: A research approach*, London: Routledge.

Hill, R. and Stewart, J. (1999) 'HRD in small organisations', *Human Resource Development International*, 2, 2: 103- 23.

Hitt, M. (1998) 'Twenty-first century organizations: business firms, business schools, and the Academy', *Academy of Management Review*, 23, 2: 218- 24.

Investors in People UK (1996) *Investors in People the Revised Indicators: Advice and guidance for practitioners*, London: IiP UK.

Jennings, P., Banfield, P. and Beaver, G. (1996) 'Human resource development in small firms: a competence based approach', *Strategic Change*, 5, 2: 89- 105.

Keep, E. (1989) 'There's no such thing as society . . . some problems with an individual approach to creating a learning society', *Journal of Education Policy*, 12, 6: 457- 71.

Kessels, J. (2001) Interviewed by Jean Woodall, *Human Resource Development International*, 4, 3: 383- 90.

Lawrence, P. R. and Lorsch, J. W. (1967) *Organization and Environment*, Cambridge, MA: Harvard University Press.

Lee, M. (2001) 'A refusal to define HRD', *Human Resource Development International*, 4, 3: 327- 41.

McGoldrick, J., Stewart, J. and Watson, S. (2001a) 'Theorizing human resource development', *Human Resource Development International*, 4, 3: 343- 56.

McGoldrick, J., Stewart, J. and Watson, S. (eds) (2001b) *Understanding Human Resource Development: A research approach*, London: Routledge.

March, J. G. and Simon, H. G. (1958) *Organizations*, New York: Wiley.

Marsick, V. and Watkins, K. (1990) *Informal and Incidental Learning in the Workplace*, London: Routledge.

Matlay, H. (1996) 'Paradox resolved? Owner/manager attitudes to, and actual provision of, training in the small business sector of the British economy', *19th ISBA Conference*, Birmingham, 20- 2 November.

Matlay, H. (1999) 'Vocational education and training in Britain: a small business perspective', *Education and Training*, 41, 1: 6- 13.

Matlay, H. (2000) 'Evaluating training initiatives and support: lessons from Britain', *ISBA Conference*, Leeds, November.

Matlay, H. and Hyland, T. (1997) 'NVQs in the small business sector: a critical overview', *Education and Training*, 39, 9: 325- 32.

Morgan, G. (1990) 'Paradigm diversity in organizational research', in J. Hassard and H. Pym (eds) *The Theory and Philosophy of Organizations*, London: Routledge.

Mumby, D. K. and Clair, R. (1997) 'Organizational discourse', in T. A. Van Dijk (ed.) *Discourse as Structure and Process*, vol. 2, London: Sage.

Nohria, N. and Eccles, R. G. (1992) *Networks and Organizations*, Boston, MA: Harvard University Press.

Parker, I. (1992) *Discourse Dynamics*, London: Routledge.

Parsons, T. (1951) *The Social System*, London: Routledge and Kegan Paul.

Pettigrew, A. (1985) *The Awakening Giant: Continuity and change in ICI*, Oxford: Basil Blackwell.

Pettigrew, A., Arthur, M. and Hendry, C. (1990) *Training and Human Resource Management in Small and Medium Sized Enterprises: A critical review of the literature and a model for future research*, Sheffield: Training Agency.

Pfeffer, J. (1981) *Power in Organisations*, Boston, MA: Pitman.

Pondy, L. R., Morgan, G. and Dandridge, T. C. (eds) (1983) *Organizational Symbolism*, Greenwich, CT: JAI Press.

Potter, J. and Wetherell, M. (1987) *Discourse and Social Psychology*, London: Sage.

Preece, D. (1995) *Organizations and Technical Change*, London: Routledge.

Ram, M., Sanghera, B., Abbas, T. and Barlow, G. (2000) 'Training and ethnic minority firms: the case of the independent restaurant sector', *Education and Training*, 2, 4/5: 334-41.

Reed, M. I. (1992) *The Sociology of Organizations*, Hemel Hempstead: Harvester Wheatsheaf.

Revans, R. W. (1980) *Action Learning: New techniques for management*, London: Blond and Briggs.

Rogers, C. (1983) *Freedom to Learn*, Columbus, OH: Charles E. Merrill.

Sadler-Smith, E., Down, S. and Field, J. (1999) 'Adding value to HRD: evaluation, Investors in People and small firm training', *Human Resource Development International*, 2, 4: 369-90.

Sambrook, S. and Stewart, J. (1998) 'HRD as discursive construction', paper presented to Lancaster-Leeds conference, Emergent Fields in Management - Connecting Learning and Critique, July.

Scott, W. R. (1987) *Organizations: Rational, Natural and Open Systems*, 2nd edn, Englewood Cliffs, NJ: Prentice Hall.

Simon, H. (1957) *The New Science of Management Decisions*, New York: Harper.

Sinclair, J. McH. and Coulthard, R. M. (1975) *Towards an Analysis of Discourse: The English used by pupils and teachers*, Oxford: Oxford University Press.

Spradley, J. P. (1979) *The Ethnographic Interview*, London: Holt, Rinehart and Winston.

Storey, D. J. (1994) *Understanding the Small Business Sector*, London: Routledge.

Storey, D. J. and Westhead, P. (1997) 'Management training and small firm performance. Why is the link so weak?', *International Small Business Journal*, 14, 4: 13-24.

Training (1998) *1998 Industry Report, Training*, 33, 10: 37-82.

Trehan, K. and Rigg, C. (in preparation) *Making Sense of Silence in Groups*.

Van Dijk, T. A. (ed.) (1997) *Discourse as Structure and Process*, vol. 1, London: Sage.

Vickerstaff, S. and Parker, K. T. (1995) 'Helping small firms: the contribution of TECs and LECs', *International Small Business Journal*, 13, 4: 56-72.

Vince, R. (1996) 'Experiential management education as the practice of change', in R. French and C. Grey (eds) *Rethinking Management Education*, London: Sage.

Walton, J. (1999) *Strategic Human Resource Development*, London: Financial Times and Prentice Hall.

Watson, T. (1994) 'Managing, crafting and researching: words, skill and imagination in shaping management research', *British Journal of Management*, vol. 5, special issue June: 577-87.

Watson, T. (2000) 'Book reviews', *Human Relations*, 53, 4: 559-97.

Weick, K. (1995) *Sensemaking in Organisations*, Thousand Oaks, CA: Sage.

Welch, B. (1996) *Developing Managers for the Smaller Business: A report on training and development needs*, London: Institute of Management.

Westhead, P. and Storey, D. (1997) *Training Provision and Development of Small and Medium Sized Enterprises*, Research Report 26, London: HMSO.

White, O. F. and McSwain, C. (1983) 'Transformational theory and organizational analysis', in Gareth Morgan (ed.) *Beyond Method*, Beverley Hills, CA: Sage.

Wilson, D. C. and Rosenfeld, R. H. (1990) *Managing Organizations*, London: McGraw-Hill.

Wolcott, H. F. (1995) 'Making a study more ethnographic', in J. Van Maanen (ed.) *Representation in Ethnography*, London: Sage.

Woodilla, J. (1998) 'Workplace conversations: the text of organizing', in D. Grant, T. Keenoy and C. Oswick (eds) *Discourse and Organization*, London: Sage.

5 The big business of strategic human resource management in small business

Graham Beaver and Kate Hutchings

Objectives

This chapter examines the role for human resource management (HRM) in small business. Much of the current literature has suggested that the employment relations and/or management of human resources in small business is fundamentally different from that of large business and this can primarily be attributed to the lesser financial and time resources available to small businesses. We acknowledge that many small businesses may have too few employees to ever viably consider the creation of an actual HRM department or even allocate one individual to the role of HRM functions, yet effective management of human resource is necessary for any organisation. We do not suggest that what is good for a large business may not necessarily be good for a small business. However, it is our contention that there is still much that small business may learn from HRM literature and practice and that HRM policy and practice may inform small business through its strategic focus on people development.

Small business and HRM

Previous HRM research has focused primarily on large businesses with very little attention given to managing human resources in small businesses (exceptions include Deshpande and Golhar 1994; Flanagan and Deshpande 1996). Moreover, HRM texts do not devote enough attention to relevant people management for small businesses, despite the fact that small businesses owners often rank HRM as the second most important management activity for them next to organisational management (Hornsby and Kuratko 1990). For example, a recent sixth edition of a text on strategic management (Scholes and Johnson 2002) that runs to over a thousand pages devotes only one page to discussion of small business! For their part, small business textbooks devote only a miniscule percentage of their discussion to HRM with most of the focus being given to finance or marketing, and the problems, motives and prospects for small business (Curran 1991; Goss 1991). Yet, given that human resources, like other organisational assets, must be a key consideration for small businesses that are attempting to enhance their competitive advantage (King *et al.* 2001: 3; see also Senge and Fulmer 1993; Ulrich and Lake 1990), greater attention also needs to be given in the literature to exploring how small businesses may maximise their human resource potential and strategic positioning. This is even more important when it is believed that the greatest demands on organisations today are time compression, uncertainty and the need for continuous change (Kinnie *et al.* 1999: 232) and that there is growing empirical evidence linking HRM activities, organisational performance and long-range planning (Becker and Gerhart 1996; Ichniowski *et al.* 1996).

Clearly the lack of focus in the literature on small business, and the lack of application of HRM policy and practice utilised by small businesses in the literature that does address HRM and small businesses, is of concern given the enormous people and economic significance of small businesses in major industrialised nations. In the United Kingdom, Australia and New Zealand, the vast majority of businesses are small, and most of those are family and owner operated. In North America 90 per cent of all businesses are small to medium size while in the United States only 2 per cent of organisations employ more than 100 people (Heneman and Berkley 1999). Further, small businesses are the fastest growing segment of the economies of most industrialised nations. While it should not be assumed that all small businesses are embryonic large corporations, small and medium businesses do play an important role in the development of economies in that they stimulate competition, develop new technologies and products and are prime creators of employment (McLarty 1999: 103; see also Westhead and Birley 1995). In the European Community alone, small to medium enterprises account for around 99 per cent of companies and the employment of almost 30 million people, with their share of employment ranging from 40 per cent to 65 per cent across Europe (Kerr and McDougall 1998: 66). So, there are far-reaching social and economic ramifications of not maximising the human potential located within small businesses.

As the majority of literature investigating small business and HRM makes reference to specific organisational case studies, this chapter deliberately takes an overarching approach in not being organisational-specific or industry-specific in its focus. Moreover, the arguments advanced throughout are designed to be as applicable to an owner-operated business or family-run business as they are to the businesses at the larger end of the spectrum of small business. We take as our definition of small business that used in the Workplace and Industrial Relations Survey (WIRS) and Australian Workplace and Industrial Relations Survey (AWIRS). These surveys define small businesses as organisations that employ 100 people or fewer. The North American National Organisational Survey (NOS) defines small businesses as organisations that employ 450 people or fewer, while the European Commission defines small business as 49 employees or fewer and refers to those with fewer than 10 employees as very small or micro enterprises. (At a US Congressional Committee, 700 definitions were presented as to how a small business should be defined: Watson and Everett 1996.) Moreover, in advocating strategic planning as well as implementation within the spirit of entrepreneurial innovation for small businesses, our focus is not national-specific but rather addresses the synergies between HRM and small businesses across the United Kingdom, Europe, North America and Australia.

Chapter overview

This chapter begins with an examination of the development of HRM from its early days as personnel management, through to strategic HRM and the place for small business within this discipline and profession. Though HRM has a very broad agenda, this chapter will limit its focus to discussion of some of the key functional areas of HRM, namely recruitment and selection, training, rewards and performance appraisal, as well as giving consideration to the most recent development in HRM, diversity management. Following the theoretical overview of HRM, a section is included on organising and resourcing that considers the value of human resource planning. Recruitment and selection is addressed from the perspective of the importance of a vision in human resource acquisition for small business. The section on training and development examines the importance of value adding through building competence. In examining performance management, consideration is given to effectiveness and efficiency and the usefulness of appraisal for small business. The section on reward management examines the lack of extrinsic rewards in small business and the obstacles to reward management. Finally, the chapter examines a newer field (and one of increasing importance) in HRM, namely diversity management. The role of international HRM and cross-cultural management for developing global consciousness in small business is addressed.

From personnel management to strategic HRM

Throughout the twentieth century, the study of people management changed quite dramatically. In the early part of the century we were exposed to the views of Taylor's scientific management through to Mayo's Hawthorne studies. By the 1950s and 1960s organisations began to focus on individual needs and motivation (Robbins *et al.* 2000). It can be argued that at this time we witnessed the advent of personnel management and advances in recruitment and selection practices, performance appraisal and training. Study of individuals was divided between the personnel and industrial and organisational psychologists and organisational behaviouralists. However, by the 1970s the discipline of HRM emerged. While encompassing the traditions of the aforementioned psychologists and behaviouralists, the focus was broader than earlier work and also included concerns for health and safety and individual satisfaction (Schuler 2000: 241). Industrial relations that had hitherto been quite separate from personnel management because of its implied adversarial approach, now came under the auspices of the new HRM (for an excellent review of the historical development of HRM, see Torrington 1998; for a similar account that examines development within Australia and includes a broader industrial relations focus, see Gardner and Palmer 1997).

By the early 1980s a focus on strategy was added and more recently issues of international consideration such as managing internationally, labour availability, global competition and business ethics have come under the domain of HRM (Schuler 2000: 241-2). It has to be argued that in many nations, particularly developing ones, although there has been a renaming of personnel departments as

HRM departments, the functions and mindset remain very much one of the old personnel management. Yet, the distinctions between the two have been hotly debated. Storey (1994) presents 27 points of difference between personnel and HRM and there has been some antagonism between those that advocate HRM and those that adhere to the principles rooted in industrial relations. Industrial relations was more able to effectively operate alongside personnel management, which made no apology about being another arm of management, whereas HRM advocates suggest that they are working in the interests of employees and that there should be little room for conflict within organisations.

Ideological divides

Most fundamentally, this divide results from an underlying ideological difference between the two schools of thought. The industrial relations advocates' perception is that HRM is simply a tool of management and does not represent the workers' interests and inherent right to engage in industrial action can be in conflict with, or adversarial to management. The HRM people argue that employees and employers need to work together for the good of an organisation and that it is in the interests of both to avoid conflict with the other that ultimately will be destructive to the economic health of the organisation. As Schuler (2000: 241) asserts, personnel management had as its guiding principle a focus on attracting, training and motivating workers, whereas HRM sees these goals as critical to achieving the broader focus of bottom line goals of productivity, competitiveness, competitive advantage, survival and workforce flexibility. To this end, HRM is said to involve all management decisions and actions as they affect the nature of the relationship between employees and the organisation (Beer *et al.* 1984: 1) as it seeks to enhance company performance, employee needs and societal well-being (Schuler 2000: 241). Further, it is said to encompass aspects of international business, organisational behaviour, personnel management, industrial relations and strategy (Schuler 2000: 241). For a discussion of some of the more recent debates in HRM and frameworks in HRM, see Schuler 2000. (For an excellent review of the context of HRM, see Jackson and Schuler 1995; for some very readable texts on North American, British and Australian HRM, see Anthony *et al.* 2002; Dessler 2000; Fisher *et al.* 1999; Kramar *et al.* 2000; Maund 2001; Nankervis 2002).

The introduction of strategic HRM

In the early 1980s attention began to be focused on the role of strategy for HRM. Following the crises between personnel management and HRM, academics and practitioners grasped strategy with both hands, often viewing it as a panacea for the continuing problem besetting the discipline of HRM, namely that it was viewed as marginal to other core business functions like accounting and research and development. Strategy served to legitimise HRM and put it on the map as a first-order strategy in organisations, well worthy of its place alongside other first-order functions within organisations and equal in importance to those other resources of money and fixed assets. As Torrington (1998: 28) notes, people have embraced the concept of strategy because it is perceived as sexy. Purcell and Ahlstrand (1994, cited in Torrington 1998: 28) view it as presupposing importance while others, including Guest, Kamoche, and Schuler, have predicted an increase in the status of HRM if it successfully links its practices with the strategic goals of organisations (Torrington 1998: 28).

The advent of strategic HRM (SHRM) was to witness an integration of HRM and other business functions. As Schuler and Jackson (1999) note, the concern of SHRM is to ensure that HRM is strategically integrated with the strategic needs of an organisation, HRM is consistent across policy areas and HRM is used by line managers as part of their everyday work. From this it could also be construed that HRM departments will contract over time as increasingly the HRM strategic functions are performed by line managers and the more routine work of the old personnel managers, such as payroll and recruitment, is contracted out.

HRM's contribution to small business

Literature has consistently highlighted the lack of HRM application in small businesses. Partly, this can be accounted for by the fact that large organisations are more likely to have the resources to employ HR specialists (Morissette 1993; Ng and Maki 1993) or to devote time and resources to implementing HRM practices. It has also been suggested that small businesses are less likely to be unionised (have more 'control' over their human resource decisions) and hence are not bound by the 'constraints' of HRM practice applicable to large organisations, or employ family members and do not feel compelled to provide the same conditions to which large organisations are legally bound. (For a discussion of the implications of declines in industry bargaining, see Kinnie *et al.* 1999.) Further, it can be argued that many managers of small businesses do not have human resource training and knowledge of their own and hence do not implement HRM best practice within their organisations. (For a good practical guide to HRM practice and policy for the small business entrepreneur, see Sullivan 1997.) All these factors result in what is viewed as a lack of strategic employee management within the majority of small businesses (Marlow and Patton 1993, cited in Wagar 1998: 14). Compounding these perceptions of small business operations is the significant absence of concrete data on human resource practices in relation to small business (Flanagan and Deshpande 1996; Rowden 1995). Where there has been research it has suggested that the marked heterogeneity of employment relations said to be characteristic of the small business has meant that its people management has been distinctly different from large businesses (Kinnie *et al.* 1999; Scase 1995; Storey 1994).

It is argued that heightened exposures to market pressures in some industries have resulted in much of the decision-making in small business needing to be relatively short term (Rainnie 1989, cited in Kinnie *et al.* 1999). This means that for most small businesses, flexibility is greater and conflict is potentially lower than within large organisations, but the opportunity for long-range planning that would maximise efficiency and effectiveness and the ability to attract, retain and motivate the best human resources is also potentially reduced. Moreover, the absence of strategic planning also will often coincide with a lack of attention to innovation and entrepreneurship with the business generally, and in regard to human resources, specifically.

Small business and strategy

The research that has addressed HRM in small businesses has acknowledged the resource constraints upon small businesses and has focused on what is current practice within organisations with a view to suggesting improvements. Lynas and Healy (1999: 245) suggest that there has been a lack of concern for addressing HRM as a concept for identifying factors leading to growth and success or failure and decline. There is a perception that there is a lack of a strategic focus within small businesses in that they generally do not adopt an integrated set of policies consistent with a strategic approach that is favoured by some larger organisations (Wagar 1998: 14). (For a discussion of small businesses that are implementing new management ideas, see Bacon *et al.* 1996.) Moreover, research that is being carried out is not sufficiently addressing how small businesses may develop, and profit from, systematic planning and implementation.

While it would be untrue to suggest that there is universal acceptance of the value of strategy, there is general agreement that the successful entrepreneur is an advocate of planning (Lynas and Healy 1999: 255). For small business, strategic planning can be used as a process for guiding a business through the transition from simple to more complex and for an owner-manager or supervisor to reflect on the prerequisites for successful development (Lynas and Healy 1999: 255). Much of the literature that does address small business and HRM has focused heavily on the need for training and development of both managers and employees and there has been much attention given to the role of the supervisor in engendering an organisational culture consistent with the principles of HRM in its broadest definition. This literature has focused on the personal capability of the supervisor in developing the organisation and has highlighted the importance of prior experience, occupational background, training and education, and attitudes to change. Clearly if small businesses are to maximise their human resource potential, such organisational learning needs to be generated throughout their businesses, but it must be accompanied by development of innovative strategic thinking and implementation of HRM goals.

Organising and resourcing

Though thousands of small businesses are established each year in the industrialised world, only a small number remain in operation within ten years of their inception. A number of factors account for this, including the owners' lack of knowledge of basic business operating procedures; lack of market research into customer demand for the product or service being offered; and insufficient equity in the business. A further factor contributing to the failure of much small business is a lack of attention being given to the development of a business plan, goals and objectives and HR organising and resourcing for the new venture.

The importance of business plans and goals and objectives

Historically, HRM has been viewed as a second order strategy of businesses. That is, business and competitive strategies were seen as the first order or key strategies of organisations while HRM functions were viewed as being secondary features of business planning that were used to support the first order strategies. However, in recent times it has been argued that because of the value of human assets to organisations, HRM should be deemed a first order strategy to be weighted in equal importance to competitive strategies and finance and budgeting (Thompson 1991). That is, HRM strategy advocates implementing HRM planning as a major function not a tactical development of the other business functions and that ideally this should be done at the inception of a business to ensure that its human resources are affectively deployed and the goal of organisational growth is met (for a good review of how to strategically grow a small business, with specific reference to family businesses, see Jacques 1996; King *et al.* 2001). The aims of HRM strategy, then, are to enable organisations to achieve strategic objectives; ensure all business planning processes recognise the value of people; appreciate HRM implications of strategic management; integrate corporate business objectives and HRM objectives; and design and manage organisational structure, culture and policy (Stone 1998: 20- 1).

A framework for strategic management incorporating HRM involves developing a mission statement that answers questions of what businesses the organisation is in; determining goals that are general and long term; and establishing objectives that are short term and measurable. It should also encompass a complete SWOT analysis that incorporates HRM as a functional unit of analysis. (For a discussion of the problems of linking HR to corporate strategy, see Brown and Forester 1996.) It has been argued that 'time has become the competitive strategy for the firm' (Schoenberger 1997: 45) and that success in business is dependent upon being able to make the best use of resources in the shortest time frame possible, but at particular junctures of business operations, namely the start-up phase, much time does need to be expended. Assuredly, it can be difficult for small businesses that do not have the time to plan but making an investment in planning can be a contributing factor to ensuring that the business does not encounter financial ruin down the track. It should be noted though that strategy is not synonymous with planning. Thinking does not have the same mindset as planning - innovation and responsiveness are also required.

HR planning and job design

From the outset, organisations need to pay attention to human resource planning (HRP) and job design if they are to ensure a strategic approach to their human resources. Despite the monetary and time costs involved in doing so, small businesses will profit in the long run from such short-term investment. Ng and Maki

(1993), utilising Canadian data, found that small and large firms differed in their ranking of the importance of HRM issues. While large businesses highlighted adjustment, development and identifying functions, the small businesses highlighted the retaining function (payroll, health and safety, public relations, holidays), the obtaining function (recruitment and hiring) and the identifying function (HRM planning and job evaluation). Moreover, in a 1990 article Hornsby and Kuratko (1990) surveyed small businesses on what they viewed as being most important issues for them in relation to their human resources. The top six issues were wage rates, availability of quality workers, government regulation, training, benefits, and job security. Being able to achieve efficiency and effectiveness in respect to these key HRM issues is in no small part determined by careful attention being given to HR planning.

The translation of organisational strategy into specific selection processes that are designed to ensure that the organisation has the right person for the right job and fit with overall business goals and objectives, begins with the business forming a view or a vision of what it wants to be like and development of strategies to ensure that it gets there. This is part of a strategic HRM approach and is known as human resource planning. In essence, HRP attempts to ensure that there is a match between the knowledge, skills and abilities a business will need in its future and those that it believes it will have available. While HRP is usually designed to be formal and detailed (Kramar *et al.* 2000), it also needs to be flexible enough to respond to changes in labour supply and other external factors as well as organisational change. Like all aspects of strategic planning, there needs to be room for manoeuvre and responsiveness to internal and external change. Engaging in HRP ensures that an organisation is able to respond to technological change; plan training and development; allow for demographic changes in the workforces; calculate critical resources (including succession planning and career pathing of employees); respond to government influences; have HRM input into strategic business planning; evaluate the effects of HRM policies; link individual and organisational goals; integrate HRM and industrial relations; and contribute to organisational expansion and diversification (Kramar *et al.* 2000; Stone 1998).

Strategic planning and job design need to be closely related for maximum outcomes. Job design involves the process of analysing, describing and recording the characteristics and qualities of jobs and specifying the skills and other requirements necessary to perform those jobs. From this, job descriptions and job specifications may be developed (Dessler 2000; Nankervis 2002). Job design and analysis serve several purposes, including understanding where a job fits within an organisation; determining recruitment needs; deterring worth of jobs and pay equity; ensuring fit with legislative conventions relating to pay; providing realistic job previews; providing selection information; aiding reporting relationships between employee and supervisor; establishing career paths; identifying redundancies; and guiding CV preparation. Job design is linked to other key HRM activities, namely recruitment and selection, training and organisation development, rewards and remuneration, and performance management. Further, undertaking comprehensive job analysis ensures that organisations are able to respond to their internal and external environment in relation to their human resources. These environmental factors include management goals; technology; the technological environment; the political environment, the economic environment; and the social environment (Kramar *et al.* 2000). (For a discussion of how to collect job analysis information, see Nankervis 2002.)

Recruitment and selection

Having developed a vision for their business and undertaken job design, the next task that falls to the small business operator is to ensure that the right people are selected for the right job in the business. It has been argued that the selection and retention of a competent and qualified workforce is a vital issue in managing and operating a small business (Baker and Aldrich 1999; Deshpande and Golhar 1994; Stevenson *et al.* 1999). Surveys indicate that about 25 per cent of small businesses view the lack of qualified workers as a threat to their expansion and very survival (Mehta 1996). Yet, while some of the larger 'small' businesses do employ quite substantial number of employees and have need for effective recruitment and selection policies (Hornsby and Kuratko 1990: 9), recruiting and keeping good employees has always been a major challenge for small businesses (Mathias and Jackson 1991). This is also exacerbated by the small size of the organisation, meaning that small businesses often have a high number of single incumbent jobs and employees typically perform multiple roles with unclear boundaries regarding respective job role responsibilities (May 1997).

The difficulties in attracting and retaining high quality employees can be partly explained by the difficulties that small businesses have in competing with large corporations for the 'best' employees (Stewart and Knowles 2001: 98) because of their incapacity to offer the same extrinsic rewards and job status as the larger businesses (Curran 1988). The problems, however, also relate to the element of cronyism that is inherent in many small businesses' hiring and firing practices. This reflects the existence of a non-bureaucratic 'family' culture that limits proceduralism in favour of personal relationships as a basis of employment relationships (Scott *et al.* 1989 cited in Kinnie *et al.* 1999) and a very informal approach to recruitment (Curran *et al.* 1993). While this may reduce costs for many small businesses, it also contravenes the logical advantages of a strategic approach to recruitment and selection.

Research by Curran *et al.* (1993), Millward *et al.* (1992) and Scase and Goffee (1982) has found that whereas larger organisations have relied on very formalised methods and bureaucratic procedures by specialist HRM departments, small business managers or owners have often handled recruitment and associated human resource issues without relevant skills and have relied upon a very informal process. Although a small business may need to acquire additional employees to fuel its growth, employee attraction strategies may be used on a sporadic, ad-hoc basis (Heneman and Berkley 1999: 54) and decisions are often made on the basis of informal contacts (Ram 1998: 20). It should be noted, though, that more formal practices are used in 'knowledge-intensive' or professional service-based small companies (Alvesson 1993; Slatter 1992). The attraction difficulties faced by small businesses are more likely to be addressed through enhanced recruitment techniques than through any other method (Rynes and Barber 1990; Heneman and Berkley 1999).

Recruitment in small businesses

Recruitment is a two-way process in which information is given and received by both applicants and the organisation. A strategically developed recruitment process is essential because it allows an organisation to determine its short- and long-term HRM needs, develop appropriate recruitment methodology, evaluate the effectiveness of the organisations' recruitment strategies, and increase organisational effectiveness in respect to decreasing employee turnover and maximising the potential pool of applicants and success rate at acquiring the best person for the right job (Kramar *et al.* 2000; Stone 1998). Recruitment may be undertaken internally or externally to the organisation. By and large, small companies have used internal recruitment because of its reduced costs. Internal recruitment methods commonly used by small businesses include use of bulletin boards, newsletters, job postings and word of mouth (Heneman and Berkley 1999). These methods have the advantages of improving morale and security and being a motivator for good performance, identifying long-term interests and ensuring that the employer has a good appreciation of the knowledge, skills and abilities of applicants. However, they are disadvantageous in that they can also contribute to poor morale through infighting, it may mean that the best talent is not being accessed and often necessitate very advanced training programmes, an area in which small businesses are usually also deficient (see Schuler *et al.* 1992: 162).

The alternate approach, external recruitment, may utilise methods such as advertising; use of professional employment agencies; customer contacts, staff contacts; special event recruiting; and unsolicited or cold-call applications. The external methods preferred by small companies are advertising, walk-ins and contacts, all of which are reasonably cost-efficient (Heneman and Berkeley 1999: 54). While these external methods allow the small business to attract new ideas and skills into the business, reduce the need for training, and potentially advance equal employment opportunity goals, they also have the disadvantages of creating problems of fit for the business as well as exacerbating morale problems and decreasing the incentive value of promotions. However, where contacts are used (potentially opening the small business up to accusations of cronyism) the issue of fit is less usual. It has been consistently argued in the literature that although the methods used by small businesses are not as sophisticated as those used by large businesses and do result in deficiencies as noted above, they continue to be the preferred methods because of issues of size necessitating organisational fit. That is, it is argued that employers in small businesses are seeking workers that have the capacity to 'fit in' with a particular style and process of working rather than just the technical requirements of the job (Holliday 1995; Kitching 1994; Ram 1998).

Selection in small businesses

Selection is the process of gathering information for the purposes of evaluating and deciding who should be hired as well as working towards the short- and long-term interests of the individual and organisation (Schuler *et al.* 1992). Measurement in the selection process includes two issues - criterion and predictors. Criteria used to measure job success include output measures; quality measures; lost time; turnover; trainability, promotability; and ratings of performance (Kramar *et al.* 2000). There are numerous selection tools (predictors) that organisations may utilise including work samples; reference letters; cognitive ability tests; CVs; application blanks; job ability tests; interviews; graphology; and palmistry. The most commonly used methods in small businesses are interviews and application blanks (Heneman and Berkeley 1999: 54). While application blanks are lower cost they do not score very highly on predictability of job performance in terms of their reliability and validity as measurement tools (see Dessler 2000). Interviews do score highly if they are structured (Tharenou 1994), although they can be quite cost-intensive, particularly if large numbers of applicants are interviewed and there are several staff members on the interview panel. (For a discussion of what works and why, potential errors and potential bias in selection methods, see Schuler *et al.* 1992.)

It has also been argued that the most beneficial outcomes in hiring, and long-term organisational effectiveness of those hired, results from the use of multiple recruitment and selection methods (see Kramer *et al.* 2000). While small businesses may not have the requisite technical skills and resources to undertake sophisticated, multiple methods of recruitment and selection methods tested for reliability and validity, they could consider engaging specialised recruitment agencies to find suitable employees for them, and to ensure that potential employees are given realistic job previews to ensure that they are likely to be retained by the organisation once hired (Phillips 1998). Though this probably will not be an option (or even a consideration) for the smallest owner-operated and family businesses such as petrol stations, general stores and off-licences, it certainly should be given serious thought by the larger small businesses that have a commitment to retaining, motivating and developing their employees over the long term. As Heneman and Berkley (1999: 55) note, to fill vacancies, small businesses can focus on employee referrals and temporary help agencies. However, to gain long-term employees, it will be important that businesses provide more advanced methods and make written job offers, provide hiring bonuses and offer benefits like training and promotion opportunities (Heneman and Berkeley 1999).

HRM and training

For small businesses to develop strategic HR planning processes that link recruitment and selection to training and development (and performance appraisal and rewards), it is essential to ensure that the company is able to attract, retain and motivate high quality employees. Arguably, highly motivated, developed staff with effective transferable skills are more likely to be able to meet the demands of the fast changing work environment which is typically associated with small business (Kerr and McDougall 1998: 65). According to Curran *et al.* (1996) small businesses experience problems in providing training for both owner-managers and workers. Two of the indicators of a systematic approach to training are the existence of a training plan/policy and a specific budget for training (Jameson 2000: 44), both of which are usually conspicuously absent in many small businesses. Again, partly lack of funds is at the root of the problem. Hall (1989) notes that an inability to provide requisite collateral levels or profit track record can constrain the small company in its attempts to attract reasonable finances to underpin development, which may also include development of human resources. Further, it has been suggested that small businesses do not have the time or experience to implement training programmes or the army of HRM specialists at their disposal as have large corporations (Vickerstaff 1992).

It must be acknowledged that there are financial limitations facing small businesses and that the constraints, motivations and uncertainties facing smaller firms differ from those facing larger firms (Westhead and Storey 1996: 18) but it has been suggested that top performing companies are distinguished by their higher spending on training and development. The proportion of the working population employed in small to medium businesses, together with the personal and wealth creation implications for individuals in this sector not fulfilling their potential, emphasises the importance of the creation of company cultures that encourage and value organisational learning, training and skills application (Kerr and McDougall 1998: 72). Moreover, integrating training and development activities into key business decisions and activities is crucial. The benefits of doing so include increased flexibility from being able to transfer people with core skills to different parts of the operation; the prevention of a shortage of key management skills; the focus on devising the company's own methods and techniques of operation which relate to its particular demands; and the good atmosphere and satisfaction among people working effectively towards recognisable goals (Kerr and McDougall 1998: 72-3). Further, given that small businesses face open-ended change, which is unknowable and unpredictable, and the essential challenge to the small business owner or manager is learning how to cope with such change (Wyer and Mason 1998: 112), training and development and the creation of innovative managers are even more crucial (for a discussion of change situations, see Stacey 1990, 1993).

Human resource development

Human resource development (HRD) encompasses the broad set of activities that improve the performance of individuals and the organisations. The central notion is that HRD may involve traditional training, organisational development and career development. Training encompasses the fostering of learning among organisational members. Education activities are designed to improve the overall competence of an employee. Development goes beyond education to encompass lifelong learning. So, at its most basic, HRD increases workforce competence, skills development and quality, as well as motivation and commitment to the organisation and the development of teams. At its most sophisticated, organisational learning provides employees with skills in responding to change, and an appreciation for lifelong learning. Strategic HRD is concerned with linking training and development to organisational objectives, and responding to changes in technology and other factors in the external environment (see McLagan 1989). Reasons why strategic HRD may not occur in small businesses include cost; ill-defined strategic objectives; lack of managerial support for the value of training; neglect of long-term plans; and no analysis undertaken of the needs for training (Bacon *et al.* 1996). There is wide acceptance that owner-managers and supervisors in small businesses determine the ethos and strategic direction for the whole company and the appropriateness of training (Hendry *et al.* 1991; Jennings *et al.* 1996; Smallbone and Wyer 1994). However, the process of convincing owner-managers in small companies of the benefits of training is made difficult by the volume and spread of small companies (Kerr and McDougall 1998: 66).

At the crux of the difficulties of training in small businesses is training that is provided tends to be ad hoc, ill conceived and occurs in the course of normal routines (Hendry *et al.* 1998). This means that small businesses generally do not undertake a training needs analysis and do not have a sense of organisational or person variables that determine needs or what particular jobs require. Added to this is the problem that the training that is provided is rarely measured for effectiveness that results in it being of little value. Various kinds of subjective assessments are used by owner-managers of small businesses to assess the value of workforce training informally (Jameson 2000: 44). While the proximity of owner-managers to employees may make informality viable in the smallest businesses, as companies grow, flexible, holistic processes of learning and the informal approach to staff development may become inadequate. As Thomson *et al.* 1998 (cited in Kerr and McDougall 1998: 67) note, it is important that learning and development strategies employed are ones that nurture the creative solutions, personal and intuitive insights, networking and emphasis in effectiveness and short-term realism which are important to small businesses but are sufficiently measurable to allow for potential growth. Further, as Jameson (2000: 48) argues, whether or not an organisation is in a state of growth can affect attitudes towards, and participation in, training. Thus, an expanding organisation will have managers more disposed towards offering training and employees more disposed towards engaging in such training.

Training and development

Training needs to be measurable in order to be able to assess its effectiveness. Therefore, training objectives should include terminal behaviours and standards about how behaviour should be performed, such as in terms of quality, quantity and time (see Kramar *et al.* 2000). Training may be provided on-the-job (OJT) or off-the-job. Small businesses overwhelmingly use OJT because of its low cost and their preponderance to use ad-hoc training, where provided. While OJT has the benefit of maximising transfer of knowledge, it is also deficient in that the supervisor may not be an expert trainer and evaluation of effectiveness is much more difficult. For small businesses to utilise external trainers in-house would go some way towards reducing the problems associated with OJT and would not prove as cost-intensive as off-the-job training. Job instruction training and apprenticeships are the most common forms of OJT in small businesses. Off-the-job training is more costly for smaller companies and can be difficult to organise, but it also offers expert training, minimal interruptions to daily work and can be quite efficient for small companies if they participate in 'central' courses. Where this method is utilised by small companies it tends to be limited to seminars and classroom teaching rather than the potentially more useful simulations and programmed instructions (for a discussion of the principles of learning, see Field and Ford 1995; for an evaluation of training methods, see Kirkpatrick 1975).

Self-education of employees is rarely supported by small businesses because of financial constraints and the more advanced forms of training characteristic of organisational learning that promote lifelong learning are also very rarely utilised in small businesses. Further, management development is often neglected in small companies. Given that the organisational culture of a small business often reflects the motivations, attitudes, values and abilities of the owner-manager (Smallbone and Wyer 1994), exposure to training and development would ensure that owner-managers and managers in small businesses are provided with some of the requisite skills for coping with the change demands placed on modern organisations. Moreover, the development of managers may contribute to organisational learning through improvements to organisational practices being embedded in the organisation and becoming part of organisational culture through transition from one generation of employees to the next.

Literature suggests that it is not clear why some small businesses rather than others adopt a strategic approach to HRD, placing emphasis on integrating their learning activities with their business strategy, on regularly identifying and responding to learning needs, and reviewing such activities in the light of the business plan (Kerr and McDougall 1998: 67). It is clear the implementation difficulties facing those that do not adopt a strategic approach to HRD include budgetary constraints; lack of detailed pre-planning; and insufficient HR planning integration with overall strategic business plans (or absence of a strategic business plan). Moreover, the implications of a lack of strategic HRD in small businesses are more far-reaching than not meeting existent organisational needs. It also suggests that organisations are not prepared to meet competitiveness in the external environment, and that there is a lack of individual and organisational effectiveness in the long term. Moreover, not paying attention to strategic HRD in the short term translates into a lack of career pathing and succession planning and problems in creating a strategic performance appraisal system in the long term.

Performance management and appraisal

The hardest task in respect to HRM of small businesses is to convince owners and managers that there is much to be gained in the long term if financial and time investments are made in the short term. Of all the functional aspects of HRM, it is most difficult to convince small business managers of the need for taking a strategic approach to developing formal performance appraisal systems. Partly, the choice is cost related but it also results from the over-confidence of small business managers that employees are prepared to trade-off extrinsic benefits that are seen to exist in large businesses for the intrinsic benefits they perceive as characteristic of small businesses.

Performance management involves a series of processes focused on managing employee performance. It includes work and job design, reward structures, the selection of people for work, the training of these employees, assessment of work performance and policies associated with rewarding and improving performance. Thus, like other HR functions, performance management is in no small way related to all other HR functions. It is but one part of a performance management system.

Performance appraisal

Performance appraisal is the HRM activity by which organisations assess the extent to which employees are performing their jobs effectively. The purposes of perform-ance appraisals are to improve performance; identify potential candidates for promotion; provide feedback to employees; communicate between supervisor and subordinate; assist HR planning; and develop management (Beer 1981). A formal performance appraisal system encompasses a method for gathering appraisal data, identification of standards of criteria for analysing data, knowledge of the validity and reliability of the method being utilised for appraisal, understanding of the characteristic of the rater and ratee, a defined process for utilising the information acquired, and an evaluation of the appraisal and its stated objectives (Stone 1998). While small businesses may recognise the value of performance appraisals, very few utilise formal appraisal systems. Most small businesses communicate with employ-ees in a personalistic style that places little emphasis on formal and standardised methods and techniques. Assessments of performance are usually made on the basis of employee conversations with the owner, family and co-workers (Kickul 2001: 333), although the process may be more explicit in the larger 'small' companies that have a hired manager with prior HRM experience.

There are six usual methods used in performance appraisals including comparative standards; absolute standards; objectives based; direct or objective indices; accom-plishment records; and means based (see Schuler *et al.* 1992). The form that is used is determined by what is being measured; what people are, what people do, or what people achieve (Kramar *et al.* 2000). Whichever method is used, it is important that it has been tested for validity and reliability and standards are measurable. Interviews are the most commonly used form of undertaking a performance appraisal and may utilise four styles: tell and sell (directive); tell and listen; problem-solving; or mixed. Appraisal interviews should include a review of job responsibilities; a review of performance standards; a review of the employee's performance; a discussion of strengths and weaknesses; setting of goals and targets; a discussion of career plans; and development of an action plan (Kramar *et al.* 2000). The major advantage of such formalised approaches is that they allow employees to actively engage in their own setting of goals and objectives and to work with a supervisor to improve their performance.

Performance appraisal in small businesses

As most small businesses do not engage in formal appraisal systems, they open themselves up to accusations of being subjective in their assessment of employees' performance and bias in their appraisal. It should be noted, however, that in small businesses in the professional service areas and high technology sector, there might be greater job autonomy and more formal appraisal. This does not reflect management strategy per se but rather the nature of the work in this particular market environment (Kitching 1997; Rainnie 1989; Scase 1995). Further, informal conversations with employees and cursory summaries of their performance do not provide much scope for development of career plans and management potential from within an existing workforce. Divergence in management abilities across small businesses also means divergence in potential to develop employees as the role of the supervisor is key to small business performance. This is supported by Jennings and Beaver's (1997) finding that emphasises that small business success or failure hinges on managerial skills and decision-making. As they argue, the role of small business managers being, in general, more multifaceted than their large company counterparts, makes them a key factor at both the strategic and operational level (for a discussion of problems with performance appraisals, see McGuire 1980; Serpa 1984; Saul 1992; Yager 1981).

The other difficulty that small businesses face in not implementing formal performance appraisal systems is that employees' understanding of the psychological contract and the conditions they have been offered (rewards and promotion prospects) are a matter of perception and what is offered may be changed by management at any time. This has consequences for employee satisfaction and performance as well as turnover (Phillips 1998). Though there are certainly costs to a small business of implementing a formal performance appraisal system, the short-term costs may be counteracted by long-term reductions in turnover, absenteeism, poor job performance, job dissatisfaction and hostile attitudes towards management by employees. So, in developing formal performance appraisal systems, small businesses not only are able to ensure that performance management may become strategically aligned with organisational goals, but also increase accountability, decrease underutilisation of human resources, address concerns of productivity, and decrease employees' concerns about fairness and accuracy.

Reward management

It has been consistently argued that the rewards offered in small businesses differ markedly from those in larger businesses. Ram (1998) argued that pay determination is usually an individualistic affair in small businesses and rarely pursued in a systematic manner. Further, pay is not usually regularly reviewed, pay increases are normally a product of individual bargains and most small businesses have no recognised pay structure (Curran *et al.* 1993; Ram 1998). In sum, issues associated with pay are opaque at best (Gilman *et al.* 2002: 54). Yet while small businesses may not have taken a strategic approach to developing monetary rewards, it is also often argued that many individuals join small businesses for non-monetary rewards such as the sense of organisational loyalty and commitment they find and that the work itself may be viewed as a means of self-expression and self-development (Benveniste 1987; Ram 1998). While it is recognised that small businesses may not viably compete with large organisations in terms of extrinsic compensatory rewards, Golhar and Deshpande (1997) maintain that the ability to adequately provide competitive compensation (at least internal pay equity) and employee participation initiatives are crucial factors associated with the effective and efficient operations of small businesses.

Defining rewards

An organisation's reward system may be defined as the need to attract, retain and motivate employees (Kramar *et al.* 2000). A total reward package includes base pay (possibly award-set or minimum standards) + performance-based pay (if applicable) + compulsory employer-provided benefits (such as superannuation) + discretionary employer-provided benefits (such as bonuses). While the ability to attract, retain and motivate individuals is partly explained by the value that money has for individuals, people are often willing to perform work for non-monetary gains such as status and prestige, job security, responsibility and variety, power, affiliation, or softer rewards such as travel or camaraderie. These non-monetary rewards often explain an individual's choice to take one job over another, or to choose one organisation over another when the monetary gains may be higher elsewhere. Rewards may be defined as extrinsic and intrinsic. Extrinsic rewards are those that receive external recognition, such as pay, bonuses and promotion. Intrinsic rewards are those that may not be recognised by others but hold considerable worth to the individual, such as job variety, and autonomy.

Some forms of rewards are useful in attracting employees, yet it is acknowledged that other forms of rewards are required to retain and motivate employees. Ting (1997) suggests that factors of non-monetary motivation decrease in effectiveness when implemented without consideration to pay satisfaction. Yet, it is also argued that pay satisfaction is not sufficient in itself and that pay equity within an organisation is often more important a linkage between compensation and employee loyalty/ retention and compensation (Lewis 1997; McShulskis 1997). It is suggested that rewards such as hiring bonuses, paid holidays, and benefits will induce applicant attraction (Gomez-Mejia *et al.* 1995) while promotion possibilities and new employee training were significantly related to retention rates (Heneman and Berkley 1999). While motivational factors such as organisational culture, customer focus, teamwork and problem-solving are cited as having a positive relationship in the context of implementing quality improvements, job enrichment is viewed as the best way of increasing employee motivation and productivity (Appelbaum and Kamal 2000; Grensing 1996).

Though small businesses in the professional service and high technology sectors offer high rates of pay, reflecting the market power of such individuals (Ram 1998: 22), most small businesses offer more to their employees in terms of intrinsic rewards, though these may not include the job enrichment cited as the key factor in motivation (Grensing 1996). Small businesses often use non-traditional benefits to give employees a feeling of greater control over the destiny of their work lives. Benefits may include more responsibility and autonomy, latitude in direction of product marketing, flexibility in handling personal matters, leave and leisure-time activities. Other rewards offered can include liberal dress codes, personnel counseling, assistance with tax preparation, subsidised childcare and welfare programmes.

In many industrialised nations, a key determiner of pay rates and benefits is the award systems that set minimum rates of pay for particular jobs, occupational, industries and sectors. Moreover, legislation also establishes minimum conditions that organisations need to provide. These conditions usually include workers' compensation, superannuation schemes, sick leave, holidays and holiday pay, and long service leave. In some nations, organisations are also required by law to provide paid maternity leave and carers' leave. However, it should be noted that a small number of organisations fail to provide the minimum standards legislated by government to their employees. While small businesses are noted for offering non-traditional benefits, unfortunately they are also overly represented among those businesses that do not provide minimum legal standards. While small businesses should be providing their employees with minimum conditions, they are not as open to litigation as large corporations. Essentially, the onus falls to employees (where unionisation does not exist in the workplace) to make themselves aware of their entitlements under the law and to seek redress where these standards are not being met. However, where those employees are very young, uneducated, illegal immigrants or immigrants with poor language skills, employers can usually count on the employees remaining uninformed of their rights.

Performance and pay

Reward planning and management requires organisations to consider four key issues: determing the value of jobs; establishing a pay structure; building a link with performance; and communication and administration. One of the most neglected aspects of this process in small businesses is determining the value of jobs and relates to the lack of initial HR planning and job analysis characteristics of small businesses. Determining the value of jobs entails evaluating a job from job analysis, considering compensable factors, designing a system for evaluation and determining who will do the evaluation e.g. management or peers. From this initial analysis it is then possible to rank and classify jobs, and tie this to the development of selection criteria and other HRM functions (Schuler *et al.* 1992).

Employees need some acknowledgement of their accomplishments and validation of task accomplishment is a strong predictor of employee satisfaction (Appelbaum and Kamal 2000: 736). Hence, performance appraisal also has an important link to rewards, particularly where performance-related pay and promotion are offered within an organisation. Without a valid and accepted performance appraisal system, diminished motivation and lowered performance may result. Again it should be noted that the performance appraisal system should also take account of the value of non-monetary or intrinsic rewards such as prestige, job recognition and job enrichment and variety. Building a link between pay and performance needs to involve the development of outcomes to be sought and may entail performance-based pay systems, merit pay plans, individual incentive plans, and managerial incentive plans (that focus on the workgroup rather than specific individuals) (see Kanter 1989; Lawler 1990; Schuster and Zingheim 1992).

Communicating rewards

The management and administration of a reward system also has the potential to be a significant form of employee communication. The rewards are clear indications of human resource values, goals and priorities of the organisation. There are three primary reasons why it is important: it ensures the organisation is aware of business trends; it ensures links with overall business objectives of the organisation; and it ensures that employees are aware of how their pay and benefits are determined and how the organisation fits relative to its competitors (for a discussion linking rewards to other HR functions and the external environment, see O'Neill 1995). There are four important aspects raised by this. First, whether employees should be involved in their own pay determination, e.g. a flexible approach. Second, whether there should be pay secrecy or whether pay rates for particular grades of work should be published as they are in the public sector (market loadings not negated). Third, whether pay equity has an impact on absenteeism and turnover. Fourth, whether all employees should receive annual salaries or whether organisations should have a mix of salaried and performance-based pay employees (see Lawler 1990).

There are non-monetary approaches that may be used to gain firm attractiveness in obtaining and keeping valuable human assets. Appelbaum and Kamal (2000: 758) argue that job enrichment, employee recognition, pay equity and managerial skill affect job satisfaction in small business. It is acknowledged that small businesses do not have the financial resources available to offer monetary rewards competitive with larger organisations. However, we suggest that there are practices that small businesses can employ that will ensure that they meet some non-monetary rewards for their employees and are responsive communicators and are of minimal financial cost to the business.

Small businesses can improve their practices in respect to how they communicate benefits and rewards to their employees. They have been known to rely on informal techniques to assist employees to understand the psychological contract (Kickul 2001: 330). Uncertainty and ambiguity about remuneration need to be removed. While in small businesses the promises made to employees may not be made explicit through formal HRM procedures (like handbooks) as they are in large organisations (Aldrich and Langton 1997), promises can be made explicit by being actioned. For instance, promises made may satisfy an employee's extrinsic needs by pay and bonuses and benefits being tied to performance, and promises made may satisfy an employee's intrinsic needs in the form of increased responsibilities and opportunities for personal growth that may lead to promotion. Doing so would ensure that small businesses can minimise negative feelings and attitudes of employees towards the business, increase levels of commitment and minimise absenteeism and turnover. Employees who feel that their organisation gives them challenges and opportunities or more responsibility, freedom to develop new skills, and autonomy and control, are likely to demonstrate more loyalty toward their employer and hence contribute to the growth of the business. Thus, for small businesses to communicate better with their employees and action opportunities for their employees are critical factors in building a committed and quality workforce and organisation (Golhar and Deshpande 1997).

In addition to removing ambiguity about rewards, small businesses can also ensure that they provide feedback to their employees, both constructive criticism at the time of errors being made and praise when a job is well done. If a manager has no time to give praise, then it should be delegated to someone else. Given the value stowed on independence and autonomy of owner-managers and the concern for loss of control through delegation (Wyer and Mason 1998: 122) this may take some time to infiltrate the organisational culture. Moreover, Appelbaum and Kamal (2000: 760) suggest that small businesses should hire managers that have the skill to implement incentive programmes and ensure that existing managers understand the value of incentives so that they show commitment to accomplishing tasks. Despite the investment involved, the savings realised through lower employee turnover and anticipated benefit to revenues through more efficient functioning should more than compensate (Appelbaum and Kamal 2000: 760).

Further, instituting communication mechanisms that inform employees about how decisions are made and implementing procedures that allow employees to challenge or appeal decisions made by the business (Kickul 2001: 331) also contributes to employees' intrinsic self-worth. Kickul (2001: 331) suggests that small businesses can openly communicate to employees what they can reasonably expect in terms of organisational inducements and practices through open-book management (see Case 1996). By sharing an array of organisational information (promises and obligations as well as financial and marketing practices), Kickul (2001: 331) argues that small businesses help their employees recognise their contribution and significance to the success of the business. Effective communication between employees and management also must entail information from employees being acted upon by management and efforts made to bring employees on board to implement required changes (Appelbaum and Kamal 2000: 759).

Managing diversity and thinking globally

From the late 1970s most industrialised nations began to implement employment policies targeted at removing discrimination in workplaces on grounds of gender, marital and pregnancy status, race, age, disability, religious belief or political persuasion. These policies were designed to ensure that all individuals had equal employment opportunity in respect to recruitment and selection, training and development, pay and other rewards, and promotion opportunities. Legislation was also enacted to ensure that individuals would not be subjected to sexual or other harassment in the workplace and could take legal action against perpetrators of such harassment. By the mid-1980s most industrialised nations had also brought in affirmative action policies that suggested or mandated organisations to employ techniques and methods to create equal employment opportunity (for an extended discussion of the rationales for such legislation, see Anthony *et al.* 2002; Fisher *et al.* 1999; Kramar *et al.* 2000). While it may be argued by some that small businesses are not as concerned with implementing such policies due to their nepotistic hiring practices, close proximity to their employees, their size, and lesser unionisation, legislatively they are just as obligated to comply as are large corporations. Beyond just the legislative compliance to which organisations must adhere, there is a moral and economic imperative to manage diversity and think globally.

Managing diversity

The effects of internationalisation and the changing nature of the labour market (partially because of increased international migration) mean that business owners can no longer be assured of the culturally and ethnically homogenous workforces that characterised businesses in the past (Gudmundson and Hartenian 2000: 27). This means that there is now an onus on employers and supervisors to manage increasingly diverse workforces that much of the popular press has argued is intrinsically good for organisations (London *et al.* 1993; Rice 1994). Managing diversity refers to valuing differences between stakeholders and developing and implementing policies to manage those differences (Kramar *et al.* 2000). Managing diversity can be argued to be a moral issue, but it is also an economic imperative for organisations in the sense that managing the needs of a diverse workforce can contribute to an organisation's ongoing survival. Diversity issues confronting organisations include the obvious legislative requirements of equal employment opportunity and anti-discrimination as well as concerns for tolerance of individual difference, communicating with and motivating ethnically diverse populations, managing workers with family responsibilities, conflict resolution among diverse workforces, managing older workers, managing career paths diversely, managing diverse teams, and meeting the needs of those with disabilities (Kramar *et al.* 2000). Further, being effective at managing diversity can contribute to an organisation's competitive advantage through the arguments of costs, resource acquisition, marketing, creativity, problem-solving and system flexibility (Cox and Blake 1991: 47).

Though small businesses may not be confronted with the same demands to manage diversity as larger organisations that have much greater numbers of employees and consequently the likelihood of more diversity, it is also in the interests of small businesses to develop an appreciation of diversity and to engender an organisational culture that supports diversity. Benefits to organisations of thinking diversely include breadth of perspectives in decision making; larger talent pools in acquisition; and greater marketing to ethnically diverse communities domestically and internationally (Benibo 1997; Cox 1991; Gudmundson and Hartenian 2000). Potential disadvantages include: difficulties in recruiting, training and managing a diverse workforce; and increased potential for organisational conflict (Gudmundson and Hartenian 2000; Milliken and Martins 1996; Motwani *et al.* 1993). Despite the disadvantages, the ever-increasing diversity of modern industrialised nations suggests that there are on-going strategic advantages in employing a diverse workforce. While many small employers may argue that it is cost prohibitive to provide special conditions or facilities for employees with 'divergent' needs, there is no increased financial cost in simply showing respect for difference within their workplaces. Moreover, it may make those organisations more competitive (as employers and businesses) in the future (Edwards *et al.* 1991).

Thinking globally

Increasing numbers of organisations are recognising that effectively managing their human resources also necessitates recognition and incorporation of the global context (Schuler 2000: 39). While we would not suggest that the vast majority of small businesses would ever be in a position, or indeed have the desire to, take their businesses offshore, it is almost impossible in an age of internationalisation to conceive of any business as being purely domestic in its focus. Though most small businesses may never sell their products internationally or establish subsidiaries in other nations, they are affected by global fiscal and monetary trends, fluctuations in stock markets and swings in economic conditions. Small businesses will also increasingly find that some, if not most of, the products or services they buy and sell, or the components from which they make their products, are produced overseas. Further, the increasing international mobility and cultural diversity of workforces will mean that thinking globally will be essential to business survival, and to this end, there is much that small businesses may learn from the disciplines of international human resource management and cross-cultural management.

The essence of international human resource management (IHRM) is knowledge of conditions in a variety of nations and knowledge of how to manage both within and across them (Schuler 2000: 251). Strategic international human resource management (SIHRM) is the collective of HRM issues, functions and practices that result from the strategic activities of multinational organisations and that impact the international concerns and goals of those enterprises (Schuler *et al.* 1992). SIHRM includes issues associated with people management through acquisitions and mergers, expatriate selection and preparation, creation of global thinking managers, managing, motivating, leading and negotiating in other nations, and corporate social responsibility. While management of expatriates and the human resource aspects of mergers and acquisitions will never be necessary for most small businesses, the cross-cultural management aspects of SIHRM do have application to domestic small businesses and all managers may benefit from cross-cultural competence (see Elashmawi 2001; Fatehi 1996; Ferraro 1998; Mead 1998; Schneider and Barsoux 1997).

In essence, cross-cultural differences arise from culturally divergent attitudes and behavior and differences in understanding, interpretation and application. Culture may impact on the values people have in the workplace, the manner in which decisions are made, negotiations are conducted, jobs are designed and disputes resolved (Kramar *et al.* 2000). (For an examination of cultural differences, see Hofstede 1980; Trompenaars and Hampden-Turner 1997.) As such being able to appreciate and work with differences is essential to achieving organisational harmony and is dependent upon undertaking a comprehensive analysis of the culture of an organisation and its HRM practices. In so doing, Cox and Blake (1991) argue that it will be possible to uncover sources of potential bias unfavourable to some, and to identify ways that corporate culture may place some members at a disadvantage. In recognising possible sources of disadvantage either in an existing business or one that is in its start-up phase, it then becomes possible for the organisation, its employees and its supervisors to move forward to an appreciation of diversity consistent with global consciousness. While these more proactive aspects of SIHRM are usually characteristic of large organisations (and primarily those in the public sector) it is not beyond the means of small businesses to also implement such thinking and to benefit strategically and economically from doing so.

Bibliography

Aldrich, H. and Langton, N. (1997) 'Human resource management practices and organizational life cycles', in Babson College, *Frontiers of Entrepreneurship Research*, Wellesley, MA: Babson College Center for Entrepreneurial Studies.

Alvesson, M. (1993) 'Organisations as rhetoric: knowledge-intensive firms and the struggle with ambiguity', *Journal of Management Studies*, 30, 6: 997- 1015.

Anthony, W. P., Perrewe, P. L. and Kacmar, K. M. (2002) *Human Resource Management: A strategic approach*, 4th edn, Fort Worth, TX: Harcourt College Publishers.

Appelbaum, S. H. and Kamal, R. (2000) 'An analysis of the utilization and effectiveness of non-financial incentives in small business', *Journal of Management Development*, 19, 9: 733- 63.

Atkinson, J. and Meager, N. (1994) 'Running to stand still: the small firm in the labour market', in J. Atkinson and J. Storey (eds) *Employment, the Small Firm and the Labour Market*, London: Routledge.

Bacon, N., Ackers, P., Storey, J. and Coates, D. (1996) 'It's a small world: managing human resources in small business', *International Journal of Human Resource Management*, 7, 1: 82- 100.

Baker, T. and Aldrich, H. (1999) 'The trouble with gurus: responses to dependence and the emergence of employment practices in entrepreneurial firms', in Babson College, *Frontiers of Entrepreneurship Research*, Wellesley, MA: Babson College Center for Entrepreneurial Studies.

Bartlett, C. and Ghoshal, S. (1991) *Managing across Borders: The transnational solution*, London: London Business School.

Becker, B. and Gerhart, B. (1996) 'Impact of human resource management on organizational performance: progress and prospects', *Academy of Management Journal*, 39, 4: 779- 801.

Beer, M. (1981) 'Performance appraisal: dilemmas and possibilities', *Organizational Dynamics*, Winter: 27.

Beer, M., Spector, B., Lawrence, P. R., Mills, D. Q. and Walton, R. E. (1984) *A Conceptual Overview of HRM: Managing human assets*, New York: Free Press.

Benibo, B. (1997) 'A technology-contingency framework for a productivity-oriented workforce diversity', *SAM Advanced Management Journal*, Spring: 28- 32.

Benveniste, G. (1987) *Professionalizing the Organization: Reducing bureaucracy to enhance effectiveness*, San Francisco, CA: Jossey Bass.

Browne, M. and Forester, J. (1996) *Principles of Strategic Management*, Melbourne: Macmillan.

Case, J. F. (1996) *Open-Book Management: The coming business revolution*, New York: HarperCollins.

Cox, T. (1991) 'The multicultural organization', *Executive*, 5, 3: 34- 47.

Cox, T. and Blake, S. (1991) 'Managing cultural diversity: implications for organizational competitiveness', *Academy of Management Executive*, 5, 3: 45- 56.

Curran, J. (1988) 'Training and research strategies for small firms', *Journal of General Management*, 13, 3: 24- 37.

Curran, J. (1991) 'Employment and employment relations in the small enterprise', in J. Stanworth and C. Gray (eds) *Bolton 20 Years On: The small firm in the 1990s*, London: Paul Chapman.

Curran, J. and Stanworth, J. (1979) 'Self-selection and the small firm worker: a critique and alternative view', *Sociology*, 13, 3: 427- 44.

Curran, J., Kitching, J., Abbot, B. and Mills, V. (1993) *Employment and Employment Relations in the Small Service Sector Enterprise: A report*, Kingston-upon-Thames: ESRC Centre for Research on Small Service Sector Enterprises, Kingston University.

Curran, J., Blackburn, R. A., Kitching, J. and North, J. (1996) *Establishing Small Firms' Training Practices, Needs, Difficulties and Use of Industry Training Organisations*, London: HMSO.

Deshpande, S. P. and Golhar, D. Y. (1994) 'HRM practices in large and small manufacturing firms: a comparative study', *Journal of Small Business Management*, 32, 2: 49- 56.

Dessler, G. (2000) *Human Resource Management*, 8th edn, Upper Saddle River, NJ: Prentice Hall.

Edwards, A., Laporte, S. and Livingston, A. (1991) 'Cultural diversity in today's corporation', *Working Woman*, 16, 1: 45- 61.

Elashmawi, F. (2001) *Competing Globally: Mastering multicultural management and negotiations*, Boston, MA: Butterworth-Heinemann.

Fatehi, K. (1996) *International Management: A cross-cultural and functional perspective*, London: Prentice Hall International.

Ferraro, G. P. (1998) *The Cultural Dimension of International Business*, 3rd edn, Upper Saddle River, NJ: Prentice Hall.

Field, L. and Ford, B. (1995) *Managing Organizational Learning: From rhetoric to reality*, Melbourne: Longman.

Fisher, C. D., Schoenfeldt, L. F. and Shaw, J. B. (1999) *Human Resource Management*, 4th edn, Boston, MA: Houghton Mifflin.

Flanagan, D. J. and Deshpande, S. P. (1996) 'Top management's perceptions of changes in HRM practices after union elections in small firms: implication for building competitive advantage', *Journal of Small Business Management*, 34, 4: 23- 34.

Forster, J. and Browne, M. (1996) *Principles of Strategic Management*, Melbourne: Macmillan Education Australia.

Gardner, M. and Palmer, G. (1997) *Employment Relations: Industrial relations and human resource management in Australia*, 2nd edn, South Melbourne: Macmillan Education Australia.

Gilman, M., Edwards, P., Ram, M. and Arrowsmith, J. (2002) 'Pay determination in small firms in the UK: the case of the response to the National Minimum Wage', *Industrial Relations Journal*, 33, 1: 52- 67.

Goffee, R. and Scase, R. (1995) *Corporate Realities: The dynamics of large and small organisations*, London: Routledge.

Golhar, D. Y. and Deshpande, S. P. (1997) 'HRM practices of large and small Canadian manufacturing firms', *Journal of Small Business Management*, 35, 3: 30- 8.

Gomez-Mejia, L.R., Balkin, D. B. and Cardy, R. L. (1995) *Managing Human Resources*, Englewood Cliffs, NJ: Prentice Hall.

Goss, D. (1991) *Small Business and Society*, London: Routledge.

Grensing, L. (1996) 'When the carrot can't be cash', *Security Management*, 40, 12: 25- 7.

Gudmundson, D. and Hartenian, L.S. (2000) 'Workforce diversity in small business: an empirical investigation', *Journal of Small Business Management*, 38, 3: 27- 36.

Hall, G. (1989) 'Lack of finance as a constraint on the expansion of innovatory small firms', in J. Barber, J. S. Metcalfe and M. Porteous (eds) *Barriers in Growth in Small Firms*, London: Routledge.

Heneman III, H. G. and Berkley, R. A. (1999) 'Application attraction practices and outcomes among small businesses', *Journal of Small Business Management*, 37, 1: 53- 74.

Hofstede, G. (1980) *Culture's Consequences: International differences in work-related values*, Beverly Hills, CA: Sage.

Holliday, R. (1995) *Investigating Small Firms: Nice work?* London: Routledge.

Hornsby, J. S. and Kuratko, D. K. (1990) 'Human resource management in small business: critical issues for the 1990s', *Journal of Small Business Management*, 28, 3: 9- 18.

Ibrahim, A. B. and Ellis, W. H. (1993) *Entrepreneurship and Small Business Management: Text, readings and cases*, Dubuque, IA: Kendall/Hunt.

Ichniowski, C., Kochan, T. A., Levine, D., Olson, C. and Strauss, G. (1996) 'What works at work: overview and assessment', *Industrial Relations*, 35, 3: 299- 333.

Jackson, S. E. and Schuler, R. S. (1995) 'Understanding human resource management in the context of organizations and their environments', *Annual Review Psychology*, 46, 237- 64.

Jacques, E. (1996) *Requisite Organization: The CEO's guide to creative structure and leadership*, 2nd edn, Arlington, VA: Cason Hall.

Jameson, S. (1998) 'Employment and employee relations', in R. Thomas (ed.) *The Management of Small Tourism and Hospitality Firms*, London: Cassell.

Jameson, S. M. (2000) 'Recruitment and training in small firms', *Journal of European Industrial Training*, 24, 1: 43- 9.

Jennings, P. and Beaver, G. (1997) 'The performance and competitive advantage of small firms: a management perspective', *International Small Business Journal*, 15, 2: 63- 75.

Jennings, P. L., Banfield, P. and Beaver, G. (1996) 'Human resource development in small firms: a competence-based approach', *Journal of Strategic Change*, 5, 2: 89- 105.

Kanter, R. M. (1989) *When Giants Learn to Dance*, London: Unwin.

Kerr, A. and McDougall, M. (1998) 'The small business of developing people', *International Small Business Journal*, 17, 2: 65- 74.

Kickul, J. (2001) 'Promises made, promises broken: an exploration of employee attraction and retention practices in small business', *Journal of Small Business Management*, 39, 4: 320- 35.

King, S. W., Solomon, G. T. and Fernald Jr, L. W. (2001) 'Issues in growing a family business: a strategic human resource model', *Journal of Small Business Management*, 39, 1: 3- 13.

Kinnie, N., Purcell, J., Hutchinson, S., Terry, M., Collinson, M. and Scarbrough, H. (1999) 'Employment relations in SMEs market-driven or customer-shaped?', *Employee Relations*, 21, 3: 218- 35.

Kirkpatrick, D. L. (1975) *Evaluating Training Programs*, Washington, DC: American Society for Training and Development.

Kitching, J. (1994) 'Employers' work force construction policies in the small service sector enterprise', in J. Atkinson and D. J. Storey (eds) *Employment, the Small Firm and the Labour Market*, London: Routledge.

Kitching, J. (1997) 'Labour regulation in small service sector enterprise', unpublished PhD thesis, Kingston University, Surrey.

Kramar, R., McGraw, P. and Schuler, R. S. (2000) *Human Resource Management in Australia*, 4th edn, South Melbourne: Longman.

Lawler, E. (1990) 'Pay for performance: a motivational analysis', in H. Nalbatian (ed.) *Incentives, Cooperation and Risk Sharing*, Savage, MD: Rowman and Littlefield.

Lewis, B. (1997) 'Used strategically, money can really talk to motivate and reward employee', *Infoworld*, 19, 41: 104.

London, A., Daft, R. and Fugate, A. (1993) *Multicultural Diversity*, Fort Worth, TX: Dryden Press.

Lynas, M. and Healy, S. (1999) 'HRM in the small business', in N. Cornelius (ed.) *Human Resource Management: A managerial perspective*, London: International Thomson Business Press.

McGuire, P. J. (1980) 'Why performance appraisals fail', *Personnel Journal*, September: 742-62.

McLagan, P. (1989) *Models for HRD Practice*, St Paul, MN: ASTD Press.

McLarty, R. (1999) 'The skills development needs of SMEs and focus on graduate skills application', *Journal of Applied Management Studies*, 8, 1: 103-11.

McShulskis, E. (1997) 'Well-paid employees are loyal employees', *HR Magazine*, 42, 11: 22.

Marlow, S. and Patton, D. (1993) 'Managing the employment relationship in the small firm: possibilities for human resource management', *International Small Business Journal*, 11, 4: 57-64.

Mathias, R. L. and Jackson, J. H. (1991) *Personnel/Human Resource Management*, 6th edn, St. Paul, MN: West.

Maund, L. (2001) *Introduction to Human Resource Management: Theory and practice*, Basingstoke: Palgrave.

May, K. (1997) 'Work in the 21st century: understanding the needs of small businesses', *Industrial Organizational Psychologist*, 35, 1: 94-7.

Mead, R. (1998) *International Management: Cross-cultural dimensions*, 2nd edn, Oxford and Malden, MA: Blackwell Business.

Mehta, S. N. (1996) 'Worker shortages continue to worry about a quarter of small businesses', *Wall Street Journal*, 27 June: B-2.

Milliken, F. and Martins, L. (1996) 'Searching for common threads: understanding the multiple effects of diversity in organisational groups', *Academy of Management Review*, 21: 402-33.

Millward, N., Stevens, M., Smart, D. and Hawes, W. R. (1992) *Workplace Industrial Relations in Transition: The ED/ESRC/PSI/ACAS Surveys*, Aldershot: Dartmouth.

Morissette, R. (1993) 'Canadian jobs and firm size: do smaller firms pay less?', *Canadian Journal of Economics*, 26, 1: 159-74.

Motwani, J., Harper, E., Subramanian, R. and Douglas, C. (1993) 'Managing a diversified workforce: current efforts and future directions', *SAM Advanced Management Journal*, Summer: 16-21.

Nankervis, A. (2002) *Strategic Human Resource Management*, 4th edn, South Melbourne: Nelson.

Ng, I. and Maki, D. (1993) 'Human resource management in the Canadian manufacturing sector', *International Journal of Human Resource Management*, 4, 4: 897-916.

O'Neill, G. (1995) 'Framework for developing a total reward strategy', *Asia Pacific Journal of Human Resources*, 33, 2: 103-17.

Phillips, J. M. (1998) 'Effects of realistic job previews on multiple organizational outcomes: a meta-analysis', *Academy of Management Journal*, 41, 6: 673-90.

Purcell, J. and Ahlstrand, B. (1994) *Human Resource Management in the Multi-divisional Company*, Oxford: Oxford University Press.

Rainnie, A. (1989) *Industrial Relations in Small Firms*, London: Routledge.

Ram, M. (1994) *Managing to Survive: Working lives in small firms*, Oxford: Blackwell.

Ram, M. (1998) 'Managing autonomy: employment relations in small professional service firms', *International Small Business Journal*, 17, 2: 13- 30.

Rice, F. (1994) 'How to make diversity pay', *Fortune*, 8 August: 78- 85.

Robbins, S. P., Bergman, R., Stagg, I. and Coulter, M. (2000) *Management*, Sydney: Prentice Hall.

Robinson, S. L. (1996) 'Trust and breach of the psychological contract', *Administrative Science Quarterly*, 41: 574- 99.

Rousseau, D. M. (1995) *Psychological Contracts in Organizations: Understanding written and unwritten agreements*, Thousand Oaks, CA: Sage.

Rousseau, D. M. (1998) 'The "problem" of the psychological contract considered', *Journal of Organizational Behavior*, 19: 665- 72.

Rousseau, D. M. and Tijoriwala, S. A. (1998) 'Assessing psychological contract: issues, alternatives and measures', *Journal of Organizational Behavior*, 19: 679- 95.

Rowden, R. W. (1995) 'The role of human resource development in successful small to mid-sized manufacturing business: a comparative case study', *Human Resource Development Quarterly*, 6, 4: 355- 73.

Rynes, S. L. and Barber, A. E. (1990) 'Applicant attraction strategies: an organizational perspective', *Academy of Management Review*, 15: 286- 310.

Saul, P. (1992) 'Rethinking performance appraisal', *Asia Pacific Journal of Human Resources*, 30, 3: 25- 40.

Scase, R. (1995) 'Employment relations in small firms', in P. Edwards (ed.) *Industrial Relations: Theory and practice*, Oxford: Blackwell.

Scase, R. and Goffee, R. (1982) '"Fraternalism" and "paternalism" as employer strategies in small firms', in G. Day, L. Caldwell, K. Jones, D. Robbins and H. Rose (eds) *Diversity and Decomposition in the Labour Market*, Aldershot: Gower.

Schneider, S. and Barsoux, J.L. (1997) *Managing across Cultures*, New York: Prentice Hall.

Schoenberger, E. (1997) *The Cultural Crisis of the Firm*, Oxford: Blackwell.

Scholes, K. and Johnson, G. (2002) *Exploring Corporate Strategy*, 6th edn, London: Financial Times and Prentice Hall.

Schuler, R. S. (2000) 'Internationalisation of human resource management', *Journal of International Management*, 6: 239- 60.

Schuler, R. S. and Jackson, S. E. (1999) *Strategic Human Resource Management: A reader*, London: Blackwell.

Schuler, R. S., Smart, J. P. and Huber, V. L. (1992) *Human Resources Management in Australia*, 2nd edn, Sydney: Harper Educational.

Schuster, J. and Zingheim, P. (1992) *The New Pay: Linking employee and organisational performance*, New York: Lexington.

Scott, M., Roberts, I., Holroyd, G. and Sawbridge, D. (1989) 'Models of customer- supplier relations', *Journal of General Management*, 22, 2: 56- 75.

Senge, P. M. and Fulmer, R. M. (1993) 'Simulations, systems thinking and anticipatory learning', *Journal of Management Development*, 12, 6: 21- 34.

Serpa, R. (1984) 'Why many organisations - despite good intentions - often fail to give employees fair and useful performance reviews', *Management Review*, July: 41- 6.

Slatter, S. (1992) *Gambling on Growth: How to manage high-tech firms*, Chichester: John Wiley.

Smallbone, D. and Wyer, P. (1994) 'SMEs and exporting - developing an analytical framework', paper presented at the Small Business and Enterpise Development Conference, Manchester.

Stacey, R. D. (1990) 'Dynamic strategic management', in M. Armstrong (ed.) *The New Manager's Handbook*, London: Kogan Page.

Stacey, R. D. (1993) *Strategic Management and Organisational Dynamics*, London: Pitman.

Stevenson, H. H., Roberts, M. J., Grousbeck, H. I. and Bhide, A. (1999) *New Business Ventures and the Entrepreneur*, Boston, MA: Irwin McGraw-Hill.

Stewart, J. and Knowles, V. (2001) 'Graduate recruitment: implications for business and management courses in HE', *Journal of European Industrial Training*, 25, 2/3/4: 98- 108.

Stone, R. (1998) *Human Resource Management*, 3rd edn, Brisbane: John Wiley.

Storey, D. J. (1994) *Understanding the Small Business Sector*, London: Routledge.

Sullivan, W. (1997) *Human Resources for Small Business: What you need to know about*, New York: John Wiley.

Tharenou, P. (1994) 'Selecting the right people for the right jobs: the utility of personnel selection', in K. M. McConkey and H. Wilton (eds) *Australian Psychology: Selected applications and initiatives*, Carlton South, VIC: Australian Psychological Society.

Thompson, F. (1991) 'Management control and the Pentagon: the organizational strategy-structure mismatch', *Public Administration Review*, 5, 1: 52- 66.

Thomson, A., Mabey, C. and Storey, J. (1998) 'The determinants of management development', *International Studies of Management and Organization*, 28, 1: 91- 113.

Ting, Y. (1997) 'Determinants of job satisfaction of federal government employees', *Public Personnel Management*, 26, 3: 313- 34.

Torrington, D. (1998) 'Crises and opportunity in HRM', in P. R. Sparrow and M. Marchington (eds) *Human Resource Management: The new agenda*, London: Financial Times and Pitman.

Triandis, H., Kurowski, L. and Gelfand, M. (1994) 'Workplace diversity', in H. Triandis, M. Dunnettee and L. Hough (eds) *Handbook of Industrial and Organizational Psychology*, Vol. 4, Palo Alto, CA: Consulting Psychologists Press.

Trompenaars, F. and Hampden-Turner, C. (1997) *Riding the Waves of Culture: Understanding cultural diversity in business*, 2nd edn, London: Nicholas Brealey.

Ulrich, D. and Lake, D. (1990) *Organization Capability: Competing from the inside out*, New York: John Wiley.

Vickerstaff, S. (1992) 'The training needs of small firms', *Human Resource Management Journal*, 2, 3: 1- 15.

Wagar, T. H. (1998) 'Determinants of human resource management practices in small firms: some evidence from Atlantic Canada', *Journal of Small Business Management*, 36, 2: 13- 23.

Watson, J. and Everett, J. (1996) 'Do Small Businesses have High Failure Rates?', *Journal of Small Business Management*, 34, 4: 45- 62.

Westhead, P. and Birley, S. (1995) 'Employment growth in new independent owner-managed firms in Great Britain', *International Small Business Journal*, 13, 3: 11- 34.

Westhead, P. and Storey, D. (1996) 'Management training and small firm performance: why is the link so weak?', *International Small Business Journal*, 14, 4: 56- 64.

Wyer, P. and Mason, J. (1998) 'An organizational learning perspective to enhancing understanding of people management in small business', *International Journal of Entrepreneurial Behaviour and Research*, 4, 2: 112- 28.

Yager, E. (1981) 'A critique of performance appraisal systems', *Personnel Journal*, February: 129- 33.

Part II

Approaches to HRD in small organisations

INTRODUCTION

Part II of the book is concerned with what we have termed 'approaches to HRD'. We readily admit that this is an ill-defined term. Our meaning is associated with scale and scope; in other words, approaches are generalised and mostly organisation-wide ways of dealing with learning and development. That is not to say that what we define as an approach, rather than a method, cannot be applied to a single occupational group, or some other limited category. It is to say though that an approach, in contrast to a method, implies greater investment of resource at the organisational level.

The chapters themselves perhaps define the term best through their specific examples. Chapter 6 by Vikki Smith and colleagues illustrates this point very well with their focus on the government-supported Employee Development Programmes. These programmes are intended to promote cultures supportive of continuous learning and development through 'empowering' individual employees to choose their own subjects and topics of learning. They can also be seen as a direct application of large(r) firm logic to the small organisation context. The research reported by Smith and colleagues suggests some reasons to doubt the appropriateness of this logic. A different government-supported and promoted programme, that of national standards for HRD practice, provides the focus for Chapter 7 by Eugene Sadler-Smith and Jonathan Lean. This chapter is concerned with comparing and contrasting small organisations and large(r) organisations. The results suggest areas of commonality and difference, and also that size may not always be a significant factor. In that respect, the chapter lends some support to Chapter 5, which closed Part I. The chapter does though highlight a factor which is probably related to size, that of the availability of specialist expertise as being potentially significant. Relating this to the arguments on context in Part I, the non-availability of such expertise may be a significant feature of the social context which characterises small organisations.

Chapters 8 and 9 are both co-authored by Paul Iles with Maurice Yolles and Elaine Eades respectively. As well as having a co-author in common, both chapters are concerned with the focus of knowledge transfer, and in particular two forms supported by government. Both chapters add further reasons for questioning the large(r) firm logic which informs government-promoted and supported programmes. Chapter 8 in particular also questions the assumed homogeneity of small organisations, and of HRD practices within them. The theme of the localised and situated nature of knowledge creation is also explored and, to some extent at least, supported in both chapters. Thus, in common with Chapters 6 and 7, and with Part I as a whole, these two chapters can be said to emphasise the significance of context in achieving successful outcomes from HRD in small organisations.

Chapter 10, by Sally Sambrook, examines the topical and growing use of e-learning as an approach to HRD. Many of the issues emerging in earlier chapters are found to affect e-learning in the same way that they affect other approaches to HRD. Some examples include perceptions of and attitudes to learning and development per se, the availability of and investment in specialist expertise and necessary resources, and the cultural barriers associated with context. The problems associated with application of large(r) firm logic are also supported in the results of the research reported here.

Sambrook's chapter on e-learning has another connection with the other chapters in this part, and that is a focus on an approach which has been or is promoted by government. An emerging theme of this part of the book therefore is that government-promoted and supported programmes and approaches consistently apply large(r) organisation logic. A second theme seems to be that such application is a fundamental error, which may go some way to explaining the recurrent failure of take-up and/or effectiveness of government attempts to increase the quantity and quality of HRD in small organisations. Additional themes include the following:

- Factors other than size affect the social context of small organisations.
- Examples of the above include the non-availability of specialist expertise.
- The relationship between e-learning and knowledge creation is significant for HRD practice in small organisations.
- New approaches to HRD such as e-learning do not of themselves side-step or overcome established obstacles to learning and development in small organisations.

6 Employee-led development in SMEs

Positioning practice

Vikki Smith, Denise Thursfield, John Hamblett and Rick Holden

Objectives

This chapter aims to develop our understanding of employee development (ED) in small and medium sized enterprises. ED programmes seek to encourage learning and development of employees through the workplace. Roughly speaking such programmes may be differentiated from the more traditional types of training initiatives in three ways. First, participation is on a voluntary basis. Second, individuals choose what they learn. Third, learning is undertaken in an individual's own time.

ED initially achieved prominence through programmes in a number of large organisations, the most notable being the Employee Development and Assistance Programme (EDAP) established by the Ford Motor Company in 1988. Similar initiatives have been implemented by, for example, Lucas Varity, Peugeot, Rolls Royce Cars, Coats Viyella, Zeneca and the Rover Group (www.niace.org.uk). In this chapter we focus our attention on ED in SMEs. Our aim in this respect is twofold. First, we want to challenge the assumption that ED is not a suitable initiative for SMEs. Given the strength of such a belief within conventional wisdom, this is a worthwhile task. Our second, and related, task is to build a tentative, analytical framework adequate to the task of making sense of the empirical data we have generated while investigating the workings of ED in SMEs.

The chapter unfolds as follows. First, we offer a section comprising three distinct, though related, elements. Herein we give a necessarily schematic description of the orthodox account of ED. This is followed by the identification of a number of weaknesses which we consider characterise this orthodox account. We close this section with some comments on ED within the specific context of SMEs. The second section takes the form of a brief methodological discussion. We subsequently present three case studies. The case studies provide the data, the characteristics of ED practice in SMEs, from which our framework is drawn. By way of conclusion we revisit our critique of the orthodox account of ED and highlight how the framework assists a more plausible understanding of the practical diversity of ED within SMEs.

Employee Development

Although the need to encourage adults 'back into learning' has a long pedigree (see, for example, Field 2000; Hodgson 2000), throughout the 1990s the debate on widening participation in learning has been infused with vitality and significance. In this regard, the publication of *The Learning Age* (DfEE 1998) provides a clear indication of the extent to which the Labour government has brought a creative dimension to the debate about the United Kingdom's involvement in, and practice of, adult learning. Widening participation and social inclusion feature in this agenda in an attempt to bridge the 'clear divide between those who benefit from education and training and those who do not' (Hillage *et al.* 2000: xii), be they in employment or not.

Although ED schemes predate New Labour's lifelong learning policy reappraisal it is only in the debate leading to the publication of *The Learning Age* that such programmes can be seen to have achieved national recognition (DfEE 1996; Kennedy 1997; Fryer 1997). Within the emergent lifelong learning agenda SMEs have become a priority (DfEE 1999, 2000; DTI 2001). The rationale behind this focus lies in the notion that

> provision of learning opportunities at work remain patchy and still skewed towards those who are already learners, have achieved through learning or have qualifications to their names. This is especially true for those working in small and tiny businesses.
>
> (Fryer 1999: 31)

Ford's Employee Development and Assistance Programme introduced in 1988, is widely perceived as the forerunner of such programmes in the United Kingdom (Maguire and Horrocks 1995; Beattie 1997). Prior to this time EDAP had been established in the United States by Ford, evolving out of a collective bargaining agreement between the company and the United Automobile and Aeronautical Workers (James 1996). Since 1989, schemes similar to EDAP have been adopted more widely across a range of sectors.

Interest in ED has continued to grow. The DfEE (1997) estimated that the number of schemes increased from around 50 in 1993 to over 500 by 1997. By 1998, Parsons *et al.* (1998) indicated further growth, estimating that around 2000 organisations were involved in England, a fourfold increase on an estimate in 1995. More recent figures (Berry-Lound *et al.* 2001) suggest that over 1500 organisations have ED and indicate that some attrition may have taken place.

Principles of ED

Although there are no agreed standards and little consistency in workplace practice (Thompson 1999), the TUC (1999) has proposed a set of ingredients essential to a successful ED programme. Such schemes, it argues, should centre on voluntary participation. Further, the activities undertaken should be additional to that needed in employees' current work role. It is the TUC's view that ED should be egalitarian in nature with a common entitlement to participation. Diversity is seen, also, as a guiding principle with participants undertaking activities via a variety of learning pathways. There is a recognition that such learning will take place, generally, in employees' own time. Although they do not discount the need for guidance, for the TUC the emphasis should be placed on self-directed, personal development. Finally, such schemes should be based on cost-sharing, with individual participants and employers contributing to fees and relevant leaning resources.

The orthodoxy

A dominant discourse can be identified in respect of ED programmes. The popularity of such programmes is explained, in large part, with reference to the promise they hold for mutual benefit (Industrial Relations Service (IRS) 1993; Maguire and Horrocks 1995; DfEE 1996). A powerful assumption is that ED can help establish a learning culture within an organisation. The DfEE, a significant player in the promotion and advocacy of ED, notes that:

> Experience suggests that these schemes bring business benefits and are very successful in promoting a culture of learning . . . there is a significant pay-off both for employers and employees. The learning encourages more thoughtful activity in the workplace. It allows a greater insight into what employees are capable of achieving. Most importantly, it gives them confidence to do more, to innovate and to ask more informed questions.
>
> (DfEE 1996: 1)

A further factor in the mutuality argument is that ED schemes are egalitarian, opening up access to learning opportunities to those denied them in the past. Again the DfEE (1996: 1) argues that 'ED schemes generate participation from employees who do not normally participate in other training and development activities, encouraging them to rediscover a taste for learning'.

As such, ED schemes can be seen as a cost-effective mechanism in promoting a number of desired attributes among the workforce. The desired attributes are not confined, moreover, to the acquisition of skills and competencies. As Berry-Lound *et al.* (2001) suggest, the orthodoxy attitudinal change in the form of an increased identification with the company culture is conceived of as a major contribution to a rise in profitability and/or efficiency. This view resonates with the review undertaken by Frank *et al.* (1998). Here we read of the supposed, synergistic relationship obtaining between individual and organisational development. At the individual level, ED is deemed to facilitate a return to learn for non-traditional learners. By such means levels of skill and confidence are enhanced allowing for a generalised process of empowerment. Relatedly, at the inter-individual level, ED initiatives are believed to facilitate the development of better organisational communication, employee relations and so on (see, for example, Thompson 1999; Forrester *et al.* 1995).

The orthodoxy: three points of criticism

Elsewhere we have offered a critique of the orthodox position defined above (e.g. Hamblett and Holden 1998; Holden and Hamblett 1998; Thursfield and Hamblett

2001). Here we want to offer a summary of our major points of concern. These we will offer, schematically, under the headings, 'learning', 'rationality' and 'mutuality'. The first two of these, we claim, share the common flaw of reductionism. The last, seems to us, to represent a chaotic abstraction.

Let us begin with the cardinal notion of 'learning'. Here we have three, intimately related, points of criticism to make concerning the manner in which that concept is employed by the orthodoxy. First, and most obviously, it is a concept that has no closely determined boundaries within the discourse in question. Moreover, it appears to grow or shrink as occasion demands. Such being the case, questions of the most fundamental kind, such as 'Who determines what counts as learning?' or 'How do we know what or when workers are learning?', are answered in a less than convincing way. Second, various types or modes of 'learning' are represented in a reductive fashion. So, for example, although there is much talk of 'informal learning', and 'experiential learning' the processes that are deemed to comprise these categories refer more or less exclusively to work-related tasks and competencies. What is evacuated from these categories is any acknowledgement that by 'informal' means and 'experience' workers learn highly significant lessons concerning matters of social process such as the exercise of power in hierarchical organisations, and the often dubious morality of employers who seek to disguise attacks on their terms and conditions of employment beneath a transparent veneer of sweet-sounding rhetoric. Finally, we would suggest, the concept 'learning' is used too often to identify and to stigmatise 'non-learners'. For the orthodoxy, conventionally, 'learning' is synonymous with participation in such schemes as ED. Therefore, those who do not 'participate' are deemed to be 'non-learners'. This proposition supports a second, and equally dubious, claim: as participation in officially sanctioned 'learning' activities is assumed to represent rational behaviour, non-participation is taken as evidence of some kind of irrationality.

This leads to our second area of criticism. This concerns the manner in which the concept 'rationality' is used by orthodox commentators. An assumption that employees are rational actors is necessary to preserve the integrity of the orthodox account. We would not disagree. We would contend, however, that the model of 'rationality' utilised by orthodox commentators is thin and self-serving. We can best express our objection through reference to the work of Charles Taylor (1964, 1996). Elsewhere we have drawn a finer representation of Taylor's work (see, for example, Hamblett *et al.* 2001). For our purposes here, a thumbnail sketch must suffice. 'Rationality' is intimately bound up in the processes of sense-making and choice-making; we are fully human, rational agents in so far as we have the propensity and the ability to make an informed evaluation of a given state of affairs, and the desire (which may be frustrated) to act in accordance with that evaluation. Thus far, the orthodox commentator may be in happy agreement. However, for Taylor the process of evaluation is not homogenous. Rather it must be subdivided in two distinct types: strong evaluation and weak evaluation. Simply put, the latter represents making a choice between given alternatives on the basis of desire. The former, however, involves critical reflection on the given and on the nature of desire. Put slightly differently, strong evaluation is the specifically human ability to evaluate our desires, and to conceive of some desires as more or less desirable than others. We maintain that the orthodox account excludes the notion of 'strong desire'. The practical significance of this error is that for orthodox accounts there is no way in which, systematically, to include the moral aspect of evaluation into the reckoning. In other words, there is no principled way of explaining a refusal to participate in a learning and development activity other than by recourse to such dubious notions as 'irrationality'. On the contrary, we have argued, such a refusal may well illustrate a case of strong evaluation, where an employee has measured the opportunity on offer against a more or less well-defined idea of 'how things *ought* to be'.

Finally, given the nature of the objections we have raised thus far, it would be odd indeed were we to feel comfortable with the notion of 'mutuality' upon which so much rests for the orthodoxy. In theoretical terms any defence of this concept must be made to turn on the definition of interests. The fundamental question is this: are interests objective entities which exist independently of our understanding of them, or are they 'subjective' states of affairs? If the former is the case, then it is perfectly possible for agents to be mistaken about what constitutes their 'interests'. If the latter holds true, an agent's 'interests' are precisely what she or he says they are, no more no less. These are mutually exclusive propositions. The problem for the orthodoxy is that in its (under-developed) defence of 'mutuality' it moves from one position to the other as the argument appears to demand. We want to say, therefore, that at the level of theory, 'mutuality' is logically inconsistent. We will not however, delve further into this complicated debate. Instead, we will draw a point of more immediate practical significance. For 'mutuality' to work (regardless of how one conceives 'interests') it must have a root in the experiential reality of workplace actors; mutuality to be 'mutuality' must be experienced as such. Five years of fieldwork have for us, generated precious little in the way of supporting evidence for the strong claims of this notion.

ED and SMEs

The momentum for ED has, historically, tended to support the proposition that 'small firms are less likely to offer formal training opportunities to their adult employees, and if they do, they appear less willing for that training provision to encompass non-task specific skills' (Keep 1999: 3). Similarly, Payne (1996) intimated that such schemes were more suited to larger organisations and any championing of ED by trade unions (Dundon and Eva 1998) is unlikely to reach many small organisations. Data generated by Parsons *et al.* (1998) seemed to confirm that ED was mainly confined to medium- large firms. However, in the light of findings from Firth and Goffey (1997), Parsons *et al.* (1998) do acknowledge that small firms can profit greatly from ED. So, although the contention is that SMEs are unlikely to be attracted into participation, in terms of 'mutual benefits' no difference is acknowledged; the same 'orthodox' account is employed in relation to any 'exceptions'.

These judgements, we suggest, require qualification both empirically and conceptually. First, our experience in the field in the latter half of the 1990s suggests that SMEs, often through TEC-led consortia and reflecting funding priorities (e.g. European Social Fund, ADAPT), have become important players in ED. More recently our somewhat anecdotal evidence has received support from Berry-Lound *et al.* (2001) who indicate that by 2001 the growth in the number of ED initiatives was largely confined to SMEs. These authors record a distinct rise in organisations of fewer than 100 employees running ED programmes; a result, they suggest, of TECs targeting SMEs and at a time when the number of total schemes since 1998 appeared to be eroding.

Second, existing small business research alerts us to avoid simplistic assumptions that SMEs are simply *small* large businesses (Storey 1994; Hill 2001). Our current understanding of learning and development in SMEs is poor and under-developed. It is undoubtedly the case that research evidence (for example, Westhead and Storey 1997; Matlay 1999) indicates SMEs, formally, invest minimal amounts in the training and development of their employees. On the face of it learning opportunities for employees in SMEs are least evident. Increasingly, though, doubt is cast upon the validity of such 'measures' of learning within an SME context. Hill and Stewart (1999) suggest SMEs, probably unwittingly, develop unique, fit for purpose, models of HRD and where an array of informal learning processes are likely to be of some considerable significance. Other studies suggest SMEs may offer considerable learning advantages. Hendry *et al.* (1995), for example, note the numerous reviews of organisational learning which all neglect size as a critical factor and that this bias overlooks advantages that small size (simpler and easier internal communications, for example) may bring. In a similar vein, Harrison (2000) concludes that SMEs may be better equipped to come close to a notion of 'learning organisation', often 'sub-consciously', simply because of the power of informal learning fostering a climate of continuous development.

Our review of the orthodox argument in respect of ED suggests it must be viewed as inherently problematic. Further complication is added when we consider ED practice in SMEs, a context in which learning and development more generally represents contested terrain. However, our critique of ED should not be interpreted as suggesting that it is impossible, or even unfeasible, for both employers and their employees to benefit from the introduction of ED schemes, or their likes. Particularly, we do not wish to convey that such is the case within SMEs where we can identify both elements of the problem and genuine potential in relation to widening participation in learning. Our point is that it is impossible to defend a *necessary* relationship of the kind suggested by the orthodoxy obtaining between 'learning' and the putative (mutual) benefits. Simply put, the orthodox discourse offers neither the right kind of theoretical framework, nor even a theoretical argument with the strength to support such intemperate predictions. Whether or not any particular scheme offers benefits of a mutual kind is a highly contingent matter that can be ascertained only by empirical investigation. It is in an attempt to draw a degree of order out of this empirical complexity that we seek, through our fieldwork, a crude typology of ED 'ideal types' in SMEs.

Methodology

Our involvement in ED programmes stretches back to 1996. During this time, as independent researchers contracted to undertake various pieces of 'evaluation research' (Clarke and Dawson 1999), we have generated a considerable body of data. This chapter, directly, draws on only a small proportion of these data. However, an emergent picture has been influential in shaping and steering our research effort.

Our methodology for this chapter, therefore, involved revisiting evaluation data on a series of organisations participating in ED. These data were collected between 1997 and 2000. Qualitative in nature, the data attempt to shed light on the characteristics, perceptions and behaviours of the community that made up each organisation visited. For the purposes of this exercise we adopted a multiple case study approach which then provided the basis for 'ideal type' analysis (Weber 1949). A multiple case study approach was adopted to enable emerging themes across the case studies to be drawn together (Yin 1989), thereby providing more compelling evidence than a single case study. The process of abstraction into ideal types follows that adopted by Doorewaard and Meihuizen (2000):

> Our analysis aims at the reconstruction of HR strategies in an 'ideal typical' way. Based on a qualitative analysis of case documents and interviews, we have extracted particular insights concerning distinct HR practices . . . Subsequently, we have interpreted these insights and we have translated them into representations of particular sets of HR practices . . . In so doing, our methodology is tributary to the core idea of Weber's method of constructing 'ideal types'.
>
> (Doorewaard and Meihuizen 2000: 44- 5)

The benefit of the process of constructing ideal typical statements is that it provides a framework for 'simplifying the multiple and complex realities, highlighting key aspects as a means of enabling individuals to analyse and compare their own practices and consider possible alternatives' (Sambrook 2000: 167). In effect the ideal types have a mirror function: they serve as models for comparing real practices. In constructing the ideal types theoretical insights, in this instance concerned with HRD and ED in SMEs, can be sharpened. The case study abstractions into ideal types provides an indication of relationship between organisation policy choices in the context of differing interpretations of the ED discourse.

ED in practice: three case studies

Case 1

Case 1 is a small business providing river trips and cruises. Led by two managing partners it employs twenty-two full-time employees with a further twenty-plus joining the company on a seasonal basis. A strong commitment to training within the organisation is evident. The company was awarded Investors in People in 1993. However, subsequently the IiP model has been viewed more circumspectly. The company chose not to seek re-accreditation. The view of the partner interviewed was that IiP had little to contribute to 'learning for life'.

An ED programme was introduced in 1997. It was launched and promoted as a programme to encourage personal development - for all staff. While investment in training was regarded as essential this had not necessarily embraced all staff. If ED could reach some of these it would help generate inclusivity and the ability of company as a whole to respond accordingly to changes etc. ED was positioned as sitting comfortable alongside the 'Deming' principles that the partners were actively pursuing in their approach to managing the business. The partner's 'vision' in respect of ED was to 'encourage people to be doing things, to be learning, to be receptive to change and to be more flexible'. Furthermore, it was perceived as something which could engender good will and reinforce key company values: 'it puts us in a good light . . . it's not a huge amount of money . . . yet it promotes tremendous good will . . . a willingness . . . and belief in what we're doing'.

The ED programme was launched via a presentation to all staff. It has been administered by a steering group of three, incorporating one of the partners, a co-ordinator in the office (a manager with personnel/training responsibilities) and a co-ordinator on the river (one of the boat skippers); £150 per year was made available to all staff. Some minor restrictions operated; the programme would support an individual 'learning' to swim but not simply 'to swim'. Overall, the programme was kept as 'informal' as possible so that staff didn't get 'bogged down in rules'. Although initiated prior to a TEC programme of ED the company was able to enjoy TEC financial support between 1997 and 1999; equivalent to fifty per cent of the employer contribution. The programme was set to continue beyond TEC support.

Participation in the ED programme has been very high. Year on year participation has ranged between 40 and 60 per cent, while over the three-year period virtually all full-time employees have at some time undertaken a learning activity using the programme. All sections and age levels of staff have participated. Some success has also been achieved in encouraging one or two seasonal staff to take part. Activities undertaken have been varied (including tank driving, scuba diving and trampolining) but IT-related activities have been the most popular, having been accessed by 38 per cent of staff at some point in the three years of the programme. Interviewees cited two main benefits from their participation. The first of these referred to interaction inside and outside the business. In other words, the social side of learning, the 'banter at work' and the value of meeting new people, making new contacts and so on. Second, interviewees identified the benefit of developing an interest when not working. At periods in the year work in Case 1 could be very intensive and involve long hours. Being able to develop an interest in times of relative quiet was valued.

One employee, whom we call 'Ron', provides an interesting vignette. Ron was 56 years old. He had spent much of his earlier working life in the army. He was using his ED monies to learn about welding. Ron looked the sort of bloke who could bend steel rods with his bare hands. A recent accident meant that he was unable to do his normal job. When we interviewed Ron he was folding napkins for use in the cruise parties taking place in the run up to Christmas. It was clear this wasn't Ron's choice of job but there was no doubting the good spirit in which it was being undertaken and the desire of Ron to pull his weight even though incapacitated through injury. For Ron the ED programme summed up why he liked working for the company.

At an organisational level it would appear that the ED programme has become part of the way Case 1 does things - entirely consistent with its general workplace culture. The high level of overall participation is testament to the commitment of staff to pursue personal development. ED has contributed to the social side of organisation development: 'people are doing things which is great . . . people have talked about it which is great . . . people have done unexpected things which is wonderful'.

It has encouraged some staff to get back into formal learning, outside of work, after a lengthy gap. ED, it would appear, contributes in a small way to the competence of staff in terms of their day-to-day jobs but more significantly to a sense of continuous development and vitality within the organisation and a commitment and sense of loyalty to 'their business'.

Case 2

Case 2 is a luxury car dealership operating independently but part of a larger group. The firm employs a total of sixty-five staff located on two separate sites - the dealership itself and a car maintenance bodyshop. The dealership workforce consists of sales, administrative staff and ancillary workers. The bodyshop employs mechanics and car valeters. The company achieved IiP status in 1997 and has been re-accredited with ISO9000 on an annual basis for the last few years.

The ED programme commenced in 1999, part of a wider TEC-led initiative. Formally the objectives associated with the company's engagement in the ED programme incorporated showing staff they were valued; an opportunity for staff to grow and develop; a more motivated workforce and improved team working. Underpinning these formal objectives were two key business imperatives. First, customer satisfaction was perceived as critical and the company was constantly monitoring their performance on this criteria. Second, there was a recognised need to provide employees with IT skills in both the dealership and the bodyshop.

The ED programme was open to all employees. Participants were required to contribute ten pounds (subsequently donated to charity), which the firm viewed as a symbol of an individual's commitment. Co-ordination of the programme was the responsibility of the company secretary, who reported directly to the MD. A total of eighteen employees had participated in the ED programme. The strong commitment to IT resulted in the firm placing restrictions on employees' choice of course. The only options available were a half-day Chamber of Commerce Internet training course and an RSA Level One IT course provided by a franchise of the local college. Management were circumspect about a notion of ED bringing benefits through non-work-related learning:

> There were lots of courses they could go on, but we said if you want to learn the guitar or something, that's up to you. They may be more fulfilled personally, but what they do has to relate to a benefit to us . . . I cannot see how bungee jumping or basket weaving would benefit the dealership.

Dealership employees had mainly taken the Internet course. They generally expressed satisfaction with the programme and identified personal benefits which had accrued. For example: 'We started off with the basics . . . and if you ended up going on, searching for this, searching for that . . . it gives you a bit of confidence and you feel you could carry on from there'.

At the bodyshop participants in particular highlighted the value of the general IT course. First, it was giving them what they felt to be valuable skills in terms of 'using the computer better' and second, the prospect of the qualification was attractive. Participants generally pointed out that an IT-skilled workforce was better for the company than an unskilled workforce: 'We've only been offered what they think will benefit the company'.

Participants throughout the company lacked any real understanding of ED and the controls placed on participants' choice of course has resulted in the programme being perceived as primarily work-related training: 'You mean if I was at a different company I could go on a fishing course. I can't imagine this company paying me to do that'. Not surprisingly, there was no perception of 'ownership' of ED among participants.

At an organisational level management pointed to IT-trained staff as more able to adapt to changes in the workplace, both with respect to communication and sales, and the development of computerised maintenance technology. However, take-up of the scheme had, from management's point of view, been disappointing. Other residual benefits were identified as an increase in participants' sense of commitment to the company as a result of the opportunity they had been offered, and an improvement in staff motivation. While the company pointed to reductions in turnover, high customer satisfaction ratings etc., there is very little basis for attributing to ED any contributory role. There is minimal evidence of employees at Case 2 being 'converted' to learning through ED. In the main, participants can be described as 'experienced learners'. All had taken part in various forms of work-related training, many had taken night school classes and had qualifications ranging from NVQ to degree level. The programme appeared to have done little to tempt those with no qualifications and little prior experience of learning.

The company had not embraced the concept of ED and, to all intents and purposes, the programme was employer led in the direction of meeting company identified training needs. A failure to capture the essence of ED appears to have resulted in the programme having minimal impact. At the margins ED may assist in the IiP re-accreditation process but it provides no support for a notion of ED adding value 'post IiP'.

The future of ED at the company, once TEC funding ceased, was unclear. It appeared unlikely that the programme would continue unless other forms of funding materialised.

Case 3

Case 3 manufacture a range of pneumatic equipment, such as air pressure pumps, for the automotive industry. The company employs 130 staff. Approximately 100 staff work on the shop floor and include skilled and semiskilled operatives, assemblers and dispatch staff. The remainder are managerial and white-collar staff. The company is not unionised but a works council operates which incorporates representatives from the shop floor. An application for IiP status in 1997 proved unsuccessful but the intention was to reapply.

An ED programme was introduced in 1999, part of a wider TEC-led initiative. Formally, the aim was 'to increase the morale of the current workforce and promote the company as one that is interested in developing employees potential in areas that do not relate to their daily work'. The need to boost morale appears to have been the key driver, acknowledged by both management and shop floor representatives. The company had undergone a series of upheavals in recent years: a take-over and a major restructuring, significant management changes and a series of what were described as 'unfinished initiatives'.

The programme was promoted and communicated through team briefings, the company's quarterly newsletter and a range of TEC promotional leaflets and posters. Senior management introduced some distance from the regulation of the programme by the appointment of two co-ordinators - the training officer and a shop floor leading hand. The programme was initially open to all staff, who were free to choose any activity provided that it was not directly work related. Up to £100, 50 per cent of which was refunded by the TEC, was available to each participant. Nearly half the workforce expressed interest in taking part. This level of interest was greater than anticipated and take-up was capped at twenty (15 per cent), with a draw determining who would be the programme participants. Although leisure and sport-related activities predominated, activities pursued also included aromatherapy, IT, languages and driving.

Individual participants, although somewhat unclear as to the rationale behind the programme's introduction, were enthusiastic about their involvement. For many of the ED participants at Case 3, although they had had recent experience of training initiatives internally, it had been some considerable time since they had experienced any formal education. Positive experiences were recounted relating to 'learning new things', 'meeting new people' and 'a sense of achievement'. While acknowledging that they had been the 'lucky ones' and that there was a level of disappointment from those that were not picked, nevertheless the chance to embark on a programme of learning had been appreciated by these participants, one individual noting: 'It's been brilliant - I want to write a letter to somebody to say thank you for this opportunity'.

Any sense of 'ownership' of the ED by those able to access the programme, however, was not evident. It was the first year that the opportunity had been given to employees of Case 3 and thus there had been little chance for it to embed into the culture of the organisation. Of more significance, though, was the restriction of the opportunity to just twenty staff. Although every employee had been eligible this had not been a company-wide opportunity. Furthermore, it was perceived as a one-off initiative. Significantly perhaps it had not featured in works council deliberations. The decision about whether ED would continue resided with the MD. Hence, the ownership of the programme sat very firmly with the MD and had been handed down to employees at his discretion.

Thus, at an organisational level the impact of the ED is difficult to gauge.

Management acknowledged a number of individual 'success stories' and a level of interest (and anticipation about a possible second year) in the programme. However, disappointment was evident in terms of the types of courses chosen by individuals: 'too much leisure and not enough college development'. Management remained sceptical about the programme's overall value, unconvinced that offering 'golf lessons' was anything more than 'a perk for a few staff'.

It was the view of the MD that tangible and measurable benefits to the organisation as a result of the courses taken were not seen to be evident or forthcoming: 'morale was our main reason for going for it and there's no visible change, not even from the people who were actually successful. They've not outwardly changed their view of [the company]'.

This ambivalence about the benefits of ED translated into uncertainty about the future of the programme. Although no decision had been made at the time of the evaluation senior management disappointment regarding take-up and apparent lack of benefits implied that it was far from certain that a second year would be undertaken.

Towards a framework of ED in SMEs

The case studies presented here suggest that employee development can, and does, have a valuable and significant role to play in SMEs. The benefits of ED accrue to both employer and employee, although these may be diffused unevenly between the two parties. The distribution of benefits among participants depends upon the underlying ethos of each scheme and the mode of implementation and execution. Our aim in this section is to scrutinise the characteristics of the above case studies in order to formulate a framework of ED practice.

Here would be a good place to enter a caveat with respect to our framework. The framework we offer is, in important ways, formulated with the specificity of SMEs in mind. We would not claim a universal applicability for our model. We could make the same point by saying that our model does not travel well, or easily, into the sphere occupied by large, complicated institutions. Without wishing to enter a technical debate concerning how best to conceptualise 'SMEs' we will draw upon a small number of related notions, conventionally held to distinguish SMEs. These are the significance of management style in a context defined by the relative absence of complex hierarchical relationships and the consequent under-development of formal processes and procedures. Having said this, we now move to the framework.

The contours of the very evident differences in ED practice hinge upon a number of features. First is the operation of the scheme, in particular the involvement of employees in decision-making and day-to-day charge. We might refer to this, differently, as the context within which ED is introduced. Second is the inclusiveness of the programme and participation rates. Our third criterion concerns the approach adopted to the concept of learning. What, for example, counts as learning and what courses are available to participants? A shorthand way of summing these three factors would be to refer to them as comprising the underlying ethos of the schemes in practice. Finally, the extent to which the benefits of ED are shared between employer and employee is considered.

Broadly, following the three case studies presented, we suggest three 'ideal type' schemes. We have labelled these 'Fringe Benefit', 'Learning and Development' and 'Backdoor Training'. We do not suggest that all ED programmes in all SMEs will replicate exactly these ideal types. We are however, confident in our assertion that the criteria we propose can be used to distinguish between three qualitatively different 'patterns' of ED.

Fringe Benefit approach

A Fringe Benefit approach to ED might be seen operating as follows. Management are driven by their reading of market pressures, or whatever, to author a series of more or less radical changes within their organisation. Customarily, such changes will include down-sizing and work reorganisation. In turn, these may well mean an intensification of work for employees either in the form of speed-up, or the extension of overtime working. Because the forces which are perceived to drive these changes can be characterised as the need to exert downward pressure on labour costs, the rewards offered to employees as compensation for this intensification of effort are experienced, often, as inadequate. Most managers are aware of this and the negative impact it has on morale and motivation. As a result they are sensitive to any (low cost) suggestion which may help them readjust the effort- reward bargain in ways more favourable to their employees. A TEC-sponsored and part-financed ED scheme, under these circumstances, can come to be seen as just such a 'fringe benefit'.

We can illustrate the Fringe Benefit approach with reference to Case 3. Although the day-to-day operation of ED is run by employee co-ordinators, ownership and control of the programme remains firmly with the MD. This gives the scheme a top-down character. With respect to the issue of inclusivity, the programme is highly selective and participation limited to a lucky few. Although the approach to learning appears to be conceptualised in a broad manner, management disappointment with the choices made indicates that this aspect of the scheme is built on flimsy foundations. In terms of the benefits to arise from this scheme, these are limited to a minority of employees. While there are gains to both management and participants, these are limited due to the restricted nature of the programme. Any benefit to the firm will be, inevitably, partial. We could even hazard a guess that some resentment among those turned down could create tension in the future.

Significantly, and as evident from the case material, the programme was intro-duced following a significant period of 'upheaval'. We have demonstrated elsewhere that tensions between ED and the less benign aspects of change can dilute the impact of ED (Thursfield and Hamblett 2001). Here we argue that such tensions highlight the fragility of the Fringe Benefit approach. Simply put, no ED scheme can be expected to compensate employees for a raft of powerful, negative changes to their experienced terms and conditions of employment. In some cases, in these conditions, ED can be seen as making a bad situation worse, as the introduction and development of the scheme becomes, itself, an extension to the contested terrain; another source of potential disharmony and misunderstanding.

Learning and Development approach

Far more positive and robust, in our view, is the Learning and Development approach. Such an approach might be seen as engendering a number of positive developments. In addition to encouraging a number of employees to re-engage in formal learning, ED might be charged with promoting a more open and participative working culture. And, following such an argument through, ED may more genuinely enhance morale and motivation.

Case 1, we suggest, is an example of a Learning and Development ED programme. The scheme is operated by a steering group that includes participants. It is informal, open to all employees, and has achieved almost universal participation. The concept of learning is wide and few restrictions are placed on the choice available to participants. Significantly, both symbolically and substantively, the programme contributes to the logic of strategic development within the organisation.

Thus, we have an example of a different type of ED, a model defined by a perception of ED as an integrated element in the promotion of socially sustainable learning and development.

Backdoor Training approach

This approach, we suggest, largely rejects the rhetoric of mutuality and sees in ED an opportunity to supplement or even replace training by taking advantage of a small, but none the less attractive, financial subsidy. It provides an example of how ED can, in effect, be hijacked to satisfy a very different purpose to that enshrined in the orthodox accounts of ED.

This 'type' is exemplified by Case 2. In this organisation ED is top-down in its operation with little or no input from participants. While it may be open to all employees, few have taken up the offer. Those who have engaged with the scheme are, furthermore, skilled learners who may well have taken courses elsewhere if this programme had not been offered. Perhaps most significant is the narrow conceptualisation of learning. Learning is something that is of use to the company and any benefit to the individual is secondary. The restriction of available courses to IT training is diametric to the very concept of ED.

While the small number of employees who have taken up this training have undoubtedly benefited in terms of development and enjoyment, the impact on the workforce in general has been minimal. The likely benefits to the company are also negligible due to the low participation rate and resentment on the part of employees who feel they have been denied the opportunity to engage in a real ED scheme.

Conclusion

In our conclusion we draw together a number of the issues raised above. First, we return to the idea of ED in SMEs. Second, we revisit the criticisms we have levelled at the 'orthodox' account of ED. We want to do this here, however, with particular reference to SMEs. It is our intention, finally, to facilitate these discussions by reference to our cases and the ideal types we take them to represent.

We begin with the idea of 'learning'. The reader will recall that our criticism of the orthodox conception was that it was applied in an inconsistent way and that it was reductionist. With specific regard to the latter, we pointed out that employees 'learned' through their workplace practice of the power-saturated nature of the employment relationship. Put slightly differently, we would argue that through their experience of what managers do to them employees see the gap between the rhetoric of officially sanctioned 'learning' and the practical manipulations employed to further the dominant interests. We suggest that this is most clearly demonstrated in Case 2 and the Backdoor Training approach we have identified on that basis. Here, not only is participation low, but also interpretations generated by a number of those who did participate suggest a further diminishing of trust, a hardening of the lines that separate 'them' and 'us'. In short, 'learning' engaged in as a result of reflecting, critically, on the introduction of ED and the mode of its operation has served to deepen existing division.

In contrast, we have identified the Learning and Development approach based on Case 1. 'Learning', here, is defined more broadly and by more democratic means. What constitutes 'learning' is left, pretty much, to the employees to decide for themselves. Moreover, the operation of the scheme includes formal and meaningful input from employee representatives. Significantly, ED in this case has been introduced by a management, defined historically, by their open and inclusive style. Such being the case, ED offers further practical evidence of their desire to promote a 'high trust' relationship within the workplace. The illustrative evidence offered in Case 1 demonstrates the degree to which they were succeeding in that endeavour.

One significant point we want to underline, here, is the singular importance of management style in SMEs, and the relatively unmediated impact this has on ED in that context. In an environment defined by under-developed procedures, crude formal mechanisms of regulation and rudimentary hierarchies, the introduction of ED will reflect the key features of what might be called, the 'prevailing ethos'. We see this clearly with respect to the three models and their cases discussed above. The manner in which learning is defined, and the way ED is regulated, tells us much about how the management conceives of the employment relationship.

This point can be finessed, however, by reference to the idea of 'rationality'. We claimed, above, that within the orthodox account employees were 'rational' insofar as they were viewed as 'weak evaluators'. After Taylor (1996) we claimed that this was an invalid reduction of the concept 'rational'. Human agents are also 'strong evaluators'. That is, human agents have the ability and the propensity to reflect, critically, on their desires and to weigh some as more desirable than others according to their understanding of what counts as morally right. Evidence from our cases can be seen to support this view.

Let us look at Case 3, which underpins the Fringe Benefit approach. We reported that the company had undergone a series of upheavals in recent years. These included a take-over and major restructuring, significant management changes and a series of what were described as 'unfinished initiatives'. Within this context, ED was seen by management as a low-cost addition to the effort- reward bargain, a reasonably cheap way to give employees 'something back'. At first blush such an attitude appears laudable enough. However, on closer inspection this Fringe Benefit approach reveals the workings of a reduced understanding of 'rationality'.

For management it would appear that the equation is a simple matter of quantity. Learning becomes an addition to the balance of effort and reward. However, evidence suggests that employees fit judgements concerning ED into a framework of interpretation that is neither one-dimensional nor temporal. They have a learning history that speaks of radical change, a process to which they were subject and within which they felt relatively disempowered. Reflections on this process are the reflections of strong evaluators, they are defined by an irreducible moral imperative. The choices that are made cannot be reduced to a process whereby employees select between a range of possible learning opportunities, no matter how wide that choice may be. 'Choice' of a qualitatively different kind is invoked when employees decide whether or not it is *right* within the prevailing state of affairs to engage with the process at all.

This discussion leads us to the basic notion of 'mutuality'. We want to argue, further, that the notion of mutuality can be seen in a clear light when viewed through the lens offered by SMEs. This is because the lack of bureaucratic distance between owner and employee suggests a greater scope, potentially, for the generation of mutuality. The argument is familiar enough. Unencumbered by the structural and procedural complexities definitive of large organisations, managers within SMEs are more able to engage with employees in an informal way and at a personal level. 'Informal' and 'personal', here, would stand for such ideas as the ability to get to know employees, through closer contact. In turn, such notions would be extended to cover propositions concerning the existence of 'high trust' relationships wherein the aspirations and desires of employees are expressed, freely, and are understood, clearly.

However, the case study evidence demonstrates the fragility of this view. While it is arguable, at least, that Case 1 illustrates that mutuality can be attained, the other two cases illustrate its absence. How do we deal with this conflicting evidence? Our answer involves two moves. The first is to reduce the strength of definition and the second reclassifies the concept. Our weaker definition excludes the idea of 'interests' and reduces mutuality to a state of affairs concerned solely with mutually recognised benefits. Following this, our reclassification seeks to recast mutuality as a descriptive category. By virtue of these two moves we can claim that whether mutuality exists or not is an empirical question. Thus, questions concerning mutuality cannot be answered theoretically.

In this chapter we have used our case studies to achieve two closely related ends. First, we have used our argument to demonstrate a number of key weaknesses identified in the orthodox view of ED. In an effort to address those weaknesses we have expanded the boundaries of two central concepts, 'learning' and 'rationality'. We have reduced and reclassified the idea of 'mutuality' and have demonstrated, via empirical means, the implausibility of a monolithic model of ED. Second, and relatedly, we have used our empirical evidence to develop a rudimentary typology of ED as we have found it practised in SMEs, a typology that goes some distance to depicting and explaining the practical diversity of ED within this specific context.

Bibliography

Beattie, A. (1997) *Working People and Lifelong Learning: A study of the impact of an employee development scheme*, Leicester: NIACE.

Berry-Lound, D., Rowe, V. and Parsons, D. J. (2001) *Research into Recent Developments in Employee Development Schemes*, Research Report 310, Sheffield: DfES.

Clarke, A. and Dawson, R. (1999) *Evaluation Research: An introduction to principles, methods and practice*, London: Sage.

Department of Trade and Industry (DTI) (2001) *Opportunity for All*, White Paper on Enterprise, Skills and Innovation, Cm 5052, London: The Stationery Office.

DfEE (1996) *Employee Development Schemes: What impact do they have?*, Sheffield: DfEE.

DfEE (1997) *Successful Strategies for Employee Development Scheme*, Sheffield: DfEE.

DfEE (1998) *The Learning Age – A renaissance for a new Britain*, Cm 3790, London: The Stationery Office.

DfEE (1999) 'Small and medium enterprises: their role in the economy', *Labour Market Quarterly Report (Skills and Enterprise Network)*, November 1999, Sheffield: DfEE.

DfEE (2000) *Skills Issues in Small and Medium Sized Enterprises*, Skills Task Force Research Paper 13, Sheffield: DfEE.

Doorewaard, H. and Meihuizen, H. E. (2000) 'Strategic performance options in professional service organisations', *Human Resource Management Journal*, 10, 2: 39-57.

Dundon, T. and Eva, D. (1998) 'Trade unions and bargaining for skills', *Employee Relations*, 20, 1: 52-72.

Field, J. (2000) *Lifelong Learning and the New Educational Order*, Stoke-on-Trent: Trentham.

Firth, D. and Goffey, L. (1997) *Employee Development Schemes: The benefits of participation for employees in small firms*, Research Report 39, Sheffield: DfEE.

Forrester, K., Payne, J. and Ward, K. (1995) *Workplace Learning: Perspectives on education, training and work*, Aldershot: Avebury.

Frank, F., Garrod, P., Hunter, L. and Percy, K. (1998) *Reaching the Non-Traditional Learner through Employee Development Schemes: The Lancaster Employee Development Consortium*, Lancaster: Lancaster University.

Fryer, R. H. (1997) *Learning for the Twenty First Century*, First Report of the National Advisory Group for Continuing Education and Lifelong Learning, London: NAGCELL.

Fryer, R. H. (1999) *Creating Learning Cultures: Next steps in achieving the learning age*, Second Report of the National Advisory Group for Continuing Education and Lifelong Learning, London: NAGCELL.

Hamblett, J. and Holden, R. J. (1998) 'To boldly go? Questioning orthodox accounts of employee development', *Human Resource Development International*, 1, 2: 149-70.

Hamblett, J., Holden, R. J. and Thursfield, D. (2001) 'The tools of freedom and the sources of indignity', in J. McGoldrick, J. Stewart and S. Watson (eds) *Understanding Human Resource Development*, London: Routledge.

Harrison, R. (2000) *Employee Development*, London: IPD.

Hendry, C., Arthur, M. B. and Jones, A. M. (1995) *Strategy through People: Adaptation and learning in the small-medium enterprise*, London: Routledge.

Hill, R. (2001) 'Researching HRD in small organisations', in J. McGoldrick, J. Stewart and S. Watson (eds) *Understanding Human Resource Development*, London: Routledge.

Hill, R. and Stewart, J. (1999) 'Human resource development in small organisations', *Human Resource Development International*, 2, 2: 103-23.

Hillage, J., Uden, T., Aldridge, F. and Eccles, J. (2000) *Adult Learning in England: A review*, Institute for Employment Studies (IES)/National Organisation for Adult Learning Report 369, Brighton: IES.

Hodgson, A. (2000) *Policies, Politics and the Future of Lifelong Learning*, London: Kogan Page.

Holden, R. J. and Hamblett, J. (1998) 'Learning lessons from non-work-related learning', *Journal of Workplace Learning*, 10, 5: 241- 50.

Industrial Relations Services (IRS) (1993) 'Employee Development Programmes: towards a learning culture', *Employee Development Bulletin*, 37, Industrial Relations Review and Report, January.

James, P. (1996) 'Employee Development Programmes: the US auto approach', *Personnel Review*, 25, 2: 35- 49.

Keep, E. (1999) *Employer Attitudes towards Adult Training*, Skills Task Force Research Paper 15, Sheffield: DfEE.

Kennedy Committee on Widening Participation (1997) *Learning Works: Widening participation in further education*, Coventry: FEDA.

Maguire, M. and Horrocks, B. (1995) *Employee Development Programmes and Lifetime Learning*, Working Paper 6, Leicester: Centre for Labour Market Studies, Leicester University.

Matlay, H. (1999) 'Vocational education and training in Britain: a small business perspective', *Education and Training*, 41, 1: 6- 13.

NIACE (1997) *History of EDPs in the UK* [Internet], Leicester: NIACE. Available from: http://www.niace.org.uk/research/edp/edphist.htm (accessed 15 March 2002).

Parsons, D., Cocks, N. and Rowe, V. (1998) *The Role of Employee Development Schemes in Increasing Learning at Work*, DfEE Research Report 83, Sheffield: DfEE.

Payne, J. (1996) 'Who really benefits from Employee Development Schemes?', in P. Raggatt, R. Edwards and N. Small (eds) *The Learning Society*, London: Routledge.

Sambrook, S. (2000) 'Talking of HRD', *Human Resource Development International*, 3, 2: 159- 78.

Storey, D. J. (1994) *Understanding the Small Business Sector*, London: Routledge.

Taylor, C. (1964) *The Explanation of Behaviour*, London: Routledge and Kegan Paul.

Taylor, C. (1996) *Human Agency and Language, Philosophical Papers*, Vol. 1. Cambridge: Cambridge University Press.

Thompson, A. (1999) 'A beautiful paradox: Employee Development Programmes in the UK', *Lifelong Learning in Europe*, 4, 2: 86- 92.

Thursfield, D. and Hamblett, J. (2001) 'Mutuality, learning and change at work: the case of employee led development', *Employee Relations*, 4, 23: 337- 51.

Trades Union Congress (TUC) (1999) *Guide to Workplace Development of EDS*, London: TUC.

Weber, M. (1949) *The Methodology of the Social Sciences*, translated and edited by E. Shils and H. Finch, New York: Free Press.

Westhead, P. and Storey, J. (1997) *Training Provision and the Development of Small and Medium Sized Enterprises*, Research Report 26, Sheffield: DfEE.

Yin, R. K. (1989) *Case Study Research*, London: Sage.

7 The practice of HRD in smaller firms

Eugene Sadler-Smith and Jonathan Lean

Introduction

This chapter examines the practice of human resource development in smaller firms and explores, through empirical research, some of the extant notions of small firm HRD. We shall begin by considering some general aspects of HRD activities (conceptualised in terms of the systematic approach) and HRD methods (the means by which HRD is facilitated) in order to provide context and to inform the research aims. We shall then focus on HRD in smaller firms by examining HRD as a policy intervention, the effect of size and organisational characteristics on small firm HRD, barriers to HRD in smaller firms and finally, the attitude and role of the owner-manager in facilitating HRD. This review of the field will provide the conceptual backcloth for our empirical investigations. Through exploring these issues we hope to provide a descriptive framework that may form a basis for further theoretical and empirical elaboration of small firm HRD. The chapter should be seen in the context of a field of inquiry in which

(i) some have argued there has been a noticeable paucity of research;
(ii) researchers and HRD specialists have been 'content to offer solutions which were more relevant to the business strategies of larger firms';
(iii) the majority of owner-managers have been sceptical towards government involvement in their affairs, including the provision of HRD initiatives.

(Matlay 2000: 326)

The research is important in an economic environment in which the majority of workers in the United Kingdom are employed in small and medium sized firms, and in a political context in which enterprise and small business management is high on the agendas of European governments. Within this political and economic landscape there is increasing recognition by companies that people and their skills are an important factor of production and that learning is a crucial source of competitive advantage (Iles 1996: 72). Against this backdrop HRD has a key role to play in enhancing performance in organisations of all sizes, but in order to manage small firm HRD and maximise its potential we must at first understand it.

Background

One of the central axioms of HRD practice is the systematic approach (Figure 7.1), and it is this that forms the basis both for our review of the field and for the design and development of the measurement tools that we employed in the empirical work; hence it is a central precept of our research. Our review of the field falls into three sections: HRD activities (through a process-based view of learning and development), HRD methods (how learning and development can be facilitated) and HRD in smaller firms (an examination of some of the extant notions of learning and development in smaller firms).

HRD activities

The systematic approach to HRD (sometimes referred to as the 'training cycle' - including the selection and use of particular training methods) is central to much HRD policy and practice. Many organisations use the systematic approach as a convenient and rational heuristic for solving the operational and strategic issues associated with training and developing their workforces. The systematic approach is now embedded as a *modus operandi* for many practitioners, and is embodied in the United Kingdom's national occupational standard for training and development. In the latter context it was referred to as the TDLB (Training and Development Lead Body) Standard (Employment Occupational Standards Council 1995). The programme for establishing the National Standard was launched in 1986. The TDLB was the lead body with the remit to set a National Standard for training and development that could be used as a basis for national qualifications (such as National Vocational Qualifications or NVQs). The National Standard has many

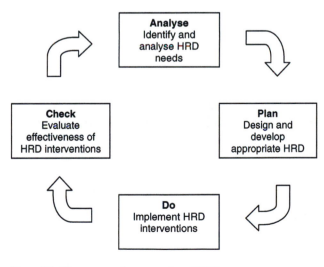

Figure 7.1 The systematic approach to HRD.

potential uses: for example, it may be used as the basis for job descriptions, recruitment and selection, for accreditation and also to provide a vehicle for identifying training needs and evaluating training (Sanderson 1995: 122). The development and use of the National Standard in the United Kingdom has parallels in the United States where the issue of trainer certification is a long-running concern. Supporters claim that certification provides a guarantee to potential employers that trainers have the appropriate skills and thus can perform to an established standard (Lee 1998).

UK national standards have often been derived in response to central government interest in the performance of particular occupational groups, for example managers. Occupational standards represent an informal arm of government policy towards the management of organisations and employment and may be derived through functional analyses of the particular role or tasks concerned. Their development is usually conducted under the auspices of a lead body that has the authority to consult, establish best practice and commission developmental work (Sanderson 1995: 119). However, such an approach is not uncontested, for example in his critique of the national standard for personnel management (the personnel equivalent of the TDLB Standard), Gibb (1995) bemoaned the apparent imaginative interpretation of trends rather than data-based analyses in the formulation of the Personnel Standards Lead Body model of personnel/human resource management. One interpretation of his argument is that what might be a politically driven derivation of an occupational standard presents a danger in that the orthodoxy that quickly becomes established may not have demonstrated its validity, for example on the grounds of utility, logic or practice. These issues may be further compounded if the political and stakeholder influences that affect the content of the standard emanate from a small number of powerful groups. Moreover, Grugulis (1997: 429) noted in general that comparatively little independent research has been conducted in the area of NVQs and occupational standards. Our research may be seen, in part, as a response to these concerns and perceived shortcomings.

The National Standard

The TDLB Standard is a representation of HRD that is derived from a process-based view of practice (i.e. the systematic approach). This approach itself has evolved in part from the instructional systems design (ISD) methodologies that were developed as a means of designing and developing training in the United States. In the decades following the Second World War these methods were adopted in the United Kingdom by the armed forces and a number of large organisations (see, for example, British Gas/Futuremedia 1984). The epitome of the systematic approach is embodied in Irwin Goldstein's *Training in Organisations* first published in 1974 (Goldstein 1993). At its simplest the systematic approach may be represented as a four stage operational cycle consisting of identify and analyse needs, design training, deliver training and evaluate training (see Buckley and Caple 1992). Variations on this 'analyse-plan-do-check' theme are well described in the HRD, human resource management and organisational behaviour literatures, for example: Anderson (1993: 20), Buckley and Caple (1992: 29), Craig (1995: 4), Gibb and Megginson

(2001: 150), Mullins (2002: 698), Stewart (1999: 135) and, at a more strategic level, Walton (1999: 29).

The TDLB opted to use a simple four-stage version of this approach and base the content of the standard on a functional analysis of each stage. They adopted the training cycle because 'it describes systematically and comprehensively the whole training and development process; it is familiar to all sectors and parts of the training community; most training and development roles can be located within it' (Employment Occupational Standards Council 1995: 5). As noted earlier, such standards are often derived by functional analysis in which the analyst asks, at repeatedly finer levels of resolution, the question: 'what is the purpose (or function) of a given job or occupation?' The approach is atomistic and reductionist and the results of this analysis may then be expressed in the conventional competence framework of units (for example: 'Prepare and present demonstrations and information and provide advice to support learning'); elements (for example: 'Present information to groups of trainees'); performance criteria (for example: 'Visual aid equipment is regularly maintained and fit for use when required'); and range statements (for example: 'Projection systems and non-projected display systems'). The framework provides a benchmark of competence at three levels, and those who opt for assessment may achieve an NVQ at Level 3, 4 or 5. As well as being a generic job description of an HRD practitioner's role the standard may be offered as a model of acceptable practice.

In the light of 'feedback from users, on-going consultation and market research' a revised standard was issued in 1995 that used 'plain English, eliminated overlaps, had a strategic focus and explicitly acknowledged values and ethics' (EOSC 1995: 2). Leaving the details of revisions aside, the TDLB Standard appears to have been the subject of comparatively little empirical or critical analysis. As a generic standard it is assumed to be universally applicable, since the TDLB 'spans all industries and occupations and it has produced standards and qualifications which are accepted nationally by all parties having an interest in training and development' (EOSC 1995: 2) and as such should encompass small firms as well as larger ones. Stewart (1999: 90) suggested that there is evidence for the content validity of the training standards when he noted that there appears to be 'some congruence between the roles specified in NVQs and those included in the analyses of Bennett and Leduchowicz (1983) and that of Pettigrew and his colleagues [1982], at the level of face validity at least'. In a similar vein Harrison (1997) mapped the roles identified by Pettigrew against the Standard. Since small firms were not addressed explicitly in the research by Bennett and Leduchowicz (1983) and Pettigrew *et al.* (1982) the strength of the presumed link between NVQ roles and empirically identified roles in this sector is not clear.

Critiques of the competence-based approach

Criticisms relating to the lack of cognisance taken of the complexity and contingency of managerial work that have been levelled at other applications of competence-related approaches (see Burgoyne 1993; Du Gay *et al.* 1996) could also be said to apply to the functional analysis of the HRD practitioner's role, and by extension to the National Standard. Some have proposed that standards in general may be perceived as reductionist and atomistic (Transform 1991); furthermore Harrison (1997: 137) added that 'such neat and tidy definitions do not adequately indicate what the trainer or developer should do or how best to do it'. She pointed out some difficulties with this type of approach, for example the failure to recognise contextual factors, not distinguishing between training and development, reductionism and ignoring relationships. She went on to discuss the importance of context: 'it [success in employee development] needs an understanding of the particular organisation and the knowledge and skills needed to deal with its culture and politics'. The theme of much of the criticism may be summarised succinctly as an emphasis of measurable outcome at the expense of context and process ('making the measurable important rather than measuring the important'). In the United States critics of the standardisation and certification route have claimed that certification can deal only with the most basic aspects of training and does not include the more complex facets of the field (Lee 1998). However, we prefer to exercise caution and not opt for outright rejection; the need for certain core occupational standards can be acknowledged and accepted both for political reasons (in relation to the desire to 'professionalise' the HR/HRD role) and practical expediency (in relation to the undoubted value of the standard as a comprehensive description of a particular conceptualisation of HRD). In our view the challenge is to influence and work with the standards, to apply and build upon them. A well-worn aphorism is that treated as absolutes the standards make a poor master; used appropriately they can be a good servant. For us, in researching HRD in smaller firms, their value lies in the fact that they provide a comprehensive description of a model of HRD, with the added advantage of having a degree of consensus associated with them (thus permitting a broader contextualisation of our findings).

HRD methods

In parallel with the developments described above, recent years have seen the range of HRD methods available to practitioners greatly enhanced through technological developments (for example, computer-based training and more recently e-learning) and the application of HRM principles (for example, the integration of learning and work). As a result of a number of influences (down-sizing, de-layering and the promulgation of HRM models of practice) HR practitioners no longer have primacy of role in the delivery of HRD; line managers or subject experts (for example, consultants, equipment manufacturers and suppliers and providers) conduct training, often in an on-the-job situation (Bachler 1997). This has transformed the role of trainers from instructors to mentors and facilitators whose purpose it is to guide employees and employers to the best and most timely solutions from the available HRD alternatives (Leonard 1996). One problematical issue is that in order to be executed effectively the systematic approach to HRD requires a level of HRD knowledge that may not be present in the smaller firm. A lack of knowledge of HRD may allow the supply-side of the relationship to dominate (because owner-managers may not be able to make informed and effective HRD decisions) - see Hill and Stewart (1999).

Provider-focused vs client-focused approaches

The reality for many small organisations is likely to be far removed from the managerial/theoretical ideal presented in the systematic approach. For example, it is often argued that many organisations of all sizes subscribe, to a greater or lesser degree, to a provider-focused (as opposed to client-focused) approach. Choosing from 'menus' of training courses may supplant training needs identification to such an extent that what is *available* takes precedence over what is *needed* (and it is debatable whether anything *is* actually better than nothing). Mumford (1995: 17) noted that much off-the-job training comes about through marketing of courses in 'in-company training course catalogues, brochures from training centres of business schools or leaflets from conference organisers' and not through careful analyses of training needs. This concurs with Mole's (1996: 19) description of much management training as 'genre training' in which 'the tone is prescriptive, the advertised package is a solution to a universally pre-existent problem and that the solution itself is comprehensive and absolute'. As an HR director Mole was able to offer an insider's critique of management training. He cited a number of weaknesses in provision as he perceived it:

- *Post hoc* rationalisation of training problems on the basis of the available solutions.
- The 'commoditisation' [*sic*] of training courses and homogeneity of solutions.
- 'Mimetic isomorphism' - by which he meant that particular types of training may become perceived wisdom and achieve almost panacea-like status.

Mole (1996) argued against a 'course menu' approach to training provision that tends towards being provider/supply-focused. He argued for a more customer-led approach. There are parallels perhaps between his perception of the management training industry and some small firm support initiatives in the United Kingdom, and these arguments have been extended and explored by a number of authors. For example Sadler-Smith *et al.* (2000) described a collaborative model of learning and development and its implementation in a number of smaller firms. The central precepts of this approach were the identification and prioritisation of individual and organisational learning needs by trained assessors and the design and implementation of a bespoke learning programme (i.e. client-focused as opposed to supply-driven) in order to meet the most important needs as perceived by the assessors and owner-managers.

Flexible learning

In recent decades many organisations have turned to alternative methods of delivery that do not rely on traditional methods of face-to-face contact between trainer and trainee. For example, open and distance learning (ODL) is an approach in which 'the learner is: not continuously and immediately supervised by a trainer or a tutor; does benefit from the services of a training/tutorial organisation; utilises [training] materials in a variety of formats' (Stewart and Winter 1995: 202). Stewart and Winter (1995: 203- 4) charted ODL's rise from correspondence courses in the early years of the twentieth century, through the establishment of the Open University in the 1960s to the adoption of distance learning techniques by industry in the 1980s. They cited three reasons for this growth:

- concerns about making training more responsive to the needs of business in order to 'improve national economic performance';
- active promotion by government;
- developments in information technology.

Stewart and Winter (1995) also noted that although the use of distance learning had grown recently they argue that it has 'not become the major force in education and training predicted by its commentators'. Brown (1997) presented a series of case studies drawn from 'real, practical examples from industry and education' in the United Kingdom. His commercial case studies (Lloyds Bank, Trustee Savings Bank, British Telecom, Abbey National, Barclays Bank and Reuters) all described the development of bespoke materials, often delivered by highly capital-intensive delivery systems using the latest information and communications technologies (ICT) and aimed at target audiences numbering in hundreds if not thousands of trainees dispersed over many sites. At British Telecom the benefits were overtly presented as economies of scale: 'the costs and benefits really only show up when a company-wide perspective is taken' (Brown 1997: 48) as they are for Barclays: 'irrefutable proof exists that distance learning can *enrich and enhance the cost-effectiveness* of more traditional training methods' (Christian-Carter 1997: 72, italics added). Curran *et al.* (1996: xi) noted 'distance learning should be given more attention because it would support in-house training and reduce lost production where workers train away from the firm'. Curran and Stanworth (1989: 17) saw distance learning as an appropriate delivery mechanism for small businesses' 'continuing education' since it could effectively overcome the barrier of the 'resistance of small business owners to having any contact with formal educational institutions'. For many small firms the resource constraints under which they may operate (for example little slack time, limited financial resources, lack of HR expertise and environmental uncertainty) can impose limits upon the feasibility of such approaches.

HRD in smaller firms

HRD in small firms has been subjected to analyses from a number of fields of management, including the marketing, strategy, small firm academic communities and as well as scholars of HRM, organisational behaviour and HRD (see, for example, Curran and Stanworth 1989; Curran *et al.* 1996; Gibb 1995; Gorman *et al.* 1997; Goss and Jones 1992; Hendry *et al.* 1995; Hill and Stewart 1999; Joyce *et al.*

1995; Westhead and Storey 1996). In the late 1980s Curran and Stanworth (1989: 18- 20) highlighted the lack of research on the 'character, availability and effectiveness' of small business education as being a major weakness in the field and argued that the assessment of training effectiveness in small firms should be a major area for future work. Over the intervening period there have been a number of substantial and important contributions to this debate (for example, Curran *et al.* 1996; Hendry *et al.* 1995; Westhead and Storey 1996).

HRD as intervention

Gray (1998: 27) traced the use of HRD as an SME policy intervention back to the 1970s and interpreted many of the mass training programmes as the UK government's preferred form of intervention to encourage the growth of entrepreneurs. Hogarth-Scott and Jones (1993: 21) observed that training providers would often make little attempt to 'selectively target their promotional activities or the content of their service. Instead they tend[ed] to view small firms as homogeneous in nature and consequently offer a standardised approach'. This reflects Mitra and Formica's (1995) observation that providers (including universities) are good at 'generalised solutions and the application of abstract principles [but] companies want specific answers to specific questions - and they want them now' (1995: 286). Gibb (1995: 18) argued that the nature of the training on offer to small businesses is heavily influenced by a tradition of business education geared almost exclusively to students and large firms. The content of much 'off-the-shelf' training he contends is largely irrelevant to owner-managers in small firms and can contribute to the perception on the part of entrepreneurs of business education and training as being 'academic' and divorced from the 'real world'.

The effect of size and organisational characteristics

A number of researchers have explored the issue of HRD and size of firm and other related factors. Sadler-Smith *et al.* (1998: 84) in a survey of 700 SMEs in south-west England found that patterns of training and development showed clear evidence of relationships with size of firm. An alternative perspective was adopted by Goss and Jones (1992) who linked the type of training undertaken to organisational structure (monarchic, diarchic and polyarchic). They noted differences in training practice between these three structural types, with complexity of organisational structure having a clear effect on the sophistication of the training provision (from 'restricted' through 'instrumental' to 'sophisticated').

Barriers to HRD in smaller firms

Hill and Stewart (1999) and Sadler-Smith *et al.* (2000) have both argued that the resource constraints within many smaller firms might mean that they sometimes fail to maximise the potential of learning. Matlay (2000) in his large-scale study of HRD in smaller firms identified two groups of factors that affect the provision of training in small firms. Direct factors included market position (nominated by 92 per cent of respondents as a limiting factor), economic conditions (88 per cent) and availability of relevant training (81.5 per cent). Indirect factors included costs of training (45.5 per cent) and time constraints (38.5 per cent). A minority of firms identified lack of in-house instructors (28.5 per cent), lack of trainee motivation (25.5 per cent) or trainee interest (12.5 per cent) as limiting factors (Matlay 2000: 334). Hendry *et al.* (1995: 153) highlighted affordability, ownership and control, fear of poaching (since lack of growth may lead some individuals to seek promotion within the sector rather than the firm), limited horizons and the pressures of growth as constraints on occupational learning in small firms:

> The greatest obstacle to extended occupational learning in the small firm is size itself. New job challenges through promotion opportunities and expanded roles, by definition, are limited in the absence of growth. Attention then turns away from the individual firm to progression via job opportunities in the sector.
>
> (Hendry *et al.* 1995: 156)

In this context the attitude of the owner-manager towards learning and her/his perception of the threat of 'poaching' or career progression outside the firm are crucial.

The attitude and role of the owner-manager

Matlay's (2000) research suggests that owner-managers take virtually all of the important decisions related to workforce training (as well as retaining control of most of the other functions relevant to the management of their firms). From a sample of 2000 firms with fewer than 100 employees he observed a modest decrease in owner-manager decision-making with firm size and a concomitant small increase in the role played by other personnel (including HR specialists). Curran *et al.* (1996) in their research found that the owner-manager appeared to take on the HRD role by default. Walton (1999: 335) commented upon the degree of dependence of the HRD commitment and effort upon the 'attitude of the person running or owning the organisation'. The educational experiences of some owner-managers in small firms may reinforce a generally negative attitude to education and training that can make it difficult to convince these key stakeholders of the value of training. Research by Hogarth-Scott and Jones (1993) and the CBI survey of 1986 (reported in Pettigrew *et al.* 1990) suggested that management training was held in low esteem by respondents in their sample of firms of fewer than 200 employees. In a fiercely competitive market with high rates of mortality among businesses, financial pressures are likely to be a key determinant of the priority given to training provision within small firms. Gray (1998: 31) speculated that the opportunity costs of attending training for many entrepreneurs might be too high to justify the expenditure. Owner-managers need to be convinced of the potential benefits of HRD (or any other activity) where opportunity costs may be incurred. Theoretically at least, flexible modes of delivery (such as distance learning) may have zero or lower opportunity costs than do conventional approaches. Hendry *et al.* (1995) identified a general reluctance in

SMEs to spend money on training with the allocation of resources for training being ad hoc up to the point at which the firm reaches about one hundred employees in size. In terms of training delivery methods Hendry *et al.* (1995) found owner-managers favouring practical in-house training to meet specific local needs. An overriding operational concern was the perceived lack of time for training that militated against external (i.e. off-the-job and off-site) training.

Aims and objectives

The aim of this research was to build upon the previous work that has attempted to describe HRD practices in smaller firms. In order to achieve this aim we identified three broad research objectives:

- Use the National Standard for Training and Development as a basis for exploring HRD practices within smaller firms (Study 1).
- Explore the frequency of use and managers' perceptions of the effectiveness of a range of HRD methods (Study 1).
- Examine the HRD roles and responsibilities within smaller firms (Study 2).

Study 1

Based upon previous research and theorising, Study 1 aimed to examine the relationships between size of firm and HRD activities and HRD delivery methods by testing the following propositions:

Proposition 1 (P1)

The importance accorded to the activities embodied in the National Occupational Standard for Training and Development will show a positive relationship with size.

Proposition 2 (P2)

The frequency of use of off-the-job HRD methods will show a positive relationship with size.

Proposition 3 (P3)

The frequency of use of on-the-job HRD methods will show a negative relationship with size.

Method

Participants

The study was cross-sectional and data were collected by means of a postal questionnaire survey mailed to 800 firms in south-west England (comprising the counties of Cornwall, Devon, Somerset, Avon and Dorset). Respondents were selected randomly from a commercially available database.

Instrument and procedure

The survey form consisted of a number of sections with a separate accompanying letter stating that a small donation to charity would be made for every completed questionnaire received. The sections of the survey form pertinent to the present study were:

- *Respondent information:* number of employees, sector (manufacturing, service or construction).
- *Training activities:* respondents were asked to indicate the importance they attached to each of twenty separate HRD activities (referred to in the questionnaire as training activities) for training in their company. These were scored on a five-point scale from very important (five) to very unimportant (one). The twenty individual items were based upon the units of the UK National Occupational Standard for Training and Development (EOSC 1995). Two units from the standard were omitted since they dealt with recruitment and appraisal and these are not normally included in the systematic approach as exemplified in the HRD literature. In a footnote to this question it was stipulated that by 'training' the survey was referring to any type of training activity (for example, on-job training) and not only formal activities such as training courses.
- *Training methods:* respondents were asked to indicate the frequency with which they made use of a number of delivery methods for workforce training in their businesses from a list which comprised computer-based training; distance learning packages; formal taught courses (off-site); formal taught courses (on-site); job rotation; on-job instruction (OJI); training videos; and work shadowing. The question was scored on a five-point scale ranging from very frequently used (scored five) to very infrequently used (scored one). The questionnaire was mailed to the manager responsible for training in each of the firms sampled; this person was taken as being a knowledgeable key informant (Shortell and Zajac 1990) and hence provided a valid source for measuring HRD as an organisational process.

Results

Characteristics of sample

The number of usable questionnaires received was 278 (representing a response rate of 35 per cent). Firms were categorised into four size groups as follows: micro firm: 0-9 employees; small firm: 10-49 employees; medium firm: 50-249 employees; large firm: 250 employees or more. The sample characteristics were as follows:

- *Size*: micro, $N = 38$ (13.7 per cent); small, $N = 71$ (25.5 per cent); medium, $N = 55$ (19.8 per cent); large, $N = 114$ (41.0 per cent).

- *Sector*: construction, $N = 44$ (15.8 per cent); manufacturing, $N = 102$ (36.7 per cent); service, $N = 132$ (47.5 per cent).

HRD activities

In order to simplify the interpretation of the data those items that comprised the HRD activities were subjected to a principal components (factor) analysis. The suitability of these data for factor analysis was confirmed by the results of Bartlett's test of sphericity ($\chi^2 = 3039.25$, df = 190, $p < 0.001$). There were four principal components (factors) with eigenvalues greater than one, and these represented 62.91 per cent of the total variance. Based upon the content of those items which loaded at or above a salient value of 0.40, and using the highest loading in those instances where items cross-loaded at or above this value, the four extracted factors were labelled as follows:

- Factor 1: assessing performance
- Factor 2: planning and evaluating HRD
- Factor 3: implementing HRD
- Factor 4: designing HRD.

These four factors, their respective items and the associated factor loadings are shown in Table 7.1.

The factor structure which emerged is not entirely consistent with that predicted from the model of the systematic approach that was used by the TDLB in the design of the UK National Standard (from which one might have predicted the four factors consisting of analysis, design, implementation and evaluation - see Figure 7.1). Training needs analysis and evaluation of training combined to form a single factor (Factor 2). In this regard it is worthy of note that the context-input-results-output (CIRO) evaluation framework of Warr *et al.* (1970) drew explicit links between analysis and evaluation - a conceptualisation borne out empirically by these data. Implementing HRD and designing HRD emerged, as expected, as separate factors. Assessing performance, which is not normally included in traditional models of the systematic approach (but is subsumed within evaluation), emerged as a separate factor, thus vindicating its treatment as such in the National Standard. For the purposes of subsequent analysis the four factors were treated as internally consistent scales and their individual items summed and divided by the number of items loading at the salient level on the relevant factor in order to compute mean scores.

The mean scores and inter-correlations for the four factors are shown in Table 7.2. Also included in Table 7.2 are the correlations with size. Given the large size range within the sample it was decided to compute the correlations with the $\log_{10}$ of the number of employees. As may be seen from Table 7.2 the inter-correlations between the four HRD activities were statistically significant. More importantly three of the scales showed positive relationships with firm size ($p < 0.0001$). Assessing performance was the only HRD activity that failed to show a statistically significant correlation in this regard.

Table 7.1 Matrix of factor loadings for HRD activities

Variable	Loading
Assessing performance	
Designing systems to collect evidence of competence	84
Collecting evidence of competence	82
Identifying employees' prior training and educational achievements	66
Assessing individual employees' training performance (e.g. by testing)	55
Planning and evaluating HRD	
Identifying the type of training that's important to your company's success	- 83
Improving the quality of training in your company	- 65
Identifying the right type of training for the improvement of individual employees' performance	- 64
Evaluating the training plan for your company	- 63
Devising overall plans for implementing training in your company	- 59
Evaluating training carried out in your company	- 59
Negotiating and agreeing individual training requirements with your employees	(- 32)
Implementing HRD	
Carrying out training by demonstration and instruction	92
Carrying out individual training by coaching and mentoring	89
Carrying out training in groups by presentations and other activities	56
Supporting and guiding individual employees' training and development	48
Monitoring and reviewing individual employees' training progress	41
Designing HRD	
Designing and developing training materials (e.g. worksheets, manuals)	- 78
Designing training activities (e.g. workshops, classes, etc.) to meet the needs of your employees	- 65
Creating a climate in your company which is conducive to learning	- 55

Note
Zeros and decimal points omitted from factor loadings.

In order to further investigate the relationships with size (and for example to identify any non-linear effects) a multivariate analysis of variance was conducted (since the four dependent variables were inter-correlated) with size (four levels) and sector (three levels) as the independent variables. There are several statistical techniques available to test the significance of main effects and interactions. Tabachnik and Fidell (1996: 400- 1) recommended that when dealing with unequal cell sizes (which is a feature of these data) Pillai's test is generally regarded as a robust criterion. Using this method (Pillai's trace = 0.17) the combined dependent variables were significantly related to size ($F = 3.97$; df = 12; $p < 0.0001$). There was no main effect of sector ($F = 1.23$; df = 8; $p = 0.28$), nor any interaction between size and sector in their effect upon the combined dependent variables ($F = 0.96$; df = 24; $p = 0.51$). The results of the uni-variate analysis for each main effect along with *post-hoc* comparisons (Scheffé's test; $p < 0.05$) are shown in Table 7.3.

As may be seen from Table 7.3 the uni-variate analyses of variance revealed statistically significant effects of size for all four dependent variables. The *post-hoc*

Table 7.2 Means, standard deviations and inter-correlations for HRD activities and correlations with size (log $_{10}$)

	Mean (sd)	(2)	(3)	(4)	Size (log $_{10}$)
Assessing performance	3.71 (0.71)	0.55*	0.56*	0.52*	0.09
Planning and evaluating HRD	4.30 (0.58)		0.56*	0.60*	0.34*
Implementing HRD	4.08 (0.58)			0.61*	0.21*
Designing HRD	4.08 (0.66)				0.34*

Note
* $p < 0.001$.

Table 7.3 Means and standard deviations for HRD activities by size (Pillai's trace = 0.17; F = 3.97; df = 12; $p < 0.0001$)

	Size				MANOVA
	Micro	Small	Medium	Large	$F_{3, 263}$
Assessing performance	3.51 (0.67)	3.67 (0.70)	3.91 (0.68)	3.70 (0.72)	3.14*
Planning and evaluating HRD	3.92 (0.56)$_{ijl}$	4.15 (0.54)$_k$	4.37 (0.64)$_i$	4.50 (0.50)$_{jkl}$	9.75***
Implementing HRD	3.84 (0.51)$_{ij}$	3.97 (0.64)	4.20 (0.56)$_i$	4.16 (0.55)$_j$	3.92**
Designing HRD	3.83 (0.51)$_{il}$	3.80 (0.81)$_{jk}$	4.20 (0.56)$_j$	4.28 (0.57)$_{kl}$	8.02***

Notes
Subscripts refer to statistically significant subgroup differences at 0.05 level (Scheffé's test); * $p < 0.05$; ** $p < 0.01$; *** $p < 0.001$.

comparisons did not reveal any statistically significant subgroup differences for Factor 1 (assessing performance). For Factor 2 (R^2_{adj} = 0.12) there was a monotonic relationship with size; larger firms gave greater emphasis to planning and evaluating HRD than did their smaller counterparts. For Factor 3 (R^2_{adj} = 0.08), implementing HRD, there were statistically significant subgroup differences between the micro-firms and the medium and large firms, with the micro-firms giving less emphasis to this activity than their larger counterparts. For Factor 4 (R^2_{adj} = 0.10) there were statistically significant subgroup differences between the micro/small group of firms and the medium and larger firms, with the micro/small firms according less emphasis to the designing of HRD than their larger counterparts. With the exception of Factor 1, these results provided support for Proposition 1.

HRD methods

As with the previous measures, it was decided to simplify the interpretation of the HRD methods by attempting to identify latent groupings within the items. (This section represents a reanalysis of data reported by Sadler-Smith *et al.* (2000) in which the items were not grouped.) In order to achieve this a principal components (factor) analysis was conducted. The results of this suggested that two factors accounting for 42.11 per cent of the variance should be extracted. The solution was rotated to simple structure using an orthogonal (varimax) rotation. The resultant factor matrix is shown in Table 7.4.

Factor 1 comprised HRD methods that rely upon learners being away from their place of work in order to acquire knowledge and skills; hence this factor was labelled off-job HRD. Conversely, Factor 2 comprised methods of delivering HRD though, or in proximity to employees' work (on-job instruction, job rotation and second-ments); hence this factor was labelled on-job HRD. Mean scores were computed for each of these factors and a paired samples t-test revealed statistically significant differences between mean scores for frequency of use of on-job HRD (mean = 3.05, sd = 0.73) and off-job HRD (mean = 2.52, sd = 0.84) ($t = -8.91$; df = 277; $p < 0.001$). The relationship between HRD methods and size was investigated further by means of multivariate analysis of variance with size and sector as independent variables and HRD methods as the combined dependent variable. Using the method outlined in the previous section (Pillai's trace = 0.10) the combined dependent variables (on-job HRD and off-job HRD) were significantly affected by size ($F = 4.49$; df = 6; $p < 0.0001$). There was no main effect of sector ($F = 2.16$; df = 4; $p = 0.07$) although this did approach significance at the 5 per cent level. There was no statistically significant interaction between size and sector in their effect upon the combined dependent variables ($F = 1.09$; df = 12; $p = 0.34$). The results of the uni-variate analysis for each main effect along with *post-hoc* comparisons (Scheffé's test; $p < 0.05$) are shown in Table 7.5.

The uni-variate analyses of variance revealed a statistically significant effect of size upon frequency of use of off-job HRD methods ($F_{2, 263} = 8.14$; $p < 0.001$). The *post-hoc* comparisons revealed statistically significant subgroup differences between the large firms and the medium, small and micro firms. These results provided support for the proposition that the frequency of use of off-job HRD methods will show a positive relationship with size (Proposition 2). The uni-variate analyses of variance did not reveal any statistically significant effect of size upon on-job HRD methods and hence

Table 7.4 Matrix of factor loadings for HRD methods

Variable	Loading
Off-job HRD	
Videos	78
Distance learning packages	74
Formal taught courses (on site)	54
Computer-based training	48
Formal taught courses (off site)	(39)
On-job HRD	
Work shadowing	71
Job rotation	67
On-job instruction (OJI)	64

Note
Zeros and decimal points omitted from factor loadings.

Table 7.5 Means and standard deviations for HRD methods by size (Pillai's trace = 0.10; F = 4.49; df = 6; p < 0.0001)

Size	Size				ANOVA
Size	Micro	Small	Medium	Large	$F_{3,\,263}$
On-job HRD	3.09 (0.95)	2.97 (0.90)	3.09 (0.71)	3.06 (0.85)	0.68
Off-job HRD	2.27 (0.66)$_i$	2.41 (0.67)$_j$	2.87 (0.62)$_k$	2.51 (0.73)$_{ijk}$	8.14*

Notes
Subscripts refer to statistically significant sub-group differences at 0.05 level (Scheffé's test); * p < 0.001.

these results did not provide support for the proposition that the frequency of use of on-job HRD methods will show a negative relationship with size (Proposition 3).

Further detailed analysis at the item level was conducted for off-job and on-job HRD and the results are shown in Figures 7.2 and 7.3. The most frequently used methods of off-job HRD were traditional 'taught' training courses. Perhaps disappointingly for advocates of distance learning these data suggest that this method (for which many HRD advantages have been claimed - see Buckley and Caple 1992: 176-7) appears only to have a peripheral role in HRD delivery in firms of all sizes. This is perhaps a key finding in terms of small firm support policy (given many recent initiatives in the UK) and raises questions about why this pattern was observed. Possible reasons may include lack of awareness of the espoused benefits of distance learning, cost of materials and delivery systems (although no longer so prohibitive if personal computer-based), the perceived lack of social interaction associated with self-instruction or available packages not meeting firm-specific

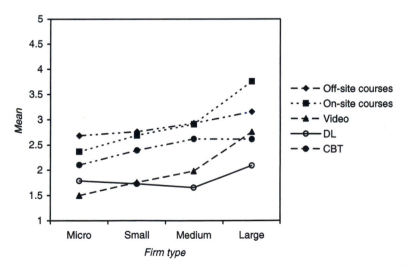

Figure 7.2 Mean frequency of use for off-job HRD by size.

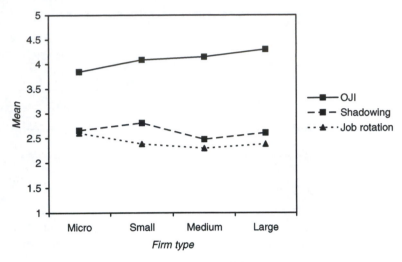

Figure 7.3 Mean frequency of use for on-job HRD by size.

learning and development needs. As may be seen from Figure 7.2 there is a general increase in the reported frequency of use of off-job HRD with firm size, with notable increases in the frequency of use of on-site courses and video-based training in the large firms. The latter may be explained by the assertion that such organisations are the most likely to have dedicated training staff and facilities with which to provide on-site bespoke training courses and the financial resource to invest in video-based corporate training packages (given that the cost of the latter is likely to be prohibitive to the smaller firms). With respect to the frequency of use of the specific on-job HRD methods, it may be seen that on-job instruction is by far the most frequently used and, somewhat surprisingly showed an increase in its usage with size (though this was non-significant). Work shadowing and job rotation were used less frequently than on-job instruction.

Study 2

Having examined the HRD processes in the previous study (in terms of activities and methods), in Study 2 we aimed to explore the HRD roles and responsibilities within smaller firms. There were no specific research hypotheses for Study 2, however the broad research question was defined as: 'which stakeholders have the major responsibilities for the principal activities within the HRD process?'. Our expectations were that the bulk of the responsibility would be borne by owner-managers with the delivery of on-job instruction being the responsibility of line managers or co-workers. The stakeholders for the purposes of this study were defined as owner-managers, HRD specialists (for example, training officer/training manager), line managers, employees and external providers.

Method

Participants

As with the preceding study a cross-sectional design was employed with data collected by means of a postal questionnaire survey mailed to 500 firms with 250 or fewer employees in south-west England (comprising the counties of Cornwall, Devon, Somerset, Avon and Dorset). Respondents were selected randomly from a commercially available database.

Instrument and procedure

The survey form was four pages (A4) and consisted of a number of sections with a separate accompanying letter stipulating that a small donation to charity would be made for every completed questionnaire received. The sections of the survey form pertinent to the present study were:

- *Respondent information:* number of employees; sector (manufacturing, service, construction or other).
- *Training activities:* respondents were asked to indicate, by ticking the appropriate box on the survey form, who in their company was responsible for carrying out each of twenty separate HRD activities (referred to in the questionnaire as training activities). The question was in a multiple response format; hence it was possible for respondents to report that more than one individual stakeholder was responsible for a given activity. The individual items were based upon the UK National Occupational Standard for Training and Development (EOSC 1995). The questionnaire was mailed to the manager responsible for training in each of the firms sampled.

Results

Characteristics of sample

The number of usable questionnaires received was 135 and represented a response rate of 27.0 per cent. The sample characteristics were as follows: construction, $N = 37$ (27.4 per cent); manufacturing, $N = 43$ (31.9 per cent); service, $N = 40$ (29.6 per cent) and other 15 (11.1 per cent). The size range was from 2 to 250 employees and the median size was 25.50 employees.

HRD activity and stakeholder responsibilities

The results of the survey are shown in Table 7.6. The figures in each cell represent the percentage of respondents who indicated that a given stakeholder has responsibility for a specific HRD activity in their organisation. The overall pattern that emerged was one in which the principal responsibilities for HRD activities lies primarily with owner-managers, with a degree of secondary responsibility for line

Table 7.6 Responsibilities for HRD practices in small and medium sized firms

	Owner-manager	Training manager/officer	Line manager	Employee	External provider	Nobody
1 Identifying the type of training that's important to your company's success	82	24	36	30	8	1
2 Identifying the right type of training for the improvement of individual employees' performance	62	23	46	30	9	4
3 Devising overall plans for implementing training in your company	72	28	16	6	7	7
4 Designing training activities (e.g. work-shops, classes, etc.) to meet the needs of your employees	41	28	20	6	22	17
5 Designing and developing training materials (e.g. worksheets, manuals, etc.)	38	26	23	9	23	17
6 Co-ordinating training provision with external training providers (e.g. Training and Enterprise Councils, colleges, etc.)	53	32	12	5	9	13
7 Creating a climate in your company which is conducive to learning	75	28	33	15	2	10
8 Negotiating and agreeing individual training requirements with your employees	62	21	44	22	5	4
9 Carrying out training in groups by presentations and other activities	38	28	24	8	27	28
10 Carrying out training by demonstration and instruction	49	25	48	24	23	5
11 Carrying out individual training by coaching and mentoring	41	21	55	23	11	10
12 Supporting and guiding individual employees' training and development	60	31	49	10	4	7
13 Monitoring and reviewing individual employees' training progress	63	28	50	13	7	6
14 Assessing individual employees' training performance (e.g. by testing, etc.)	34	20	35	7	17	23
15 Designing systems to collect evidence of competence	30	22	18	4	11	30
16 Collecting evidence of competence	37	17	36	9	8	24
17 Identifying employees' prior training and educational achievements	58	29	33	8	2	4
18 Evaluating the training plan for your company	67	24	11	1	6	15
19 Improving the quality of training in your company	74	28	20	7	9	9
20 Evaluating training carried out in your company	62	25	19	9	11	17

managers and some employee responsibility, but very little involvement for HRD/ HRM specialists and external providers. Even taking a liberal threshold of a 30 per cent response for each given activity it is the owner manager who had the prime responsibility for eighteen out of twenty HRD activities. At this level of salience other significant responsibilities are taken by line managers (in identifying training needs and negotiating requirements, and facilitating training through demonstration, instruction, coaching and mentoring) and by employees in identifying training needs. The only activities in which owner-managers had a secondary role to line managers was with respect to carrying out individual training by coaching and mentoring and assessing individual employees' training performance.

The data presented in Table 7.6 suggest that there appears to be little effort accorded to the designing of training activities and materials, or to the issue of competence assessment (perhaps because the respondents were not involved in these activities or the persons responsible were not identified in the design of the survey question, for example an external assessor). The latter is supported by the higher level of effort devoted to carrying out training by demonstration, instruction, coaching and mentoring, i.e. on-job HRD. The data also suggest that relatively more activity is devoted to broader strategic and contextual issues related to learning than to operational issues. For example, if one takes an arbitrary criterion of 70 per cent to indicate high involvement, strategic HRD activities such as identifying training needs (82 per cent), overall HRD planning (72 per cent), the creation of a learning climate (75 per cent) and continuous improvement of HRD (74 per cent) appeared to be of importance (and engaged in principally by owner-managers). The extent to which this is due to biases in the perceptions of respondents (primarily owner-managers) is not clear. Nonetheless, the significant finding is the dominance of owner-manager's role in the HRD process; their contribution far outweighs that of others who have a potential role to play (i.e. line managers and employees). These data help to more clearly describe HRD roles and responsibilities in smaller firms, they do not however tell us anything about the quality, efficiency or effectiveness of the learning and development that takes place, the HRD decision process that owner-managers engage in and HRD's relationship with measures of individual and organisational performance (these may be topics worthy of further investigation). The findings are commensurate with our expectations and with previous research on the entrepreneurs' desire for autonomy, fear of external control and the desire to manage one's own business (Delmar 2000: 144).

Conclusions

This chapter has examined the practice of HRD in a sample of smaller firms in terms of activities, methods used and roles and responsibilities. The aim of the chapter was to consolidate and extend our knowledge of small firm HRD. The overall picture that emerged from the two studies was as follows:

- HRD activities fell into four principal groups: assessing performance, planning and evaluating HRD, implementing HRD and designing HRD, and with the exception of assessing performance, all of these activities showed statistically significant positive correlations with firm size.

- HRD delivery methods fell into two principal groups: first, off-job HRD (which showed a clear positive relationship with size, and in which traditional training courses were the dominant method of delivery); second, on-job HRD (in which on-job instruction was the method of choice for the delivery of HRD across the firms surveyed in preference to off-job learning and irrespective of size of firm).
- Distance learning appeared to have a peripheral role to play as an HRD method.
- Owner-managers had the prime responsibility for virtually all HRD activities, while line managers had the main responsibility for carrying out HRD through demonstration, instruction, coaching and mentoring and assessing individual employee's training performance.
- There was little evidence of any activity related to the collection of evidence of competence.

These findings are summarised diagrammatically in Figure 7.4.

These results highlight the need for future HRD research to consider broader HR issues such as employee recruitment and selection. For example, it is not clear if

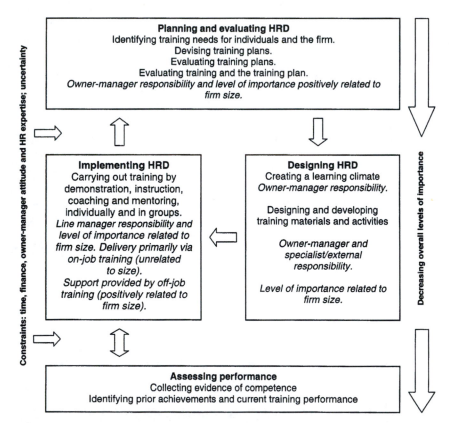

Figure 7.4 A descriptive framework of small firm HRD.

small firms recruit those individuals that have been (informally) assessed through the selection process as not needing additional training. In a highly resource constrained internal environment owner-managers may be more likely to employ individuals who are able to perform effectively and quickly with minimal induction training or additional skills development needs (hence reducing costs). Loss of any investment made in knowledge and skills development may also be a very real fear among owner-managers in a labour market in which employees may find it more feasible to exit in order to secure career progression rather than achieve this within the firm. The threat may be exacerbated if key individuals have the potential to leave to set up in competition with their former employer. Therefore the assessment of current skill levels is likely to be crucially important; in this scenario questions may be raised about the status accorded subsequent skills development.

These findings and those of the other research that we have cited have some implications for practitioners and policy-makers:

- The observation that HRD activities showed statistically positive correlations with firm size suggests that existing skills gaps in the small firm sector may continue and underlines the continued need for policy intervention to encourage training and development activities in order to sustain the competitiveness of smaller firms.
- The findings from Study 2 demonstrated the central role played by owner-managers in HRD. An important question arising from these results is therefore 'Who trains the owner-managers?' One way in which the quality of training and development activities might be improved is by targeting owner-managers for training in the development and delivery of effective HRD.
- Line managers had a role to play in the delivery of learning in the workplace and this raises the question of whether such individuals have optimum skills for facilitating learning. Coaching and mentoring skills for line managers may be a crucial area for further development (perhaps as a generic need).
- The results of the research indicated that the use of distance learning by all firms is limited. Therefore policy-makers and developers of flexible learning materials must ask whether this is simply a failure in communication and presentation of the potential benefits of such methods, or whether the concept is more fundamentally flawed. It is our view that distance learning should be pursued as an intervention, but that further work is needed in order to

(i) reduce the costs to firms (particularly to the smallest firms)
(ii) develop the specific sectoral, functional and business relevance of the materials
(iii) convince owner-managers of its potential value and cost-effectiveness in supporting learning in the workplace.

Few would claim that distance learning is a panacea and research is needed to establish how it can best support more favoured approaches such as on-the-job training in smaller firms.

Walton (1999: 325) provided a succinct perspective on HRD in smaller firms. He argued that the attention that has been given to the analysis of training within SMEs has conflated the presence or absence of training with learning. He commented that the pre-occupation with training (perhaps a manifestation of the supply side perspective of government-funded and other small firm support initiatives) gives a 'narrow and distorted view of the realities of both what is being learned and how it is being learned'. One of the main lessons from small firm HRD research is that a broader perspective is required in order to generate greater insight; too much of the emphasis for too long has been on a supplier-driven conception of learning (for example as formal taught courses). This narrowness of vision of small firm HRD is one that is shared by some researchers, managers and policy-makers and has constrained the growth of our understanding of the field and may overlook much of the most valuable learning that goes on in small firms.

Bibliography

Anderson, A. H. (1993) *Successful Training Practice*, Oxford: Blackwell.

Bachler, C. J. (1997) 'Competencies all trainers need', *Workforce*, 76, 6: 94- 6.

Bennett, R. and Leduchowicz, T. (1983) 'What makes for an effective trainer?', *Journal of European Industrial Training*, 7, 2, monograph.

British Gas/Futuremedia (1984) *The Systems Approach to Training*, London: British Gas.

Brown, S. (ed.) (1997) *Open and Distance Learning: Case studies from industry and education*, London: Kogan Page.

Buckley, J. and Caple, C. (1992) *The Theory and Practice of Training*, London: Kogan Page.

Burgoyne, J. (1993) 'The competence movement: issues, stakeholders and prospects', *Personnel Review*, 22, 6: 6- 13.

Christian-Carter, J. (1997) 'Implementing distance learning in Barclays Bank', in S. Brown (ed.) *Open and Distance Learning: Case studies from industry and education*, London: Kogan Page.

Craig, M. (1995) 'Techniques for investigation', in S. Truelove (ed.) *The Handbook of Training and Development*, Oxford: Blackwell.

Curran, J. and Stanworth, J. (1989) 'Education and training for enterprise: some problems of classification, evaluation, policy and research', *International Small Business Journal*, 7, 2: 11-22.

Curran, J., Blackburn, R. A., Kitching, J. and North, J. (1996) *Establishing Small Firms' Training Needs Practices, Difficulties and Use of ITO's*, Research Studies Report RS 17, London: HMSO.

Delmar, F. (2000) 'The psychology of the entrepreneur', in S. Carter and D. Jones-Evans (eds) *Enterprise and Small Business: Principles, practice and policy*, Harlow: Financial Times and Prentice Hall.

Du Gay, P., Salaman, G. and Rees, B. (1996) 'The conduct of management and the management of conduct: contemporary management discourse and the "constitution" of the competent manager', *Journal of Management Studies*, 33, 3: 263- 82.

Employment Occupational Standards Council (EOSC) (1995) *The Training and Development Lead Body: National Occupational Standard for Training and Development*, London: EOSC.

Gibb, S. (1995) 'The lead body model of personnel management', *Human Resource Management Journal*, 5, 5: 60- 74.

Gibb, S. and Megginson, D. (2001) 'Employee development', in T. Redman and A. Wilkinson (eds) *Contemporary Human Resource Management*, Harlow: Financial Times and Prentice Hall.

Goldstein, I. (1993) *Training in Organisations*, Pacific Grove, CA: Brooks Cole.

Gorman, G., Hanlon, D. and King, W. (1997) 'Some research perspectives on entrepreneurship education, enterprise education and education for small business management: a ten year literature review', *International Small Business Journal*, 15, 3: 56-77.

Goss, D. and Jones, R. (1992) 'Organisation structure and SME training provision', *International Small Business Journal*, 10, 4: 13-23.

Gray, C. (1998) *Enterprise and Culture*, London: Routledge.

Grugulis, I. (1997) 'The consequences of competence: a critical assessment of the Management NVQ', *Personnel Review*, 26, 6: 428-44.

Harrison, R. (1997) *Employee Development*, London: Institute of Personnel and Development.

Hendry, C., Arthur, M. B. and Jones, A. M. (1995) *Strategy through People*, London: Routledge.

Hill, R. and Stewart, J. (1999) 'Human resource development in small organisations', *Human Resource Development International*, 2, 2: 103-23.

Hogarth-Scott, S. and Jones, M. A. (1993) 'Advice and training support for the small firms sector in West Yorkshire', *Journal of European Industrial Training*, 17, 1: 18-22.

Iles, P. (1996) 'International HRD', in J. Stewart and J. McGoldrick (eds) *Human Resource Development: Perspectives, strategies and practices*, London: Pitman.

Joyce, P., McNulty, T. and Woods, A. (1995) 'Work-force training: are small firms different?', *Journal of European Industrial Training*, 19, 5: 19-25.

Lee, C. (1998) 'Certified to train', *Training*, 35, 9: 32-40.

Leonard, B. (1996) 'Distance learning: work and training overlap', *HR Magazine*, 41, 4: 40-8.

Matlay, H. (2000) 'Training and the small firm', in S. Carter and D. Jones-Evans (eds) *Enterprise and Small Business: Principles, practice and policy*, Harlow: Financial Times and Prentice Hall.

Mitra, J. and Formica, P. (1995) 'Innovative player in economic development in Europe', *Industry and Higher Education*, October: 285-92.

Mole, G. (1996) 'The management training industry in the UK: an HRD director's critique', *Human Resource Management Journal*, 6, 1: 19-26.

Mullins, L. J. (2002) *Management and Organisational Behaviour*, Harlow: Financial Times and Prentice Hall.

Mumford, A. (1995) *Effective Learning*, London: Institute of Personnel and Development.

Pettigrew, A., Jones, E. and Reason, P. (1982) *Training and Development Roles in their Organisational Setting*, Sheffield: Manpower Services Commission.

Pettigrew, A. M., Arthur, M. B. and Hendry, C. (1990) *Training and Human Resource Management in Small to Medium Sized Enterprises*, Sheffield: Training Agency.

Sadler-Smith, E., Sargeant, A. and Dawson, A. (1998) 'Higher level skills training: meeting the needs of small businesses', *International Journal of Training and Development*, 1, 4: 216-29.

Sadler-Smith, E., Down, S. and Lean, J. (2000) 'Modern training methods: rhetoric and reality', *Personnel Review*, 29, 4: 474-90.

Sadler-Smith, E., Gardiner, P. Badger, B., Chaston I. and Stubberfield, J. (2001) 'Developing small firms through collaborative action', *Human Resource Development International*, 3, 3: 285-306.

Sanderson, G. (1995) 'Objectives and evaluation', in S. Truelove (ed.) *The Handbook of Training and Development*, Oxford: Blackwell.

Shortell, S. M. and Zajac, E. J. (1990) 'Perceptual and archival measures of miles and snow's strategy types: a comprehensive assessment of reliability and validity', *Academy of Management Journal*, 33, 4: 817-32.

Stewart, J. (1999) *Employee Development Practice*, London: Financial Times and Pitman.

Stewart, J. and Winter, R. (1995) 'Open and distance learning', in S. Truelove (ed.) *The Handbook of Training and Development*, Oxford: Blackwell.

Tabachnick, B. G. and Fidell, L. S. (1996) *Using Multivariate Statistics*, New York: HarperCollins.

Transform (1991) *Developing the Developers*, London: Association for Management Education and Development.

Walton, J. (1999) *Strategic Human Resource Development*, Harlow: Financial Times and Prentice Hall.

Warr, P., Bird, M. and Rackham, N. (1970) *Evaluation of Management Training*, Aldershot: Gower.

Westhead, P. and Storey, D. (1996) 'Management training and small firm performance: why is the link so weak?', *International Small Business Journal*, 14, 4: 13- 24.

8 HRD and knowledge migration in SME–academic partnerships

The technology translator project

Paul Iles and Maurice Yolles

Introduction: HRD and SMEs

Most research and theory-building in HRD is associated with large organisations. However, most firms in the United Kingdom employ fewer than fifty people. The 'official' view sees the sector as not facing any specific issues that differentiate it from large firms; HRD, of a formal 'enterprise training' kind, is seen as necessary to facilitate growth (e.g. Gray 1993). SMEs are therefore seen as scaled-down large firms, and SME HRD as scaled-down large firm HRD. However, UK government-supported enterprise training programmes have often not had the impact on performance anticipated (e.g. Storey 1994; Gray 1993, 1998; Stanworth and Gray 1991). There is little evidence that small business-owners are particularly attracted to such training, either for themselves or their staff, and many have argued that such training has often not been cost-effective, nor has it had the impacts desired. Some have argued that this is due to the lack of education, inward-looking orientation and lack of perspective of many owner-managers (Watkins 1983) or their individualism, stress on personal independence and desire for control (Stanworth and Gray 1991; Storey 1994). Such factors may all contribute to the rejection of outside advice and training provision. In addition, very small 'micro-businesses' in particular may lack time, as well as sufficient clarity over diagnosing training needs.

Others have argued that SMEs, especially sole traders and micro firms, are very different from larger organisations, being disadvantaged not only in relation to financial and labour markets, information, and compliance with regulation and reporting requirements, but also in terms of the cultural and personal motivations of owner-managers and their need for a wide range of skills in managing informal relationships. These are not often taught in formal training courses (e.g. Stanworth and Gray 1991). For other firms, perhaps in the 'growth corridor' of fast growth SMEs with between fifteen and twenty-four employees (Stanworth and Gray 1991; Stanworth *et al.* 1992), there may however be a need to introduce formal management approaches to HRD, often perhaps because such firms are linked into complex supply- production- distribution chains and networks with larger businesses, and are often open to much more influence from large firms, including influences over HRD practices. Formal HRD may have a positive impact here, as Wang *et al.* (1997) show. However, few studies have looked at how SMEs actually manage their own

HRD (Thomson *et al.* 2000). There is some evidence that many trainers focus on the past, on critical analysis, on knowledge, on passive understanding, on detachment, on symbols, on neutral communication and on concepts. However, entrepreneurs typically focus on the future, on insight, on creativity, on active engagement, on emotional involvement, on events, on personal communication and on problems and opportunities (Gibb 1987). Entrepreneurs' stress on 'charisma' may contrast with the stress on order, rationality and predictability emphasised in much formal training (Curran and Stanworth 1989). As a result, there may be a greater receptiveness among SMEs to more informal development processes and more personalised development experiences, such as those provided by consultants and mentors (Curran *et al.* 1996). SMEs do engage in HRD, but not necessarily formal training, and such individualised, personalised and consultant-like relationships may help owner-managers identify appropriate training and knowledge needs and develop appropriate skills (Stanworth *et al.* 1992). This implies that the cognitive gap in worldviews between SMEs and academia may be wide, and needs bridging in ways that go beyond formal enterprise training.

Thus this review of HRD in SMEs shows that, whereas SMEs are typically not, as the 'official' view suggests, large firms scaled-down needing formal enterprise training to grow, neither are they uniform and homogenous with respect to HRD. This suggests that consultant-like support from a knowledge broker may be attractive, especially as our review of knowledge management suggests that the roles of knowledge broker, facilitator, networker and intermediary will become increasingly important for HRD in general. This conceptualisation underpinned the development of the technology translator project designed to facilitate the development of knowledge-broking skills in business support roles.

Case study: the technology translator project

The initial aim of this project was to identify the profile of a technology translator (TT), able to bridge the gaps between SMEs and the 'knowledge base' (KB) of universities, research institutes and large companies. The project was supported by a wide range of players in the region, including the DTI Regional Innovation Unit. A regional innovation centre, MIC, was asked to lead the project, funded under the Objective European Social Fund, with local universities and business links as main partners. The objectives of the project were to:

• Define the core competencies of translators, taking into account best practice.
• Collate and develop appropriate training materials around these core competencies.
• Strengthen networks between intermediaries.
• Pilot training modules and methodology.
• Enhance the skills of intermediaries working in the SME/business support areas.

'Technology' was defined very broadly, referring not only to tools and procedures but also to organisational and managerial knowledge more broadly.

Participants were drawn from a variety of backgrounds, including innovation and technology counsellors or business counsellors; local authority investment officers; higher education advisers with Business Link; self-employed consultants or trainers in business advice or product development; SME proprietors; employees of the local Graduates into Employment Unit; a business director with local innovation centres; development managers or managers, technology counsellors with Business Link; and programme managers with local university teaching company schemes.

In the context of the programme, the knowledge base referred to the home of the potential solution to the SME's business problems. This included not only universities and research institutions, but also large companies and business and professional associations. Altogether, seven one-day modules in the form of workshops were delivered in North-west England by workshop leaders from local universities, the DTI Innovation Unit, a regional Business Link and a local project aimed at developing higher skills for business. After piloting materials and delivery in 1998, all workshops were delivered in January and February 1999 at weekly intervals. The course was not intended to be accredited. Later, seven similar module programmes were run in 2000 in Yorkshire (three) and the East Midlands (two).

The first module, managing relationships, was intended to improve the skills of intermediaries in building relationships with SMEs. The second module, analysing needs, focused on understanding SME business development through the systematic use of analytical and diagnostic tools. The third module, creativity, developed an understanding of the innovation process. The fourth module, the group project, developed a framework for operating as a TT. The fifth module, innovation, focused on the application of creative skills to improving SME competitiveness. The sixth module, navigating the KB, examined the processes involved in finding third party (KB) solutions. This theme of managing relationships with the KB and with third parties, such as universities, was extended in the seventh module, which sought to equip translators with appropriate tools and techniques.

What is knowledge management?

In order to appreciate the rationale behind the TT project, and the conceptualisation of the TT as a knowledge broker, it is first necessary to explore the growing importance of knowledge and knowledge management to the economy in general and to the SME sector in particular. For Bassi (1997), knowledge management (KM) is the process of creating, capturing and using knowledge to enhance organisational performance, such as documenting and codifying knowledge and disseminating it through databases and other communication channels. KM is often seen as involving the recognition, documentation, and distribution of both explicit and tacit knowledge residing in organisations' employees, customers and other stakeholders (Rossett and Marshall 1999). It is often asserted that this requires new ways of thinking and acting, new policies and practices, new technologies and new skills (Davenport and Prusak 1998; Stewart 1997), and thus new roles for HRD (Nijhof 1999; Toracco 1999). However, there is less agreement over what specific changes are necessary in organisational structure, culture and behaviour to facilitate KM. One of the purposes of this chapter is to develop a conceptual model of knowledge migration, seen as a key dimension of KM, based on a critical analysis of the TT project.

KM and HRD

Rossett and Marshall (1999) have looked at the role of HR professionals in KM, surveying KM-related practices as reported by 122 US HR professionals in 1998. Organisational culture and policies, access to information, developing enabling technologies and the need to learn about KM were seen as key issues for HR.

About 70 per cent of respondents worked in organisations that captured some knowledge, such as best practices or lessons learned, mostly by paper-based formats. Only 16 per cent worked in organisations using technology-based systems to capture and access knowledge, mostly consultancy firms. These appeared also to be more likely to have access to formal KM systems comprised of people and technology dedicated to capturing, distributing and maintaining knowledge. HR professionals rated their units more highly than the larger organisations in which they resided. Problems were reported over information overload, restricted access to information, and managerial command and control systems.

In the United Kingdom, Scarbrough (1999) and Scarbrough *et al.* (1999), surveying HRM and KM for the IPD, argue that technology alone cannot fully capture and manage innovative thinking in an organisation, and that HR needs greater attention. A technology-driven view, focusing on flows of information and groupware, intranets and IT tools, was becoming dominant, losing sight of people and sidelining HR. KM however is a process, not a technology, linked to changes in the ways people work. A supportive culture is seen as necessary, with performance management systems that link rewards to individual contribution to projects, creating an internal market for knowledge. There may need to be appropriate HR mechanisms, such as good practice in selection, training and reward, and a role in managing change and overcoming resistance to sharing information. As interest in KM grows, HRD may become increasingly sidelined in favour of IM and IT, yet has much to offer KM. In part, this seems to be because many HRD practitioners are insufficiently informed about the implications of KM for HRD, including HRD in SMEs, and may not appreciate how adopting a KM perspective will transform their role away from a direct trainer towards a more consultant-like knowledge intermediary or broker role.

However, though regarded as valuable and helpful by participants in many ways, the TT project represents only a limited break with traditional HRD approaches. It is based in part on a traditional OD approach to developing consultancy skills in facilitators of learning. Though it may indeed be the case that SME support staff will benefit from enhancement of such skills, such an approach does not address how KM may change our conception of HRD and OD. In addition, the TT project appears to rest on a rather mechanistic, linear conception of innovation as a process of diffusion (e.g. Van de Ven 1986). It is therefore necessary to develop a more adequate conceptualisation of KM and HRD in SMEs that builds on the strengths of the TT project but responds more effectively to the challenges posed by KM.

Developing a model of knowledge migration

The technology translation process could be seen as a process of knowledge migration from source (the KB, specifically HE in this instance) to destination (the SME) (Figure 8.1). Knowledge can be seen as potentially able to migrate in both directions. The reasons for selecting the term 'knowledge migration' rather than 'knowledge management' are developed later, as are the terms knowledge accommodation and knowledgeable action, depicted in Figure 8.2.

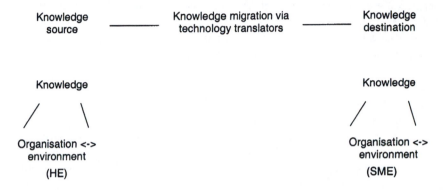

Figure 8.1 Technology translation and knowledge migration.

Source: adapted from Steenhuis and de Boer (1999: 86).

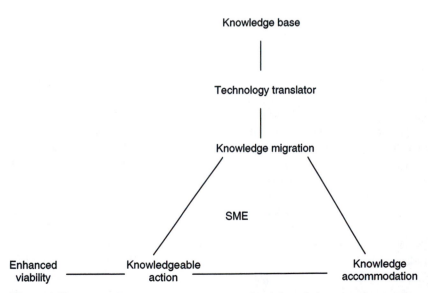

Figure 8.2 Three knowledge cycle phases connected with knowledge migration.

Viable and knowledge management: a theory of viable knowledge creation

Our reviews of HRD in SMEs of the implications of KM for HRD have identified the need to develop knowledge intermediaries and brokers to support SMEs. One approach to KM that may be sensitive in particular to partners' differences in perspectives is viable systems theory (VST).

A viable system is an active, purposeful, and adaptive organisation, able to operate in complex situations and survive. Since complex situations entail variety differentiation, in surviving a viable system responds to changing situations by generating sufficient variety through self-organisation to deal with the situational variety it encounters (called requisite variety). It is often said in the cybernetic literature that variety is a measure of complexity (Yolles 1999a).

Viable organisations seek ways of improving their ability to survive in complex situations. This is often coupled with the idea that they have fluid knowledge banks; organisational survival hinges upon an ability to create and manage knowledge. Knowledge creation/recognition is therefore of prime importance to organisations such as universities and SMEs and to potential partnerships.

The idea of knowledge creation is closely related to that of learning. Learners (individuals or organisations such as universities and SMEs in partnerships) will undertake viable learning if there is an ability to maintain stable learning behaviour. The caveat is that the learner is able to adapt to changes in a given learning environment that alters the learning situation. Whether a learner can adapt to the changes in the learning environment is a function of that learner's plastic limit. In the systems literature, when perturbations push it beyond this limit, the system either changes its form (incrementally through morphogenesis, or dramatically through metamorphosis) or 'dies'. As an example of this, an SME- university partnership which is struggling for the reasons outlined earlier 'dies' in this context when one party leaves the partnership prematurely (fails?), because new learning behaviours cannot be established. If a viable organisation survives, then it is able to change its form and adapt.

Knowledge creation is associated with different *worldviews*, seen as relative to the institutions that one is attached to in a given society, and changing as institutional realities change. Thus, worldviews involve perspectives of the perceived behavioural world that are determined by cultural and other attributes of viewers. Through socialisation, views are formed within the institutions one is attached to in a given society, and they change as the institutional realities change. Worldviews may be shared by a group of people, though when this occurs the individuals each retain their own realities while using common models to share meaning. Further, worldviews have boundaries that are generated within the belief system and cognitive space of their viewholders, and as a result we can explore worldviews in terms of their knowledge attributes.

Two types of worldviews may be defined: informal (weltanschauung) and formal (paradigm). By formal we are referring to the expression of ideas through language. Formalisation enables a set of explicit statements (propositions and their corollaries) to be made about the beliefs and other attributes that enable expression in a self-consistent way. Informal worldviews are more or less composed of a set of undeclared assumptions and propositions, while formal ones are more or less declared. Both are by their very nature bounded, and thus constrain the way in which perceived situations can be described. Paradigms can change (Yolles 1999b), so that the nature of the constraint is subject to a degree of change - however bounded it might be. Consequently, the generation of knowledge is also constrained by the capacities and belief systems of worldviews. Specifically in this context, both SMEs and universities may have different weltanschauungs and different paradigms: different assumptions, propositions and belief systems.

Worldviews interact, especially in partnerships, alliances and joint ventures, and following the cybernetic tradition, this interaction can be placed in a cognitive domain that drives a purposeful adaptive activity system. The system has form, and thus has structure, process and associated behaviour. This is assigned to an energetic behavioural domain. The knowledge-related cognitive domain is the 'cognitive consciousness' of the system that it drives. According to Yolles (1999b), the two domains are connected across a gap that we refer to as the transformational or organising domain, and this may be subject to surprises, such as often occur in partnerships and joint projects. It is strategic in nature, and operates through information (Figure 8.3). The three cognitive, organising and behavioural domains are analytically and empirically independent. This model can be applied to any purposeful adaptive activity system by distinguishing between cognitive, strategic, and behavioural aspects of a situation, such as a partnership between SMEs, universities and TTs.

There are properties associated with each of these domains, perhaps most simply expressed in terms of Table 8.1 derived from Yolles (1999b). Associated with each is a cognitive property that guides organisations in the way that they function and survive. Exploration of the nature of cognitive influence associates this with the process of *knowledge migration*, that is the movement of knowledge between worldviews (such as between universities and SMEs) that is subject to redefinition every time it migrates. Since cognitive influences and purpose are ultimately dependent upon such knowledge migration, then epistemology becomes an important consideration in terms of how organisations are able to survive. We are deliberately

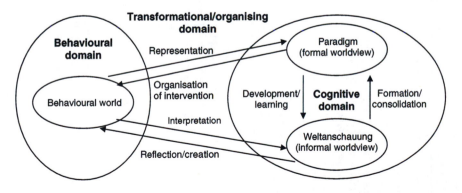

Figure 8.3 The relationship between the behavioural and cognitive domains in a viable system.

Table 8.1 Relationship between human cognitive interests, purpose and influences

Cognitive interests of the behavioural domain (data)

Technical	Practical	Critical deconstraining
Work: this enables people to achieve goals and generate material well-being. It involves technical ability to undertake action in the environment, and the ability to make predictions and establish control.	*Interaction:* this requires that people as individuals and groups in a social system gain and develop the possibilities of an understanding of each other's subjective views. It is consistent with a practical interest in mutual understanding that can address disagreements.	*Degree of emancipation:* for organisational viability, the realising of individual potential is most effective when people: • liberate themselves from the constraints imposed by power structures • learn through participation in social and political processes to control their own destinies. Autonomy and interdependence rather than dependence result.

Cognitive purposes within the organising domain (information)

Cybernetical	Rational	Ideological
Intention: this is through the creation and strategic pursuit of goals and aims that may change over time. It enables people through control and communications processes to redirect their futures.	*Logico-relational:* enables missions, goals and aims to be defined and approached through planning. It involves logical, relational and rational abilities to organise thought and action, and thus to define sets of possible systemic and behaviour possibilities.	*Manner of thinking:* an intellectual framework through which policy-makers observe and interpret reality. This has an ethical and moral orientation. It provides an image of the future that enables action through 'correct' strategic policy.

Cognitive influences within the cognitive domain (knowledge)

Social	Cultural	Political
Formation: enables individuals/groups to be influenced by knowledges that relate to the social environment. This has a consequence for social structures and processes that define social forms that are related to intentions and behaviours.	*Belief:* influences occur from knowledges that derive from the cognitive organisation (the set of beliefs, attitudes, values) other worldviews. It ultimately determines interaction and defines logico-relational understandings.	*Freedom:* influences occur from knowledges that affect the polity determined, in part, by thoughts about the constraints on group and individual freedoms, and in connection with this, how to organise and behave. It ultimately impacts on ideology and degree of emancipation.

using the term 'knowledge migration' here rather than the more conventional knowledge management to emphasise the unplanned, emergent and unpredictable nature of knowledge flows; knowledge is not simply a thing to be managed or mobilised in the ways often implied in the KM literature.

A viable model of knowledge creation and management in SME: academic partnerships

The most influential framework for knowledge creation has been developed by Nonaka and Takeuchi (1995), who distinguish between two types of knowledge, explicit and tacit (Table 8.2). Tacit knowledge includes cognitive and technical elements. Cognitive elements operate through mental models, working worldviews that develop through the creation and manipulation of mental analogies. Mental models (like schemata, paradigms, perspectives, beliefs and viewpoints) help individuals perceive and define their world. The technical element of tacit knowledge includes concrete know-how, crafts and skills. However, explicit knowledge is about past events or objects 'there and then', and is seen to be created sequentially by 'digital' activity that is theory progressive. An alternative perspective on the distinction between explicit and tacit knowledge, to be developed in this chapter is also presented in Table 8.2.

All knowledge is worldview local and belief related. Knowledge can be redefined as patterns of meaning that can promote a theoretical or practical understanding that enables the recognition of variety in complexity. These patterns are often developed through a coalescing of information. If information is seen as a set of coded events,

Table 8.2 Typology of knowledge

Expression of knowledge type	*Explicit knowledge*	*Tacit knowledge*
Nonaka and Takeuchi	Objective Rationality (mind) Sequential (there and then) Drawn from theory (digital) Codified, formally transmittable in systematic language. Relates to past.	Subjective Experiential (body) Simultaneous (here and now) Practice related (analogue) Personal, context specific, hard to formalise and communicate. Cognitive (mental models), technical (concrete know-how), vision of the future, mobilisation process.
Alternative	Formal and transferable, deriving in part from context related information established into definable patterns. The context is therefore part of the patterns.	Informal, determined through contextual experience. It will be unique to the viewer having the experience. Not transferable, except through recreating the experiences that engendered the knowledge for others, and then the knowledge gained will be different.

then consistency with Nonaka and Takeuchi (1995) occurs when they say that explicit knowledge is codified.

The creation of explicit knowledge is often seen as a process of storing and indexing information. However, these patterns can also occur mentally as tacit knowledge. Knowledge also enables context to be defined in a richer way, and this affects both data processing and the distillation of information into new knowledge by enriching existing patterns. The model leads to questions about our understanding of knowledge creation, and has consequences for the way in which we see knowledge development in organisations, such as how and through what means are the patterns of meaning formed that enable data to be processed and information to be coalesced.

Nonaka and Takeuchi's (1995: 8) SECI cycle of knowledge creation is illustrated in Figure 8.4. This offers a model of conversion between tacit and explicit knowledge that results in a cycle of knowledge creation. The conversion process involves four processes - socialisation, externalisation, combination and internalisation - all of which convert between tacit and/or explicit knowledge. Socialisation is the process by which synthesised knowledge is created through sharing of experiences as people develop shared mental models and technical skills. Since it is fundamentally experiential, it connects people through their tacit knowledges. Externalisation comes next, and occurs as tacit knowledge is made explicit. Here, the creation of conceptual knowledge occurs through knowledge articulation in a communication process that uses language in dialogue and collective reflection. The use of expressions of communication are often inadequate, inconsistent and insufficient, leaving gaps between images and expression, while promoting reflection and interaction and triggering dialogue. The next process is combination, where explicit knowledge is transformed through its integration by adding, combining and categorising knowledge. This integration of knowledge is also seen as a systemising process. Finally, in the next process explicit knowledge is made tacit by its internalisation. This is a learning

From/to	Tacit	Explicit
Tacit	*Socialisation* Creates *synthesised* knowledge through the sharing of experiences, and the development of mental models and technical skills. Language unnecessary.	*Externalisation* Creates *conceptual* knowledge through knowledge articulation using language. Dialogue and collective reflection needed.
Explicit	*Internalisation* Creates *operational* knowledge through learning by doing. Explicit knowledge like manuals or verbal stories helpful.	*Combination* Creates *systemic* knowledge through the systemising of ideas. May involve many media, and can lead to new knowledge through adding, combining and categorising.

Figure 8.4 The SECI cycle of knowledge creation.

Source: Nonaka and Takeuchi (1995).

process, which occurs through the behavioural development of *operational* knowledge. It uses explicit knowledge, like manuals or verbal stories, where appropriate.

A constructivist view of knowledge creation and migration

The age of complexity has led some, particularly soft systems thinkers, away from positivist perspectives. Alternative paradigms are described by Guba and Lincoln (1994), who propose what may be constituted as a cross between post-positivism and critical theory paradigms. Here, there are no observers, only viewers; their views, like their behaviours, are worldview derived. Worldviews also interact with each other. This interaction occurs through a semantic communication process and, from Habermas (1987), occurs in a framework of meaning called the lifeworld.

In this view, there is no absolute real world that can be separated out, because viewers create it and interact with their creation. There is therefore no absoblute separation between viewers and the behavioural world around them. Since what constitutes reality is determined through worldviews, it changes as worldviews change. In each worldview, we build our view of what we perceive to be the world through our mental models. We may believe that we share them with others, but they will be incommensurable to some degree (Yolles 1999b) because the models may involve different conceptual extensions, or the same conceptual extension may take on meanings that are qualitatively different. We are never aware whether these shared models are related, except by attempting to draw meaning from others' explanations provided through language, or by comparing what we expect from the behaviour of people in a situation with what we perceive that they are doing.

Prediction is local, but it requires that people are prepared to constantly modify their view of the world around them. They consistently need to realise or release the information potential inherent in the complex situations that they see around them. We may propose that there is an Other, rather than an Observer, also a potential or actual viewer. In a social context, such as a partnership, a viewer (e.g. academic) has a worldview that interacts with the worldviews of others (e.g. entrepreneurs), either directly or indirectly (through some of their apparent constructions). The creation of viewholder-local knowledge (knowledge that is personal and therefore local to the viewer) results. Since this knowledge tells us about reality, then reality is a local phenomenon. This is also the case if one considers only a situation involving a single worldview. In this case, reality is constructed as a result of the interaction between viewers and the information around them, again seeing reality as locally generated. This in turn leads us to questions about what constitutes information, what constitutes knowledge, and the role of the viewer in defining it.

Knowledge, epistemology and knowledge creation

Adopting a critical epistemology, we can see that tacit knowledge is informal, determined through contextual experience, and unique to the viewer having the experience (Table 8.2, alternative). It is therefore not transferable, except through recreating the experiences that engendered the knowledge for others, and then the knowledge gained will be different. Tacit knowledge is therefore the result of self-learning. Explicit knowledge may be identified as formal, deriving in part from context related information established into definable patterns. Context formally exists as part of these patterns. Formal knowledge is transferable if the medium of transfer enables the transferral of meaning. Explicit knowledge can be a consequence of self-learning tacit knowledge, or received as knowledge transfer. HE- SME partnerships often attempt to transfer explicit knowledge in this way; the TT project is no different in this respect, seeing the TT as a 'translator'.

The proposition here that the knowledge creation cycle occurs as a continuous cycle is, however, quite different from Nonaka and Takeuchi (1995; see also Figure 8.2). No structural adaptability is considered with the SECI cycle, which supports a positivist epistemology because each phase in the process is predetermined by the prior phase, and, other than through conditioning, there is no mechanism by which one phase can be spontaneously enabled.

As an example of this, is conceptual knowledge to be assigned to the externalisation phase, developed only after socialisation, or can it develop independently without socialisation and be externalised? Perhaps, though, this might be through process of socialising with oneself? Our mental models centre on our conceptualisations, and these are not often made explicit. When we are unable to explain things that we believe, we create concepts that enable us to help ourselves, a process that Cohen and Stewart (1994) call collapsing chaos, which reduces complexity. It would also seem to be the case that externalisation, leading to new theories and generalisations, offers a sound rational positivist logic. However, we are aware that such rational approaches tend to be unrepresentative of the way that patterns of belief can change the nature or relevance of knowledge. Returning to the socialisation process, Nonaka and Takeuchi (1995) acknowledge that knowledge is belief based. However, beliefs may develop into knowledge without the benefit of the socialisation process. In any case, socialisation itself may be suspect as a way of developing models that share common meaning, as is often aspired to in HE- SME partnerships.

A viable approach to knowledge creation in SME–HE partnerships

The structured spiral of knowledge creation (Nonaka and Takeuchi 1995) appears to adopt a positivist perspective. An alternative approach is possible, linking closely with VST. In addressing this, we note that each of the three domains identified in Table 8.1 has associated with it its own knowledge process, one connected with cognition, one with organising, and one with behaviour. This notion is consistent with Marshall (1995), whose interest lies in knowledge schema. Marshall identifies three types of knowledge:

- *identification knowledge:* the facts and concepts making up the knowledge domain
- *elaboration knowledge:* the relationships between the individual knowledge components and the way they are organised
- *execution knowledge:* the conceptual skills and procedures required to execute an activity.

Marshall himself does not attempt to address knowledge creation, though we shall do so through our own model. We consider that in social situations, knowledge creation occurs through a process of knowledge migration from one worldview to another, involving a process of knowledge identification. The basic knowledge cycle model (Figure 8.5) links to Table 8.1 and Figure 8.2, and depicts the three fundamental phases of the knowledge creation process: knowledge migration, knowledge accommodation and knowledgeable action. Migration is associated with the cognitive domain, accommodation with the organising domain, and action with the behavioural domain. Each process has an input and an output. A control process also is able to condition each process through actions on the inputs or on the processes themselves. Knowledge migration is conditioned through cognitive influence, knowledge accommodation though cognitive purpose, and knowledgeable action through cognitive intention.

The control process involved with knowledge migration (Figure 8.6) occurs through the development of interconnections between the worldviews of the actors in a given suprasystem, such as a TT partnership, and is the result of semantic communication. As part of the process of knowledge migration, new knowledge is locally generated within the actor. While this may be seen as part of a socialisation process, it may also be seen as actor local spontaneous when the process of knowledge migration operates as a knowledge creation trigger.

Newly migrated knowledge may be shared and re-shared within the suprasystem, because the new knowledge created by one actor will have a local definition, different for others. As a result, the originally migrated knowledge will need re-migration in a feedback loop. This is fundamentally consistent with the notion of paradigm incommensurability, since every worldview will have its own distinct

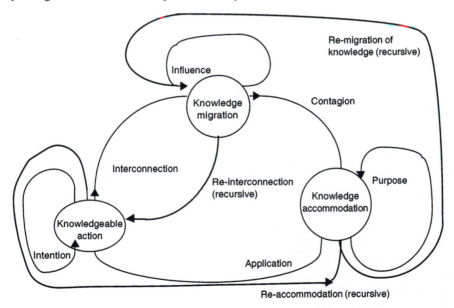

Figure 8.5 The knowledge cycle.

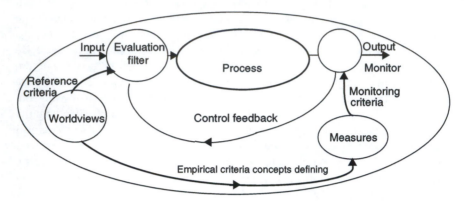

Figure 8.6 Basic form of the control model.

pattern of meaning that will be different from every other one. This does not stop the knowledge from being 'contagious' to relevant others within a given suprasystem, such as a TT Partnership, through a continuous semantic communication process involving recursive migration (that is re-migration and re-re-migration) of knowledge. Each recursive knowledge migration has the potential of new knowledge creation for each actor (TT, KB, SME) in the suprasystem. As knowledge is migrated, it is likely to pass through a morphogenic process, and sometimes a metamorphic one that makes it new to the group.

Knowledge management is inherently a political, not neutral, process. Polity, a core aspect of politics, acts as a filter on knowledge migration, concerned with an organised condition of social (or civil) order. Polity is connected to politics through the latter's interest in the causal relationships relating to behaviour. Within the context of knowledge about the creation of order, we can talk of polity knowledge, connected to what Marshall (1995) refers to as elaboration knowledge (relating to the relationships between the individual knowledge components and the way they are organised within a schema). Polity knowledge relates to the relationships between individual knowledge components as perceived by an actor to be possessed by the other actors, and the relative way that they are organised. It would thus seem to be an active recogniser of identification knowledge, i.e. the concepts and patterns of meaning that make up knowledge. When polity knowledge is applied to other actors, it enables us to make decisions, sometimes involving 'false' assumptions not representative of the identification knowledge of other actors. This can inhibit the process of knowledge migration, since recognition of knowledge differences is needed before knowledge migration can occur. Partnerships between SMEs and universities offer a rich source of such potential false assumptions, frictions and misunderstandings. For SMEs in particular, it may be difficult to identify the most appropriate source of help in HE, and it may be difficult to contact individuals. The quality and depth of information held by SMEs on academic expertise may be very variable. Academics may seem to SMEs to be focused on problems, not solutions, with a poor reputation for delivery. They may seem to use an exclusive language, assuming pre-knowledge on the part of the SME (e.g. references back to previous research, theory and models). They may not seem to use business language and may seem to lack business understanding, to have very slow cycle times, and to be focused on very small-scale issues (e.g. Ruana 1999).

Towards a research agenda for studying knowledge creation and migration in SME–HE partnerships

A number of issues for further research are raised by the model outlined in Figures 8.5 and 8.6 and by reflection on the TT project. A process of knowledge accommodation may follow knowledge migration. Accommodation of migrated knowledge by a relevant other is essential in order to harness it within a behavioural world. Knowledge accommodation by relevant others (e.g. SMEs) is dependent upon knowledge contagion to these others. However, this is filtered through knowledge that activates weltanschauung-derived ideology and ethics. In addition, the evaluation reference criteria derive from knowledge about intention and logico-relational cognitive purposes. Interestingly, this connects with Marshall's (1995) idea of planning knowledge - the knowledge of which pathways to select in order to achieve a solution.

Contagion can be evaluated by examining to whom knowledge has been passed, and whether it has been retained for use (e.g. by SME from HE). Cultural and social influences can be evaluated by examining the parties' respective beliefs, values and attitudes (cognitive organisation). One way of doing this is to examine resistance to the adoption of new patterns of cognitive organisation (e.g. resistance by the SME to new technologies or by HE to new modes of learning). Social influences represent knowledges about the way in which social processes operate. This dimension can be measured in terms of the reticence that actors have to the introduction of new social meanings.

The process of knowledgeable action may be dependent upon the application of knowledge. Knowledgeable action occurs with awareness of what is being done within a behavioural world, and is dependent upon knowledge application to the tasks that are perceived to require to be addressed within the situation. This is filtered through knowledge that activates weltanschauung derived emancipative capabilities that enable knowledgeable action to occur. The evaluation reference criteria derive from knowledge about actor interests through work and interaction, related to Marshall's (1995) idea of execution knowledge, seen as the computational skills and procedures required to execute a behaviour.

Measures within this control loop with respect to knowledgeable action can occur by examining the environment in which that action has occurred. Work and interaction knowledge that conditions knowledgeable action can be explored by examining how work and interaction processes change with the introduction of new knowledge. Knowledge about emancipation can be determined through in-depth questioning of relevant others, such as the academic, TT and SME representatives taking part in joint partnerships.

When the above control loops operate to make process changes, morphogenic changes occur in the knowledge phases of our knowledge cycle. When the control processes are complex and control action fails, knowledge process metamorphosis can occur (Yolles 1999b). As an example of a metamorphic change, a new concept may be born during the process of knowledge migration: a new way of working by the SME, a new way of facilitating learning by HE, a new mode of consulting by the TT.

There are parallels between our proposed knowledge cycle and that of Nonaka and Takeuchi (1995). In the former, knowledge can be created spontaneously within a migration process, and any socialisation process that occurs is through communication that may be seen to act as a trigger for new knowledge. Unlike Nonaka and Takeuchi, our cycle is not required to be monotonic and continuous, relative to a conditioning process. Rather, the process of continuity is transferred to the communication process, and knowledge creation is cybernetic, passing through feedback processes that can change the very nature of the patterns of meanings that were initiated through semantic communications.

Central to this analysis of knowledge creation and a proposed research agenda on SME- HE partnerships is the knowledge typology shown in Figure 8.7. It derives from the knowledge creation cycle, defined in terms of the processes of knowledge migration, accommodation, and knowledgeable action. Knowledge migration occurs

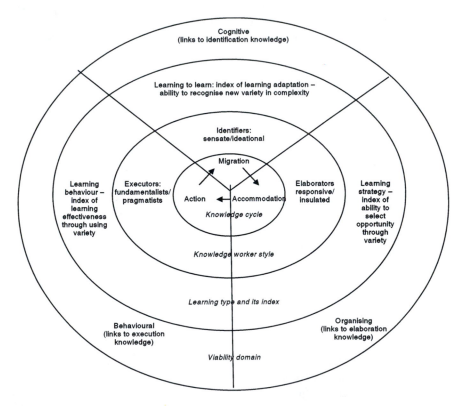

Figure 8.7 Knowledge typology.

through the development of interconnections between the worldviews of the actors in a given suprasystem (such as an SME- HE partnership) and is the result of semantic communication. As part of the process of knowledge migration, new knowledge is locally generated within the actors.

Associated with each phase of knowledge creation are, it is proposed, different types of knowledge workers. Thus, those who are particularly good at migrating knowledge, whether from HE to SME or vice versa, are seen as knowledge identifiers. Following the notions of Sorokin (Yolles 1999a), we can classify two cultural classes of identifiers, sensate and ideational. Sensate culture is to do with the senses, and can be seen to be utilitarian and materialistic. Ideational culture relates to ideas; an example might be the adherence to say spirituality or ideology. The accommodation phase of knowledge creation has associated with it those who might be called elaborators. It is possible to classify two polar types of elaborators, those who are responsive to new knowledge, and those who are not. There may be responsive elaborators among TTs, SMEs and HE (i.e. open to new ideas and approaches) and non-responsive elaborators, closed to new approaches. Finally, closely associated with the phase of knowledgable action are executors. Two types of executors may exist. Fundamentalists adhere to notions very strictly, while pragmatists provide for some degree of leeway in the way that adhere to notions. So, there may be fundamentalist executors in both sectors (e.g. academics and entrepreneurs who implement actions only within previously defined parameters) and pragmatist executors in both sectors, willing to cross boundaries and categories. It should be pointed out at this juncture that it is not necessary to be fundamentalist. For example, identifiers may not be only sensate or ideational types. They may be able to mix sensate and ideational perspectives, in a condition that Sorokin refers to as idealistic. The same ideas can apply to executors and identifiers. Clearly, these ideas and propositions need testing through further empirical research on HRD in SMEs and on HRD partnerships in general (e.g. Iles and Yolles 2001a, 2001b; Iles *et al.* 2001).

Bibliography

Bassi, L. J. (1997) 'Harnessing the power of intellectual capital', *Training and Development*, 51, 12: 25- 30.
Cohen, J. and Stewart, I. (1994) *The Collapse of Chaos: Discovering simplicity in a complex world*, London: Viking.
Curran, J. and Stanworth, J. (1989) 'Education and training for enterprise: some problems of classification, evaluation, policy and research', *International Small Business Journal*, 7, 2: 11- 22.
Curran, J., Blackburn, R., Kitching, J. and North, J. (1996) *Establishing Small Firms' Training Practices, Needs, Difficulties and Use of Industry Training Organisation*, DfEE Research Studies, London: HMSO.
Davenport, T. H. and Prusak, L. (1998) *Working Knowledge: How organisations manage what they know*, Boston, MA: Harvard University Press.
Fivaz, R. (2000) 'Why consciousness? A causological account', *Systems Research and Behavioural Science*, 17, 6.
Gibb, A. (1987) 'Enterprise culture: its meaning and implications for education and training', *Journal of European Industrial Training*, 11, 2.

Gray, C. (1993) 'Stages of growth and entrepreneurial career motivation', in F. Chithaden, M. Robertson and D. Watkins (eds) *Small Firms – Recession and recovery*, London: ISBA and Paul Chapman.

Gray, C. (1998) *Enterprise and Culture*, London: Routledge.

Guba, E. G. and Lincoln, Y. S. (1994) 'Competing paradigms in qualitative research', in N. K. Denzien and Y. S. Lincoln (eds) *Handbook of Qualitative Research*, Thousand Oaks, CA: Sage.

Habermas, J. (1987) *The Theory of Communicative Action*, Vol. 2, Cambridge: Polity Press.

Iles, P. A. and Yolles, M. (2001a) 'Across the great divide: HRD, technology translation and knowledge migration in bridging the knowledge gap between SMEs and universities', *Human Resource Development International*, 4, 1: 1-35.

Iles, P. A. and Yolles, M. (2001b) 'International HRD alliances in viable knowledge migration and development: the Czech Academic Link Project', *Human Resource Development International*.

Iles, P. A., Yolles, M. and Altman, Y. (2001) 'HRM and knowledge management: responding to the challenge', *Journal of Research and Practice in HRM* (special issue on knowledge management), 9, 1: 3-33.

Lester, T. (1996) 'Mining your organisation's knowledge base', *Human Resources*, July-August.

Lloyd, B. (1996) 'Knowledge management: the key to long-term organisational success', *Long Range Planning*, 29, 4.

Marshall, C., Prusak, L. and Shpilberg, D. (1996) 'Financial risk and the need for superior knowledge management', *California Management Review*, 38, 3.

Marshall, S. P. (1995) *Schemas in Problem Solving*, Cambridge: Cambridge University Press.

Marshall, S. P., Christensen, S. E. and McAllister, J. A. (1996) 'Cognitive differences in tactical decision making', in *Proceedings of the 1996 Command and Control Research and Technology Symposium* (pp. 122-32), Monterey, CA: Naval Postgraduate School.

Nijhof, W. J. (1999) 'Knowledge management and knowledge dissemination', in *Academy of Human Resource Development 1999 Conference Proceedings*, Vol. 1, Arlington, VA: Academy of HRD.

Nonaka, I. and Takeuchi, H. (1995) *The Knowledge-Creating Company: How Japanese companies create the dynamics of innovation*, New York: Oxford University Press.

Rossett, A. and Marshall, J. (1999) 'Signposts on the road to knowledge management', in *Academy of Human Resource Development 1999 Conference Proceedings*, Vol. 1, Arlington, VA: Academy of HRD.

Ruana, N. E. A. (1999) 'Theory in "theory to practice": voices of practitioners', in *Academy of Human Resource Development 1999 Conference Proceedings*, Vol. 1, Arlington, VA: Academy of HRD.

Scarbrough, H. (1999) 'Science friction', *People Management*, 5, 7: 68-74.

Scarbrough, H., Swan, J. and Preston, J. (1999) *Knowledge Management: A literature review*, London: Institute for Personnel and Development.

Stanworth, J. and Gray, C. (eds) (1991) *Bolton 20 Years On: The small firms in the 1990s*, London: Paul Chapman and Small Business Research Trust.

Stanworth, J., Purdy, D. and Kirby, D. (1992) *The Management of Success in 'Growth Corridor' Small Firms*, Milton Keynes: Small Business Research Trust.

Steenhuis, H. J. and de Boer, S. J. (1999) 'Global corporations and international technology transfer', in *Proceedings I, 3rd International Symposium a Multinational Business Management*, Nanjing, China.

Stewart, T. A. (1997) *Intellectual Capital: The new wealth of organisations*, London: Nicholas Brealey.

Storey, D. (1994) *Understanding the Small Business Sector*, London: Routledge.

Sveiby, K. E. (1997) *The New Organisational Wealth: Managing and measuring knowledge-based assets*, San Francisco, CA: Berrett-Koehler.

Thomson, A., Mabey, C., Storey, J., Gray, C. and Iles, P. A. (2000) *Changing Patterns of Management Development*, Oxford: Blackwell.

Toracco, R. J. (1999) 'A theory of knowledge management', *Academy of Human Resource Development 1999 Conference Proceedings*, Vol. 1, Arlington, VA: Academy of HRD.

van de Ven, A. H. (1986) 'Central problems in the management of innovation', *Management Science*, 32: 590- 607.

Wang, K., Marshall, J., Alderman, N. and Thwaites, A. (1997) 'Management training in small and medium sized enterprises: methodological and conceptual issues', *International Journal of Human Resource Management*, 8, 1: 44- 65.

Watkins, D. (1983) 'Development, training and education for the small firm: a European perspective', *European Small Business Journal*, 1, 3: 29- 44.

Yolles, M. I. (1999a) *Management Systems: A viable approach*, London: Financial Times and Pitman.

Yolles, M. I. (1999b) 'Towards a viable systems theory of joint ventures', *Systemist*, 21, 2: 63- 80.

9 Knowledge migration in an academic–SME partnership

How useful is the Teaching Company Scheme as a vehicle for HRD in SMEs?

Elaine Eades and Paul Iles

Objectives

- To test knowledge migration models using a specific case study of an SME.
- To identify the potential effectiveness of Teaching Company Schemes (TCS) as a model/process for HRD in SMEs.
- To identify blockages/barriers to the effectiveness of the TCS process.
- To identify the skills required by TCS Associates and Academics in managing the process.

Theoretical context

As Thomson *et al.* (2001) and Iles and Yolles (Chapter 8 in this book) point out, a prevailing view of HRD in SMEs is that such firms do not face any specific HRD issues separate from large firms; all they require is formal 'enterprise training' in business and commercial skills to assist their successful growth into large firms, with all their benefits in terms of employment opportunities. Such a view is often held by government, with a plethora of initiatives launched to upgrade skills in SMEs. However, as Iles and Yolles point out, such a view suffers from an over-homogenous, undifferentiated view of SMEs (SMEs are not just scaled-down large firms, and are not just different from large firms, but also differ among themselves). Such a view also suffers from a limited view of appropriate HRD interventions, confined to formal training solutions.

As Walton (1999) points out,

> Until comparatively recently, there has been little attempt in the HRD literature to differentiate between larger and smaller organisations and to address the impact that size and associated resource constraints might have upon both size and desired approaches to learning.
>
> (Walton 1999: 324)

Such firms are unlikely to have a specialist HRD function, department or staff, and may be resistant to formal training for a variety of reasons such as its cost, long-term focus, irrelevance, scepticism over its links to business performance and concerns over poaching staff (Wang *et al.* 1997).

As Walton (1999), also argues, it is by no means clear that formal training is the most suitable course for SMEs; a focus on training may have diverted attention from broader HRD issues. Curran *et al.* (1996) have called for a focus on informal, incidental and accidental processes of learning in SMEs and on learning and tacit skills. This approach seems to be in tune with recent emphases on knowledge management and tacit skills in SMEs (e.g. Iles and Yolles 2001a, 2001; Iles *et al.* 2001; see also Chapter 8 in this book). Rowden (1995) for example in case studies of three American SMEs observed that 'development' was more often facilitated by coaching, mentoring, job enrichment, autonomous team-working and on-the-job training rather than by planned, formal training programmes.

Some kinds of small firm, especially sole traders, self-employed individuals and micro firms with few employees, seem fundamentally different from large firms - not only are they disadvantaged in relation to access to information and compliance with the regulatory environment (e.g. Stanworth and Gray 1991) but also their behaviour is often governed as much by personal and cultural motivations as economic and commercial logic (e.g. desires for independence, control, autonomy, a balanced lifestyle). They may have a preference for informal, on-the-job training and more personalised, consultancy-like advice and support, rather than off-site, externally supplied formal enterprise training (e.g. Gibb 1987; Curran and Stanworth 1989; Gray 1993, 1998; Watkins 1983).

However, many larger small firms have developed much closer relationships with their SME suppliers and distributors and much closer learning links with their clients and customers (Hendry *et al.* 1991). SMEs differ in terms of size, sector, product/ service, ownership/control, age, stage of development, and customer base, all affecting their HRD needs and resourcing requirements and influencing the nature, course and effectiveness of HRD interventions (Walton 1999). SME size affects ease of staff release, numbers of dedicated HR staff, and dependence on an owner-manager. Owner-managed, family firm and entrepreneurially driven SMEs may be more dependent on how the central figure(s) perceive HRD. Gaining the attention of such figure(s) becomes a priority, and Iles and Yolles (2001a; Chapter 8 in this book) discuss how 'technology translators' may play a role in such cases by helping to migrate knowledge between an HRD provider (e.g. a university) and the SME. In contrast, partner and freelance-based SMEs (e.g. consultancies) may employ staff with high levels of pre-existing skills and knowledge and be committed to using professional networks and a range of HRD providers to update skills and qualifications. SMEs who rely on one or a few large firm customers can be in an uncertain position of 'subcontractor vulnerability', with their training focused on meeting specific customer needs.

Of particular interest are growth-oriented SMEs entering increasingly into long-term partnerships with large firm customers and 'learning chains', where the customer takes substantial responsibility for its associates' learning needs (Stanworth *et al.* 1992). Such SMEs may, following Walton (1999), make use of a variety of HRD strategies. They may use consultants and part-time HRD support, e.g. from universities, or 'technology translators' (Iles and Yolles 2001a; Chapter 8 in this book) and forge business links through sector-specific networks and support systems such as mentors, business links, personal business advisers, secondments and exchanges. Such SMEs, as constituent elements of commercial networks and supply- production- distribution chains, may recognise the need to manage their relationships with large firm customers and develop their staff. Fast growth businesses seem to show particular interest in training and development (Thomson *et al.* 2001). Larger SMEs tend to have more formal development policies and give a higher priority to management development, and are more likely to assess training needs. Business efficiency pressures, the firm's growth strategy, and the need to motivate and retain staff were cited in a survey by Thomson *et al.* (2001) as the main drivers of training, alongside pressure from large companies and competitive pressures. The average number of days training reported was similar to large firms, but higher for 'growth' firms and for those firms giving high priority to development and with an explicit development policy. Larger SMEs were more likely to use consultants, formal induction, in-house training, external courses, assess training needs and set performance targets. Most HRD was triggered by personal initiative, senior management decision and informal discussion with one's boss, rather than through formal appraisal. Management development policy was usually set by the CEO/MD, once again indicating that the owner-manager is often the gatekeeper of HRD policy and practice. Only in the larger, growth-oriented firms was a specialist employed to implement and develop policy.

Mabey and Thomson (2001) report on two complementary surveys of management development in the small business sector. These covered both 'provider' (HR manager) and 'consumer' (manager) perspectives on HRD. Both reported an average of 6.4 days per year spent on formal management development, very similar to a similar survey of larger companies (Mabey and Thomson 2000) and a significant improvement on the 4.6 days reported in 1996 (Thomson *et al.* 2001). Around eight days of informal development was reported, rather more than in the larger companies. More medium sized than small companies reported that their firms had a written policy statement. The smaller companies reported that the initiation of development policy lay with the CEO. In the medium companies, a much greater role was played by a central HR department. In the smallest companies, the CEO also played a much greater role in policy implementation, while a budget for management development was much more common in medium sized than small companies. Small companies tended to use more informal methods of development, medium sized more formal. External seminars were the most used formal method, followed by in company training. Job rotation, shadowing and coaching were most used in smaller companies. Medium sized companies were more likely to use mentoring, secondment and planned on-the-job development. All SMEs cited managing people, teamwork and customer focus as high priorities for development; smaller firms also cited functional and technical skills. Most businesses held regular performance appraisals to discuss individual development needs, but this was less often a trigger to training than staff initiative, informal discussion, and senior management decision. Medium sized organisations generally used national training programmes more extensively than smaller businesses, especially IiP, NVQ, Modern Apprenticeships and the New Deal. Smaller firms were more likely to use the University for Industry (UFI) and Management Standards than medium sized firms. Very small organisations were most likely to report positive benefits from these programmes (except for UFI) and small organisations the least. IiP and Management Standards were seen as having the most positive impact on performance. In general, a positive view of managerial development in small firms emerged from this survey, (though with a low response rate), with a high level of comparability between consumer and provider perspectives.

In general, growth-oriented firms specialising in value added exchanges with other firms as specialist suppliers of components, tools or business services often recognise that they face major HRD challenges and seem prepared to take up more structured approaches to HRD, focused on business efficiency and managing structural change. They may therefore be oriented to accepting alternative approaches to 'knowledge migration' and HRD interventions than formal training, including the 'technology translator' approach of Iles and Yolles (2001a; Chapter 8 in this book). The case study describes one such alternative approach to structured HRD in SMEs, also involving knowledge migration between a university and an SME, namely the Teaching Company Scheme. First, we describe the research context and the Teaching Company Scheme process before discussing the case study company.

Research context

What is TCS?

TCS is a UK government scheme, operational since 1975, that enables firms of all types to take advantage of the wide range of expertise available in the knowledge base (universities, research institutes, etc.). Through TCS, partnerships are formed between staff in knowledge bases and UK companies. These partnerships are called TCS programmes. TCS programmes are part-funded by government grants, and are managed by the Teaching Company Directorate (TCD). At the heart of TCS programmes are innovation projects that are central to the strategic development of the company partners. The projects are implemented by senior staff from both the company and the knowledge base, with the help of recently qualified graduates. The aims of all TCS programmes are to improve the competitiveness of the company partner, enhance the career of the graduate, and promote the business relevance of the knowledge base partner.

As at March 2000, there were over 700 TCS programmes in the United Kingdom; 90 per cent of these were taking place with small or medium sized companies. According to Lord Sainsbury, Minister for Science and Innovation, 'TCS is one of our best mechanisms for technology transfer'.

TCS and HRD

The TCS programme which is the subject of the case study is unusual, in that it has HRD as its focus. Although the origins of TCS lie in the engineering sector, less than half of the current programmes have an engineering focus. Nearly a quarter are now focused on information and communication technology, and the subject of almost 10 per cent of the projects is classified as being 'Social Sciences'. While the categor-isation system by TCS is not broken down effectively by function, the TCS programme in what we refer to as 'Cranbrook and Co Ltd' is the first HRD programme in north-west England, and may have been the first such programme in the United Kingdom. Why are so few companies identifying the need for programmes in the HRD arena? The failure of organisations to recognise the fact that there is potentially a relationship between good people management and development practices and bottom-line performance has long been a depressing feature of UK industry. Many large, sophisticated, blue chip organisations are only just beginning to accept that it is human assets and capabilities which hold the key to competitive advantage. The Chartered Institute for People and Development (CIPD 2001) paper *The Case for Good People Management* summarises recent research relating to the link between personnel and development practices and organisational performance. It concludes that there is overwhelming evidence that progressive personnel practices improve business performance. It is perhaps disappointing for HR practitioners and academics that the CIPD finds it necessary to make these claims, which may appear self-evident. However, difficulties in devising acceptable measures and attributing causality to human factors, combined with the short-termist, accountancy-led approach of UK industry, make such exercises inevitable.

If large organisations, with HR directors and significant resources, have not seen HRD as the crucial factor in their growth and success, it is perhaps not surprising that small organisations have not done so either. Many small organisations have no HR function to speak of, and may regard people management issues as 'common sense'. Small organisations, precariously placed, may see their salvation in finding new products or investing in new technology, while a long-term investment in people development is less likely.

Why might the TCS programme provide an effective framework for an HRD intervention?

If knowledge migration occurs through the development of inter-connections between the worldviews of the company and the knowledge base, and is the result of semantic communication (see Chapter 8 in this book) then the TCS programme, with its structured two-year project and reporting arrangements can be seen to both instigate and promote these inter-connections. In a TCS programme, the placement of a supported graduate in the company for the duration of the programme could be expected to lead to effective knowledge migration in terms of the increased likelihood of embedding 'knowledgeable behaviour'. Thus, in contrast to the 'one-off' consultancy approach, the academic partner meets the graduate weekly and has formal meetings with all partners monthly. The academic partner is committed to the achievement of outputs, not just the promotion of ideas. Implementation is seen as a crucial aspect of the partnership. As the academic partner becomes immersed in the company situation, alternative implementation strategies can be negotiated and agreed upon - challenging the worldviews of all partners at times. Knowledge elaboration through sharing mutual meanings is thus promulgated. The graduate is placed full time at the company, and is able to contextualise the concepts and approaches encouraged by the academic partner. From a more prosaic perspective, perhaps the TCS framework, with its generous financial support and access to expertise, may provide sufficient incentive for the company to take the longer term view necessary for strategic HRD.

Additionally, there is a strong case for arguing that the TCS programme framework encourages a holistic, rather than a piecemeal approach, enabling the company to introduce organisational innovations in carefully aligned, complementary stages ('horizontal integration'). Combined with the appropriate contextualisation of the 'knowledge', this presents a strongly supportive set of circumstances for the potential effectiveness of HRD initiatives.

From the perspective of the research approach, the TCS framework represents action research at its most fundamental. The objectives or outcomes agreed for the company, are the focus of the programme, but these are obviously subject to review as the company's situation changes. This 'action research' is designed to effect change in the organisation and the views and perspectives of all three 'partners' (academics, company and graduate) are also likely to change significantly.

Case study

Cranbrook Ltd is a manufacturing company in the engineering sector, employing 160 staff and operating from two sites (one main, one subsidiary) in north-west England. A family business for over one hundred years, the company was subject to a 'buy-in' of its then chief executive officer in the early 1990s. He put in place a recovery plan, which included the development of sophisticated management information systems for monitoring production efficiency. After a period of seven years, the CEO was becoming increasingly concerned and frustrated at the company's failure to grow and develop as envisaged, and identified a TCS programme as potentially useful after attending a local seminar. Initially, engineering academics were dispatched to discuss the programme, but it quickly became clear that engineering expertise was not at issue.

The CEO identified through initial interviews with the two authors of this chapter, the following key factors as hindering the company's further growth and development:

- the lack of proactive culture and change management capability of the existing management and supervisory team
- the company's location, limiting the recruitment of good quality managers experienced in the automotive sector
- the low effectiveness and efficiency of existing production practices, and under-utilisation of plant
- high cost structure relative to competitors, and severe rates of absenteeism.

He recognised that the automotive sector was subject to ever increasing customer demands for higher specification, higher levels of technology, and adherence to national and international quality and environmental standards. The managers and supervisors, in his view, were characterised by a willingness to work very 'hard, but not smart', a lack of willingness to be proactive, and a lack of the ability to apply lessons learned to other situations.

Initial data gathering by the knowledge base (the two authors then at Liverpool John Moores University Business School) followed. This included a series of individual interviews with the whole senior management team and a sample of supervisors. These semi-structured interviews were carried out by the two academic partners, with one taking notes (no tape-recording took place). Every interviewee was guaranteed confidentiality. The questions asked focused upon perceptions of what the company currently did well, and did badly; what problems the company faced, internally and externally; what barriers existed; what skills and qualities were present and what were needed; and how people worked together and communicated. Specific questions were focused on how staff were recruited, how training needs were identified and met, and how people knew what was expected of them at work.

The academic partners then analysed the data gathered and identified the following issues as significant:

- difficulties in recruitment of high calibre managers
- lack of trust within the senior management team
- managerial and supervisory weaknesses in staff management, including motivation, delegation and objective setting
- ineffective performance management systems
- lack of shared understanding over Company objectives and priorities
- a pervasive 'blame culture'
- lack of communication within and between teams
- ad hoc approach to the identification and meeting of training needs.

Overall, there was no coherent approach to people management. There was no specific personnel/HR function identified in the company, with the operations manager taking on this role in addition to the health and safety function.

Two-year TCS programme

After some difficult initial feedback to the CEO, the following two-year TCS programme was agreed, including ten main tasks.

1 Induction of TCS Associate

The associate would follow an induction programme with the university, including in-depth discussion with academic supervisors. An induction programme would also be designed by the company, monitored by the industrial supervisor. Additionally, training modules provided by TCS and focusing on project-management skills would be included.

2 Design of audit tools and attitude survey

These would be used to evaluate the specific problems, issues and opportunities of the organisation in relation to the management and supervisory system. These same tools would be used to measure changes over the period of the TCS programme.

3 Establish a shared strategic vision

The strategic and business plans of the company would be reviewed with respect to the existing human resources, their planned development, and the awareness of the shared vision across the management team (this activity was supported and facilitated by a member of the university's Business Strategy Group). A full business strategy plan and linked HR strategy/plan would be produced.

4 Analysis of senior management team (SMT)

A development centre approach was planned (focusing on both individuals and the team), including personality profiles and team dynamics. This was to result in a senior management team development plan linked to the business strategy.

5 Team building activities with senior management team

Individual and group development exercises were to be specifically designed by the academic supervisors to forge together the SMT, including issues such as:

- trust and communication
- personal strengths and team membership evaluation
- personal skills and styles.

NB: In reality, the above steps were taken instead with the second tier of managers for operational reasons. The work with senior managers was due to commence in 2002, after a change of personnel.

6 Design and develop a competence framework

Based on business strategy and HR plans, the core competences required by the business would be identified. Individual job roles would be examined and specific job competences identified. The framework would be used to formalise behavioural standards and skill requirements, linked to individual and company training plans. The framework was designed by the Associate, with significant consultation at every stage with appropriate individuals and focus groups.

7 Design and implement performance management system

The competence framework would underpin the performance management system, might include payment review, and would include an appraisal/performance review process. This would be based on clear allocation of responsibilities, clear objective setting and formal feedback systems.

8 Systematic training needs analysis

This would involve an evaluation of the ongoing training needs of the management and supervisory teams against the competency framework above. This would be achieved by individual interviews, focus group sessions, examination of secondary evidence, and self and peer assessment exercises.

9 Appraisal/performance review system

This would now be designed, with the knowledgeable contributions of managers and staff, to reflect the strategic development needs of the business, the competence framework and the performance management system. It would need to take account of:

- job objectives
- personal development objectives
- individual motivation
- organisational performance targets
- qualitative and quantitative performance measures
- priorities.

All appraisers would need to be appropriately trained in interview skills, objective setting, and training needs identification. Appraisers would need to be made aware of and supported in their role in this process.

10 Evaluation and review

Formal review of the competence framework, appraisal system and performance management process would be the major focus of the final stages of the programme, leading to recommendations for amendments and the planning and implementation of these recommendations. (Suggested tasks, initially scheduled in the programme but removed due to TCD misgivings about overloading the Associate, included a review of rewards/recognition and equal opportunities.)

A TCS Associate was appointed after a rigorous selection process. The Associate was an HRM graduate with previous placement experience in the automotive sector.

Progress against the plan

At the time of writing (late 2001) the Associate has been in post for fifteen months. All of the planned tasks have been completed on or before the schedule (with the exception of the Senior Management Team Development Centre) and a number of agreed additional tasks have also been completed. These include a company staff restructuring exercise, a small redundancy exercise, revision of the disciplinary procedure, and various training initiatives.

The company now has a clear organisational structure, with reporting responsibilities clearly outlined. All managers and supervisors have job descriptions, individual objectives and performance targets, based on the company competence framework. Appraisers have been trained, appraisals carried out, and training needs identified. A company training plan, a dynamic document, is publicised on the intranet and on the staff notice board. The company has gained the IiP Award and secured quality awards relevant to its needs. A training database has been created and placed on the intranet, and sixteen new internal training modules have been designed as a result of the training needs analysis.

A major turning point in the programme related to the two-day team leadership and management event staged with sixteen managers and supervisors (see Tasks 4 and 5).

Prior to the event, participants completed a number of questionnaires relating to team roles, negotiation styles, learning styles, conflict handling etc. Additionally, the event designers (the authors) considered previous data collected, such as the business/HR strategy and competence framework. The aim was to enable managers to improve the performance of their team against business development plans. Specifically, the objectives were that participants would be able to:

- identify characteristics of effective teams;
- evaluate their own contribution during structured exercises;
- evaluate the overall effectiveness of the team process;
- identify and analyse communication skills, particularly in relation to conflict management and negotiation;
- receive and discuss feedback relating to their profiles, based on previously completed questionnaires;
- plan development activities for their own team and for themselves.

This was the first occasion that this group of staff had all met together off-site, and with none of the senior management team present they were encouraged by the facilitators to speak freely (a confidentiality agreement was negotiated at the beginning of day one).

Activities during the event included the following:

- analysis of current organisational context (linked to previously held business strategy event);
- exercises to identify characteristics of effective teams;
- diagnosis of current team effectiveness;
- feedback and discussion relating to team role performance;
- self-assessment and discussion relating to conflict management and learning styles;

- individual and group feedback exercise;
- identification of 'desired future state';
- action planning (for individual, team and company).

Having analysed the previously completed questionnaires, the course facilitators found the overall profiles very interesting. For example, in team role preference, the group exhibited an overwhelming preference for the roles of *Implementor* and *Complete/Finisher* and, by a similarly striking proportion, their least preferred roles were overwhelmingly *Resource Investigator* and *Plant*. Not one participant of the sixteen had 'Resource Investigator' in their top two preferred roles.

According to Belbin (1981), the *Implementor* typically offers practical common sense, self-control, discipline, hard work and efficiency. They may, however, be somewhat inflexible at times and slow to respond to new possibilities. The *Completer/ Finisher* typically offers follow-through, attention to detail and conscientiousness. This can be accompanied by a reluctance to delegate and a tendency to anxiety. The roles which few (or none) of the group were comfortable to take were also interesting. The *Resource Investigator* is typically an enthusiastic extrovert, good at developing contacts and explaining opportunities, and a consummate communicator, while the *Plant* is typically an innovator, providing ideas and solving problems.

The team profile as a whole indicated an imbalance, with a relative lack of members with enthusiasm and willingness to explore new opportunities and develop creative problem solving approaches. Similarly, when learning styles were analysed (Honey and Mumford 1992), the overall profile showed a marked preference for the *Reflector* and *Theorist* styles, while *no* team members had a preference for the *Activist* style, and few had a *Pragmatist* preference.

Of the preferred styles, *Reflectors* like to stand back and ponder experiences thoroughly, collecting all appropriate data before concluding. They can be over-cautious. *Theorists* think problems through in a logical way, assimilating facts into coherent theories, and may distrust 'lateral' thinking, feeling uncomfortable with subjectivity.

Activists tend to involve themselves fully and without bias in new experiences, being willing to 'try anything once'. *Pragmatists* are also keen to try out new ideas and techniques, but with a focus on their application. These attributes may then be lacking in this group.

If the results of the learning styles and team roles are considered together, it is possible to hypothesise that the dominant behavioural attribute of this team was *caution*. Was there an unwillingness to take risks? What was it about the company and the way in which people were selected and managed, which might impact on behaviour? And if the possible attributes of Activists, Resource Investigators and Plants are regarded as desirable for the company, how was it that such behaviour was not being reinforced or rewarded?

An exercise involving an analysis of 'building blocks' to develop team effectiveness resulted in the identification of areas where improvements in team working could most profitably be made. The items scoring most highly were, in order,

- better co-operation, less conflict
- more openness
- more appropriate leadership.

Actions and implementation

The final group exercise and plenary session resulted in an ambitious action plan, supported by all participants. The action plan was an attempt to identify what steps needed to be taken by the company, its managers and staff in order to improve performance. Some recommendations were specific and immediate, others more long term. The action plan was put before the senior management team.

The impact of this two-day event was marked. The discussions during the two days had identified that these managers felt unable to contribute effectively in terms of new ideas. They felt that they were actually discouraged from meeting to discuss issues, and felt that the company was characterised by control, blame and lack of communication. Several managers felt that the atmosphere was 'intimidating'.

As a direct result of this event, seven process improvement teams were set up, staffed by volunteers identified during the two-day event. Each focused on a product or process, and were facilitated in their group meetings by the TCS Associate. Process improvements, and resultant savings, were identified almost immediately, and there began to be a formally quantified link to the TCS Programme. A Works Council was established, and the defunct suggestion scheme relaunched.

Two months after the team-building event, the CEO left the company by mutual consent, and there has been a restructuring of the senior management team. The TCS Associate is now HR Manager. The TCS is now fundamental to the Company's business strategy, and has enabled the reduction of a significant level of costs, with a handful of redundancies.

As part of all TCS programmes, tangible benefits have to be agreed and logged formally. So far, the tangible benefits, in terms of systems and procedures put in place (identified by the company) include:

- business strategy formalised and shared with all staff
- HR strategy agreed, based on above
- Investors in People Award achieved
- organisation training plan and budget produced
- competence framework in place
- appraisal system in place
- works council established
- suggestion scheme introduced
- pay bands reduced from fourteen to three
- staff restructuring completed
- internal newsletter introduced
- intranet developed and expanded.

Evaluation of effectiveness of programme

- The initial audit was carried out in 2000, and at the time of writing was about to be repeated. Initial evidence suggests that significant reductions have occurred in absenteeism; overtime payments have been reduced and production efficiency has improved. Wastage rates and scrap are down, while quality and environmental standards are still being achieved.
- The attitude survey, also completed in 2000, was due to be repeated, with some additional questions included. These results should throw light on the extent to which staff at all levels have perceived a change in the way people are managed in the company.
- Anecdotally, staff say they feel that they now have a voice, and that there is a new spirit of co-operation. It would be interesting (and is planned) to repeat the questionnaire used to inform the team effectiveness event, to identify whether or not any significant changes have actually taken place.
- The process improvement (PI) teams, formed as a result of the team-building exercise, have produced significant results in terms of improved efficiency and cost savings. They are dynamic, forming and re-forming around new products and processes as necessary. In a new (to this company) initiative, the four most skilled operators are put onto each new production job for a three-day period. This is followed by a half-day brainstorming session away from the shop floor and involving the production manager, facilitated by the HR or Quality manager. The objective is to identify the most efficient methods, machine settings, ergonomics and procedures for the job, involving the staff on the factory floor.
- Financial incentives have been introduced for suggested improvements in practice. These have resulted in improvements in efficiency in several areas.
- The Works Council provides a new forum for discussion, involving shop floor workers for the first time. Representatives are elected by their peers and are given facilities and time to consult with them (no trade union is formally recognised).
- A company intranet contains the latest information on sales and productivity, updated weekly. The company training plan and new HR policies are also accessible on the intranet, with terminals at most work spaces and in the staff canteen.
- Charts showing training and meeting schedules are now sited in communal space, and an internal newsletter produced. This contains company-related information, e.g. orders sought/gained, developments etc. as well as personal news items about staff.
- Specific cost-savings quantified by the Company (in late 2001) due to the implementation of the HR TCS programme (annual gross saving) total over £300,000. This includes cost reductions due to:

  - process improvements identified and implemented by P I groups
  - reduction in overtime costs due to improvements in internal communications

- reduction in costs due to lower absenteeism
- materials reduction.

Analysis

The TCS project at Cranbrook Ltd. has specific outcomes against which its effectiveness is to be evaluated. The programme has not yet been completed: however, it has met (and exceeded) its objectives to date. The company attributes significant cost savings and efficiency improvements to the TCS project, as well as reductions in absenteeism, improved team working and internal communications. Such changes in behaviour among staff would support the suggestion that knowledge migration has been effective to date (Iles and Yolles).

Cranbrook Ltd. is a medium sized enterprise, and is growth oriented. As a company specialising in value added exchanges with other firms, as suppliers of components to major automotive manufacturers, they are well aware of the need to focus on business efficiency and quality, and this requires structural change which is ongoing. The initial recognition, by the company, of the need to focus on HRD issues, and its willingness to engage in such an 'alternative' approach as a TCS in this area ensured an initial commitment to the project which was essential for its success. Such commitment is crucial in overcoming the potential barriers to the success of TCS projects.

Barriers to success

The placement of a relatively recent graduate in any organisation needs appropriate management. The TCS Associate should be regarded as a member of staff of the company, to all intents and purposes, and any references to the Associate as 'student' or 'trainee' can undermine his or her position. Additionally, the position that the Associate holds, with structured access to senior managers and a supportive academic supervisor, can potentially lead to resentment among staff without these 'privileges'. Associates need to be able to apply theory, concept and knowledge operationally within the organisational context. This can assist them in 'mediating' between perceived differences in approach (or worldviews?) of their academic supervisor and their industrial supervisor. They can, if not well managed, be seen as 'an extra pair of hands', and thus be diverted from the programme of objectives (although the TCS reporting on management arrangements are designed to identify and prevent this). It is possible for TCS Associates to initially feel isolated, being affiliated wholly to neither 'camp'. Universities can help here, and LJMU Business School TCS Centre has established a network of associates with regular meetings, social events and a 'mentor' system of pairing experienced associates with new starters.

Promoting effective knowledge migration requires specific approaches and skills on the part of the academic, the associate and the industrial supervisor. The academic has to learn to be a true 'business partner', speaking and understanding the language of the business. Small organisations often suffer potential business crises, and need to act quickly. Academics need to appreciate this, while trying to ensure that the activities engaged in still form a coherent approach. Those academics who are collecting research data have to accept that in this actions research approach the end objective is change - and this may mean that initial data gathered are less useful than expected. However, the business can not be held back for research purposes! There may well be a rough and tumble in the factory that is unlike any situation the academic may have faced before, and a need for a greater level of assertiveness. Resilience will be required, and a willingness to rethink strategies in response to changing circumstances. A willingness to be flexible in approach is essential.

Associates require a flexible approach also. They need to be able to persuade and convince others, as gaining support for their project is essential. They need also to be prepared to listen to the voices of experience within the company, and be confident enough to stand their ground if, having listened, they disagree. They need to develop good working relationships with both their work colleagues and their academic supervisor, who can be invaluable as a sounding board.

Industrial supervisors need to be open to new ideas and approaches (responsive elaborators: see Chapter 8), and preferably have good coaching skills, as they will be the day-to-day contact for the associate under their guidance.

If we refer to the model from Chapter 8, it may be hypothesised that the TCS programme requires knowledge identifiers, responsive elaborators and pragmatic (rather than fundamentalist) executors. These, ideally, would be present in all three areas of the TCS partnership - the academic, the associate and the company.

The TCS programme itself may lead us to offer an adaptation of the Iles and Yolles model (Chapter 8) where the technology translator is not a consultant but is in fact the Associate (graduate); see Figure 9.1.

Although the case study company engaged in a TCS programme focusing on HRD, this is extremely rare. However, all TCS programmes aim to bring about organisational learning in some form. Whether the initial subject of the knowledge migration is engineering design, information technology or biotechnology, organisations and individuals will need to engage in learning. Perhaps there are few overtly 'HRD' TCS programmes, but could it be said that *all* TCS programmes, implicitly, involve HRD interventions? Since the involvement of academic partnership in the TCS programme, 'HR' issues from other TCS programmes are regularly being

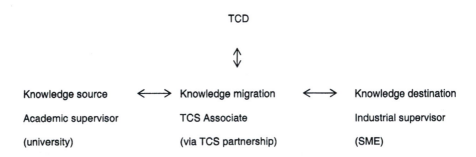

Figure 9.1 TCS partnerships as a process of knowledge migration.

referred for their support, and HRD interventions have taken place in these organisations, albeit not as part of the TCS programme.

It may be that academics involved in drawing up TCS programmes, in collaboration with the organisation, do not immediately identify HRD as making a significant potential contribution. However, once 'technical' systems have been put in place, difficulties in implementation and lack of appropriate organisational development approaches can limit project effectiveness.

Learning points

It is our view that the Teaching Company Scheme could provide an effective framework for HRD in small organisations. Features of the TCS programme which support this view include the two-year time frame; the placement of a supported graduate (Associate) actually within the company to embed the knowledge and spread 'knowledgeable action'; the agreed, measurable outputs and project management frameworks; and the financial support from government grants.

Skills required of partners in the programme include flexibility of approach, openness to new ideas, assertiveness, negotiation and persuasiveness, and the ability to understand the language and needs of the business. This has implications for the selection and development of associates, academics and industry partners. Although this particular TCS programme unusually focused explicitly on HRD, it may be that most, if not all, TCS programmes aim to provide a vehicle for organisational learning, and as such, HRD implications should be considered at the programme planning stage.

In order to promote the use of TCS schemes as vehicles for HRD in small organisations, we consider it necessary to:

- ensure HRD issues are identified at the programme planning stage;
- publicise the results of effective HRD TCS schemes, such as Cranbrook Ltd.;
- identify companies who could potentially benefit and raise awareness of the possibilities of TCS in HRD;
- encourage academic supervisors from an HRD background to take part in TCS programmes;
- devise appropriate qualitative and quantitative measures relating to the effectiveness of HRD TCS programmes;
- encourage the practice (current at LJMU Business School) of involving HRD specialists at an early stage in programme planning, by adopting a "team" approach to academic supervision;
- develop good practice in academic supervision of TCS projects, e.g. seminars, coaching, sharing best practice examples.

A fuller analysis of the effectiveness of the TCS project was due to take place at the end of the two-year programme in 2002.

Bibliography

Belbin, M. (1981) *Why Management Teams Succeed and Fail*, London: Heinemann.

CIPD (2001) *The Case for Good People Management*, London: Chartered Institute for People and Development.

Curran, J. and Stanworth, J. (1989) 'Education and training for enterprise: some problems of clarification, policy, evaluation and research', *International Small Business Journal*, 7, 2: 11- 22.

Curran, J., Blackburn, R., Kitching, J. and North, J. (1996) *Establishing Small Firms' Training Practices, Needs, Difficulties and Use of Industry Training Organisation*, DfEE Research Studies, London: HMSO.

Gibb, A. (1987) 'Enterprise culture: its meaning and implications for education and training', *Journal of European Industrial Training*, 11, 2.

Gray, C. (1993) 'Stages of growth and entrepreneurial career motivation', in F. Chithaden, M. Robertson and D. Watkins (eds) *Small Firms – Recession and recovery*, London: ISBA and Paul Chapman.

Gray, C. (1998) *Enterprise and Culture*, London: Routledge.

Hendry, C., Jones, A., Arthur, M. and Pettigrew, A. (1991) *HRD in Small to Medium Sized Enterprises*, Employment Department Research Paper 88, Sheffield: Employment Department.

Honey, P. and Mumford, A. (1992) *The Learning Style Questionnaire*, Maidenhead: Peter Honey.

Iles, P. A. and Yolles, M. (2001a) 'Across the great divide: HRD, technology translation and knowledge migration in bridging the knowledge gap between SMEs and Universities', *Human Resource Development International*, 4, 1: 1- 35.

Iles, P. A. and Yolles, M (2001b) 'International HRD alliances in viable knowledge migration and development: the Czech Academic Link Project' (accepted with revisions *Human Resource Development International*).

Iles, P. A., Yolles, M. and Altman, Y. (2001) 'HRM and knowledge management: responding to the challenge', *Journal of Research and Practice in HRM* (special issue on knowledge management), 9, 1: 3- 33.

Mabey, C. and Thomson, A. (2000) *Achieving Management Excellence: A survey of UK management development at the millennium*, London: Institute of Management.

Mabey, C. and Thomson, A. (2001) 'Management development in the small business sector: a report at the millennium', *Training and Management Development Methods*, 15: 417- 24.

Rowden, R. (1995) 'The role of human resource development in successful small to mid-sized manufacturing businesses: a comparative case study', *Human Resource Development Quarterly*, 6, 4: 355- 73.

Stanworth, J. and Gray, C. (1991) (eds) *Bolton 20 Years On: The small firms in the 1990s*, London: Paul Chapman and Small Business Research Trust.

Stanworth, J., Purdy, D. and Kirby, D. (1992) *The Management of Success in 'Growth Corridor' Small Firms*, Milton Keynes: Small Business Research Trust.

Storey, D. (1994) *Understanding the Small Business Sector*, London: Routledge.

Thomson, A., Mabey, C., Storey, J., Gray, C. and Iles, P. A. (2001) *Changing Patterns of Management Development*, Oxford: Blackwell.

Walton, J. (1999) *Strategic Human Resource Development*, London: Financial Times and Pitman.

Wang, K., Marshall, J., Alderman, N. and Thwaites, A. (1997) 'Management training in small and medium sized enterprises: methodological and conceptual issues', *International Journal of Human Resource Management*, 8, 1: 44- 65.

Watkins, D. (1983) 'Development, training and education for the small firm: a European perspective', *European Small Business Journal*, 1, 3: 29- 44.

10 E-learning and small organisations

Sally Sambrook

Introduction

Small organisations make a significant contribution to the economy through employment and GDP growth (Matlay 2000: 324). However, while employers in small firms offer fewer training opportunities to their employees, they also complain of skills shortages (Matlay 2000: 315). Although many training programmes and initiatives have been implemented in the United Kingdom, Curran *et al.* (1993) found little evidence of training and development in small firms. However, the 'blame' does not necessarily lie solely with employers: employees may not wish to participate, considering training and development to be of little relevance to their work. Therefore, it is important to consider both employer and employee perspectives on learning within the small firm context. Various factors influence training and development in small and medium sized enterprises, including size, sector, stage of life cycle and skills supply strategy (Hendry *et al.* 1991). There are also numerous triggers for training and development, such as new recruits, acquiring new technology, growth, management culture, and workforce expectations (Hendry *et al.* 1991). The way training is organised and provided depends, for example, on the value attached to it, the type of training, the cost, and the pace of change (Harrison 1997). Abbott (1994) found that lack of financial resources and time made training very difficult, but not necessarily absent or low - some firms engage in informal learning, which is not considered as proper 'training'. Determining the level of training depends on how training is defined. Harrison (1997) distinguishes between 'high' training, which is planned and strategic, and 'low' training which is unplanned and informal, but argues that the type does not matter: the key question is - does it raise the skills base? Many factors considered as barriers to HRD in small organisations - such as access problems and time constraints - could potentially be resolved by electronic learning. However, while e-learning may offer new opportunities, it can also create other barriers. From the employer perspective, these can be lack of resources and lack of trust. From the employee perspective, these can be lack of confidence and IT skills. In addition, the use of ICTs, in general, to support any form of small firm activity is limited, let alone its use to support e-learning.

The purpose of this chapter is to explore the existing and potential role of electronic learning in small organisations.

The key aims of the chapter are to:

- define lifelong learning, organisational learning and work-related learning;
- define e-learning and computer-based learning;
- explore the uses of e-learning in small organisations;
- present findings from a two-year research project examining computer-based learning in the SME context from employer and employee perspectives;
- identify factors (both inhibiting and enhancing) that influence e-learning, particularly in SMEs;
- identify further research required.

Some key concepts

First, let us consider learning. *Learning* is very much in vogue, whether it is lifelong, work-related, traditional or electronic. Honey (2001b) suggests that learning has become 'respectable' and is enjoying centre stage as the undisputed key to sustainable performance and competitive advantage. Exploring learning in its broadest sense, whether within or without work, the 'Declaration on Learning' (Learning Declaration Group 1998, 2000) does attempt to raise awareness of the various purposes, processes and problems associated with this complex phenomenon. In this document, the declaration is made that 'the capacity to learn is an asset which never becomes obsolete'. Honey (2001c) notes the paradox that the more other skills become outdated, the more it becomes necessary to *continue* learning.

The theoretical context for this chapter is provided by four key concepts associated with learning - lifelong learning, organisational learning, work-related learning and electronic or e-learning. The four are linked in the conceptual framework illustrated in Figure 10.1. Each will be explored to provide the reader with a

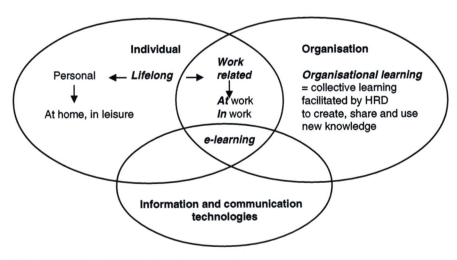

Figure 10.1 A conceptual framework.

basic understanding of the individual concepts, their interrelationships and relevance to small organisations.

Lifelong learning

Lifelong learning can be described as learning 'from cradle to grave'. Some would argue that learning is *nothing but* lifelong, as it is ongoing, natural and inevitable (Stewart 1992). However, others argue that lifelong learning cannot be a continuous activity - we just wouldn't cope with all the information processing and change - but occurs as 'an oft repeated continual activity' (Honey 2001b), suggesting learning occurs in regular bursts, on a need-to-know basis. Honey (2001d) goes on to describe a lifelong learner as someone who is willing, able and empowered to learn.

'Lifelong learning' is defined by Brandsma (1997: 10) as a continuous process of personal development for everyone, whether in work or not, encompassing formal and informal activities, and making demands upon the social structures in which learning takes place. However, the OECD (1996: 15) suggests lifelong learning has broader objectives, including strengthening democratic values, cultivating community life, maintaining social cohesion, and promoting innovation, productivity and economic growth. These were reiterated in an EU Memorandum (European Commission (EC) 2001a), and the concept was redefined as: 'all learning activity undertaken throughout life, with the aim of improving knowledge, skills and competences within a personal, civic, social and/or employment-related perspective' (EC 2001b). This implies that learning is not just about work life, but about an individual's whole life, from birth, through youth, encompassing leisure time, domestic labour, and employment, to retirement and the 'third age'. This European definition includes aspects such as social inclusion and citizenship. However, the focus here is on the need to learn and continue learning within the changing context of working in small firms. As large organisations de-merge, de-layer and down-size - and given the problems already identified in the introduction - how is lifelong learning being facilitated in the context of small organisations?

At a national level, the United Kingdom is encouraging lifelong learning (DfEE 1998), highlighting the changing nature of work, the need for reskilling as traditional industries decline and new technologies emerge, and the need for *everyone* to engage in ongoing learning. This last point raises the question of access - how can those distanced from work-based training or adult education centres and higher education institutions access quality learning? To address this, the UK government launched the University for Industry (UfI). The UfI was established to help enhance the competitiveness of British industry by stimulating demand for lifelong learning among businesses (particularly SMEs) and individuals and improving access to relevant high-quality learning resources. The UfI - now renamed learndirect to overcome the criticisms that it is neither a *university*, nor *for* industry - aims to encourage lifelong learning by drawing upon developments in education and training technology. This takes the form of establishing learndirect centres - located in public places such as libraries, local colleges and hospitals, as well as within other businesses - and commissioning computer based learning materials to be used in these centres. By providing such centres in local communities, existing and potential employees would be able to access personal and work-related learning, to enhance both their attitudes to learning and their personal knowledge and skills. In addition to such centres, work organisations are an important partner in the learning society, providing opportunities for both formal and informal learning. Just as individuals need to continue learning, so too do organisations.

Organisational learning

To achieve competitive advantage and survive, it is argued that organisations need to develop their learning capacity, that is - manage their individual and collective learning processes, become learning organisations and engage in knowledge management (Argyris and Schön 1978; Porter 1990; Senge 1990; Nonaka 1991; Moingeon and Edmondson 1996). As the pace of change accelerates, new learning is required to both keep up-to-date and compete - whether at national, regional, organisational and even individual level. In recent research, a key reason cited for aspiring to become a learning organisation was the need to cope with technological change, to compete (Sambrook and Stewart 2000). Paradoxically, the technology that creates the escalating change can also create solutions, by offering new means of learning to cope with the change. For example, technology such as the Internet provides e-commerce solutions to small firms but requires significant individual and organisational learning: employees need to develop new skills and organisations need to develop new patterns of working and communicating. Yet, e-learning could provide the means of supporting employee and organisation development.

Constant changes in the business environment require organisations to be able to respond quickly and effectively, by improving existing products and services or by innovation (Nonaka 1991). Thus, to be able to respond to the ever-increasing rate of (technological) change, an organisation's capacity to learn can be identified as a core competence for firms in the new millennium. However, organisational learning is not a new concept. The notion that organisations could adapt through processes of learning was introduced by Argyris and Schön (1978). 'Organisational learning is a process in which members of an organisation detect error or anomaly and correct it by restructuring organisational theory of action, embedding the results of their inquiry in organisational maps and images' (Argyris and Schön 1978). This suggests organisation members - owner-managers and employees - identify problems and respond accordingly, and this learning often becomes codified, captured and written down, becoming part of the organisational memory. The ability to quickly detect and correct errors, adjust organisational activities and remember from past mistakes could be considered characteristics of small, informal, flexible firms. This contrasts with large firms, characterised as being slow to respond and change (Kanter 1989).

Newer concepts, such as the learning organisation (Senge 1990), learning-oriented organisations (Tjepkema *et al.* 2002), the knowledge creating company (Nonaka and Takeuchi 1995) and knowledge management (Drucker 1995; Bassi 1997; Scarbrough 1999) reflect the ongoing search for ways of enhancing organisational learning capacity. While organisational learning requires individual employee learning (Kim 1993), employee learning in itself is not enough to ensure learning at an organisational level. Individual learning needs to be identified, captured, shared and used to improve organisational actions. Structures need to be in place to transform individual learning into organisational learning. However, small firms might resist formal structures, and learning might be retained within individuals, particularly owner-managers, reluctant to share both their 'mistakes' and new knowledge - again depending on attitudes to learning, management styles and organisational culture. A feature of organisational learning is the ability to harness all forms of learning. This requires organisations to facilitate employee learning, whether through formal training interventions or, increasingly, through informal learning activities, embedded in work processes. In small organisations much learning is informal.

Work-related learning

The term work-related learning is used to mean all forms of learning activity that take place within the work context. Organisations are important partners in European and national economies and can provide a range of opportunities for learning. Large organisations develop an HRD infrastructure to provide training and development opportunities internally and thus provide access to formal forms of learning. For example, the Learning and Training at Work 1999 survey (DfEE 2000) demonstrates that the proportion of employers providing off-the-job training increases with the size of the employer's workforce. This would suggest that greater opportunities for formal training exist in large organisations than in small organisations. However, recent research suggests that there are new approaches evident in large organisations that also emphasise the shift towards *learning*, and more informal forms of learning - rather than training (Sambrook and Stewart 2000). For example, 'implicit learning' (Chao 1997), 'incidental learning' (Marsick and Watkins 1997) and 'informal/accidental learning' (Mumford 1997) can be significant processes within the organisation context. Given the lack of HRD infrastructure within small firms, it is possible that these informal forms of learning could be more relevant in this context, depending of course upon organisational culture, managerial style and the extent of a learning infrastructure (Watkins and Ellinger 1998).

While there are pressures to find new ways of providing learning opportunities within the work context, it is interesting to note the subtle differences between conceptions of learning *at* work and learning *in* work (Sambrook and Betts 2001). At the Second European Conference on Human Resource Development Research and Practice, the subtitle was 'perspectives on learning at the workplace', (http://www.ufhrd.org). Several papers focused on (more formal) learning activities conducted at the place of work (rather than off-site). Others explored how (more informal) learning could be integrated with the actual process of working, thus helping to remove the barrier of workplace learning being viewed as solely 'going on courses' and helping to recognise the value of 'finding things out on-the-job'. The various forms of work-related learning are illustrated in Figure 10.2.

Outside work

E.g. learning that is related
to work but takes place
away from work, such
as at college or in
training centres

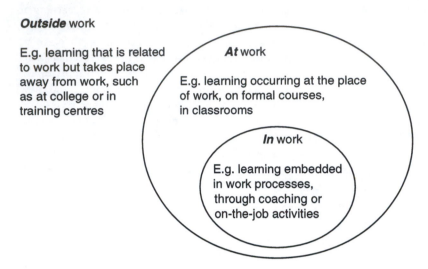

Figure 10.2 Work-related learning.

The increasing pressure to enhance learning to achieve competitive advantage is particularly problematic in small organisations, which often lack any formal HRD infrastructure (Hill and Stewart 2000; Hyland and Matlay 1997). This would suggest that smaller organisations lack HRD expertise to harness opportunities for learning in and at work, and therefore have to look outside the organisation, turning to external training provision, with the associated problems already identified. It would be useful and interesting to investigate how much, and what type of, work-related learning occurs in SMEs. For example, how many employees (including owner-managers themselves) engage in learning outside the place of work, such as attending management development programmes at evening classes in a local college? Or, how many are engaged in a combination of learning outside and at work, through day release to achieve NVQs, or through work-based learning in the form of apprenticeships, for example? While it might be relatively easy to identify such figures, it might be more difficult to assess how much learning in work occurs, through informal processes such as coaching, team briefings and the traditional 'sitting by Nellie'. Often, this form of learning is not considered as 'proper' learning, which is perceived as taking place at education and training institutions, and results in formal qualifications. Jones and Goss (1991) suggest that there is much informal training in SMEs and it makes a vital contribution to the business.

Initial training and formal qualifications, however, once perhaps satisfying the skills and knowledge requirements of a whole career span, are now soon out-dated. This requires all employees to become lifelong learners in the context of work. Not only are work-related skills and knowledge necessary, but also the skills and attitudes associated with lifelong learning - self-awareness, confidence - together with access to relevant forms of learning. This requires a positive orientation to learning. In addition to orientations to learning and the provision of learning opportunities *within* organisations, there is also the phenomenon of prior orientations to learning. Orientations to learning can be compared with orientations to work (Watson 1995). Both are shaped by external social factors (such as family, class, education and peers), individual, internal factors (such as cognitive ability, motivation, values and expectations) and structural factors within the economy (such as number and types of jobs available). A key question is: what are owner-manager and employee orientations to learning in small organisations? As noted earlier, both tend to demonstrate negative attitudes to training and development. The next question is: how can a positive orientation to learning in and at work be developed, to encourage owner-managers and employees to harness opportunities for learning?

Attitude is one problem, another is access. However, when learning occurs *within* work, 'access' - as such - is no longer a problem. Within-work learning, such as shadowing, mentoring, coaching, project work and secondments, can impact on performance as much as traditional forms of training and development. The key issue is the need to release and realise all opportunities for learning in work to ensure organisations can adapt to change to compete and survive. Recently, the advent of information and communication technologies has provided new opportunities for individual and organisational learning. So, in the next section, we turn our attention to electronic learning.

Electronic learning

Electronic learning, often abbreviated to e-learning, can be defined as any learning activity supported by information and communication technologies (ICTs). There are debates concerning the labels, for example whether ICT-based learning is the same as computer-based learning, or is the same as e-learning. The differences are related to the different channels through which the materials are delivered (see Figure 10.3). Online materials are Internet-based and use the world wide web channel. Intranet materials, which can look like those available on the world wide web, are delivered through an internal network of personal computers. Floppy disks and CD-ROMs are used on stand alone personal computers (PCs), that is not connected to a wider network. This debate over labels will not concern us here. E-learning is taken to mean any form of electronic technology - as opposed to chalk and blackboard technology - to support learning.

At the one end of the continuum, this could include the simple use of floppy disks and CD-ROMs on stand-alone PCs. For example, a health and safety course could be purchased, and employees could take it in turns to work from the disk at their PC. Or, the material could be taken away from the workplace and used by sales people 'in the field' or even at home. Moving towards more sophisticated technology, this could take the form of local intranet provision, delivered over a network of interconnected computers, but with no access outside this. Towards the other end of the scale, there is full access to Internet and world wide web services, drawing upon a full range of multimedia, such as interactive material, links to other sites and resources, downloadable streaming videos and communication systems, such as

Blackboard   Stand-alone PC Networked PC Online   WAP

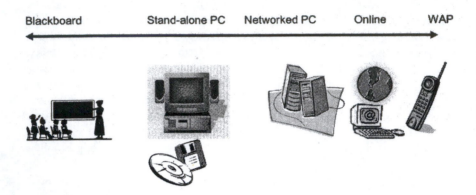

Figure 10.3 Forms of electronic learning.

help lines, email, chat rooms and video-conferencing. Here, material is installed on a network and can be accessed from several terminals. However, this might constrain learning, in that it has to occur at the place of work on a networked PC. Looking ahead, new technology is wireless, such as the WAP telephone, which will facilitate *mobile* or m-learning.

As already mentioned, access to learning opportunities is a major issue, and one which new technologies can help solve. E-learning offers learning 'any time, any place, any how'. However, it also creates further barriers - such as lack of hardware, fear of technology, and learner isolation. With the surge of learning software - often referred to as *learnware*, that is the training materials (content) and programming (process) - there is a further danger that learners are unable to select appropriate learning materials, that is, of relevant content and suitable level. This is especially important, given that even trainers find it difficult to judge the quality of training materials (Carr 1990). Currently, e-learning materials are criticised for merely taking text-based materials and transferring them into electronic format without exploiting the potential of the new medium. For example, e-learning could be 'better' than traditional training in that it has the potential to offer tailor-made learning - tailored to both the learner's knowledge and skills needs and their preferred learning style (Honey 2001a).

The concepts of lifelong learning, organisational learning, work-based learning and e-learning continue to emerge in the growing HRD literature. However, much of this literature is built upon the understanding of these concepts in large organisations, and many question whether such understanding can then be translated directly into the small firm context. The next section explores learning in small organisations and examines the relevance and usefulness of these concepts in this context.

Learning in small organisations

While large organisations provide much employment - and training - across Europe, in many areas it is the *small* firm that provides the majority of opportunities for employment, learning and development. Growth-oriented small businesses make a major contribution to economic development and employment generation within local communities and national economies (Smallbone and Wyer 2000). For example, the European Commission recognises that the fate of SMEs is vital to regenerate areas where traditional industries have contracted due to fierce global competition (EC 1998). Small firms play an important role, representing around 99.8 per cent of all businesses active in the European Union, and accounting for 68 per cent of total employment and 63 per cent of business turnover (Matlay 2000). Yet, Matlay (2000) also notes the paucity of HRD research in small firms, due to a lack of interest, lack of funding and preference for investigating in larger enterprises. There is some debate about whether HRD is different in small organisations. As Iles and Yolles note,

> Some argue that small firms do not face any particular HRD issues compared to large firms, but need HRD to help them grow. HRD is often then translated into formal 'enterprise training', often involving systematic instruction in business, managerial, and functional skills. This 'official' view sees the SME sector as not facing any specific HRD issues that differentiate it from large firms . . . From this perspective SMEs are seen as scaled-down large firms, and SME HRD as scaled-down large-firm HRD.
>
> (Iles and Yolles 2002: 29)

Yet others note that government-supported enterprise training programmes have not had the expected impact on performance (Storey 1994; Gray 1993, 1998). Others argue that there are differences between training and development practices relative to organisation size, and there is limited use in applying 'large firm' training solutions in small firms: small firms are not simply scaled-down versions (Hill 2002). For example, Westhead and Storey (1997) found that training in small businesses was different from that conducted in large firms. Small firms tend to focus on the informal transfer of work skills and knowledge between individual employees, while large firms tend to engage in externally provided training which leads to formal qualifications. So, while there is much research into HRD practices in large organisations, 'there appears to be little agreement as to how much training should be or has been provided in small firms' (Matlay 2000: 327).

The development of SMEs, through the development of owner-managers and employees, is an important subject. Smallbone and Wyer (2000) provide a useful review of growth and development in the small firms, identifying external and internal constraints - including culture, people and managerial style. Gray and Lawless (2000) identify, however, that the most important constraint on small business growth lies in the career motivations and personal expectations of each individual small firm owner and manager. For example, many owner-managers are in business for 'lifestyle' reasons, rather than growth. However, there are other factors influencing HRD in small firms. Despite problems defining the terms 'SME' and 'training and development' (Storey 1994), several studies have been conducted to explore training in SMEs. Abbott (1994) investigated employer and employee perspectives on training, finding that the SME sector is not homogeneous, with different sectors having different training needs. Matlay (1999) assessed the take-up of government initiatives such as Investors in People and NVQs in the United Kingdom and found a lack of awareness of initiatives aimed specifically at small organisations. Hyland and Matlay (1997) also identified barriers to training, mainly time and lack of relevant provision. Matlay (2000: 334) identifies factors directly affecting the provision of training in small firms as the market position of the firm, prevailing economic conditions and the availability of relevant training. Factors indirectly affecting training provision include the cost of training, time constraints, lack of trainee cover, lack of in-house trainers, lack of trainee motivation and lack of trainee interest. Small organisations often lack any formal HRD infrastructure, and the training and development role is carried out, if at all, by owner-managers, although this is dependent on the management styles of the owners, managers and/ or families involved (Gray and Lawless 2000). Small organisations thus often have to resort to 'formal' government initiatives to provide training opportunities, where the 'formality' of provision is often incongruent with the informality and spontaneity of SMEs (Hill and Stewart 2000). Keep and Mayhew (1997, cited in Matlay 2000) found that small firms are less inclined to develop their employees and any training offered was more likely to be informal and short term.

The lack of relevant training and development provision noted by Hyland and Matlay (1997) presents an even more significant barrier to small organisations in rural, peripheral regions.

Facing internal and external resource constraints, such as problems of lack of time and lack of local provision, the growing availability of ICTs and computer-based learning offer potentially accessible, affordable and flexible solutions for learning and development within SMEs. Access to learning, training and development in small organisations is a major issue, and one which new learning technologies could solve, in that e-learning offers learning 'any time, any place, any how'. However, 'little empirical research has addressed the specifics of ICT adoption, implementation and use in the context of the small firm' (Brock 2000: 384).

The use of ICTs in small organisations

The use of information and communication technologies by small organisations has been regularly monitored by the Small Business Research Trust (SBRT) since 1985. The SBRT has reported the increase from 36 per cent of SMEs having personal computers (SBRT vol. 1, no. 3) to near saturation by 1996 (SBRT vol. 12, no. 12) (cited in Gray and Lawless 2000). Brock (2000) notes that small firms use ICT more as tools to support organisational tasks like administration and accounting, rather than for formal, internal communications as in larger organisations. This suggests that most small firms underutilise ICTs potential value by restricting its use to administrative tasks. A key factor is the reluctance to formalise and decentralise - processes associated with the use of ICTs - when owner-managers tend to prefer a high degree of centralisation and unstructured structure (Brock 2000). Similarly, Lymer and Johnson (1997) note that SMEs initially used ICTs merely for accounting, but there is now increasing use of the Internet for both sales and access to information, and for improving the value chain (cited in Gray and Lawless 2000). Gray and Lawless (2000) also cite the work of McClure and Blackburn (1997), who reported distinct differences in the use of ICTs between different sectors, and identified that small firms use ICTs for four distinct activities: administration, operations, electronic communications and small firm information systems. They also found that the larger the firm, the more ICTs were used - and for more functions. However, the size of the firm does not necessarily determine levels of ICT awareness, as very small firms can be highly IT sophisticated (Gray and Lawless 2000).

Small organisations in rural, peripheral areas often face more limited markets, ranging from difficulties in accessing resources from suppliers to distributing products and services to customers, associated with the limited availability of local providers and purchasers. However, such organisations are increasingly benefiting from ICTs to support e-commerce by improving and extending communication with suppliers and customers, thus developing the supply chain beyond the local, often restricted, market. Small firms may also be more constrained in terms of the local *training* market than in urban areas. Yet, extending the use of ICTs beyond conventional e-commerce could also achieve further benefits, such as developing the demand for and supply of learning and development. However, there is currently little evidence of this. For example, to provide small organisations with information and support, the European Commission has launched its Euro Info Centre e-Business campaign, to help small firms face the challenges of e-Business (European Union 2001). However, this web site does not mention e-learning.

While computer-based learning offers potential solutions regarding access to quality learning (through flexibility of delivery mode and location, for example), it also brings certain problems, such as the level of IT skills required by learners and fear of technology. A significant barrier is the ability to judge the quality of - and hence make informed decisions about selecting and using - ICT-based resources. Given the significant factors and potential barriers to training and development in SMEs, the emergence of new information and communication technologies might offer new, and more practical, opportunities for employees, owners and managers to enhance their skills levels. However, they also pose two key problems:

- the availability of technological hardware within SMEs;
- the ability to judge (and thus select) appropriate computer based learning materials.

It is the second issue that was the focus of the research project upon which this chapter draws. However, research findings suggest that the former is a fundamental barrier.

The research project: computer-based learning in the SME context

This section presents findings from a two-year research project funded by the National Assembly for Wales and conducted at the Centre for Learning Development at the University of Wales Bangor between 1998 and 2000. The author was project manager. The project explored perceptions of the pedagogical quality of electronic learning materials designed to stimulate lifelong learning, and specifically learning relevant to business in the SME context. The lack of relevant training and development provision noted by Hyland and Matlay (1997) presents a significant barrier to small organisations in rural, peripheral regions such as North Wales. A significant feature of the Welsh economy, as in Europe, is the proliferation of SMEs. Across Wales the proportion of SMEs is 90 per cent, yet in north-west Wales this rises to 98 per cent, with 67 per cent of organisations employing fewer than fifty employees (Welsh Development Agency (WDA) 2000). In an economic analysis of the north-west Wales region (WDA 2000), two of the key issues identified are relevant to this chapter. First, there is a need to increase the skills and knowledge base - through employee lifelong learning and strengthened links between business and higher education, to help SMEs who lack their own HRD infrastructure. Second, there is a need for more effective use of ICTs to help overcome the problems of remoteness and to stimulate e-commerce and e-learning, given that around 90 per cent of small firms use computers.

The overall research question focused on how to evaluate the quality of computer-based learning materials, attempting to determine whether there was a relationship between 'good quality' learning materials and learning outcomes. The aim was to establish an approach to quality standards for computer-based learning materials, and this was interpreted as developing a quality assurance system (Sambrook *et al.* 2001). Defining quality is a complex and subjective process. Perspectives on quality vary according to whom might be using the computer based learning materials (for example, employees in SMEs) for what reasons (for statutory health and safety training or to enhance customer service skills) and how (whether individual or group based, and Internet or CD-ROM based). The research design incorporated both quantitative and qualitative methods, including a critical review of literature on pedagogical and quality issues associated with computer-based learning and the SME context, and three empirical studies seeking the perceptions of e-learning of higher education lecturers, trainers, trainees, and SME employers and employees.

Research methods

This chapter presents selected findings from qualitative research that gathered perceptions of e-learning from two perspectives - SME employers and employees.

Employer perspectives

Two sources of data gathered during this project help illustrate employers' perspectives on electronic learning. Both were related to recruitment of research subjects. The intention was to recruit SMEs in North Wales that already used computer-based learning and ask employees to evaluate their actual work-based e-learning experiences. However, this proved problematic, requiring a redesign of the final study.

To recruit potential SMEs, first, researchers were invited to an e-learning workshop in North Wales, organised by the University of Wales Swansea, and attended by SME owner-managers. The focus of the workshop was to identify training needs in SMEs. A range of issues relevant to e-learning was explored, and owner-manager views were recorded in the form of handwritten notes. These are presented later in the chapter. Second, a telephone survey was conducted between February and June 2000 to recruit participants in the research. Various sources were used to identify potential organisations within Wales, such as the Welsh Development Agency, the 'Fast Growth Fifty' network of growing enterprises in Wales, existing University of Wales Bangor (UWB) databases and directories such as Yellow Pages; 167 organisations were randomly contacted, mainly in North Wales. Of these, 13 were higher education institutions, either using computer-based learning materials or engaged in relevant research projects, and who might be able to provide SME contacts. Thus the sample size was 154 SMEs and 8 large organisations. Of the 146 SMEs contacted, the sample represented a range of activities, including accountants, solicitors, training providers, manufacturers, IT and communications companies, financial services and health care. Due to the dearth of SMEs actually using relevant technology, 8 large organisations were contacted later in the project as these were more likely to engage in computer-based training.

Only twelve organisations were able and willing to participate in the study, and three of these were large organisations from the financial services and energy sectors. Of the nine SMEs, five were training providers or local colleges, two were learndirect centres and two were other forms of SMEs - one a computer company and the other in financial services. A further forty-three organisations (including four large) expressed interest in participating at a later date, for example, once they had installed appropriate technology. However, during the life of the project, several organisations had to withdraw their participation (due to restructuring, workload pressures and lack of training, for example). This altered the shape of the final study, described later in the chapter. This also highlights the problem of designing a 'good' theoretical research question, but then finding a gap between this and the current empirical reality. It also points to the problematic nature of trying to acquire access to organisations from cold. Access is easier to achieve from known or warm contacts. Almost a half of the respondents did not use and were uninterested in e-learning.

The overall figures were:

- Twelve were able and willing to participate - i.e. currently engaged in computer-based learning - and nine of these were SMEs.
- Eight were using some form of computer-based training, but felt they 'did not use online as such' and declined to participate. An example of this was found in a firm of solicitors, using CD-ROMs for legal updates.
- Forty-three were unable to participate but were interested in participating at a later date, when they had the technology and/or appropriate learning materials. However, we were still able to gather some data regarding their perceptions of e-learning.
- Sixty-eight respondents did not use e-learning and were not interested in this

subject. This is a significant finding, suggesting either the lack of awareness of the potential of ICTs or the lack of need for electronic forms of training and development.

- Twenty-three organisations were unable to be contacted. Given the number of failed start-up ventures, these organisations may no longer be in existence.

Due to the low use of e-commerce, let alone e-learning, the final research study had to be modified. Instead of using exclusively SME employees using existing work-based materials at their own place of work, other participants were recruited to engage in a study of SME-relevant computer-based learning materials.

Employee perspectives

Employee perspectives were gathered during a research study conducted at the University of Wales Bangor. The study was conducted during June- July 2000, involving 159 participants, recruited from the North Wales area. There was a wide spread of age and experience among the participants. The learners were either existing SME employees, recent graduates engaged with experience of working within SMEs or trainees engaged in vocational training and seeking employment, which in the North Wales area is mainly in SMEs. The learning materials employed during the study were all relevant to the SME context, including an introduction to information technology, more advanced computer skills, e-commerce, bookkeeping, project management and team-building. Participants chose the learning material they wished to use, were given as much time as they required to complete the material and were then asked to complete one of the two Learner Evaluation Tools (one paper based and the other electronic). This chapter explores the qualitative comments offered by learners, and identifies the key factors influencing e-learning.

Research findings: employer perspectives

From the workshop investigation of employer perspectives, the research identified mixed attitudes to training in general, and e-learning in particular. Lack of time and resources were cited as inhibiting factors. An important factor associated with computer-based learning is the difficulty in identifying the full cost. For example, it was considered easier to identify the cost of sending an employee to college for day release, or on a training course for a day, than using computer-based methods of learning. Or, as another owner-manager argued, employees could be sitting at the computer terminal but be surfing the internet rather than engaging in work-related learning. This raises the issue of trust, as well as cost.

From the survey of 146 SMEs, only 9 organisations were able and willing to participate - that is, they were currently engaged in computer-based learning. Of those using electronic learning, there were several types. To ensure continuing professional development (CPD), the firm of solicitors was using CD-ROMs to provide updated legal knowledge. In the small financial services firm, e-learning was used to train field sales people. In the large financial services organisation, employees had access to a range of in-house courses, such as customer services, provided on the intranet, or on CD-ROMS which employees could take home to learn. A further eight organisations had the technology and were using some form of computer-based training but made comments such as 'we don't use online as such', stating they used only CD-ROMs, or IT training, 'training staff in web skills but not online specifically'. This could highlight the difficulty researching this area due to linguistic and discursive ambiguities about what constitutes *electronic* (and) *learning*. Forty-three other respondents suggested their future use of e-learning, such as 'online learning is embryonic', and 'we've only just had the Internet installed - very interested'.

Overall, it would appear that employer attitudes to e-learning vary. During the workshop discussion, although some owner-managers displayed positive attitudes to training in general, they were more negative about computer-based learning. However, during the telephone survey, although very few employers (n = 20, or 12 per cent) were currently using computer-based learning, 43 respondents (28 per cent) reported an eagerness to join the technological learning revolution. Many stated their interest in the project, but some thought the academic side was far too ahead of the practical context. Comments were made about the gap between the aims of the research project (judging the quality of computer-based learning materials) and the needs of the SME community (getting advice on how to set up and use computer-based learning in the first place). Some participants advocated a more SME-focused research agenda. Various comments were noted, including:

- 'we're interested in the project but not using online materials yet'
- 'we've only just had the Internet installed - we're very interested'
- 'we're about to appoint staff to explore online learning'
- 'online learning is embryonic . . . and something we're trying to increase over the next five years'.

Some respondents spoke about the specific problems they had encountered in trying to engage in computer-based training, and asked for help:

- 'we want help setting up online training'
- 'we're currently having IT problems'.

Other respondents, particularly training organisations, were interested in the evaluation tools to help them design and develop better learning materials:

- 'we're developing an online mentoring course and are very interested in evaluating it'
- 'we have no online learning materials ready to use yet but we're interested in the quality criteria for designing and evaluating materials'.

Figure 10.4 identifies some of the key barriers to implementing (and researching) e-learning in small organisations.

- Lack of hardware
- Lack of e-learning expertise
- Lack of time
- Lack of resources
- Lack of trust
- Difficulty in determining full cost of e-learning
- Differences in terminology/language

Figure 10.4 Barriers to implementing (and researching) e-learning in small organisations.

These findings appear to contradict earlier claims that 90 per cent of small organisation use computers - at least in terms of learning, training and development. The findings of this random, albeit small, sample, might suggest a surprisingly low use of e-commerce, let alone e-learning, among SMEs in North Wales. Alternatively, this might be a feature of the research design. However, to select or target known users would have obscured determining the extent to which electronic learning is employed in small organisations in this rural, peripheral area. This research provides a snapshot of the current reality, and although disappointing, it also reveals some reasons for not engaging in electronic learning - an important finding in itself.

Research findings: employee perspectives

When asked to describe their e-learning experiences and evaluate the computer-based learning materials, there were mixed attitudes from the 159 learners. However, the majority of responses were positive. Overall, thirty-three different factors were identified, illustrated in Table 10.1. The top eleven factors account for two-thirds (66 per cent) of the total number of comments.

Table 10.2 presents a selection of the qualitative comments. This section explores some of the emerging themes, and the connections between these factors, which appear important to learners.

The most frequently mentioned factor was *userfriendliness*, and this was particularly important to those unfamiliar with computers.

- 'I think may be it could have been explained exactly what to click on etc since there are many people who are not used to using computers.'
- '[I have] not used a computer before, so once I got started I found it very easy.'
- 'Starting the course should pose no problem for those who have used the Internet before.'
- 'Very user friendly, [I] would recommend to those with less confidence to try this course.'

Userfriendliness is especially important in the context of ICT-based learning materials where the learner could be alone and isolated, whether at home or in a small work organisation. This is also related to a learner's level of confidence, and

Table 10.1 Analysis of overall comments, ranked according to frequency of mention

Factor	Positive	Negative	Total	%
Userfriendly - e.g. ease of use, clear instructions	106	5	114	14.9
Presentation - e.g. clear, accurate, no mistakes	34	14	48	6.3
Graphics - e.g. number and quality of pictures and diagrams	22	23	45	5.9
Interest - e.g. interesting and engaging, or boring	21	21	42	5.5
Information - e.g. amount, too little or overload	28	13	41	5.4
Knowledge - e.g. knowledge gained	34	6	40	5.2
Understanding - e.g. easy or difficult to understand	31	9	40	5.2
Level - e.g. too basic or too deep	5	30	35	4.6
Type of learning - e.g. rote and memory, or deep and discussion	19	15	34	4.5
Language - e.g. easy or too difficult to read, jargon, definitions	26	7	33	4.3
Text - e.g. amount, and balance with graphics	12	21	33	4.3
Length - e.g. too short or too long	8	16	24	3.1
Navigation - e.g. moving about package and other sites	12	11	23	3.0
Structure - e.g. in chunks, logical	15	7	22	2.9
Usefulness - e.g. relevance, transferability	18	3	21	2.8
Practice - e.g. opportunity to practise, experiment, use	1	19	20	2.6
Interaction - e.g. interactive or not	8	9	17	2.2
Explanation - e.g. how well the material was explained	13	4	17	2.2
Assessment - e.g. pre-test, self-test, post-test opportunities	7	7	14	1.8
IT skills - e.g. appropriate for beginner	11	2	13	1.7
Colour - e.g. use of colour in text, to highlight key points	9	4	13	1.7
Pace - e.g. ability to progress at own pace	10	2	12	1.6
Hardware - e.g. size of screen, use of mouse	2	9	11	1.4
Examples - e.g. use of examples	3	6	9	1.2
Enjoyment - e.g. fun	7	1	8	1.0
Confidence - e.g. reduced fear of computer-based learning	8	0	8	1.0
Progress - e.g. ability to learn further	5	3	8	1.0
Feedback - e.g. on tests, wrong answers	6	0	6	0.8
Links - e.g. to other sites, content	4	0	4	0.5
Scrolling - e.g. moving about text within pages	0	4	4	0.5
Interface	2	0	2	0.3
Help - e.g. online help facility	2	0	2	0.3
Learner control - e.g. choice, self-directed	2	0	2	0.3

some participants noted their increasing *confidence* in using ICTs and computer-based learning. In addition, presentation was a factor, with another learner commenting, 'well presented for someone with little experience with computers'.

The next set of factors focus on *presentation, graphics* and *text*. One learner commented that 'the graphics were not particularly inspiring and looked like cheap clipart. Good quality graphics especially designed could be used to illustrate points better, e.g. parts of a computer'. Many commented about the use of graphics and text, including 'not enough graphics and interactivity to break up the text', 'more graphics - less text required, felt too much like reading a book' and 'the course was

Table 10.2 A selection of qualitative comments

Factor	Positive	Negative
Userfriendly	'easy to follow' 'clear how to use it' 'detailed instructions'	'I was a little unclear on how to actually commence the course' '[It] got a bit confusing towards the end'
Presentation	'well presented, good layout' 'not too bland' 'nicely laid out - not cluttered with links and options' 'good looking'	'not attractive form, format not very memorable', 'the layout of the pages was quite complicated' 'typeface was a bit small in areas' 'Arial font not the easiest to be read quickly'
Graphics	'attractive graphics' 'not too graphic heavy, not too long to load, visually very pleasant'	'no graphics', 'I prefer more of a visual experience when using the internet - diagrams etc', 'could have done with moving graphics', 'graphics seemed a bit dated', 'graphics were not very appealing or exciting', 'boring layout. Pictures - what pictures? Pictures would have been nice'
Interest	'people use the web without worrying about details, but it is interesting to learn about them' 'attractive opening pages - encouraged me to go on. The key info was highlighted, [to] catch the learner's attention' 'it was simple but not boring' 'having to interact with the package to keep interest'	'[it] gets rather tedious towards the end', 'monotony - just reading', 'nothing to encourage you or keep you focused', 'got boring', 'more detailed examples would add interest', 'could jazz it up a bit, could be monotonous to those with short attention spans'
Information	'very informative', 'lots of information', 'there wasn't too much information on each page', 'useful basic information'	'too much information', 'information overload' 'information dump', 'lack of useful information'
Knowledge	'It definitely taught me about the subject material - hence mission accomplished', 'I discovered that I already know more than I realised about this subject', 'it clarified some queries', 'I now know how web addresses are made up', 'I understand the internet much better now', 'understand	'didn't really learn anything' 'I learnt things I already knew'

Factor	Positive	Negative
Understanding	'more about computers', 'I learnt how to do specific searches', 'I know more than I did', 'I have learned the basics', 'I learnt something and it was pain free'	
	'[the] course was done in a way that was easy to understand', 'it was simple to understand', 'showed an easy way, that was the most important before going into details – making it easier to understand, especially if you're new to the subject'	'it was difficult to understand at the beginning'
Level	'perfect for my level of expertise', 'it was set at the right level'	Too basic = 'parts were too basic', 'level of info - very basic', 'not taxing enough', 'already know most of what I learnt', 'more basic than expected' and 'the course was a bit too basic for my ability'. Too difficult = 'not basic enough for a beginner', 'descriptions needed an intermediate knowledge of computers', 'assumed prior knowledge', 'very intense and heavy going'
Type of learning	'the information given in the course was easy to remember', 'the pictures helped a lot during the learning', 'it sets things out easily so it was easy to learn', 'easy to learn, option to go back and reread anything not understood first time around', 'I was able to understand clearly some thing which I had previously been taught about and had not properly [understood]', '[it] reinforced what I already knew'	'after a while I began to forget things as it all looks the same', 'I'm not sure how much of the information I will retain', 'rote learning. I didn't feel I learnt in a deep way. The test was based on memorizing words/sentences, which were not open to interpretation', 'would have liked the opportunity to put this knowledge to use, testing it out and providing a chance to consolidate the knowledge'
Language	'the language was easy to understand', 'very easy to read, uncommon within online learning', 'presented in a simple form without too much jargon', 'the course was clearly written', 'unpatronising', 'terminology was simple and new concepts introduced well'	'some words were not defined', 'a couple of terms were used before they were explained', 'a glossary could be inserted'
Text	'text presentation of material was fine', 'it was easy to read'	'cramped text', 'text book feel to design of material . . . could be more updated', 'at times the writing was too small and difficult to read', 'all text, nothing to break it up', 'there was a lot of reading. Maybe more practical work could be added', 'it had too much

Table 10.2 Continued

Factor	Positive	Negative
		writing', 'I was glad the window wasn't full screen as I find it hard to read (and find next line) when text is across the full screen'
Length	'concise', 'a bit too short', 'quick'	'[it] went on too long', 'individual sections were too long'
Navigation	'very clear to navigate through the site', 'it was easy to move from one page to the next and instructions were clear', 'easy to move around material', 'easy to find your way around'	'it was difficult to know which button to press when I wanted to continue', 'at the end of the section I wasn't clear where to go next', 'some people might find it hard to know exactly how to get through it especially if you're not used to computers and the Internet', 'seemed a little difficult to go backwards', 'it was odd moving from place to place'
Structure	'it described it very easily step by step', 'content was broken down into digestible chunks', 'the summary was good', 'blocks were of a manageable size', 'very logical'	'difficult to follow section progress', 'I felt that smaller sections would have been easier to take in', 'not always clear where I was on the course - work needs practical application', 'sometimes hard to know exactly where you were in each block'
Usefulness	'it will help me quickly retrieve info from the Internet at work', 'it was applicable to the computers I use in every day circumstances', 'I can use it in my work', 'useful when playing on computers', 'at the end of the course I have learnt something new which I would be able to use as part of my career', 'I work with a group of 5, I now understand how to resolve conflicts within the group and why it is important to work together'	'felt some of the information was irrelevant'
Interaction		'no interactive stuff - may as well have read a book - easier too! No opportunity for practice'
Assessment	'it's good to learn at your own pace, and to be able to get assessed as you're going along'	'was not enough opportunity to test yourself', 'the final test was just a replica of the questions at the end of each section - didn't evaluate how much was learned', 'the assessment sections were

Factor	Positive	Negative
		slightly misleading about whether you should answer the questions or not'
Colour	'it wasn't too much colour', 'background colour just right', 'green very easy colour to read, relaxing colour', 'bright and colourful, appealing to the eye', 'it was very attractive and colourful', 'the colour scheme made it more appealing to use without making it too garnished'	'not enough colour in the diagrams', 'key concepts could be highlighted more i.e. different colour'
Pace	'the format and descriptions allowed me to learn at a steady pace', 'interesting, unlike conventional teaching, you could go at your own pace', 'I could learn at my own pace', 'you could move along through the course at your own pace', 'able to learn at own pace – no feeling of boredom if waiting for others to understand or worry of falling behind as you might in a training group'	
Hardware	'mouse only – no need for typing'	'[it] can be slow. Course completely stuck at one point', 'just that it relied on how well the server was running!', 'it is dependent on the availability and quality of the technology available e.g. my monitor was poor, hence it made it more difficult for me'
Enjoyment	'the course was good but presented in a rather text oriented manner. As it was presented on computer, animations would have been fun and aided learning'	
Confidence	'first time to use a computer. It has given me much confidence', 'clear info made it suitable for all users. The course built my confidence in using computers in the future'	
Scrolling		'[a] let down was the nature of the scrolling and screen size of computer. Maybe easier with a location bar at [the] side that would allow to move up/down easily. Frustrating to have to scroll through material'

mainly text, which made the info difficult to absorb'. However, others thought there was a 'good balance between graphics and text'. Several comments linked the use of graphics and learner *interest* or engagement. 'More graphics might interest the user a bit more', 'lack of graphics and variety could become tedious if the course was longer', and 'more colour and pictures would have made learning more interesting'. Some comments linked the use of graphics to *understanding*, such as 'good use of diagrams to help understanding', 'there was a fair amount of graphics which made the unit easier', and 'good clear illustrations - just the right size - illustrations and other diagrams were also very basic so that they could be easily referred to and understood. I think the design of the course was suitable for the purpose'.

Some learners linked presentation and *navigation*. One noted that 'the design of all the pages was similar so that it was hard to realise that you had moved on a page'. Others complained that 'it recommended searching the web for addresses - then had trouble getting back' and 'it wasn't totally clear in the first instance that after leaving the course to perform a search, that I would be able to re-enter the course with ease'. This was an issue raised in previous studies using 'open' web-based learning materials with links to 'outside' sites. As one learner noted, on the issue of *practice*, '[I] was not able to try out things without leaving the course'. Also linked to navigation, some *hardware* problems were encountered, with comments such as 'it is dependent on the availability and quality of the technology available e.g. my monitor was poor, hence it made it more difficult for me'. Yet, one learner was impressed by the fact that the learning material used the 'mouse only - no need for typing', suggesting that poor typing skills might hinder access to ICT-based courses.

The next cluster focuses on learning: linking *knowledge, understanding, level, explanations, interest, enjoyment, language* and *access*.

- 'I learnt basic history about computers and their use in society today all in a informal, fun and interesting way'
- 'it explained aspects clearly and [these] were detailed making it easy to understand'
  'section on unique site names was quite hard and use of language here could be improved'
- '[it] was in my opinion very easy to follow and understand. The words used were suitable for my level of understanding about computers in general'
- 'easy to access but some of the terminology was difficult to read'
- 'I learned very little because I consider my self to be an advanced user, hence the course level was too low'.

This final comment highlights the importance of selecting learning materials at the appropriate level. Many learners stated that the learning material was too basic. However, other comments referred to the level as being too difficult, such as 'written by experts maybe unaware of the gulf in knowledge between them and the lay man. Seemed to presume that students had complete knowledge of computers'. This suggests that the ability of managers, HRD practitioners and learners to select learning materials of an appropriate level is crucial.

A key issue was the *type of learning*. One learner commented: 'I still find using books to learn through the most natural way, so it takes time to adapt to learning from a screen'. Another noted, '[you] need [a] tutor alongside to discuss key points - when [the] package doesn't provide [a] chance', and similarly, another learner stated 'I think learning by discussing with others - hearing about their experiences is a more fun way of learning. Communicating and finding out facts yourself [books] inspires me more'. A further factor was *usefulness* of the material, and it is likely that transfer of learning will be an important issue for managers and HRD practitioners in their evaluation and selection of computer-based learning materials.

Summarising some of the key issues to emerge in the context of *electronic* learning, one learner wrote: 'the course was good but presented in a rather text oriented manner. As it was presented on computer, animations would have been fun and aided learning'. On a similar theme, one learner complained of 'no interactive stuff - may as well have read a book - easier too! No opportunity for practice'. This could suggest that it might be easier to access books and achieve similar learning if ICT-based materials do not exploit what could be considered their added value in offering greater interactivity and opportunities to practise.

These comments help develop our understanding of what factors are important to e-learners in the SME context. Further analysis of these comments suggests that the factors can also be categorised into three levels: those specific to e-learning, those relevant to learning materials in particular, and those influencing learning in general (see Figure 10.5). Thus, this research identifying factors influencing e-learning in the SME context can also inform our understanding of the factors potentially influencing learning in general.

Conclusions

This chapter has explored concepts of lifelong, organisational, electronic and work-related learning and their implications within the SME context. It has also presented research findings from a project examining computer based learning in the SME context. This research identified factors influencing both employers' and learners' experiences of e-learning. Synthesising these two perspectives, it is useful to develop a model of factors influencing learning and development in the context of small organisations, presented in Figure 10.5. These can be constructed into a hierarchy of influencing factors, from the overall orientation to firm and employee development and barriers to learning in general (from the employer perspective) to factors influencing learning in general, using learning materials and electronic learning (from the employee/learner perspective).

A key finding is that e-learning requires a positive attitude, from both employers and employees. In addition, SME/e-learning requires significant support in terms of assisting owner-managers, who might lack the specialist knowledge and skills, to identify and acquire appropriate technological systems (hardware, specifications); engage in appropriate methods of learning/training (formal/informal, CD-ROM/ web); and identify and select appropriate learning materials (content, level, type of learning). It is both important and useful to identify the factors influencing e-learning

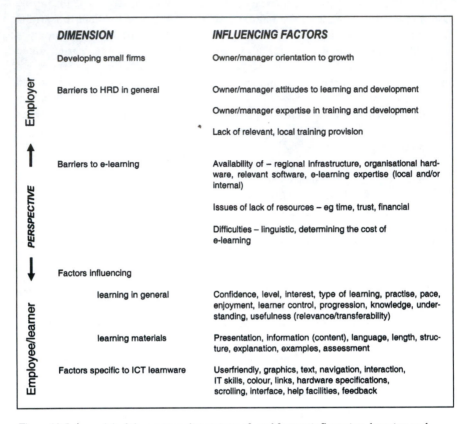

Figure 10.5 A model of the various dimensions of, and factors influencing, learning and
　　　　　development in small organisations from employer and employee/learner
　　　　　perspectives.

to help training brokers, HRD professionals, owner-managers and learners themselves identify the various potential barriers - whether attitudinal, financial or
technological. It is also important to help them better judge the quality of, and thus
select, electronic learning materials. Selecting inappropriate learnware is a waste of
resources and can discourage engagement in future learning. 'Bad' experiences of
electronic learning will do little to engender a positive employee orientation to
learning, nor will they encourage employers to invest in this new form of learning.
The most significant factor influencing learners' experiences was the extent to which
the computer based learning material was perceived as being *userfriendly*. Factors
influencing employers included the lack of trust, the difficulty determining the cost
of e-learning and the physical lack of technology.

If e-learning is to be of benefit to smaller organisations, it is both important and
useful to identify the factors - judged by learners themselves - influencing e-learning.
However, research findings suggest that the same factors could be both positive and
negative features, highlighting the complexity and subjectivity of investigating

learners' perceptions of e-learning. Yet, learning (rather than training) and particularly e-learning are becoming important issues as the national and European governments attempt to encourage lifelong learning. Learnware producers are responding with the growing supply of computer-based learning materials, yet computer interface usability is a concern. A report suggests that e-learning companies will lose large amounts of revenue due to the unusable interfaces of their products, that is interfaces that fail to recognise issues of userfriendliness and accessibility (Quinn 2001). At an organisational level, with an increasing emphasis on learning to enhance competitive advantage, it is important for owner-managers as HRD decision-makers, or other HRD practitioners, to be aware of the factors identified *by learners* to ensure effective e-learning. This is particularly pertinent in small organisations where - despite the lack of formal HRD infrastructure - computer-based learning can offer accessible and flexible learning opportunities, yet can also be greatly hindered by lack of technology, trust, time - and cost. However, a lower level of internal ICT expertise compared with larger firms with IS departments means small firms usually have to rely on external support from friends, providers and/or consultants (Brock 2000).

As employment (and learning opportunities) in large organisations decline, particularly through down-sizing, right-sizing and outsourcing, there is considerable emphasis on developing SMEs to provide employment in areas which have seen a decline in traditional industries (EU 1998) and in peripheral, regional areas such as North Wales. However, are all SMEs growing and creating more jobs? It is important to note that not all SMEs have growth as a business strategy. For many owner-managers it is the prospect of a certain kind of lifestyle, rather than growth, that provides the motivation to set up and sustain a small organisation. Thus, should national resources be targeted at growing SMEs, such as those selected into the Fast Growth Fifty Network, a network of the fifty fastest growing organisations in Wales? It is difficult to consider SMEs as a homogenous sector of the economy, so identifying the characteristics of growing SMEs, and particularly the key managers and decision-makers within them, could help determine what specific learning is needed in these organisations. For example, SMEs with growth strategies will require new knowledge and skills to innovate and compete, requiring an investment in human capital, as well as traditional venture capital.

From this albeit limited research, it possible to suggest that the extent to which e-commerce and e-learning is used in North Wales is lower than expected. This is probably in part due to the lack of national infrastructure, particularly in this rural, peripheral area. E-learning requires investment in infrastructure - both the technological infrastructure at a national and regional level, and the hardware requirements at an organisational level. The issue of 'bandwidths' is important, as narrow channels limit the extent to which new technologies such as video streaming can be used, cause time delays in downloading resources, and are more prone to loss of connections. These factors further frustrate e-learners. Technology is changing at an alarming pace, and another new feature of ICTs is the wireless phone or WAP. This may open up the possibilities for m-learning - or mobile learning - but that is another research project, and we have only just begun to scratch the surface of e-learning.

Areas for further research include:

- a more detailed survey of SMEs to determine the extent to which technology has been adopted - initially to support e-commerce, and then for e-learning;
- an investigation of the problems encountered when setting up e-learning in SMEs and the types of assistance required, for example, from government through business and training agencies;
- an investigation of the potential barriers to e-learning particular to rural regions, such as North Wales, Scotland and other parts of the United Kingdom, as well as other peripheral regions of the world.

Learning points

- HRD in SMEs is not a scaled-down version of HRD in large organisations (Hill 2002; Hill and Stewart 2000).
- Large organisations tend to have an internal training infrastructure, with a dedicated HRD budget and specialist professionals, and are also increasingly able to offer other informal opportunities for learning, such as projects and secondments (Sambrook and Stewart 2000). SMEs tend not to have the internal training infrastructure seen in large organisations, and might also be more constrained in opportunities for informal learning.
- HRD professionals in large organisations cite lack of resources (time, staff, money) as barriers to learning, but possibly have greater scope in supporting less obvious learning in work, such as informal learning through project work, secondments, coaching and mentoring (Sambrook and Stewart 2000). SME owner-managers also cite lack of resources (time, materials, staff, money) as barriers to learning, but are possibly more limited internally in terms of more innovative attempts to support learning in work.
- Both SME employers and employees demonstrate limited awareness of external provision/opportunities (Hyland and Matlay 1997). Yet, e-learning requires a positive attitude, from both employers and employees.
- E-learning requires investment in infrastructure - both the technological infrastructure at a national and regional level, and the hardware requirements at an organisational level.
- Many of these barriers could be resolved through emerging education and training technologies - electronic learning. However, this is not a panacea to overcome all of the problems associated with learning in small organisations. A key constraint is the lack of resources, and both ICT skills development and financial support to invest in ICTs is required (Brock 2000).
- E-learning in small organisations requires significant support in terms of assisting owner/managers, who might lack the specialist knowledge and skills, to

  - identify and acquire appropriate technological systems (hardware, specifications);
  - engage in appropriate methods of learning/training (formal/informal, CD-ROM/web);
  - identify and select appropriate learning materials (content, level, statutory/elective).

Bibliography

Abbott, B. (1994) 'Training strategies in small service sector firms: employer and employee perspectives', *Human Resource Management*, 4, 2: 70-87.

Argyris, C. and Schön, D. (1978) *Organisational Learning: A theory in action perspective*, Reading, MA: Addison-Wesley.

Bassi, L. J. (1997) 'Harnessing the power of intellectual capital', *Training and Development*, 51, 12: 25-30.

Brandsma, J. (1997) *Een leven lang leren: (on)mogelijkheden en perspectieven* (Lifelong learning), Enschede: University of Twente.

Brock, J. K.-U. (2000) 'Information and communication technology in the small firm', in S. Carter and D. Jones-Evans (eds) *Enterprise and Small Business*, Harlow: Pearson Education, Financial Times and Prentice Hall.

Carr, J. (1999) 'The role of higher education in the effective delivery of multimedia management training to small and medium entreprises', available at http://ifets.gmd.de/periodical/vol_2_99/james.carr.html

Chao, G. T. (1997) 'Organisation socialisation in multinational corporations: the role of implicit learning', in C. L. Cooper and S. E. Jackson (eds) *Creating Tomorrow's Organisations*, Chichester: John Wiley.

Curran, J., Kitching, J., Abbot, B. and Mills, V. (1993) *Employment and Employment Relations in the Small Service Sector Enterprise - A report*, Kingston-upon-Thames: Small Business Research Centre, Kingston University.

DfEE (1998) *The Learning Age: A renaissance for Britain*, London: HMSO.

DfEE (2000) *Labour Market Quarterly Report*, Skills and Enterprise Network, August, Sheffield: Department for Education and Employment.

Drucker, P. F. (1995) *Managing in a Time of Great Change*, New York: Truman Valley.

Ellinger, A. M. (1997) 'Managers as facilitators of learning in learning organisations', unpublished doctoral dissertation, University of Georgia, Athens.

European Commission (EC) (1998) 'Developing European SMEs: a study of European SMEs adopting the internet, ESPRIT/TBP project no. 22336, Brussels: Commission of the European Community.

European Commission (EC) (2001a) *Memorandum of Lifelong Learning*, Brussels: Commission of the European Communities, available at http://www.lifelonglearning@cec.eu.int

European Commission (EC) (2001b) *Making a European Area of Lifelong Learning a Reality*, Communication from the Commission, COM (2001)678, Brussels: Commission of the European Communities.

European Union (2001) Euro Info Centre e-Business campaign, *Helping SMEs to Face the Challenge*, http://europa.eu.int/ISPO/ecommerce/gogdigital/helpingsme.html (accessed 23/07/01).

Garavan, T. (1991) 'Strategic human resource development', *Journal of European Industrial Training*, 15, 1: 17-31.

Gass, R. (1996) *The Goals, Architecture and Means of Lifelong Learning*, background paper issued by the European Commission, Luxembourg: Office for Official Publications of the European Communities.

Gray, C. (1993) 'Stages of growth and entrepreneurial career motivation', in F. Chithaden, M. Robertson and D. Watkins (eds) *Small Firms: Recession and recovery*, London: ISBA and Paul Chapman.

Gray, C. (1998) *Enterprise and Culture*, London: Routledge.

Gray, C. and Lawless, N. (2000) 'Innovations in the distance development of SME management skills', available at http://www.nks.no/eurodl/shoen/Gray.html (accessed 03/01/01).

Harrison, R. (1997) *Employee Development*, London: IPD.

Hendry, C., Jones, A., Arthur, M. and Pettigrew, A. (1991) *Human Resource Development in Small to Medium Sized Enterprises*, Employment Department Research Paper 88, Sheffield: Employment Department.

Hill, R. (2002) 'Researching HRD in small organization', in J. McGoldrick, J. Stewart and S Watson (eds) *Understanding Human Resource Development*, London: Routledge.

Hill, R. and Stewart, J. (2000) 'Human resource development in small organisations', *Journal of European Industrial Training*, 24, 2/3/4: 105- 17.

Honey, P. (2001a) *Learning Styles: The key to personalised e-learning?*, available at http://www.peterhoney.com/articles/Article66 (accessed 09/03/01).

Honey, P. (2001b) *Identikit Picture of a Lifelong Learner*, available at http://www.peterhoney.com/article/70

Honey, P. (2001c) *A Thought Provoking Saying about Learning/Development*, available at http://www.peterhoney.com/Newsletter (11 July).

Honey, P. (2001d) *The Changing Face of Learning*, available at http://www.peterhoney.com/article/71

Horst, H., Sambrook, S., Stewart, J. and Meinicke, K. (1999) 'The role of HRD within learning (orientated) organisations in creating opportunities for lifelong learning', *ECLO International Conference*, Glasgow, May.

Hyland, T. and Matlay, H. (1997) 'Small businesses, training needs and VET provision' *Journal of Education and Work*, 10, 2: 129- 39.

Iles, P. and Yolles, M. (2002) 'Across the great divide: HRD, technology translation, and knowledge migration in bridging the knowledge gap between SMEs and Universities', *Human Resource Development International*, 5, 1: 23- 53.

Jones, R. A. and Goss, D. M. (1991) 'The role of training strategy in reducing skills shortages: some evidence form a survey of small firms', *Personnel Review*, 20, 2: 24- 30.

Kanter, R. M. (1989) *When Giants Learn to Dance: Mastering the challenges of strategy, management and careers in the 1990s*, London: Unwin.

Keep, E. and Mayhew, K. (1997) 'Vocational and educational training and economic performance', paper presented at ESRC Seminar Presentation, Cranfield University.

Kim, D. (1993) 'The link between individual and organisational learning', *Sloan Management Review*, Fall: 37- 50.

Learning Declaration Group (1998) *A Declaration on Learning*, Learning Declaration, Pearn Kandola.

Learning Declaration Group (2000) *A Declaration on Learning*, Learning Declaration, Pearn Kandola.

Lymer, A. and Johnson, R. (1997) 'The Internet and the small business: the study of implementation impacts and issues', Second International Workshop on Teleworking, Amsterdam.

McClure, R. and Blackburn, R. (1997) 'The use of information communications technologies (ICTs) in small business service firms', in *Proceedings of ISBA 20th National Small Firms Policy and Research Conference* (pp. 1212- 337), Belfast, November.

Marsick, V. J. and Watkins, K. E. (1997) 'Lessons from informal and incidental learning', in J. Burgoyne and M. Reynolds (eds) *Management Learning: Integrating perspectives in theory and practice*, London: Sage.

Matlay, H. (1997) 'The paradox of training in the small business sector of the British economy', *Journal of Vocational Education and Training*, 49, 4: 573- 89.

Matlay, H. (1999) 'Vocational education and training in Britain: a small business perspective', *Education and Training*, 41, 1: 6- 13.

Matlay, H. (2000) 'Training and the small firm', in S. Carter and D. Jones-Evans (eds) *Enterprise and Small Business*, Harlow: Pearson Education, Financial Times and Prentice Hall.

Moingeon, B. and Edmondson, A. (eds) (1996) *Organisational Learning and Competitive Advantage*, London: Sage.

Mumford, A. (1997) *Management Development: Strategies for Action*, 3rd edn, London: IPD.

Nonaka, I. (1991) 'The knowledge-creating company', *Harvard Business Review*, 69, 6: 96-104.

Nonaka, I. (1996) 'The knowledge-creating company', in K. Starkey (ed.) *How Organisations Learn*, London: International Thomson Business Press.

Nonaka, I. and Takeuchi, H. (1995) *The Knowledge-Creating Company: How Japanese companies create the dynamics of innovation*, New York: Oxford University Press.

OECD (1996) *Lifelong Learning for All*, Paris: OECD.

Porter, M. E. (1990) *The Competitive Advantage of Nations*, New York: Free Press.

Quinn, A. (2001) 'Why people can't use e-learning', available at http://infocentre.frontend.com/servlet (accessed 29/06/01).

Sambrook, S. (2000) 'Factors influencing learners' perceptions of the quality of computer based learning materials', in S. Manning and D. Raffe (eds) *VETNET ECER 2000 Proceedings: Current research in European vocational education and human resource development*, Berlin: Wissenschaftsforum Bildung und Gesellschaft e.V. [Internet].

Sambrook, S. (2001) 'Factors influencing learning in work: a comparison of two research projects', paper presented at the Second Conference on HRD Research and Practice across Europe: perspectives on learning at the workplace, University of Twente, January.

Sambrook, S. and Betts, J. (2001) *Report on the Second Conference on HRD Research and Practice across Europe: Perspectives on learning at the workplace*, University of Twente, University Forum for Human Resource Development, January.

Sambrook, S. and Stewart, J. (2000) 'Factors influencing learning in European learning oriented organisations: issues for management', *Journal of European Industrial Training*, 24, 2/3/4: 209-19.

Sambrook, S., Geertshuis, S. and Cheseldine, D. (2001) 'Developing a quality assurance system for computer-based learning materials: problems and issues', *Assessment and Evaluation in Higher Education*, 25, 5: 417-26.

Scarbrough, H. (1999) 'Science friction', *People Management*, 5, 7: 68-74.

Senge, P. (1990) *The Fifth Discipline: The art and practice of the learning organisation*, New York: Double Day Currency.

Smallbone, D. and Wyer, P. (2000) 'Growth and development in the small firm', in S. Carter and D. Jones-Evans (eds) *Enterprise and Small Business*, Harlow: Pearson Education, Financial Times and Prentice Hall.

Stewart, J. (1992) 'Towards a model of HRD', *Training and Development*, 10, 10: 26-9.

Storey, D. (1994) *Understanding the Small Business Sector*, London: Routledge.

Tjepkema, S. and Wognum, A. A. M. (1996) 'From trainer to consultant? Roles and tasks of HRD professionals in learning orientated organisations', ECLO International Conference, Copenhagen.

Tjepkema, S., Stewart, J., Sambrook, S., Horst, H., Mulder, M. and Scheerens, J. (eds) (2002) *The Role of HRD in Learning Oriented Organisations*, HRD Research Monograph Series, London: Routledge.

Watkins, K. E. and Ellinger, A. D. (1998) 'Building learning organization: new roles for managers and human resource developers', Professors' Forum, IFTDO Conference, Dublin.

Watson, T. J. (1995) *Sociology of Work and Industry*, 3rd edn, London: Routledge.

Welsh Development Agency (2000) *An Economic Strategy for North West Wales*, Welsh Enterprise Institute, University of Glamorgan; Centre of Enterprise and Economic Regional Development Research, Middlesex University; and School for Business and Regional Development, University of Wales Bangor.

Westhead, P. and Storey, D. (1997) *Training Provision and Development of Small and Medium-sized Enterprises*, Research Report 26, London: HMSO.

Part III

Applying HRD methods in small organisations

INTRODUCTION

Part III contains four chapters with a common theme of focusing on HRD methods. As discussed in the introduction to Part II, methods differ from approaches in their scale and scope. Thus, chapters in this part examine action learning, coaching, mentoring and management development. With the exception of the last, each of these could be utilised for single or multiple occupational groups. However, none necessarily implies or requires significant organisational level investment.

Chapter 11 by Alison Wilson and Gill Homan continues the examination of management development as a HRD method. Here, size is reintroduced as a potentially significant factor, even within the confines of what are commonly defined as small organisations. This lends support to the arguments in Part II against treating small organisations as homogenous. The chapter also supports and illustrates the important role of informal learning in the social context of small organisations.

Chapters 12 and 13 share a common focus on coaching and mentoring as HRD methods. David Devins and Jeff Gold report (in Chapter 12) the results of a longitudinal study examining the interesting question of the impact of an external agents seeking to work with particular social contexts. This approach can, potentially at least, impact that context by making available the specialist expertise normally available only with large(r) organisations. As the chapter makes clear though, such an approach cannot be considered either a simple or universal solution. Chapter 13 by David Megginson and Paul Stokes has a similar focus in that it examines mentoring provided by an external agent. The purpose of the mentoring was very specific with a focus on supporting attempts to enter export markets. What is clear from the interim results reported by Megginson and Stokes is that the social context within which mentoring relationships are established and developed is significant both for that relationship and the resulting success or otherwise of the method.

The final chapter of Part III, and of the book, is a study by Thomas M. Garavan and his colleagues of management development in small organisations in Ireland. Chapter 14 addresses many of the themes and issues identified in earlier chapters, including the role of size, business strategy, wider HRD practices and the attitudes of owners and managers. The research reported in the chapter differs from most of the other chapters since the design is that of a survey which utilises statistical techniques in analysing and interpreting the results. This is valuable in relation to this book in that it acts as a reminder of our eclectic position. In support of this, the results provide support from a different perspective and with different kinds of evidence for the themes just listed. So, Garavan and his colleagues also argue that organisation size, approach to HRM and attitudes of owners and managers will all impact the adoption and effectiveness of HRD methods.

This part as a whole identifies additional themes to those already included in the introductions to Parts I and II. These are as follows:

- The role and impact of industry factors and the wider political economy on the adoption and success of HRD methods in small organisations.

- The role and impact of a range and number of additional contingency factors in the success of HRD methods in small organisations.
- The importance of informal interpersonal relationships in the social context of HRD practice in small organisations.

As with Parts I and II, the individual chapters in Part III each offer additional and important insights.

Summary

The book as a whole reports a wide range of research on HRD practice in small organisations. The results of this research suggests a changing agenda for the field. Many of the chapters suggest areas for future research and these will, hopefully, form part of a new agenda. Of equal importance is the range of research methodologies and methods represented in the book. Our view as editors is this variety in perspectives and methods also needs to be part of future research on HRD in small organisations. Our hope and intention is that the book will have that influence, as well as informing current knowledge and understanding of the subject.

11 The management development needs of owner-managers in manufacturing SMEs

Mapping the skills and techniques

Alison Wilson and Gill Homan

Introduction

The economic significance of the small business sector in generating income and sustaining employment has been recognised by successive UK governments since the 1960s. Concern over the volatility of the sector in terms of the number of failures and new businesses being established on a yearly basis, has resulted in a vast array of research into various aspects of small businesses. The Bolton Committee of Inquiry on Small Firms (Bolton 1971) was tasked with investigating, for the first time, every business aspect appertaining to the small firm both in the United Kingdom and abroad. One of the Bolton Committee's conclusions, in 1971, was that in the United Kingdom 'there was a generally low level of management in small firms' and that training and "support services" could be improved to increase their chances of survival' (Stanworth and Gray 1991: 178). This was the first official recognition of the significance of the quality of management in the potential survival and growth of the small business.

However, it was not until the 1980s that management skills came to the forefront of government initiatives. This was in response to the Handy (1987) and Constable and McCormick (1987) reports, which documented the need for increased and more effective management education across all organisations. The establishment of the Management Charter Initiative (MCI) developed standards for different levels of management against which management NVQs were designed. NVQ certification is intended to improve the relevance of training and ensure that it is more closely related to skill needs. A competence-based approach with an emphasis on work-based development was thought to be more relevant to the small business sector needs.

However, in spite of successive government initiatives in the area of management development, and the plethora of courses and training programmes available to the small business sector, the lack of management skills is still being highlighted as one of the contributory factors in either failure to grow or in the cessation of small businesses (*Labour Market Survey*: see Engineering and Marine Training Authority 1998). Indeed, the White Paper *Opportunity for All in a World of Change* (DTI and DES 2001) identifies UK management as constraining private sector investment and business opportunities. This is particularly acute in smaller businesses. To understand why this occurs it is necessary to look more closely at what constitutes management and management development itself.

Much of the research and writing about management has focused on the nature and content of managerial work (Stewart 1999). It has been usual to define management in levels such as graduate, supervisory, first line, middle, senior and executive. The nature of management development has then been tailored to what are seen as the needs of the group in question. Generally, lower levels attract more technical and skills-based material, while for those at the higher levels management development tends to concentrate more on the strategic aspects of management and the 'meta' skills.

This approach has been largely devised with large organisations in mind and little attention has been paid to the nature and content of management within small businesses. That which has been undertaken points to work of a broader nature than that of managers within large organisations (Hannon 1999). A typical working day might combine strategic thinking about the direction or survival of the business with functional activities such as sales, training a new employee and lending a hand on the shop floor. Thus, it seems possible that their management development needs are likely to be equally 'mixed' and not fit comfortable with currently accepted approaches.

Management development is recognised as a key process in delivering organisational transformation and renewal. It is defined as 'a conscious and systematic process to control the development of managerial resources in the organisation for the achievement of goals and strategies' (Molander 1986). Management development is not another term for management education and training, while they are important components, management development is much more holistic in approach. The needs, goals and expectations of both the organisation and the individual form an intrinsic part of management development, account has to be taken of the political, cultural and economic context. In order for management development to be effective, however, it cannot be isolated from the organisational systems and processes, therefore the structures, systems for selection, reward and monitoring performance all play a significant part in management development.

This research, supported by the European Social Fund, focused on the management development needs of small businesses in the UK manufacturing sector. The manufacturing sector has declined significantly in terms of output and proportion of employment since the 1970s and this is a trend that is expected to continue. As most small businesses within manufacturing will be part of a supply chain, changes instigated by large businesses at the top of the supply chain have significantly affected the competitiveness of smaller companies lower down. Changes include the rationalisation of the number of suppliers; the introduction of 'lean' production methods; 'Just in Time' delivery and higher quality standards. Increased managerial effectiveness is central to the introduction of new working methods, multiskilling and managing change, and is crucial in stemming further decline in the manufacturing sector.

Objectives of the research

Much of the previous research into management development in smaller businesses has focused on management development as a holistic intervention rather than as a series of component skills and techniques perceived as important by the sector. This research aimed to ascertain the value of a range of management skills and techniques to owner-managers of SMEs. First, to develop an understanding of the skills/techniques they believed were necessary to the survival of the business. Second, to identify those skills/techniques they perceived that either themselves or their managers might personally benefit from developing. In addition, data was gathered on the type of formal and informal methods of training utilised by the sector to create an understanding of the types of developmental activities favoured by smaller businesses.

Theoretical context

There are conflicting views, but little research, into what constitutes management within the small business sector. Most writers acknowledge that it is different from management in large organisations but because of the diversity of the small business sector there is no clear theoretical direction on the way it differs. Hannon (1999), in a summary of the literature on management development processes in small businesses, refers to management within the small firm as situationally specific, and dependent on a variety of factors such as function, sector and owner-manager style. He refers to significant gaps of perception and understanding in rhetoric and practice, between owners, managers and employees, and one could add to that other stakeholders, such as providers of management development and government.

Without an understanding of what constitutes management within the small business sector it is not surprising that there is no consensus within the literature on what management development should take place (Smith *et al.* 1999), although there is a general agreement that it is the business imperative which drives it. While much research had been conducted on various aspects of small businesses, it was not until the late 1980s that a significant interest was shown in management development within small business. Since then there has been a profusion of research and a number of reasons, some of them conflicting, put forward as to why management development does not take place, or is not accorded a high priority within small businesses.

Development and organisation performance

One of the difficulties of persuading small business of the benefits of being proactive within the area of management development is the lack of quantifiable evidence that shows a link between training and development and profitability. A link that many large organisations and researchers take for granted. For example, Business Growth Training (BGT) was put in place by the Training Agency, in the early 1990s. This scheme ensured that small businesses had help with the cost of employing a management development consultant who would work in each small business and develop necessary management skills. The aim of the investment made by the training agency was to enhance company performance and therefore profit. This investment was hoped to be 'value-added', in that companies would see the benefits and include all their staff in training and development activity. Thus continuing in a cycle of improved performance/profit, and enhancing the sectors contribution to the economy. The large grant offered under the BGT scheme undoubtedly led to small businesses engaging in a larger amount of management training and development and a continued increase in training once the grant had finished. However, while it was believed that the companies who participated benefited from an overall improvement in performance, it was 'impossible to quantify' (Marshall *et al.* 1995).

Cushion (1995, 1996) and Kerr and McDougall (1999) link this lack of demonstrable evidence, to the lack of effective evaluation of management skills development in small firms. There appears to be two major factors, which prevent the conventional approaches to evaluation having utility for small businesses. The first is timescale. Many of the models of 'best practice' in evaluation put forward a multilevel strategy over time. The time horizons in smaller businesses, however, are very different from those of larger organisations (Westhead and Storey 1996) and investing in development that will impact on performance over time seems either irrelevant or a luxury to a company that is struggling to survive.

The second area of concern are the measures of success used in evaluation. As Hannon (1999) points out, these allow little room for effective comparison. Small businesses are interested in and value measures that seem to impact on their day-to-day operational practice rather than those associated with an ideal of enhanced management effectiveness per se. This view is supported by Cushion (1995, 1996), who maintains that strategies developed in and for large companies are inappropriate and that a multilevel strategy based on contingency, which allows for the impact of the owner-manager and takes a more holistic and dynamic view of learning would provide a more meaningful approach.

Barriers to participation

Much of the research in this area has focused on the reasons why management development is not accorded a high priority within smaller businesses or, indeed, does not take place at all. While undoubtedly some are specific to individual research initiatives and could, therefore, be attributed to regional or sectoral issues there are, nevertheless, consistent themes. These identify a number of structural and attitudinal constraints to participation in developing managerial competence.

There also exists a perception that the benefits of development accrue to the worker rather than the enterprise, and a real concern of giving staff valuable skills, particularly in the form of recognised qualifications, is that the staff may take the benefit of development to another organisation (Westhead and Storey 1996; Johnson 1999). Time and cost of development appear to be inextricably linked, this was the most common reason for non-participation in development given by smaller businesses in all the research reviewed. Not only does a smaller business have to justify development costs, but also the time lost to the organisation and the resultant opportunity costs (Smith et al. 1999; Wong et al. 1997; Kerr and McDougall 1999; Westhead and Storey 1996; Vickerstaff 1992; Welch 1996). This is the reason given for the low take-up of partially funded NVQs (Smith et al. 1999; Wong et al. 1997; Kerr and McDougall 1999; Westhead and Storey 1996).

Attitude is also important. Many businesses see development as an expense rather than an investment and management development as a luxury, only to be indulged in when the firm has spare money (Kerr and McDougall 1999). Consequently, management training and development is often only considered to solve a particular problem, (Hankinson *et al.* 1997; Blackburn and Kitching 1997). As Hill and Stewart (2000) point out, 'the nature of training and development in small firms mirrors the characteristics of SMEs themselves - that both small organisations and their HRD activities are essentially informal, reactive and short-term in outlook' (Hill and Stewart 2000: 109). Research has also highlighted that training can be perceived as a punishment for poor performance by the employee (Lange *et al.* 2000).

A further barrier to participation is the small business sector approach to skill shortages. It would appear that there is a strong tendency to 'buy in' to deal with skill shortages rather than invest in their own training (Childe *et al.* 2000). A contributory factor in this may be the strong resistance by family run firms to outside intervention from external organisations. Development offered by external providers, therefore, may never be considered (Smith *et al.* 1999; Westhead and Storey 1996).

Types of training and development

The critique of training in small business has included specific reference to individual approaches or types of training, some of which have been specifically designed to meet the needs of small businesses. Research has proven that these have rarely lived up to expectations. Competence-based training for example is said by Banfield *et al.* (1996) and Connor and Haydock (1997) to be perceived as driven by providers who lack understanding of small businesses. In addition it is unlikely to produce performance improvement and owner-managers do not value external certification processes (Marlow 1997; Matlay and Hyland 1997).

Open learning, which might seem to offer attractive flexibility and cost-effectiveness to small businesses was found in a small-scale DfEE research project to suffer from lack of management support which resulted in the open learners falling behind in their programmes. A need for greater understanding of what was involved in this form of learning by owner-managers was crucial to its success, and those that performed best were firms where the owner-managers themselves had experienced open learning (Temple 1995). Overall the DfEE project was considered a success with open learning offering valuable flexibility to smaller businesses provided the subject matter was driven by the perceived needs of the owner-managers themselves.

Generally, there is evidence of dissatisfaction with overall training provision (Sadler-Smith *et al.* 1998; Storey 1999). In particular there is dissatisfaction with government-sponsored agencies, as training provision for the sector tends to be generic courses and NVQ-based qualifications. Particularly frustrating is the time and effort needed to identify appropriate training from the overwhelming choice available (Marshall *et al.* 1995). It would appear that management development therefore is 'supply led, rather than demand led' (Vinten 2000: 14), which creates a dichotomy between needs and provision; Storey and Westhead (1997) attribute this to 'market failure'.

Research indicates a preference for on the job, short courses or coaching specifically relevant to needs identified at the time (Blackburn and Hankinson 1989; Marlow 1997; Quayle 1994; Vinten 2000). However, as organisations grow in size more formal approaches gain in popularity and credibility (Blackburn and Kitching 1997; Penn *et al.* 1998). It is also frequently noted that informal development takes priority over formal development within smaller organisations, because it is firm specific and on-the-job (Blackburn and Hankinson 1989; Johnson and Gubbins 1992). However, other research has raised doubts over its effectiveness in developing competence. Informal training requires particular skills on the part of the coach/facilitator transferring the requisite knowledge and skills (Hendry *et al.* 1991). In addition, Mabey and Thompson (1994) point out that a lack of knowledge of the skills of learning can render informal training inadequate. They call for strategies that foster the strengths of informal learning in small business by 'creative solutions, personal and intuitive insights, networking and emphasis on short term realism'.

One clear preference to emerge from the small business sector is for the 'personal coach' for owner-managers, usually a consultant who will work on a one-to-one basis (Lange *et al.* 2000; Blackburn and Hankinson 1989; Vinten 2000).

The influence of the owner-manager

Whether or not small businesses invest in management development is undoubtedly influenced by the owner-manager (Smith et al. 1999). As long ago as 1971 Stanworth and Curran produced research which referred to different 'entrepreneurial identities' or motivations, which they proposed influenced their business performance and willingness to engage with external resources and agencies.

The owner-manager's previous experience of training and education influences the extent to which they value it, and goes on to create and add to the place that training holds within the culture of the company. Wong *et al.* (1997) endorse the importance of the owner-manager's experience but maintain that the training culture within small business is more complex and dependent on a number of variables such as regional and labour market conditions, the ability to fill skills gaps by recruitment and the degree of organisational structure present in the company.

There are also issues around 'negative feelings' towards training and development, particularly university courses and this has been attributed partially to small business owner-managers being by their very nature individualistic, and therefore less likely to have progressed through the conventional educational system (Choeuke and Armstrong 1998). Indeed much research has shown that small business owner-managers do have a particular ethos or value system which may differ from managers working in larger organisations. Deakins and Freel (1998) and Gibb (1997) argue that the whole approach to learning for owner-managers in small business needs revisiting. They refer to 'the nature of entrepreneurial learning' as essentially different, as non-linear and discontinuous, their ability to learn from learning 'partnerships' crucial. Marlow (1997) also highlights the importance of proposed training and development interventions being 'non-threatening' to the owner-manager and Turner (1997) the significance of the owner-managers' learning style in influencing the choice of training.

Following on from this, researchers have also attempted to establish links between personal characteristics and the success or failure of small businesses, characteristics such as gender, age, work experience, educational qualifications and family background. Despite this, however, only educational qualifications have been consistently verified as being a significant variable (Berryman 1983).

The impact of growth

The significance of management structures has been highlighted as providing understanding of management development needs within the small business sector. Previous research has demonstrated that the greater the degree of structure the more emphasis is likely to be placed on training and development (Wong *et al.* 1997). When the business is very small (fewer than ten employees) the management functions are not usually formalised or differentiated from other operational business activities. Due to a high workload and the resultant pressure, training is restricted. Once the business has a single level of management between the shop floor and the owners, although training takes place it is based on operational needs rather than strategic ones. Due to the lack of an internal labour market there is no pressure to provide an integrated approach with appraisal/promotion linked to training and development of skills. Once an organisation has two or more managerial levels beneath senior/owner-manager, training and development become strategically critical to organisational development, in terms of retaining key workers and planning for internal movement (Goss and Jones 1997).

Birley and Westhead (1990) highlight the importance of internal organisational adjustments that occur as organisational structures are developed and management levels are introduced, though no standard combination or sequence of factors has been identified. Hannon (1999) also notes the distinct relationship between rapid growth and increasing formalisation of training methods. What is clear is that as small businesses grow in size a number of adjustments in processes have to be successfully negotiated. The management development needs obviously vary according to the stage the business is at in terms of growth, and account also has to be taken of the differing time frames in growth; some companies will grow at a steady rate, while for others the transitions can happen within months. Negotiating the transitional phases successfully and making the appropriate adjustments in product and market, production processes, employment and labour processes, ownership, organisational change, and location, are central to the growth of the firm (Smallbone *et al.* 1992).

Research context

As the research was partly supported by the European Social Fund, and was conducted with a number of advisory and commercial partners, time and financial constraints had to be taken into consideration in deciding the research methods to be employed. The most appropriate methodology, and one that has been used extensively by other researchers in the field (see Westhead and Storey 1996 for a review), was that of a postal questionnaire to ascertain the views of a larger number of small businesses, supplemented by in-depth interviews, nineteen in all, to provide a closer understanding of management development needs. Combining the two methodological approaches allowed the limitations of adopting a wholly quantitative or qualitative methodology to be constrained, and a more comprehensive picture of the subject being researched to be gained (Easterby-Smith *et al.* 1991).

The questionnaire was designed following extensive consultation with members of the academic community as well as personnel who worked with and in the small business sector. As this research was trying to surface owner-managers' own perceptions on management development it was important that the questionnaire used accessible language that was subject/participant led. In addition the questionnaire had to be quickly and easily answered, given the time constraints under which busy owner-managers operate. Closed and Likert-style questions were utilised in order to be able to produce responses that could be easily analysed and compared. The main focus of the questionnaire was twenty management skills/techniques which owner-managers were asked to rate on a Likert scale (0- 7). This was conducted twice, first in terms of those skills that were important to the success of their business. Second, those skills/techniques that either they or their management team would benefit from developing.

The management skills and techniques selected were derived from the NVQ management framework levels three to five and the Owner-manager Management Standards produced by Small Firms Enterprise Development Initiative. The Likert scales were considered to be most appropriate for these questions, as they are useful in measuring attitudes and feelings. While a Likert scale of 0- 5 is the most popular, the 0- 7 was adopted to allow a finer distinction around the mid-point and to allow any extreme values to be detected. Information was also gathered on the number of employees the respondent organisation employed, turnover, responsibility for training and development, and the formal and informal development tools used. Biographical information on the respondent (usually the owner) was also sought in order to contextualise owner-managers attitudes.

The questionnaire was distributed to 1000 small businesses nationwide in October 1999. Contacts were obtained through the aegis of the Forum of Private Business and the Engineering Employers Federation who both provided a random sample of their membership within the appropriate sector. In addition, some of the corporate partners to the project provided us with details of smaller companies operating within their supply chain. In total 194 (response rate of 19.4 per cent) useable questionnaires were returned by January 2000 for analysis. The questionnaire was followed up by nineteen in-depth interviews with owner-managers of small businesses of varying sizes (based on number of employees), selected from the questionnaire returns. The interviews were semi-structured in order to establish links and common themes, but also to allow areas which came up naturally to be explored. Information was sought on six main areas: history of the organisation; changes in the business environment; relationship with customers and suppliers; training and development needs; personal experience of training and development; sources of information and preference for course delivery, structure and content. All nineteen interviews were taped (with the interviewees' permission), transcribed and analysed using Ritchie and Spencer's (1994) framework methodology which is clearly laid out, rigorous and open.

Data analysis

Defining what was meant by a small firm had to be established at the outset of the research to enable effective data analysis. One of the earliest attempts to define a small firm was by the Bolton Committee (1971) which suggested taking into account a number of different statistical and economic factors such as the number of employees, the size of turnover, market share, market sector and the way the business is financed. This, alongside numerous other definitions, according to Deakins (1999), has been replaced by more workable 'single-factor' definitions. Given that the research was being partially supported by the European Social Fund, it was deemed appropriate to utilise, the then, European Union definition of an 'enterprise that employs less than 500 people'.

However, the acknowledgement by various researchers of the heterogeneity of the small business sector (Johnson 1999) precipitated analysing the data based on suitable subdivisions within the above definition. As the European Union had already provided a subdivision based on numbers employed; micro (0- 9 employees); small (10- 99 employees); and medium (100- 499 employees); this was adopted. While the research produced some interesting results based on the above classification, it became apparent that once a firm reaches 100 employees plus, they are much more akin to a large organisation. Therefore, a more interesting and fruitful analysis would be to map those management skills and techniques that were important to organisations from 0 to 100. Thus, the data in terms of the management skills and techniques was reanalysed based on disaggregating the responses in groups 0- 9, 10- 20, 21- 30, 41- 50, 51- 60, 61- 70, 71- 80, 81- 90 and 91- 100. This then allowed any distinct leverage points for specific inputs of management development to emerge and be identified. The median value, and the inter-quartile range was computed for each of the skills/techniques to give a more accurate value than the mean, which does not indicate the range of scores.

Main findings

Questionnaire data

In total 194 companies participated; the mean age of the respondents' organisations was 26 years. The majority of companies employing fewer than 10 were sole owner managed, those employing between 10 and 100 employees were, in the main, private limited companies but still controlled by the owner-manager. According to Barnett and Storey (2000) less than 20 per cent of smaller companies last more than six years, therefore the sample, if length of trading is a criteria of success, contained some well-established successful smaller businesses.

Management skills and techniques

The prime objective was to ascertain those management skills and techniques that the respondent organisations *believed* contributed to the success of their business, and those management skills and techniques *they would like* either themselves or their management team to be more proficient in. Tables 11.1 and 11.2 show the twenty skills and techniques with the median value in each of the subgroups identified above. Those skills with a median score of 5.5 or above were taken to be very significant and have been highlighted to identify similarities and differences between the subgroups. Please see the key in Figure 11.1.

It is immediately noticeable from the tables that a higher number of the skills and techniques scored 5.5 or above for contributing to the success of the business, than for requiring development. It is also apparent that once a small business reaches 51 employees those skills and techniques that contribute to business success and have a development need increase significantly. This confirms previous research by Loan-Clarke *et al.* (1999) who indicated that some form of management development has to take place within an organisation once it reaches 50 employees, because the owner-manager is not able to deal with all the managerial issues personally.

As one would expect there are certain skills and techniques that contribute to business success irrespective of the number of employees; these are sales techniques, customer care skills, quality management techniques, and cash flow and credit management. Only skills in customer care, however, showed a need for development for all businesses regardless of size.

Management skills and techniques that contribute to the success of the business

When identifying those skills that emerge as important for the first time some interesting patterns can be observed. For those smaller businesses employing up to

	Scored 5.5 or above for all subgroups
	Scored 5.5 or above for the first time
	Scored 5.5 or above intermittently
	Scored 5.5 or above for all subgroups with over 50 employees

Figure 11.1 Key for Tables 11.1 and 11.2.

Table 11.1 Management skills and techniques that contribute to the success of the business

	0–9 n=90	10–20 n=41	21–30 n=17	31–40 n=14	41–50 n=4	51–60 n=8	61–70 n=9	71–80 n=5	81–90 n=2	91–100 n=4
Sales techniques	5.7	5.7	5.7	5.5	5.5	6.2	6.7	5.7	7.0	5.5
Market knowledge/research	5.7	5.3	5.6	5.7	5.0	6.0	6.0	5.7	6.5	5.7
Customer care techniques	6.5	6.3	6.6	6.2	6.7	6.5	6.6	5.7	7.0	6.7
Quality management techniques	5.7	5.7	5.7	6.3	6.5	6.2	5.5	6.2	7.0	6.5
Cash flow/credit management	6.5	6.7	6.7	6.5	6.5	6.7	6.4	6.3	5.5	6.5
Raising capital	3.5	3.3	3.5	1.7	3.0	4.5	3.7	5.0	3.5	2.5
Financial planning/budgeting	5.2	5.4	5.2	5.0	4.5	5.5	5.0	6.0	5.5	5.5
Employment law	4.1	4.3	4.0	4.7	4.2	3.5	4.7	5.5	4.0	4.5
Health and safety at work	5.5	5.8	5.1	6.0	5.5	5.0	5.4	6.0	5.5	5.5
Recruitment and selection	4.2	4.3	4.6	3.8	5.5	5.7	4.7	5.7	5.5	3.5
Disciplinary handling	3.4	4.5	4.7	3.5	3.5	5.2	4.4	4.7	4.5	4.2
Team development	4.4	4.5	5.7	4.0	5.5	6.0	5.2	5.0	6.0	5.5
Coaching/training/skills/appraisal	4.3	4.3	4.7	4.7	5.5	5.5	4.7	5.0	4.5	4.5
Negotiation techniques	4.6	4.6	5.0	4.0	4.5	5.2	5.3	5.7	5.5	5.0
Using the Internet/email	3.6	3.7	3.1	4.0	5.8	3.9	4.2	4.3	4.5	4.5
Using computerised systems	5.0	5.4	5.6	5.5	6.0	5.5	5.4	6.0	6.5	6.0
Stock control/purchasing	5.2	4.7	5.9	5.5	5.8	5.5	5.4	5.3	6.0	5.7
Environmental regulations: compliance/risk	4.1	3.6	3.6	4.7	5.0	4.5	4.3	5.3	6.5	4.8
Managing change	5.0	4.6	4.4	5.2	5.5	5.5	5.6	6.0	6.5	5.5
Business planning and performance	5.2	5.2	5.6	5.7	4.5	5.7	5.7	5.7	6.5	6.0

Table 11.2 Management skills and techniques that require development

	0–9 n = 90	10–20 n = 41	21–30 n = 17	31–40 n = 14	41–50 n = 4	51–60 n = 8	61–70 n = 9	71–80 n = 5	81–90 n = 2	91–100 n = 4
Sales techniques	5.3	5.6	5.3	5.9	5.0	6.2	6.7	5.7	7.0	5.5
Market knowledge/ research	5.0	5.0	5.3	5.7	5.8	6.0	6.0	5.7	6.5	5.7
Customer care techniques	5.5	5.5	6.3	5.7	5.5	6.5	6.6	5.7	7.0	6.7
Quality management techniques	4.6	6.0	6.0	5.8	5.0	6.2	5.3	6.2	7.0	6.5
Cash flow/ credit management	4.8	5.1	5.5	5.4	5.5	6.7	6.4	6.3	5.5	6.5
Raising capital	2.8	2.2	3.0	1.7	2.5	4.5	3.7	5.0	3.5	2.5
Financial planning/ budgeting	3.8	4.2	4.4	4.8	2.5	5.5	5.0	6.0	5.5	5.5
Employment law	4.1	3.7	3.7	4.6	2.5	3.5	4.7	5.5	4.0	4.5
Health and safety at work	5.3	4.5	5.1	6.0	5.5	5.0	5.4	6.0	3.5	5.5
Recruitment and selection	3.4	3.9	4.7	4.6	2.5	5.7	4.7	5.7	5.5	3.5
Disciplinary handling	3.6	3.8	4.2	3.6	3.8	5.2	4.4	4.7	4.5	4.2
Team development	4.1	4.1	5.7	4.7	4.5	6.0	5.2	5.0	6.0	5.5
Coaching/training/ skills/appraisal	4.1	3.7	5.7	4.7	5.8	5.5	4.7	5.0	4.5	4.5
Negotiation techniques	4.3	3.7	4.9	4.0	4.5	5.2	5.3	5.7	5.5	5.0
Using the Internet/email	4.5	3.6	4.0	4.3	6.0	3.9	4.2	4.3	4.5	4.5
Using computerised systems	5.4	4.9	5.0	5.3	5.2	5.5	5.4	6.0	6.5	6.0
Stock control/ purchasing	4.4	3.5	5.6	3.3	5.7	5.5	5.4	5.3	6.0	5.7
Environmental regulations: compliance/risk	3.8	3.6	3.7	4.3	4.0	4.5	4.3	5.3	6.5	4.8
Managing change	4.9	4.1	4.2	4.4	5.0	5.5	5.6	6.0	6.5	5.5
Business planning and performance	4.7	4.4	5.0	5.3	3.5	5.7	5.7	5.7	6.5	6.0

twenty employees, it is apparent that the skills and techniques that are valued are those to do with the immediate gaining of and day-to-day operation of the business.

For companies employing between twenty and thirty employees those new skills that are highlighted as very significant are associated with business systems. These included stock control/purchasing, using computerised systems and business planning and performance. This could indicate that at this number of employees the workload has increased sufficiently to require systemisation in order to retain control. Similarly the fact that team development ('soft skill') becomes important for the first time, again suggests a system of work that has previously not had to be utilised.

By the time an organisation reaches between forty-one and fifty employees the people management skills emerge as a distinct leverage point, with recruitment and selection, coaching/training/skills/appraisal and managing change becoming very significant for the first time. Using the Internet/email is also highlighted at this stage although it is likely to be a spurious result given that the use of the Internet/email was still, relatively speaking, in its infancy at the time the respondents completed the questionnaire. This skill was also highlighted as being in need of development for this subgroup.

Another leverage point has been potentially identified at between seventy and ninety employees. Negotiation skills, employment law and environmental regulations (compliance and risk) show significant scores for the first time, which could be indicative of the organisation having a greater interface with the external environment. However, as the numbers of organisations within the subgroups are not as large caution is required in interpreting this result as significant.

It is noticeable that in organisations employing between fifty and one hundred employees, there are a number of skills consistently highlighted as contributing to the success of the business. These include market knowledge/research; business planning and performance; and managing change.

Management skills and techniques that require development

In terms of management skills requiring development, sales techniques and quality management techniques are identified as becoming important for the first time for companies employing between ten and twenty employees.

Between twenty and thirty employees it is interesting to note that coaching/training/skills/appraisal and team development emerge as skills requiring development, indicating a need for people development skills. However, these skills do not appear as contributing to the success of the business until the number of employees reaches between forty-one and fifty.

As with the skills contributing to the success of the business, negotiation skills, employment law and environmental regulations (compliance and risk) show significant scores for the first time (seventy to ninety employees). This could indicate an awareness of the complexity of the external environment and the need for development in skills to manage the issues.

As with the skills that contribute to business success, organisations employing between fifty and one hundred employees show greater consistency in the number of skills requiring development. Skills included are sales techniques; market knowledge/research; cash flow/credit management; managing change; and business planning and performance.

Formal and informal development

As much of the previous research had made reference to informal training being a preferred option within smaller businesses, this research set out to explore the type of developmental activities smaller businesses were undertaking. The research also looked at who took responsibility for management development and whether this affected the type of developmental activity in organisations.

As one would have expected participation in different types of developmental activities increase as the number of employees grow. Table 11.3 details the types of developmental activities the respondent businesses were engaging in, divided between formal and informal. The data analysis revealed differences between companies employing fewer than ten, from ten to fifty and from fifty-one to one hundred, the results are therefore presented broken down in this way.

It is apparent that formal methods of training and development are as popular, and arguably more popular, with organisations employing ten or more, as the informal activities. This contradicts other research findings that place great emphasis on the informality within small organisations. Across all the subgroups more respondents return a nil response for informal training and development than for formal training and development. There are a number of potential reasons for this occurrence. First, it could be attributed to the lack of skills in informal development activities as highlighted by Hendry *et al.* (1991) and Mabey and Thompson (1994).

Table 11.3 Formal and informal training and development activities

Formal	0–9 employees	10–50 employees	51–100 employees
Qualification courses run at universities/colleges	7.8%	24.4%	51.9%
Formal courses run by outside providers	10.0%	52.6%	77.8%
Distance learning courses	1.1%	6.4%	7.4%
NVQs	12.2%	29.5%	40.7%
Formal in-house courses run by outside providers	8.9%	29.5%	63.0%
Formal in-house courses run by company staff	17.8%	39.7%	55.6%
Internet-based courses	2.2%	3.8%	0.0%
None	52.2%	20.5%	0.0%

Informal	0–9 employees	10–50 employees	51–100 employees
Appraisal	12.2%	44.9%	51.9%
Coaching	16.7%	34.6%	55.6%
Promotion on a temporary basis	2.2%	7.7%	14.8%
Informal training seminars/meetings	20.0%	46.2%	74.1%
None	57.8%	28.2%	3.7%

Second, the owner-manager may be too busy to devote time to informal training, but when recognising a development need will utilise a formal approach that is cost-effective in terms of their own time. Third, previous research has highlighted training and development being utilised as a response to a problem (Blackburn and Kitching 1997), therefore, the source of expertise is unlikely to be found in-house

Responsibility for training and development

In those companies employing up to nine employees responsibility for training and development rests largely with the owner-manager, with a high proportion of respondents either not responding or declaring that no one takes responsibility. In over half of respondent organisations with ten to fifty employees, where training and development is still within the remit of the managing director or owner-manager, there is some evidence of line managers or indeed a dedicated professional taking responsibility. In the group fifty-one-to-one hundred employees, the responsibility is no longer largely with the managing director, but a greater proportion have made it the responsibility of a line manager or dedicated personnel manager. At this stage all those who responded had a dedicated person with responsibility for training and development; however, 18.6 per cent did not respond (Table 11.4).

A more detailed analysis of the data revealed some interesting differences as to the type of training and development undertaken. From the sample companies, if a dedicated professional took responsibility for training and development then the percentage of formalised in-house training increases substantially as does the use of promotion on a temporary basis as an informal training tool. When the responsibility is with a line manager their preference is for outside providers either universities/colleges or formal courses by external trainers. They would also appear to be making the greatest use of NVQs.

In-depth interviews

The interviews were conducted during January and February 2000. Participants in the interviews were located from the questionnaire where they indicated their willingness to participate in an in-depth interview. It should be borne in mind that given the difficulty of engaging small businesses in research, those that do participate are likely to be more proactive in the areas being researched.

Table 11.4 Responsibility for training and development

Formal	0–9 employees	10–50 employees	51–100 employees
Managing director	67.8%	53.8%	22.2%
Personnel or training manager	1.1%	7.7%	25.9%
Line manager	2.2%	15.4%	33.3%
No one	12.2%	5.1%	0.0%
Nil response	16.9%	17.9%	18.6%

The analysis revealed five critical factors that appear to account for similarities and differences between the small businesses that participated.

The first, which supports previous research, is that the size of the small business directly influences their training and development needs. It is of no surprise that the organisations employing under ten employees have very different requirements to those organisations employing fifty-one-to-one hundred employees.

Second, whether the organisation was static, in a growth phase or in decline influenced their development needs. There were a number of organisations that were in the invidious position of having to downsize due to the general decline in manufacturing within the United Kingdom, and obviously their priorities at the time of the interview were not with training and development. On the other hand those organisations that were growing held management development as a high priority.

Third, the reason why they were in business. There were a number within the sector employing less than ten employees that were 'working for a lifestyle'. They did not generally work more than forty hours a week and saw their company as providing the finance for them to enjoy their life outside work. They were not, therefore, interested in their organisation growing beyond its current size because of the impact that it would have on their lifestyle. There were some noticeable exceptions, for example one MD had reached retirement age but was still working in an important capacity in the organisation and rarely took holidays.

Fourth, the influence of the owner-manager as to how much importance was assigned to training and development within the organisation. There would appear to be a direct relationship between previous experience of management development and the value and importance attached to it. Those that had worked in a large organisation, prior to setting up their own business, and had therefore experienced management development placed a much higher value on the benefits of it than those who were second or third generation owner-managers and had learnt at their parent's knee. Without exception though, all managers interviewed talked about 'experience on the job' as being far more important than any formal qualification. It also appears that the training and development needs differ between owner-manager and the management teams. The latter requiring development in the generic skills, the owner-manager requiring inputs of specialised knowledge in order to stay abreast of technological, environmental and legal change.

Finally, market position would appear to be critical to attitudes displayed to training and development. Over a third of those interviewed were operating in a niche market, the external influences and resultant pressures and demands were less pressing than for those small businesses operating in a competitive or subcontracting position.

Management skills and techniques

There were a number of key management skills identified from the interviews as being areas that would justify development because of the contribution they made to the successful running of the business. As with the questionnaire results all interviewees saw customer care as being the key skill in a business. The attitude often expressed was that 'the customer is king'. Undoubtedly closely aligned to customer care was the issue of company reputation. The owner-managers saw their reputation to produce the goods that the customer wanted on time as very important and it was often commented that their reputation was more important to them than a large firm, as they would lose business much more easily if it was damaged. Linked to this were communication skills. These were seen as key in maintaining their position with customers. One owner-manager knew that his communication skills were weak and rather than develop them chose to employ a person to manage the customer interface.

Developing marketing and sales skills was an area where training and development were seen as important by owner-managers. As many of the small businesses interviewed were in a specialised niche getting to the right market was, therefore, crucial.

Developing skills in computer technology was also an area in which they were prepared to invest. Most interviewees had experienced technological advancement and realised the importance of staying ahead in technology terms if they were to remain in business. Health and safety, due to statutory requirement, was another priority area worthy of training and development investment.

All the interviewees who had personally established the business they were running talked about having business acumen and common sense to run a small company; none of them used the word entrepreneurial, but it was implied by their description of skills in 'focus', 'vision', 'drive' and 'determination'. The interviewees expressed a view that these skills were inherent rather than learned, and that it is a skill 'you either have or you don't'.

Relevance and importance of qualifications

A number of the managers interviewed had formal qualifications and valued them. Degrees were seen as instrumental in teaching the skills of thinking, application and understanding the bigger picture. Accountancy degrees were seen as potentially very useful. As one interviewee commented, 'You can't run a business by the seat of your pants, you've got to have information from the numbers'. Another commented, 'You need the ability to read a balance sheet and a profit and loss statement'.

Generally business degrees were also seen as useful, but only as a foundation, it was felt that possessing qualifications was no guarantee of being successful in operating a business. Generally there was a feeling of 'working here and gaining experience is the only real way of learning how to run a business'. One owner-manager firmly believed in starting all staff at the bottom, whether qualified or not, as being the only way to give them the knowledge of the business as well as an appreciation of the role of others in contributing to the success of the business.

Those that did not have qualifications were either in awe of formalised management development, or were disparaging about the benefits. However, those owner-managers who had younger family members working with them were very keen that their offspring should acquire relevant qualifications. This was not only to ensure the successful continuance of the business, but as insurance if the firm went out of business.

Sources of support

For those who had been on business start-up courses, their experiences appeared to vary depending on what course they had been on and one assumes on which training organisation ran the course. Some found them excellent, while others felt they were too basic to be of any real use. Regional differences would also appear to have an impact on their usefulness. One company had the benefit of not only an excellent start-up, but regular follow-up programmes (three to six monthly for the first three years, and still attended on an annual basis), the owner attributed the success of his business partially to this programme. This company was based in an area of economic regeneration with heavy government investment.

Some of the interviewees had at times used DTI grants for various courses or to make use of consultants to improve their businesses. However, most were confused as to what was available to them in the way of grants and training. Those who had explored the options were not overly impressed, saying that the paperwork involved in getting any available grants took so long to do that it negated any benefit the grant may have given them.

Professional associations appeared to perform an important function for smaller businesses. The majority of SME owner-managers interviewed said that they were members of at least one professional association. These were used for a variety of functions, often their trade magazines were seen as a very useful source of updating, both in terms of their industry and in terms of what training was available. Training run and in some cases part or fully funded by the association, was much more likely to be attended than was a TEC course. The professional associations often had help-lines which members could call if they had staffing problems, i.e. related to staff contracts, or maternity leave or new employment laws; they could also provide information on other legislation that may have an affect on the business. One of the professional organisations provided updated health and safety manuals, which the small businesses found particularly useful as they worked in a heavy industry. Professional associations were seen by the small businesses as providing a route through the minefield of government legislation and were thought to be on their side. They appeared to be the first port of call for business-related issues or concerns. All participants were paying to be members, but felt the fee was worth the service.

Many of the businesses were members of the Chamber of Commerce, but its value would appear to be limited. They felt that, as many did not sell directly to customers, as for example a high street shoe shop, they did not gain a great deal from membership. However, despite this most organisations continued to be members even if they did not attend meetings at all.

Preference for development delivery, style and content

Undoubtedly time was a major factor in smaller businesses preferences within this area. Evenings were cited as the best time for owner-managers, but for managers the preference was for day or half-day release. There was a marked division based on previous experience between those who would only value management development from a higher education institution, to those who believed industry was far better qualified to deliver appropriate training.

In terms of style and content it would appear that the development would have to be tailored to the small business sector to be really useful. There was a strong preference for short courses weighted towards practical knowledge and tailored to the needs of each specific business. Management development therefore has to be relevant to their needs at the particular time.

Many of the interviewees openly criticised the government's focus on developmental activities that were more appropriate to large organisations. There was a general consensus that the TECs had not served their purpose, only providing useful courses in basic word processing/office skills. In addition, NVQs were not valued in terms of developing managers. Business link advisers received a mixed reaction and their value would appear to be dependent on the individual adviser. Similarly, private consultants received a mixed reaction; some of the interviewees had a negative experience in which they felt they had been 'ripped off'. Others had a positive experience and although it was relatively expensive, because it was specific to their needs, it was efficient with their time. This, therefore, negated the higher cost. Without a doubt the preference was for someone to 'show them how to do it'.

As already stated experience on the job was felt to be much more important than any formal development programme, and the majority of smaller businesses interviewed talked about on-the-job training. When probed on the type of on-the-job development they were undertaking, it was learning by doing ('sitting by Nellie'). One of the participants, whose business was the youngest in the sample and was still in a growth phase, regularly utilised job rotation, as he commented, 'job movement is probably one of the most under utilised training techniques in SMEs'. However, this company was the exception and informal development seemed, in the main, to be synonymous with unstructured activities, and a 'catch as catch can' philosophy.

Informal networks as a means to share information and experience did not prove to be popular idea with this sample. The consensus was that although it would be good to mix with other small businesses there would be a real concern over confidentiality, particularly in terms of competitors.

Discussion and conclusions

The research has provided a further insight into the management training and development needs of manufacturing small businesses, and has further highlighted the complexity of the variables that influence participation in management development. It has attempted to ascertain smaller businesses perceptions of the management skills and techniques that contribute to the success of their business, and the skills and techniques they feel would benefit from development. There is no claim to the research having produced definitive answers, indeed, as with all research one of the key results is the identification of further research and this only becomes apparent once the research is either well underway or completed.

The significance of size

This study as with previous research has demonstrated the heterogeneity and the disparate needs of the small business sector. A number of key skills and techniques have been identified which were important to all smaller businesses regardless of number of employees. Skills contributing to business success were in the areas of sales, customer care, quality management and cash flow/credit management. Only skills in customer care, however, had a development need for all businesses regardless of size. It was also noted that there is much more consistency in terms of the skills required for business success and as having a development need in those organisations employing from fifty-one-to-one hundred.

It is apparent from the research that the skills that are key to the success of the business emerge over time. Not only over time, but at specific points in the growth of the small business as determined by number of employees. It would appear the successful mastery of specific skills at a time when they can leverage the business development maybe a crucial factor in survival or continued growth. Furthermore, it is also apparent that the skills are interdependent and tend to represent an aspect of business management that can be disaggregated into functionally related skills.

Those skills and techniques that contribute to the business success, for a company employing up to twenty employees, are concerned with the immediate day-to-day running of the business. Between twenty-one and thirty employees it has been possible to identify that those skills in utilising business systems become a priority. For organisations employing between forty-one and fifty employees, people management skills become important. Finally, between seventy and ninety employees another possible leverage point has been established with skills concerned with operating in an external environment. Further research is needed to either confirm the leverage points or/and identify further leverage points This is particularly important in order to identify areas that are perceived by the sector to be important, rather than areas dictated by providers.

While not as many skills and techniques were identified as having a development need and most mirrored the skills identified as contributing to business success within the same subgroups, an interesting difference was observed. Skills and techniques in people management are significant in requiring development at between twenty-one and thirty employees, whereas for business success the leverage point does not occur until between forty-one and fifty employees. This would appear to be the result of the increasing numbers of employees within the companies, necessitates skills in dealing with them, before owner-managers recognise their significance to the business.

The significance of mismatched perceptions

Expressed throughout the literature, and in the in-depth interviews with owner-managers conducted as part of this research, the terms 'timely' and 'relevant' are used repeatedly as the key factors in decisions to invest in training and development.

The difficulty appears to be a mismatch of perceptions as to what constitutes 'timely' and 'relevant' between owner-managers and providers. The owners find difficulty in articulating their exact requirements while the providers tend to have preconceived ideas of the needs of small businesses based on a narrow definition of the sector, which does not fully appreciate the extent of its diversity. Further evidence of specific needs at key leverage points may help to bridge these perceptual gaps. Any future research in this area would have to recognise the differing time frames in growth. Some companies will grow at a steady rate, while for others the transitions can happen within months.

A wider issue is the redundancy of the existing construct of management development for small businesses. The term as it is used today has largely been developed to cover holistic interventions in management development activity within large organisations. Although this research could no more than highlight this issue, it is a real and urgent area for further research. Until we fully understand how the small business owner-managers view their own development needs much of the provision that is on offer will continue to lack relevance and be offered at times inappropriate to the small business needs.

A further factor in this mismatch of perceptions could be the way in which language is used in both research and provider communication with small businesses. Particularly as the small business sector is notoriously difficult to research, due to the time constraints of owner-managers. The use of large organisation language and the language of academics is not commonplace within small businesses and can result in at best limited rapport, and at worst total lack of interest. One of the benefits of breaking down management activity into the component tools and techniques was that it enabled the owner-managers to more easily recognise and articulate what was important to them. This is yet another area that would benefit from further research.

The significance of informal training

The results of this research appear to contradict much of the existing literature on the significance of informal training in small businesses. For example there were a number of companies who showed a preference for formal methods of training but undertook no informal training. This directly contradicts research by Blackburn and Hankinson (1989) and Johnson and Gubbins (1992) who argue that informal training takes a priority over formal development methods in smaller businesses. This could be a result of lack of skills in informal training, or that formal development is more time efficient for the owner-manager, because it is provided by an external organisation or that it is a response to a crisis situation for which there is no available in-house expertise. What is of paramount importance is that informal training is essential for the transfer of business knowledge and understanding. The owner-manager will undoubtedly have the most understanding of the business, this accumulated knowledge and learned experience needs to be effectively transferred to other managers within the organisation. If owner-managers do not possess skills for disseminating and transferring this tacit knowledge, this could result in limiting growth or indeed demise of the business.

Previous research in this area tends to assume that informal training is solely learning by doing. This research has attempted to disaggregate informal training into specific activities associated with development of this nature. This in itself may be an explanation, for this research might be guilty of using the language of large organisations. Alternatively, it may be that it raised awareness of the range of informal training techniques available, many of which the small businesses were not using. Further research would be beneficial in this area.

The significance of government

The government sees small businesses as playing a very important part in the UK economy, and has invested a lot of money in attempting to overcome the barriers to management training and development in the SME sector in order to enhance their contribution to the economy. The main focus of the government measures has been to attempt to draw the SME sector into the mainstream management training and development provision, by breaking down the perceived barriers to their participation.

As this study and previous research has shown, however, this approach has not proved to be a success with the small business sector. This research may offer some insight into the reasons for the lack of success. The small businesses requirement for relevant inputs at the time they are required does not sit easily with a measured and programmed approach to delivery. If some generic development needs based on organisation size can be established, the providers of management development will be in a better position to address the needs of the small business sector at the relevant time and furthermore target small business at the appropriate moment. Thus, there may be an increased likelihood of achieving the engagement in management development, which is sought by government.

Learning points

- The importance of the small business sector to the economy is well recognised. Equally well recognised is the volatility of the sector in the sense that many smaller businesses are transient, short lived and uncompetitive. One of the key factors attributed to smaller businesses demise or failure to grow is the lack of managerial skills as opposed to the technical skills associated with the nature of the product being produced.
- A number of barriers from previous research have been identified as constraining smaller business participation in management development and are as follows: a lack of quantifiable evidence that shows a link between development and profitability; the time and cost to the organisation; a worry that trained and developed staff will be poached; training and development is often considered a luxury only to be utilised if it solves a problem; it can also be perceived as punishment for poor performance by the employee and finally there is evidence of resistance by family run firms to outside intervention. The importance of the owner-manager's previous experience of management development was also noted as being instrumental in their attitude towards development.

- There would appear to be a direct relationship between growth/size and increasing formalisation in training and development methods. Previous research has identified that training and development only becomes strategically critical to organisational development, once there are several layers of management below the owner-manager.
- This research has demonstrated, again, the homogeneity of the small business sector. Differences based on company size (number of employees) were found to affect the management development needs of the sector. The management skills and techniques were mapped in terms of importance for both contributing to the success of the business and as having a development need. Some skills and techniques were found to be important regardless of company size, but others became important at a particular point in a company's growth. Thus, potential key leverage points for specific inputs of management development emerged from this study.
- While previous research has noted the preference from the sector for informal development as opposed to formal development. This research found that companies were more likely to participate in formal development rather than informal. This could be a result of disaggregating informal development into specific activities. It would appear that informal development is largely learning by doing within the sector, and it is not, therefore, structured.
- This and previous research also established a level of general dissatisfaction with the overall training and development provision available to the small business sector, and particularly the government provision. There is a real need to establish how small business owners view their own development needs, particularly as management development is a holistic intervention developed within large organisations.
- It would appear that management development is largely led by supply, rather than demand. The terms 'timely' and 'relevant' are key to understanding why current provision has not serviced the needs of the small business sector. The small businesses requirement for relevant inputs at the time they are required does not sit easily with a measured and programmed approach to delivery. If some generic development needs based on organisation size can be established, the providers of management development will be in a better position to address the needs of the small business sector at the relevant time and furthermore target small business at the appropriate moment.

Bibliography

Banfield, P., Jennings, P. and Beaver, G. (1996) 'Competence based training for small firms: an expensive failure?', *Long Range Planning*, 29, 1: 94- 102.

Barnett, E. and Storey, J. (2000) 'Manager's accounts of innovation processes in small and medium-sized enterprises', *Journal of Small Business and Enterprise Development*, 7, 4: 315- 24.

Berryman, J. (1983) 'Small business failure and bankruptcy: a survey of the literature', *International Small Business Journal*, 11, 4: 47- 59.

Birley, S. and Westhead, P. (1990) 'Growth and performance contrasts between "types" of small firms', *Strategic Management Journal*, 11: 535- 57.

Blackburn, R. and Hankinson, A. (1989) 'Training in the smaller business: investment or expense?', *Industrial and Commercial Training*, 21, 2: 27- 9.

Blackburn, R. and Kitching, J. (1997) 'Management training for SMEs: a comparative study of three European regions', ISBA 20 National Small Firms Policy and Research Conference, Belfast.

Bolton, J. (1971) *Report of the Committee of Inquiry on Small Firms*, London: HMSO.

Childe, S., Nelder, G. and Willcock, J. (2000) 'The impact of research on manufacturing SMEs', *Industry and Higher Education*, 14, 4: 75- 90.

Choeuke, K. and Armstrong, B. (1998) 'The learning organisation in small and medium-sized enterprises: a destination or a journey?', *International Journal of Entrepreneurial Behaviour and Research*, 4, 2: 129- 41.

Connor, J. and Haydock, W. (1997) 'Management development in the small firm: do competence based approaches work?', *Enterprise and Growth in the Small Business Sector Collection of Papers by Bolton Business School*, Bolton.

Constable, J. and McCormick, R. (1987) *The Making of British Managers*, London: BIM/CBI.

Cushion, N. (1995) 'Measuring the success of small management business training', paper presented at 18 ISBA National Conference, University of Paisley.

Cushion, N. (1996) 'Evaluation of management development in the small business sector', ISBA National Small Firms Policy and Research Conference UCE, Business School, Birmingham.

Deakins, D. (1999) *Entrepreneurship and Small Firms*, Maidenhead: McGraw-Hill.

Deakins, D. and Freel, M. (1998) 'Entrepreneurial learning and the growth process in SMEs', *The Learning Organisation*, 5, 3: 144- 55.

Department of Trade and Industry and Department for Education and Skills (DTI and DES) (2001) *Opportunity for All in a World of Change*, White Paper, London: The Stationery Office.

Easterby-Smith, M., Thorpe, R. and Lowe, A. (1991) *Management Research: An introduction*, London: Sage.

Engineering and Marine Training Authority (EMTA) (1998) *Labour Market Survey of the Engineering Industry in Britain, 1998*, Report RR112A, http://www.emta.org.uk/semta.nsf/WebResearch

Gibb, A. (1997) 'Small firms' training and competitiveness: building upon the small business as a learning organisation', *International Small Business Journal*, 15, 3: 13- 30.

Goss, D. and Jones, R. (1997) 'Organisation structure and SME training provision', *International Small Business Journal*, 10, 4: 13- 25.

Handy, C. (1987) *The Making of Managers*, London: MSC/NEDO/BIM.

Hankinson, A., Bartlett, D. and Ducheneaut, B. (1997) 'The key factors in the small profiles of small- medium enterprise owner-managers that influence business performance: the UK (Rennes) SME survey 1995- 9', *International Journal of Entrepreneurial Behaviour and Research*, 3, 4: 168- 75.

Hannon, P. (1999) 'A summary of the literature on the way that management development processes in growth SMEs leads to demand, small firms enterprise development', *Small Firms Training Impact Assessment, Phase 1*, Leicester: Small Firms Enterprise Development Initiative and the Centre for Enterprise.

Hendry, C., Jones, A., Arthur, M. and Pettigrew, A. (1991) *Human Resource Development in Small to Medium Sized Enterprises*, Employment Department, Research Paper 88, Sheffield: Employment Department.

Hill, R. and Stewart J. (2000) 'Human resource development and small organisations', *Journal of European Industrial Training*, 24, 2: 105- 17.

Johnson, S. (1999) *Skills Issues in Small and Medium Sized Enterprises*, Skills Task Force Research Paper 13, Nottingham: DfEE.

Johnson, S. and Gubbins, A. (1992) 'Training in small and medium-sized enterprises: lessons from North Yorkshire', in K. Caley, E. Shell, F. Chittenden and C. Mason (eds) *Small Enterprise Development Policy and Practice*, London: Paul Chapman.

Kerr, A. and McDougall, M. (1999) 'The small business of developing people', *International Small Business Journal*, 17, 2: 65- 74.

Lange, T., Ottens, M. and Taylor, A. (2000) 'SMEs and barriers to skills development: a Scottish perspective', *Journal of European Industrial Training*, 24, 1: 5- 11.

Loan-Clarke, J., Boocock, G., Smith A. and Whittaker, J. (1999) 'Investment in management training and development by small businesses', *Employee Relations*, 21, 3: 296- 310.

Mabey, C. and Thompson, R. (1994) *Developing Human Resources*, Oxford: Butterworth-Heinemann in association with Institute of Management.

Marlow, S. (1997) 'So much opportunity - so little take up: the use of training in small firms', *Journal of Small Business and Enterprise Development*, 5, 1: 38- 48.

Marshall, J., Alderman, N., Wong, C. and Thwaites, A. (1993) 'The impact of government assisted management training and development on small and medium-sized enterprises in Britain', *Environment and Planning*, C 11: 331- 48.

Marshall, J., Alderman, N., Wong, C. and Thwaites, A. (1995) 'The impact of management training and development on SMEs', *International Small Business Journal*, 13, 4: 73- 90.

Matlay, H. (1996) 'Paradox resolved? Owner-manager attitudes to, and actual provision of, training in the small business sector of the British economy', paper given at 19th ISBA National Small Firms Policy and Research Conference, UCE Business School, Birmingham, November.

Matlay, H. and Hyland, T. (1997) 'NVQs in the small business sector: a critical overview', *Education and Training*, 39, 9: 325- 32.

Molander, C. (1986) *Management Development*, Bromley: Chartwell-Bratt.

Penn, W., Forster, R., Heydon, G. and Richardson, S. (1998) 'Learning in smaller organisations', *The Learning Organisation*, 5, 3: 128- 37.

Quayle, M. (1994) 'Management development in East Anglia', *Management Development Review*, 7, 4: 34- 40.

Ritchie, J. and Spencer, L. (1994) 'Qualitative data analysis for applied policy research', in A. Bryman and R. Burgess (eds) *Analysing Qualitative Data*, London: Routledge.

Sadler-Smith, E., Sargeant, A. and Dawson, A. (1998) 'Higher level skills training and SMEs', *International Small Business Journal*, 16, 2: 84- 95.

Smallbone, D., North, D. and Leigh, R. (1992) 'Managing change for growth and survival: the study of mature manufacturing firms in London during the 1980s', Working Paper 3, Planning Research Centre, Middlesex Polytechnic.

Smith, A., Whittaker, J., Clark, J. and Boocock, G. (1999) 'Competence based management development provision to SMEs and the providers' perspective', *Journal of Management Development*, 18, 6: 557- 72.

Stanworth, J. and Curran, J. (1971) *Management Motivation in the Smaller Business*, Aldershot: Gower.

Stanworth, J. and Gray, C. (1991) *Bolton 20 Years on: The small firm in the 1990s*, London: Paul Chapman.

Stewart, J. (1999) *The Reality of Management*, 3rd edn, Oxford: Butterworth-Heinemann.

Storey, D. (1999) *Changing the Agenda for Training in Small Firms*, OECD study reported to briefing organised by Centre for SMEs, University of Warwick Business School, in London.

Storey, D. and Westhead, P. (1997) 'Management training in small firms: a case of market failure?', *Human Resource Management Journal*, 7, 2: 61- 71.

Temple, H. (1995) 'Cost effectiveness of open learning for small firms: a study of first experiences of open learning', *DfEE Research Brief*, October.

Turner, R. (1997) 'Management accounting and SMEs: a question of style?', *Management Accounting*, 75, 7: 24- 5.

Vickerstaff, S. (1992) 'The training needs of small firms', *Human Resource Management Journal*, 2, 3: 1- 15.

Vinten, G. (2000) 'Training in small and medium sized enterprises, *Industrial and Commercial Training*, 32, 1: 9- 14.

Welch, B. (1996*) Developing Managers for the Smaller Business*, London: Institute of Management.

Westhead, P. and Storey, D. (1996) 'Management training and small firm performance: why is the link so weak?', *International Small Business Journal*, 14, 4: 13- 24.

Westhead, P. and Storey, D. (1997) *Training Provision and the Development of Small and Medium Sized Enterprises*, DfEE Research Report 26, London: DfEE.

Wong, C., Neil, J., Marshal, N., Alderman, N. and Thwaites, A. (1997) 'Management training in small and medium sized enterprises: methodological and conceptual issues', *International Journal of Human Resource Management*, 8, 1: 44- 65.

12 The value of HRD in small owner-managed organisations

The role of external coaching

David Devins and Jeff Gold

Objectives

It would seem that, for a range of different reasons, it remains problematic for external agencies and individuals to bring HRD interventions to small organisations and such difficulties continue to cause concern (Raper *et al.* 1997; Department of Trade and Industry (DTI/DfEE 2001). In spite of rhetorical recognition of the heterogeneity of small organisations, a substantial part of the difficulty relates to the important issue of how the world of a small organisation is constructed and comes to be valued. In particular, we would highlight the significant connection of the development and ongoing existence of small organisations and the identity of the owner-managers. In many respects, such managers view positively and value highly those activities that have brought them to their present position (Devins and Gold 2002). They also provide an indexical reference point of how learning has occurred and how external initiatives will be viewed. For example, many small organisations are unlikely to view positively HRD interventions which are based on generic and abstracted frameworks of how small organisations ought to learn and operate.

The aim of this chapter is to explore the extent to which coaching as an HRD activity can provide the means for working with the values and interests of small organisations. After providing an outline of why there are difficulties in bringing HRD interventions to small organisations, we shall explain the potential contribution of coaching. In particular, we outline a new view of the coaching process based on Mikhail Bakhtin's dialogism (Holquist 1990) and Lev Vygotsky's sociocultural theory of human development (Wells 1999). We then draw on primary research to explore the coaching process and assess the impact of such a process on the performance of small business managers and others. We argue that a coach as an outsider (Pawsey 2000) can gain a unique understanding of the culture of a small organisation and the way that an organisation works and learns. Further, through careful attention to values and interests, conversational space, a necessary precursor for HRD activity, can be made.

Description and analysis of theoretical context

HRD in small organisations

Despite many years of research in the small business domain following the publication of the Bolton Report (1971), uncovering the value of HRD activity in the small business context remains full of uncertainties. Various research approaches have explored the contribution to economic, organisational or the personal development of managers (e.g. Westhead and Storey 1996; Marshall *et al.* 1995; Winterton and Winterton 1997; Cosh *et al.* 1998). While the evidence of impact is variable, there are some who doubt whether a definitive answer could ever be found to the question of payback on HRD activity (Gibb 1997).

Where there is some degree of agreement is that exploring the practice and impact of HRD in the small business context is far from simple given the heterogentity of small business enterprises and their owner-managers. In spite of the relative simplicity (in organisational terms) of the smaller organisation multiple drivers of HR activity have been identified (Hendry *et al.* 1991). In common with the findings from more recent research (e.g. Vickerstaff and Parker 1995; Johnson and Gubins 1993; Curran *et al.* 1997), HRD practices in the small organisation are revealed as largely unplanned and reactive, accompanied by informal/on-the-job training activity and led by someone other than a HRD officer or expert.

This generalised view of HRD in the small business context is often accompanied by a desire by outsiders such as policy-makers and consultants to systematise and formalise in an attempt to encourage or 'improve' HRD activity. However, these approaches to encouraging HRD in small organisations often fail to relate to the interests of the managers' of these enterprises. One reason for this is that the underlying principles fail to connect with the existing small business operating environment (Down 1999; Hill and Stewart 1999; Ram 2000). Further exploration of the small business learning environment goes some way to explaining why decontextualised concepts often fail to connect with the world of the small business manager.

In most cases, small organisation learning occurs naturally in a non-contrived manner as part of an everyday process (Stuart 1984) that moves the organisation in a direction that meets the desires of the small business owner-manager and others such as his/her family. Such learning has to be work-related focusing on the problems and solutions faced by the organisation and, very often, related to its survival. As noted by Gibb (1996), 'Owner-managers learn about the process of developing their business by solving problems and grasping opportunities.' Such learning, by necessity, also draws on the help and assistance of a host of others including family and friends, and professional help such as bankers, solicitors and accountants which forms the 'network-interdependency' of a small organisation (Gibb 1997). For some years support agencies in both the United Kingdom and elsewhere have been actively promoting the concept of business networks as a mechanism through which to enhance the development of small organisations. It is argued that the network provides the small business learning environment that continually creates subjective contextual knowledge which is used by the business manager in furtherance of his/ her aims (Hendry *et al.* 1995; Hannon 1998).

The important features of such learning are that while it is often very meaningful and directly relevant to work issues, it is not recognised explicitly as learning and occurs in an ad hoc or random manner. Mumford (1987) suggested that such learning while direct and focused on work can also be accidental and unstructured. It may result in unreflective and uncritical learning which fails to move the organisation forward or keeps the organisation at a certain stage of development without the means to take it further. We therefore see many small organisations stuck in a cycle of adaptive learning rather than the generative learning (Senge 1990) necessary to meet the aspirations of policy-makers in terms of competitiveness and lifelong learning. Given the resistance to more formal training and development activity which involves time away from work and financial costs, Mumford (1987) suggested that an approach to development which occurs within work activities and has an explicit focus on learning would be more substantial. The positive aspects of interventions based on approaches such as mentoring (Deakins *et al.* 1999) and non-executive directorships (Berry and Perren 1999) are being recognised and we argue that coaching can play a significant part in a process to encourage change in smaller organisations.

Coaching

Like many other notions metaphorically transferred from other fields, coaching has been subject to a great deal of confusion and some would say mystery (Carter 2001). Originally a development within the sporting field aimed at improving performance (Evered and Selman 1989), coaching emerged during the 1970s and 1980s as a suggested management activity to enhance the development of employees with particular emphasis on the transfer of learning from formal training courses into workplace activity (Singer 1974; Megginson and Boydell 1979). It was part of a general movement to make managers more responsible for the development of their staff and retreat from the command and control ethos of managerial work. By the end of the 1980s and into the 1990s, coaching had become incorporated into various calls to change the way managers related to their staff, e.g. the Learning Company (Pedler *et al.* 1991), empowerment in organisations (Clutterbuck 1994) and human resource management (Bratton and Gold 1999). Coaching has now become one of a range of activities within organisations concerned with helping both managers and staff, such as mentoring and counselling, although the particular focus of attention in coaching is performance improvement combined with development (Megginson and Pedler 1992). However, even if the meaning of coaching is confined to performance, the apparent narrowness of this focus cannot prevent the consideration of a wide range of contextual factors which influence performance. One of the contextual factors is, of course, that a manager is accountable for the performance of staff and this has always created something of quandary for the manager *as* coach. Thus there is always the potential for recoil into stereotyped managerial behaviour (Phillips

1995). Additionally, coaching can become devalued when it is seen to be connected to, or becomes confused with, performance assessment as part of an organisation's performance management process.

In contrast, one feature of external coaching in small organisations is that a coach, as an outsider, does not have managerial responsibility for the performance of those that are being coached or helped. Further, the small organisation coach is unlikely to be able to influence any of the factors affecting the performance of the people they coach. Nor will a coach have any responsibility for assessing performance for any purpose other than as a feedback variable as part of the relationship between coach and small business manager. Small organisation coaching has some connection to what has been referred to as executive coaching (Hall *et al.* 1999). This is coaching for managers, usually working at more senior levels in organisations, often carried out by external consultants. In the United Kingdom, Carter (2001) suggests that executive coaching has arisen through the failure of more traditional sources of management development to provide feedback for senior managers who often have to operate in lonely and isolated contexts.

In some respects, this feeling of isolation is reflected in the situation of owner-managers in small organisations (Bolton 1971; Curran and Blackburn 1994). However, we would suggest that a distinguishing feature of the performance of the small organisation manager or the management team is the tight connection to the performance of the business as a whole. There are few (if any) layers of middle management lying between the owner-manager and the customer or production process. Therefore coaching in a small organisation is inevitably business coaching and considers within its remit the development of business and related issues that affect the business. Thus a coach, while not expected to be expert in all areas of business, would need to become something of a *bricoleur* in relation to small business issues (Alstrup 2000) and, most importantly, how to intervene in a non-contrived manner (Temporal 1978). Coaches in small organisations need to be tuned into the interests and desires of the small business managers.

Given the uniqueness of the small organisation, based on the values and interests of the key players, we define coaching as 'a helping process to enable small organisation managers to deal with their concerns relating to business performance'.

It is recognised that such a definition lacks the precision that is normally associated with the concept of coaching and could easily include related activities such as mentoring or even counselling. However, as we shall suggest, in small organisations there is less concern with precise meaning of terms and more concern with the way a helping relationship works with the desires and interests of the parties involved to produce actions that enable concerns to be met or dissolved.

The popularity of the coaching concept within organisations has led to the production of various models of generic skills. Salisbury (1994), for example, highlights the importance of listening, observation and non-verbal, questioning and counselling skills. Phillips (1995) suggests that awareness of personal values is significant in taking a coach beyond a mechanistic adherence to a skills checklist and flexibility in having various options rather than single solutions. Apart from generic models, larger organisations may define coaching models in terms of specified competencies. One difficulty with generic models is the inevitable abstraction with too much attention given to the skills, competencies or attributes of the coach at the expense of the making of a productive coaching relationship. There is also an implication that the coaching skills can be learnt in a mechanistic and didactic manner (Redshaw 2000). Our own preference, with respect to the peculiarities of small business organisations, is to give more prominence to the construction of a coaching relationship and its liminal and emergent features. To explicate this, we draw on various dialogic resources included in the work of Mikhail Bakhtin and Lev Vygotsky.

Coaching dialogics

In order to instigate a coaching relationship the owner-manager needs to be attracted into a conversation. As an outsider, a coach attempts to attract a manager into such a conversation with an utterance, which Bakhtin (1986) refers to as the 'real unit of speech communication'. In making an utterance, a coach will need to consider the interests and concerns of the manager to whom it is directed. However, responsive actions are never entirely predictable and the meanings that make an ongoing relationship will rely on the extent to which the coach can become attuned to the agenda and interests of the manager (Rommetveit 1990). Failure to construct conversations between the coach and the owner-manager will also fail in the short term at least, to result in the formation of a coaching relationship.

The importance of initiating and sustaining relationships with small businesses has been noted elsewhere (Lean *et al.* 1999). Indeed Bennett *et al.* (1999) suggest that those agencies which have sought to develop the most intense relations with their small business clients generally also have the highest number of respondents with a contract relationship and are able to develop the greatest fee potential. The research indicates the higher the intensity of the relationship the higher the level of satisfaction and business impact. If the relationship can be initiated, learning and development can be advanced by the coach engaging with the concerns and everyday issues of the small organisation manager and any others involved (Alstrup 2000).

It is here that Vygotsky's sociocultural theory of learning can be utilised (Vygotsky 1978). Vygotsky proposed that learning was a product of social interactions which then becomes internalised within individuals. For such learning to occur within coaching, the coach needs to assess the manager's current level of functioning and the current upper limits of functioning. Vygotsky referred to this as the Zone of Proximal Development (ZPD) which he defined as

> the distance between the actual developmental level as determined by the independent problem solving and level of potential development as determined through problem solving under adult guidance or in collaboration with more capable peers.
>
> (Vygotsky 1978: 86)

Thus through the support or 'scaffolding' (Wood *et al.* 1976) of the coach within the manager's ZPD, problems can be attempted and completed by the manager at a level beyond which he/she would be incapable alone. In this way, through a series of successful completions and quick-wins, the relationship can be advanced.

At the heart of progression are the dialogic utterances and responses of the coach and manager. One feature of such conversations within coaching is the provision of evaluative comments on the completion of tasks and learning achieved. Evered and Selman (1989) suggest that it is part of the coach's job to identify 'blind spots' so that performance can be enhanced 'beyond prior limits'. However, this has to be completed sensitively as, for small business managers, such comments also carry the potential for negative or defensive responses caused by the apparent attack on a valued identity. We have already acknowledged the identity of small organisation managers, especially owner-managers, as a significant influence on the choice of HRD interventions. For example, Gold *et al.* (1996) showed how the identities of managers in small organisations distort their responses to graduate learning projects designed to transfer new knowledge and understanding. The notion of a strong owner-manager who has built up his/her business and knows what is best can also be seen a reflection of essentialist ideas of identity based on the ideal of a self-contained individual. However, an alternative and dialogical view of identity can be employed in which owner-managers experience and define themselves through relationships with others, such as customers, suppliers, family, friends and external advisers such as a coach. Such outsiders have what Bakhtin referred to as a 'surplus of seeing' (Holquist 1990) in relation to the manager which he/she can make meaningful in a further but unfinalised definition of self. This is not to say that certain views of self cannot be preferred and/or protected by managers. However, through the dialogic relations within the manager's ZPD, managers can extend their views of self and reach new definitions of identity which can be enacted in the small business context.

These views of small organisation coaching will now be utilised to interpret a three year initiative which took place from 1997 to 2000. Details of the initiative and the evaluation of its impact now follow.

Description and analysis of research context

Developing management skills

The initiative was a development by a Training and Enterprise Council in the north of England to encourage HRD activity in small organisations. The Developing Management Skills (DMS) Programme sought to resource a coach to work with a limited number of local small organisations in order to enhance their management capability overall as well as developing the skills of individual managers and their workforce. The overall aim of DMS was 'to increase TEC penetration of the small organisation market regarding management development'.

The programme was a multifaceted intervention based primarily on the services provided by a coach but could also include structured courses and training events. The approach focused on the coach tuning into the issues which were important to small organisation managers and using them as a means to develop individual skills and organisational capability. The coach had the flexibility to work with individuals (owner-managers, directors, key staff) and teams (management teams, production teams and administrative teams) within small organisations and was not tied to one approach or a bundle of discrete HR practices. Three Business Coaches (BCs) were externally recruited to deliver the programme. One of BCs was involved in the programme at the design phase (September 1997) and had a training agency background before trading as a management development consultant. The second began in April 1998 and was previously a personal business adviser with a Business Link. The third joined the programme in June 1998 and was also a private consultant who had previously worked on TEC-funded programmes.

The programme was targeted at thirty-five local businesses. The participating companies employed between six and fifty-six employees and were drawn predominantly from the traditionally strong, although declining, engineering sector. The main characteristic of the target organisations was the uniqueness of the way their managers valued the businesses they had created and developed.

Finding the value of coaching

As indicated above, a dialogic view of coaching places emphasis on the ongoing relationship between coach and small organisation manager, formed and sustained by successive chains of utterance and response. Within conversations, each speaker adopts a particular position. In such a process, words are not used neutrally; according to Bakhtin (1986), 'at the point of contact between the word and actual reality', words are an 'expression of some evaluative position'. It is the immediacy of such communication and the sense made that provides the meanings and values of the relationship (Gardiner 2000). However, as researchers, we could not participate in such conversations. Therefore, we required a variety of methods to capture meanings and values.

A longitudinal case study approach was used based on organisations working closely with their BC (Glatthorn 1985). It drew on a multiple case design to investigate individual cases and to draw together emerging themes across individual cases (Yin 1989). Yin suggests that a multiple case approach provides more compelling evidence than a single case study and as such provides a more robust evaluation study. Each case study was embedded within individual units of analysis investigating the organisation and the manager within the organisation. The strength of this approach is that the impact of the intervention on the individual manager is combined with an added focus on contextualisation within the larger framework of the case study organisation. At the cross-case level of analysis the research used an approach based on approximate replication design (Garaway 1996). Face-to-face interviews with key personnel at twenty-five participating small organisations were undertaken to determine initial interests and baselines. Subsequent interviews were carried out at least twice annually over three years, both during and after the intervention process. This enabled an assessment to be made of the value of the process based on expectations prior to the intervention and its experiences during and after intervention. Where possible, information from managers was checked with other members of the small organisation and with the views of the BC to ensure the qualitative data were robust.

The next section reveals some of the research findings. First, we examine some of the broad themes that emerged over the three year operation of the programme. We will then use two case studies to explore the coaching process and its outcomes.

Analysis and evaluation of main findings

Initial stages

In the initial stages of the programme, BCs sought to establish relationships with small organisations. We identified three approaches which characterised the way BCs tuned into the specific requirements of small organisation managers:

- A 'visioning' process generally involving the management team in the development of a vision for the company and the development of an action plan detailing projects to help achieve the vision.
- A 'problem-centred' process which was based on the identification, and subsequent tackling of key issues of concern to the manager or management team.
- A 'sounding board' process which was based on relatively unstructured discussion of issues of concern to the manager of the small organisation.

In each approach, the BC generally adopted an inclusive stance that drew other members of the small organisation into the coaching process. The three general approaches were not mutually exclusive and the BC adopted a particular approach at a given point in time dependent upon the interests, needs or preferences of the client. It became clear that that no one approach was right or wrong and that there were a variety of factors emanating from the responses of small organisation managers which led the BCs to adopt different approaches at different times.

The visioning approach involved the manager and the management team in a collective development process. The BC facilitated the management team to determine what was needed to move from the present position to that outlined in a 'vision' and to construct an action plan with milestones and responsibilities to enable this to happen. A typical summary of the outcome of this approach was provided by one manager who noted

> we now have a list of goals (e.g. increased turnover and profit) and a set of actions to help to meet the goals . . . . for example we need to increase the number of enquiries, reduce costs and identify new product opportunities . . . we are all thinking about what we need to do to achieve these goals and taking ideas forward.
>
> (Manager, equipment installation and servicing company,
> employing 16 people)

The problem-centred approach involved the BC facilitating the identification of key issues or business priorities, analysis (largely through discussion) and the drawing up of lists of issues, problems or opportunities. After facilitation of the identification of priorities, the BC could provide further inputs (e.g. analysis, alternative models, knowledge) specifically focused to help the small organisation address the problems that had been identified. In some instances the BCs became involved in specific activities and offered hands-on support for specific issues as opposed to teasing solutions out of the managers themselves. The problem centred approach was often the focus for specific activity and the BC and managers directed their resources into specific areas. For example, managers were able to point to tangible outcomes:

- 'We have a new incentive system.'
- 'I have had personal coaching.'
- 'I have talked with Telerise [a local consultancy] about the development of a local network.'
- 'We have a system to plan production.'

The sounding board approach became apparent as greater understanding of the DMS process emerged through implementation of the programme. The sounding board activity was an unstructured approach which was largely dependent upon the manager having an agenda he or she wished to pursue with the BC. In response the BC drew on his experience and knowledge to provide his view of the 'problems or opportunities' raised by the manager. The BCs reported the implications of this approach, suggesting that the sessions 'meandered' and could have been 'unproductive' in the sense that the outcomes were neither tangible nor measurable. However the managers often suggested that they 'felt right' and were 'useful' but struggled to identify specific benefits though they remained committed to the DMS process. The following comments were gathered after six months of work with the BC:

> It is useful to have someone who is not involved in the business to bounce ideas off . . . he puts a point of view across that is different . . . it gets you to analyse things in a different manner . . . tends to be well meaning and constructive not critical.
>
> (Managing director, engineering services company, employing 25)

> It is the only time I get to talk to someone about the developments in the business . . . the coach is able to draw on a range of experiences . . . he comes up with some good ideas . . . I don't agree with everything he says but a lot of it makes a lot of sense.
>
> (Owner-manager, engineering fabrication and assembly, employing 15)

Learning-centred approach

In most cases the development of the relationship formed the cornerstone of subsequent development activity. Managers and the BCs suggested that there was a greater emphasis on the encouragement of a 'learning-centred approach' in the second and third years of DMS. Comments from managers in case study companies provide an insight into the process:

> The coach never tells us . . . he always says have you thought about not I think you should do.
>
> > (Co-owner, jewellery manufacturer and retailer, employing 19)

> The BC has given me an appreciation of what needs to be done and what I am able to do. He has helped me focus on what I need to address meetings, delegation, leadership, planning . . . . helped me to set goals . . . .. I still have problems making the time to do these things as just so much is happening . . . the BC is encouraging me to take a strategic look at the company . . . it has taken some time to recognise that change is an ongoing process and to realise that it is not a one-time event.
>
> > (Co-owner-manager, computer software company, employing 45)

A wide range of HRD activities were undertaken including the development of technical and business activity (e.g. marketing, development of IT systems, information analysis, change associated with production processes, development of financial systems and analysis and administration and ISO 9000) as well as generic management skills such as planning and co-ordinating staff. These activities resulted in changes which were unique to each small organisation. The value gained became apparent in a variety of ways. For example, the planning capability of small businesses was often challenged. In five cases, companies which had shown little previous inclination to plan ahead talked enthusiastically about the visioning approach adopted by one of the BCs. They cited achievements and outcomes in terms of a vision statement and an action plan detailing projects, responsibilities and timings. For example in one company the development of a marketing plan led to the need for more information upon which to base analysis of their competitive position. The BC supported this development through the provision of a sounding board approach, texts, references and information. In the words of the manager:

> if the BC had not been involved then the marketing plan would not get done - his visits act as a spur to get things done.
>
> > (Director, engineering manufacturer, employing 28)

In another company they developed production schedules and associated performance targets on the basis of closer examination of the production process in the company. The BC provided texts, supported the development of flow charts and helped crystallise marketing ideas in another company. The BC and production manager worked together to design the ISO 9001 system and developed reporting procedures to input analysis into the senior management meetings. The production manager adopted the visioning process, used initially by the BC, as a means to provide a focus for developing her area of control. The manager in another business suggested that the main contribution of the BC was:

to get us to recognise that we needed to review our financial performance more regularly - we set up monitoring systems and split the company into six operating units.

(Owner, engineering, employing 25)

In one instance the BC introduced a matrix to help the owner-manager in the initial diagnosis of the problems facing the business. The owner-manager adapted this to suit his needs and together with the BC identified priorities in the business. This encouraged the manager to computerise the accounts system to improve the processing and presentation of financial information. As the owner-manager stated:

the coach nudged me to get on with it . . . .it used to take 2- 3 days and now it takes ten seconds to produce the monthly accounts.

(Owner-manager, engineering, employing 15)

The manager went on to develop a website to promote the company. In another company the BC worked with a small team on the shop-floor raising productivity and employee motivation and encouraging the owner to invest in training by providing support for two members to study a computing course. In another company the BC worked with the administration staff in the company. The owner was initially distant from the DMS process but as time progressed he saw improvements in the systems and became 'more interested'.

Other cases suggested that the BC has been able to instigate regular management team meetings and to develop agendas that focused on both the long and short term and a variety of issues (accounting, marketing, production) related to the operation and development of the business. Discussions with the BC led companies to collect information and perform analyses in ways that were not previously apparent. One company developed a fledgling continuous improvement system and two other companies developed detailed production plans.

A further dimension of value was to raise awareness of HRD issues. The majority of companies became more aware of external training and development oppor-tunities and also became actively engaged.The provision of workshops and networking events associated with DMS was a key factor in this change. One attendee reported:

I learnt from the other MDs . . . we have all got our own problems and if you listen to them and how they got round them then you learn different ways of dealing with your own problems.

(Owner-manager, engineering fabrication, employing 12).

Two MDs became involved in structured courses of learning in higher education. The MD of another company attended a ten-week course on business develop-ment. The HRD needs of other staff were linked to the development needs of their businesses and steps were taken to source appropriate support. The fact that com-panies were in a position to link HRD to specific goals of the company highlighted the need for such activity. For example, one company recognised the need for product training for their telesales team and that further sales training was needed for their sales people. The BC facilitated contacts of relevant suppliers. The BCs drew other managers into the support network more widely and promoted the use of other publicly funded initiatives based on an understanding of the current situation of the manager and the business. Consequently the value became more widespread as these services become relevant and suited to the business context.

Case studies

The findings provide a testament of the general value the managers placed on DMS and the work with BCs. The majority of participants viewed the programme as a positive intervention and the contribution of the BC was valued by all but two of the owner-managers. To highlight the particular value of DMS, we now intend to focus on the stories of two participants, Andrew and Malcolm.

Andrew

Andrew is the MD of a traditional steel crafts company, which had been founded 26 years previously by Andrew's father-in-law. At the start of DMS in 1997, turnover was £350,000 and there were ten staff, all highly skilled craftsmen. About 65 per cent of production was sold as exports, mainly to the United States. When DMS began, Andrew was seeking help in managing his succession to MD. He was completing an MBA at university and wanted to move the company towards a total quality management (TQM) ethos although wider workforce development activity was not in evidence.

Soon after the start of the programme, the company faced a significant downturn in business, resulting in the loss of approximately 25 per cent of turnover. The reduced production led to a four-day week to prevent redundancies, which would have represented an attack on the company's skill base and have proved expensive because of the long service of staff.

Initially, Andrew was sceptical about DMS. He had:

> significant reservations regarding the real value of 'management development' in view of the specialised nature of the business, and having already had a fair amount of experience in applying learnt management theories and techniques in practice.

Such comments provide reference points for Andrew's interest and the criteria for his evaluation of work with the BC. Despite scepticism, however, he agreed to meet with the BC.

Andrew's main activity with the BC was the development of a business plan derived from forming a vision eighteen months into the future. The plan included the development of production schedules and performance targets based on a review and examination of the production process. However, the priority then switched to winning more orders and putting the company back on a five-day week. This required a reassessment of the plan with the coach. Andrew was soon able to claim that he had formed a supportive relationship with the coach and was holding effective meetings to deal with the difficulties faced by the company.

The relationship with the coach continued throughout the following year with meetings held every month for two hours. The basic approach was to discuss problems and present ideas with the coach acting as a 'sounding board' and 'devil's advocate'. Andrew and his fellow managers would find themselves 'stuck on key issues' and the BC would mediate, allowing emotional issues to be aired and helping consensus to be reached. The process gave Andrew a structure for talking about the development of the business and an opportunity to reflect on planned and actual activity.

Andrew gained value from the approach by providing an 'opportunity to exchange thoughts and ideas with a party unaffected by the restraining influences of the firm's strong historical and cultural perspectives'.

The BC's value is clearly indicated as someone who is outside the company. By May 2000, the company had restored the lost turnover and showed a profit for the first time in two years. Andrew attributed this to better control of costs and organisation of staff. There was also improved morale among staff. Significantly the company secured a greater share of domestic sales which had substituted for a loss of overseas turnover, although exports were also expected to rise again in the future. There had been a more proactive approach to selling and a new line of sterling silverware had been introduced. The company was seeking to target customers directly via catalogue and e-business and an Internet page which would be developed in due course. Andrew valued the longevity of DMS which was 'preferable to a two day course and instruction from a consultant'. The BC was able to help Andrew plan the process and facilitate implementation of a TQM approach. Andrew noted:

> We were fortunate that the BC was a consultant with the experience and skills to understand the importance of 'soft', qualitative as well as quantitative approaches to management problem solving. Through his facilitation, a tacit process of management development and learning occurred. This, I believe, may be of more significant value to the practising manager than more formal learning methods which usually require translation of generic models and techniques for application in a particular context.

Malcolm

The second case study concerns a company of electrical contractors supplying cable installation services to the construction sector.

The company was formed in 1984 and by 1995 had grown to employ a core workforce of twenty-five people. Malcolm was asked to join the management team to help develop the business further. While there remained aspirations to expand the business, low margins resulted in difficulties generating the funds necessary for growth. Malcolm had been visited by representatives from the TEC before 'but they had never had anything of relevance before'.

Malcolm was unsure of the nature of the input from the BC but he suggested that it might be useful to have someone to 'bounce ideas off as often you can't see the wood from the trees'. He was not expecting much change to take place in the first six months but he believed that any improvement in skills or systems should provide the company with a long-term benefit that would be reflected in financial performance.

One of the first steps taken by the BC was to talk with the three members of the management team individually to identify key issues and aspirations for the company. Malcolm suggested that these sessions got the directors to think about the business and to realise that change had to take place. Both of the founders of the business had technical backgrounds and one of them wanted to remain 'one of the boys'. This led to a tension between what 'the business' wanted to happen and what 'the workers' wanted to happen, for example in terms of quality and time-keeping. After considerable discussion it was decided that Malcolm would buy out one of the director's share of the business and become managing director.

Throughout the following year the BC visited Malcolm for two hours every six to eight weeks. These meetings were often largely unstructured. Sometimes Malcolm would raise issues with the BC and at other times the BC would put forward issues. Malcolm suggested that it was difficult to identify any specific impact but that the BC had clearly helped to focus thinking and to motivate him to consider different things and pursue different avenues. By the end of 1998, Malcolm had formed the opinion of the BC as 'very professional offering an excellent service' and he was keen to remain involved with DMS.

The sector remained highly competitive in 1999 and while turnover dropped slightly, the profitability of the company improved. Malcolm obtained a grant to develop a brochure and used the BC to bounce ideas off during the design process. The loss of the director led to increased responsibility for site supervisors and led to greater involvement and motivation of the workforce in general. The company started to access the TEC for support and conducted health and safety training and computer-aided design training for two staff. Malcolm suggested that:

> the interface with the TEC is a major benefit . . . a small company like ours has limited resources so access to funding for training is very useful . . . while we have been in contact with the TEC before we didn't get the right people but now we are as the coach is able to help us.

By the end of 1999 the company had purchased a similar business in another part of Yorkshire. Malcolm took the BC over to the new site several times. Malcolm suggested that one of the major benefits of the BC was his ability to chat with staff and to identify what they think needs to be done. This was a key part in the development process as it identified key issues and provided a basis to help to get across where the business wished to go.

By September 2000 the company had doubled turnover and the number employed and engaged staff in the development of the business. They had taken steps to improve value added element of services offered through CAD equipment and training and had developed and distributed a marketing brochure. Malcolm suggested:

> It is the first time I've had someone like this . . . I usually only deal with people in our industry and it is refreshing to get the view of an outsider . . . he [the coach] may not know the nuts and bolts of what we do but we have enough knowledge of the sector in the business so it is good to hear alternative views . . . he is constructive and not critical . . . [his suggestions] are not fanciful management theories but we talk about reasonable practical solutions.

At the end of DMS Malcolm subsequently became involved in another TEC supported project facilitating further organisational development.

Interpretation and conclusions

The importance of values

A clear theme, which emerged throughout the study, was the importance of values in a small business organisation. In many cases and especially among owner-managers, their relatives and successors, the very existence and continuation of the business are based on their wishes and desires. In many respects, attachment and adherence to what had been made in a business, whatever the outside view of that business, provided managers with the rationale to protect against the unknown such as interventions from agencies seeking to promote competitiveness and/or lifelong learning among smaller businesses.

DMS achieved some success by the way BCs orientated their actions towards their understanding of the unique interests of participants. The relationship between the BC and small business managers resulted in an expansion of the potential for business development and management learning in the majority of instances. The analysis presented in this chapter suggests that a critical factor was the way in which relationships were constructed through conversations between the BC and the small business manager. However, BCs could never be certain of eliciting positive responses to their utterances; indeed, while many of the small organisations were initially attracted to DMS, there was considerable variance in the frequency of the company visits and the time taken to establish meaningful contact. Success was not achieved in all cases. Relationships of mutual understanding failed to develop and three of the case study managers did not remain engaged in DMS over the three-year period. Frustrations emerged as the small business manager and the coach were unable to adjust to each others analysis of the problems the business faced nor to carry out an agreed course of action. The break down of the relationship resulted in dissatisfaction and managers suggested that they had reached 'a natural end' to their relationship with the BC. As Vygotsky (1987: 269) suggested, 'two people who . . . have fundamentally different perspectives often fail to achieve understanding'.

Attunement

The crucial move by BCs was to become attuned to the desires and interests of the managers and other participants (Rommetveit 1990). Further, all conversations took place in a situation and setting with a pre-history, referred to by Bahktin (1986) as 'an extraverbal context of reality', which will prevent an easy application of generic intervention formulas. For example, only one organisation seemed to fall into a 'typical' mode of working by identifying needs, formulating plans followed by implementation. In all other cases, the BCs had to adopt a process that allowed the creation of a conversational space within which a meaningful chain of utterances could be formed. It became evident to us that the BCs developed attunement to the values and interests of managers, enabling them to identify the drivers for development and the pacing of the intervention and change process. Throughout the programme, the uniqueness of the individual organisation shone through in their chosen action (Devins *et al.* 2001) and this suggests that external interventions need to better reflect the heterogeneity and diverse interests of smaller enterprises if they are to successfully engage small organisations in development activity.

Dialogue

The coaching process was heavily dependent upon discussion and dialogue between the BC and the participants. Three approaches were identified as part of the coaching process namely a visioning approach, a problem-solving approach and a sounding board approach. From a Vygotskian perspective, the various approaches created a conversational space for the work of coaching dialogics where language as well as other tools and signs mediated a higher mental functioning (Wertsch 1991). Further, such dialogues allowed the BC to assess the potential for learning and development but also the limitations for such work - i.e. a manager's ZPD. The BCs appeared to employ what Cheyne and Tarulli (1996), in their expanded view of dialogues within the ZPD, refer to as a Socratic dialogue. The BC, as a 'questioning other', recognised the maturity of the small organisation manager and gave him/her active expression in a process. Thus, both voices participated in mutual problem-solving with the potential recognition of new opportunities for HRD activity linked directly to business development. What was particularly interesting was the difficulty the BC sometimes had in making sense of what was happening. The talk of 'meandering' and 'unproductive sessions' was perhaps a reflection of the BC's disability in adopting an authoritative or expert position. Meaning and under-standing emerged over time through 'mutual inquiry' (Jauss 1989). As Cheyne and Tarulli (1996) suggest, such a dialogue provides for an 'encounter of differences that carries the potential for *inter*illumination among the voices' (emphasis in original).

Participants, through dialogue with their BC were able to work on a range of new activites and to transform their actions into thought under internalisation (Vygotsky and Luria 1994). In a successful intervention, the BCs were able to develop a supporting and trusting relationship with the small business manager. It became apparent that their conversations enabled the surfacing of specific needs that reflected the values and interests of the small business managers. It also enabled the BCs to reveal upper and lower limits of the potential of development (Wells 1999). In these respects, the findings reaffirm the view that decontextualised and generalised notions of what small business managers should know and do as managers and how they should be developed have only a very partial connection to the realities of small business worlds as constructed by small business managers themselves (Devins *et al.* 1999). As Bakhtin has written: 'All attempts to force one's way from inside the theoretical world and into actual Being-as-event are quite hopeless' (Bakhtin 1993: 12).

What Bakhtin was suggesting was that ideas such as generalised notions of HRD in small organisations, formed in a detached way from where life goes on, risk reducing others to objects and becoming 'alien' to that world. Such notions may easily be rejected. According to Bakhtin (1990), a flesh-and-blood, embodied 'presence' is crucial to the process of meaning-making. The BCs were able to prevent any 'impoverishment' by gaining an understanding of the specific goals and desires of small organisation managers and others.

The learning-centred, manager-driven process often moved the BC away from the roles adopted by a traditional consultant as people who are entitled to *know* in certain contexts (Potter 1996). While there are a number of views of consultancy which provide for a collaborative approach (Schein 1987), all models of consultation seem to work from a generative metaphor whereby the view of the expert, the consultant is seen as dominant and clients become serviceable to such views (Sampson 1993). However, while the BCs were invariably viewed as professional in their conduct and they at times provided directed guidance, the managers were often encouraged to pursue their own solutions and often came to view the BCs' as 'friends' or 'therapists' rather than 'expert advisers'. Interestingly, indication emerged that the relationship has been passed on to others when the time-bound DMS programme ended (two coaches retired and the third moved away). This was evidenced by managers' willingness to engage with other outsiders once the BC's input has been withdrawn at the end of the project. Invariably the BC had introduced a consultant or training provider and to a large extent they had shared values in terms of interventions with managers.

Learning points

Contextualisation

The perspective of coaching dialogics employed in this chapter once again underlines the need for HRD interventions to reflect the contextualised nature of owner-manager learning needs (Down 1999). BCs, as outsiders to the organisations in the DMS project reported, were successful in engaging participants in a conversation associated with the development of the business. This experience is re-enforced by the majority of organisations engaged in DMS who continued with the programme until its cessation due to time-bound funding streams. A key factor in sustaining this process of coaching dialogics was the willingness of the BC to listen to the utterances of managers and others and respond in appropriate and acceptable ways. However, as we have also indicated, this process was never entirely predictable. Fortunately, unlike some external interventionists, the BC was not obliged to 'sell' a product (such as Investors in People or a particular change/consultancy model). Instead, BCs were able to work with managers to determine a wide range of actions, which almost inevitably involved changes in systems or procedures and associated training and development activity, that were directly linked to the business problems or opportunities identified by the BC and the manager.

Scaffolding

The approach adopted through DMS facilitated the development of the core skills of owner-managers in terms of decision-making, information analysis, communication and problem-solving. However, instead of seeing these as generic skills for all owner-managers, the importance of context comes to the fore. We have explained this through the use of a ZPD and the importance of the scaffolding provided by the BC involving awareness of and sensitivity to the limits of development at a particular moment in time. There were examples of increased awareness and managers themselves talked about the benefits of 'improved confidence', 'not being scared to ask questions' or 'being more willing to delegate' as outcomes that they valued. Managers recounted the ability of the BC to help them to recognise 'blind spots' and to consider issues and ways of working not previously tried. The case studies provide examples of courses of action instigated by the manager and the BC and the value of these activities lies with the degree of fit with organisational priorities.

The value of 'outsideness'

A significant learning point for managers was that working in relationship with the BCs could enhance the value attached to the unique circumstances of their organisations. The development of the relationship was a key element of DMS as the BC and owner-manager met regularly (usually about once a month) to discuss issues. The fact that the managers made time for these meetings is evidence of their value. It also supports recognition that greater understanding about self requires the presence of another who is in dialogic relation. While managers' and BC's past experiences were critical factors at play in a dynamic relationship which evolved over time, the managers develop trust in the BC's approach and ability and through the relationship the BC's values influence the managers' values (and vice versa). We would suggest that participants in DMS came to value what Bakhtin (1986) refers to as 'outsideness' which he saw as 'a most powerful factor in understanding'. Bakhtin argued that by engaging in dialogue with others who come from another culture, it is possible to 'surmount the closedness and one-sidedness' of 'particular meanings' that exist in local understanding. By standing outside a small organisation but engaging with it through a 'dialogic encounter', trainers, consultants and coaches are able to 'raise new questions' which an organisation could 'not raise itself'. In this way, small business managers and others could find 'new aspects and new semantic depths' of their lives at work.

Bibliography

Alstrup, L. (2000) 'Coaching continuous improvement in small enterprises', *Integrated Manufacturing Systems*, 11, 3: 165- 70.

Bakhtin, M. M. (1986) *Speech Genres and Other Late Essays*, C. Emerson (ed.), Austin, TX: University of Texas Press.

Bakhtin, M. M. (1990) *Art and Answerability: Early philosophical essays by M. M. Bakhtin*, M. Holquist and V. Liapunov (eds), Austin, TX: University of Texas Press.

Bakhtin, M. M. (1993) *Towards a Philosophy of the Act*, V. Liapunov and M. Holquist (eds), Houston, TX: University of Texas.

Bennett, R. J., Robson, P. J. A and Bratton, W. J. A. (1999) 'Business Link: the influence of BL structure and local context on use and client assessment of impact and satisfaction', 22nd ISBA National Small Firms Policy and Research Conference Proceedings, *European Strategies, Growth and Development*, Leeds Business School, Leeds Metropolitan University.

Berry, A. and Perren, L. (1999) 'The role of non-executive directors in the United Kingdom', 22nd ISBA National Small Firms Policy and Research Conference Proceedings, *European Strategies, Growth and Development*, Leeds Business School, Leeds Metropolitan University.

Bolton, J. (1971) *Report of the Committee of Inquiry on Small Firms*, London: HMSO.

Bratton, J. and Gold, J. (1999) *Human Resource Management: Theory and practice*, 2nd edn, London: Macmillan Business.

Carter, A. (2001) *Executive Coaching: Inspiring performance at work*, Report 379, Sussex: Institute of Employment Studies.

Cheyne, J. A. and Tarulli, D. (1996) 'Dialogue, difference and the "third voice" in the Zone of Proximal Development', http://watarts.uwaterloo.ca/~acheyne/ZPD.html (accessed 10/12/98).

Clutterbuck, D. (1994) *The Power of Empowerment*, London: Kogan Page.

Cosh, A., Duncan, J. and Hughes, A. (1998) *Investment in Training and Small Firm Growth and Survival: An empirical analysis for the UK 1987–95*, Department for Education and Employment Research Report 36, Sheffield: DfEE.

Curran, J. and Blackburn, R. (1994) *Small Firms and Local Economic Networks: The death of the local economy?*, London: Paul Chapman.

Curran, J., Blackburn, R., Kitching, J. and North J. (1997) 'Small firms and workforce training: some results, analysis and policy implications', in M. Ram, D. Deakins and D. Smallbone (eds) *Small Firms: Enterprising futures*, London: Paul Chapman.

Deakins, D., Mileham, P. and O'Neill, E. (1999) 'Insiders v outsiders: director relationships in small companies', 22nd ISBA National Small Firms Policy and Research Conference, *European Strategies, Growth and Development*, Leeds Business School, Leeds Metropolitan University.

Department of Trade and Industry (1998) *Our Competitive Future: Building the knowledge driven economy*, CM3790, London: The Stationery Office.

Department of Trade and Industry (DTI/DfEE) (2001) *Opportunity for All in a World of Change, White Paper on Enterprise, Skills and Innovation*, Department of Trade and Industry/Department for Education and Employment, Norwich: The Stationery Office.

Devins, D. and Gold, J. (2002) 'Social constructionism: a theoretical framework to underpin support for the development of managers in small organisations?', *Journal of Small Business and Enterprise Development*, 9, 4: 111- 19.

Devins, D., Gold, J. and Marriott, S. (1999) 'Cracking the tough nuts': exploring a management development initiative for small firms, Small Business and Enterprise Development Conference, Leeds University, March.

Devins, D., Smith, V. and Holden, R. (2001) 'Creating "learning" industrial estates: addressing lifelong learning in SMEs', *Journal of Research in Post-Compulsory Education*, 6, 2: 205- 21.

Down, S. (1999) 'Owner-manager learning in small firms', *Journal of Small Business and Enterprise Development*, 6, 3: 267- 78.

Evered, R. D. and Selman, J. C. (1989) 'Coaching and the art of management', *Organizational Dynamics*, 18, 2: 16- 32.

Garaway, G. (1996) 'The case study model: an organizational study for cross cultural evaluation', *Evaluation*, 2, 2: 201- 12.

Gardiner, M. (2000) *Critiques of Everyday Life*, London: Routledge.

Gibb, A. (1996) 'What is a small business?', *Networker*, 3, Small Business Centre, Durham University.

Gibb, A. (1997) 'Small firms training and competitiveness: building upon the small business as a learning organisation', *International Small Business Journal*, 15, 3: 13- 29.

Glatthorn, A. A. (1985) *Case Study: An overview of one kind of research*, Pennsylvania, PA: University of Pennsylvania.

Gold, J., Whitehouse, N. and Hill, M. (1996) '"If the CAPS fit": learning to manage in small organisations', *Education and Training*, 38, 9: 33.

Hall, D. T., Otazo, K. L. and Hollenbeck, G. P. (1999) 'What really happens in executive coaching', *Organizational Dynamics*, 27, 3: 39- 53.

Hannon, P. (1998) 'Who are the real educators and learners? Exploring learning needs within the small firm: stakeholder transactional relationships', paper presented at the 21st ISBA National Small Firms Conference, Celebrating the Small Business, Durham University Business School.

Hendry, C., Jones, A., Arthur, M. and Pettigrew, A. (1991) *Human Resource Development in Small Organisations to Medium Sized Enterprises*, Employment Department Research Paper 88, Sheffield: Employment Department.

Hendry, C., Arthur, M. and Jones, A. (1995) *Strategy through People*, London: Routledge.

Hill, R. and Stewart, J. (1999) 'Human resource development in small organizations', *Human Resource Development International*, 2, 2: 103- 23.

Holquist, M. (1990) *Dialogism*, London: Routledge.

Jauss, H. J. (1989) *Question and Answer: Forms of dialogical understanding*, Minneapolis, MN: University of Minnesota Press.

Johnson, S. J. and Gubbins, A. (1993) 'Training in small and medium-sized enterprises: lessons from North Yorkshire', in K. Caley, E. Chell, F. Chittenden and C. Mason (eds) *Small Enterprise Development Policy and Practice*, London: Paul Chapman.

Lean, J., Down, S. and Sadler-Smith, E. (1999) 'The nature of client- personal business advisor relationship with Business Link', *Journal of Small Business and Enterprise Development*, 6, 1: 80- 8.

Marshall, N., Alderman, N., Wong, C. and Thwaites, A. (1995) 'The impact of management training and development on small and medium sized enterprises', *International Small Business Journal*, 13, 4: 73- 90.

Megginson, D. and Boydell, T. (1979) *A Manager's Guide to Coaching*, London: BACIE.

Megginson, D. and Pedler, M. (1992) *Self Development*, Maidenhead: McGraw-Hill.

Mumford, A. (1987) 'Using reality in management development', *Management Education and Development*, 18, 3: 223- 43.

Pawsey, V. (2000) 'Spiritual adviser', *People Management*, 30 March: 44- 6.

Pedler, M., Burgoyne, J. and Boydell, T. (1991) *The Learning Company: A strategy for sustainable development*, Maidenhead: McGraw-Hill.

Perren, L. (1999) 'Employment creation and small firms: reflections on Lone Henriksen's keynote address', *Journal of Small Business and Enterprise Development*, 6, 3: 219- 27.

Phillips, R. (1995) 'Coaching for higher performance', *Executive Development*, 8, 7: 5- 7.

Potter, J. (1996) *Representing Reality*, London: Sage.

Ram, M. (2000) 'Investors in People in small firms: case study evidence from the business services sector', *Personnel Review*, 29, 1: 69- 91.

Raper, P., Ashton, D., Felstead, A. and Storey, J. (1997) 'Toward the learning organisation? Explaining current trends in training practice in the UK', *International Journal of Training and Development*, 11, 1: 9- 21.

Redshaw, B. (2000) 'Do we really understand coaching? How can we make it work better?', *Industrial and Commercial Training*, 33, 2: 106- 8.

Rommetveit, R. (1990) 'On axiomatic features of a dialogical approach to language and mind', in I. Markovà and K. Foppa (eds) *The Dynamics of Dialogue*, New York: Harvester Wheatsheaf.

Salisbury, F. S. (1994) *Developing Managers as Coaches*, Maidenhead: McGraw-Hill.

Sampson, E. E. (1993) *Celebrating the Other*, New York: Harvester Wheatsheaf.

Schein, E. H. (1987) *Process Consultation*, Reading, MA: Addison-Wesley.

Senge, P. (1990) 'The leaders new work: building learning organisations', *Sloan Management Review*, Fall: 7- 23.

Singer, E. J. (1974) *Effective Management Coaching*, London: Institute of Personnel Management.

Stuart, R. (1984) 'Towards re-establishing naturalism in management training and development', *Industrial and Commercial Training*, July- August: 19- 21.

Temporal, P. (1978) 'The nature of non-contrived learning and its implications for management development', *Management Education and Development*, 9: 93- 9.

Vickerstaff, S. and Parker, K. T. (1995) 'Helping small firms: the contribution of TECs and LECs', *International Small Business Journal*, 13, 4: 56- 72.

Vygotsky, L. S. (1978) *Mind in Society: The development of higher psychological processes*, M. Cole, V. John-Steiner, S. Scribner and E. Souberman (eds), Cambridge, MA: Harvard University Press.

Vygotsky, L. S. (1987) 'Thinking and speech', in R. W. Reibner and A. S. Carton (eds) *The Collected Works of L. S. Vygotsky, Vol. 1: Problems of General Psychology*, New York: Plenum.

Vygotsky, L. and Luria, A. (1994) 'Tool and symbol in child development', in R. van der Veer and J. Valsiner (eds) *The Vygotsky Reader*, Oxford: Blackwell.

Wells, G. (1999) *Dialogic Inquiry: Towards a sociocultural practice and theory of education*, New York: Cambridge University Press.

Wertsch, J. V. (1991) *Voices of the Mind: A socio-cultural approach to mediated action*, Cambridge, MA: Harvard University Press.

Westhead, P. and Storey, D. (1994) 'Management training and small business performance: why is the link so weak?', *International Small Business Journal*, 14, 4: 13- 24.

Winterton, J. and Winterton, R. (1997) 'Does management development add value?', *British Journal of Management*, 8, special issue: 65- 76.

Wood, D., Bruner, J. S. and Ross, G. (1976) 'The role of tutoring in problem solving', *Journal of Child Psychology and Psychiatry*, 17: 89- 100.

Yin, R. K. (1989) *Case Study Research*, Newbury Park, CA: Sage.

13 Mentoring for export success

David Megginson and Paul Stokes

Objectives

This chapter draws on both past studies and theories on mentoring, as well as a funded project entitled 'Mentoring for Export Success' (MES). We describe the various stages and issues involved in setting up a Business Link funded project putting together experienced and novice exporters mainly CEOs and managing directors of SMEs in a set of pair mentoring relationships. Using data from the development and delivery of the project - which is still ongoing - we identify several key issues and challenges that have emerged from our analyses of these processes. Key issues include performativity versus reflexivity; dependence, independence and interdependence; solutions versus questions; pairs and networks.

Introduction: exploring mentoring theory

Before launching into our discussions about the MES scheme, we offer our definition of what we understand by mentoring, and then we contrast it with coaching. Mentoring is 'off-line help by one person to another in making significant transitions in knowledge, work or thinking' (Megginson and Clutterbuck 1995: 13).

This differentiates it from coaching, which is 'a process in which a manager, through direct discussion and guided activity, helps a colleague to learn to solve a problem, or to do a task, better than would otherwise be the case' (Megginson and Boydell 1979: 5).

The essence of the distinction between the two is that mentoring is focused upon significant changes for the person being helped and that in mentoring the learner sets his or her own agenda rather than having it set jointly, with strong influence from the helper.

Our brief was to carry out a research and development project which put together senior executives from different companies in a one-to-one mentoring relationship, initially for a period of six months. Our reason for making the distinction between coaching and mentoring was that an initial question we had was: is peer support of chief executives for export mentoring or is it coaching? We argue that it is mentoring, because the support concerned will not be detailed teaching, but, rather, sitting alongside the mentee and helping them explore the issues that arise when they consider moving their business into exporting. We now explore this issue by drawing on mentoring theory in order to make sense of some of the themes which emerged from the data we have collected so far. As this is done, the lessons that we took from each of these issues are summarised at the end of each section.

Theoretical background to mentoring: a selective review of the literature

Mentoring has become an important training and development tool for professional development within organisations, with significant bodies of literature in both education (Alvermann and Hruby 2000) and business (Allen *et al.* 1997; Megginson and Clutterbuck 1995; Clutterbuck and Megginson 1999; Ibarra 2000) devoted to the subject.

Earlier work on mentoring focused on relationship building between mentor and mentee (Hunt and Michael 1983; Kram 1983). At this stage, work was done to map out the broad issues that affected the mentoring relationship. These included:

- the context in which the relationship exists
- the various stages of the relationship
- the characteristics each partner seeks in the other
- the various positive and negative aspects of the relationship for the mentor, the mentee and the organisation.

As the stages in building a mentoring relationship were a key theme, commentators were keen to establish models that explained each part of the development process. Kram's (1983) life cycle model of mentoring was particularly influential here. This had four main stages:

- initiation - the contracting stages of the relationship
- cultivation - the relationship becomes stronger, richer and more developed
- separation - significant changes in circumstances mean that mentor and mentee become more distant from each other both geographically and emotionally
- redefinition - as a result of separation, the relationship either becomes redefined (e.g. as friendship) or breaks up.

The context, stages, characteristics and outcomes need to be spelled out in the design of the scheme.

Key issues

As mentoring became more popular, however, certain key issues began to emerge which meant there was a need for a more critical evaluation of mentoring. These issues are summarised below and are subdivided into relationship and mentoring scheme issues.

Relationship issues

Diversity of mentoring purposes

Research by Clutterbuck and Megginson (1999: 140) suggests that there are a number of purposes of mentoring relationships:

- develop insights
- develop mutual support systems
- enable learning
- promote networking
- perpetuate corporate cultures
- promote careers
- analyse life purpose.

As a result, it may not be useful to talk about mentoring in general terms, because different mentoring relationships may have different purposes. Indeed, the assumption that each person has only *one* mentor has been called into question (Megginson and Clutterbuck 1995; Ragins and Cotton 1999; Ibarra 2000).

Modelling desired behaviours vs corporate cloning

Some writers critical of mentoring (Covaleski *et al.* 1998; Townley 1994) have argued that the process can be seen as a form of management control which produces a tendency in mentees to conform to an ideal type of model manager in order to move up the corporate ladder. Others (Ibarra 2000) have argued that it is only by identifying people with the desired characteristics or relevant experience, and copying it, that managers can improve and develop. Ibarra (2000) in particular has argued that this does *not* necessarily mean that each person 'becomes' someone that they are not.

Mentors in this scheme need to accept that their mentee will become their own kind of exporter, not a replica of the mentor. This has had implications for mentor selection and development.

What's in it for me?

A common concern for mentors and mentees, not surprisingly, is to wonder what they themselves will get out of the mentoring relationship.

Rewards for mentees

Megginson and Clutterbuck (1995) identified the following benefits for mentees:

- business development
- focus

- development plan
- self-awareness
- change in behaviour or style
- breadth of insight
- stress management
- life purpose/life balance.

The first five items in this list will be of particular relevance to the MES scheme, and are a basis for mentee selection.

Rewards for mentors

Clutterbuck and Megginson (1999) in their research identify a range of benefits for mentors of which the following were relevant to the MES scheme:

- Personal rewards
  - satisfaction at helping others
  - friendship
  - rejuvenation.

- Learning rewards
  - intellectual excitement
  - connection to new thinking
  - understanding of other organisations
  - challenge to their own assumptions
  - development of their helping skills.

Cox (1999) discovered that mentors who found that mentoring helped their own careers were seen as the most helpful by mentees. Those mentors whose motives were altruistic were also seen as helpful, whereas those compensating for their own disadvantage in the past were seen as less helpful. Mentors expecting benefits for themselves were sought for the MES scheme.

Internal and external mentors

Much of the earlier work on mentoring was based on the assumption that mentoring was a formal process, which happened within organisations, and involved younger, less experienced members of staff being mentored by senior managers. However, these assumptions are now being challenged with many people employing consultants as mentors or deliberately seeking mentors outside their organisations (Green 1995; Christians 1999). Christians' scheme is unusual in that it paid the mentors for their services. There has also been significant growth in peer mentoring (Holbeche 1998) and co-mentoring thus challenging the traditional model of teacher and pupil. It has now been acknowledged that both parties learn from the relationship, therefore assumptions about 'what's in it for me' are changing.

The model proposed for this scheme involves peer, volunteer mentors from other companies. It is not designed as co-mentoring, as one party has considerable experience, while the other has less, so the primary helping relationship is in one direction. This basis needed to be considered and confirmed or modified to allow for the involvement of paid professional helpers.

Informal and formal mentors

Research in the United States (notably Ragins and Cotton 1999) questions whether mentors within a formal mentoring scheme can replicate the benefits of informal mentoring. This is a serious issue as we began setting up a formal scheme. However, there are two lessons to be drawn from this and related research. First, it is important that the formal mimics valuable features of the informal as much as possible (Gibb and Megginson 1993). For example in matching mentor and mentee, there needs to be as much choice as possible for both parties. Subsequent research by Viator (1999) indicates that the mentor having choice of mentee is particularly crucial. Walter (1997) in a survey for Focus Central London found that it was (by contrast) crucial for mentees to have a choice of mentors! Second, formal mentoring comes off badly in the US context because one of the expected outcomes of mentoring in the US tradition is 'sponsorship' and bringing forward the mentee's career through a kind of patronage. Sponsorship is much harder to deliver in formal mentoring relationships; indeed, so it should be. However, sponsorship is not part of the expectation of developmental mentoring in Britain and the rest of Europe (Gibb and Megginson 1993; Megginson 2000). Therefore, formal mentoring is not as disadvantaged in Europe as it would be in the United States.

Though formal, the relationships in this scheme needed to replicate features of informal mentoring - especially willing involvement by both parties, and a strong measure of choice for both parties in matching mentor and mentee. What the scheme offers and what it does not offer needed to be clearly spelled out.

Mentor behaviour

Carter and Lewis (1994) have developed four bases (resources) which contribute to successful mentoring. These four areas can be seen as the ways in which mentors can help mentees. They are:

- *Organisational:* mentors can advocate the use of position, networks and expertise within organisations to assist the mentee in achieving their goals.
- *Interpersonal:* mentors can help by using their personal access and skills to gain support and advice for the mentee.
- *Development:* identification of, and feedback on, development opportunities for the mentee is also a key task for mentors.
- *Context:* identification of purpose and goals of mentoring and how these can be supported is another important aspect of mentor behaviour.

Tranfield's (1994) work on mentoring is useful here in order to identify a possible meeting agenda. His work could be used to form a series of conversational areas that the mentor could initially explore with the mentee. These topics might include

- strategy
- image
- performance
- relationships
- organisation
- managing change.

Walter (1997) in his survey for Focus Central London suggests that mentors must

- use experience, not status
- be non-directive - encouraging self-reliance on the part of the mentee
- expect mutual learning.

In contrast to Walter's (1997) emphasis on non-directiveness, Garvey (1997) found that it is legitimate for mentors to share their own experience. This is not, however, to tell the mentee what to do, but rather to be open about their own actions and mistakes; to demonstrate trust, and to offer a window onto what will be a new experience for the mentee.

Ibarra (2000) found that effective mentors

- talked about what works
- encouraged consideration of a range of role models and offered criteria for judging them
- gave emotional and practical support
- were there for the mentee in difficult moments.

Palmer (1995) found that the mentees' three most favoured roles for the mentor were

- a sounding board
- a listener
- a critical friend.

whereas their mentors thought that they offered

- a listener
- giving encouragement
- a sounding board.

It seems that mentors overvalue the importance of encouragement. This fits with Walter's (1997) research on the importance of enhancing self-reliance. Geof Alred spoke poetically at the 1998 European Mentoring Conference of 'being listened to touching that great hunger within us'.

Borredon (1998) developed a mentor profile emphasising

- dedication to learning
- a degree of self-mastery
- ability to identify the nature and purpose of the relationship.

There is no great common prescription for an ideal mentor. However, it is suggested that they need to be listeners and capable of enhancing self-reliance and learning, rather than offering gung-ho encouragement. They need to have a clear sense of the issues on which they are going to work. They may need support to gain this clarity.

Mentoring scheme issues

Components of a mentoring scheme

Sweeney and Bloch (1994) have identified twelve components of eleven mentoring programmes and ranked them in order of importance. These components are useful as they suggest issues to address when setting up a mentoring scheme. They are:

- mentor training and development
- compatibility when pairing mentor and mentee
- monitoring and evaluating
- support for mentors (Cashmore and Sweeney (1998) spell this out)
- briefing of line managers
- creating an opportunity for the initial meeting (Arnold and Johnson (1997) show that regular contact is essential to success)
- establishing criteria for mentors
- agreeing agendas (Tranfield (1994) recommends making a development plan)
- communication to recruit participants and maintain their engagement
- training mentees
- planned use of time between meetings
- formal contract (this was seen as substantially less useful than the others).

Key items for this scheme are mentor training and development, compatibility when pairing mentor and mentee, monitoring and evaluating, support for mentors, creating an opportunity for the initial meeting and regular contact, establishing criteria for mentors, agreeing agendas, communication to maintain participants' engagement.

Matching

In matching mentors and mentees, there is a clear tension between being paired with someone too similar on the one hand - not stretching or useful - and too different on the other - there is insufficient common ground for a productive relationship to develop. This might explain why there is evidence that informal mentoring has a lower rate of turnover of mentors than formal schemes (Viator 1999). As a result, a mentoring scheme should be designed so that there are points of both commonality and difference. For example, an experienced exporter with thirty years' experience of manufacturing forklift trucks may find it difficult to relate to a start-up in the book publishing industry, and vice versa. However, if mentor and mentee were in the same or related industries, e.g. both in engineering, there may be more points of common interest. At the other end of the spectrum, two similar exporters starting up in the same industry may not result in improved exporting due to both parties having no relevant experience to share, although peer mentoring would be a possibility.

Mentoring pairs should have enough points of commonality, but choice of pairs should rest with both parties rather than scheme organisers.

Supervision

Mead *et al.*'s (1999) work on mentoring suggests that it is important to consider supervision of mentors. They argue for a safe space for mentors to develop themselves and their skills with a mentoring supervisor - clearly, this relates to the issue of what mentors themselves get out of the mentoring relationship in terms of their own skills development. Mead *et al.* (1999) offer a series of useful tips for mentors in which they argue that they, in their supervisory sessions, should

- focus on the particular and personal rather than looking for general advice on mentoring
- prepare their thinking for each session rather than trying to develop a fixed agenda
- bring important issues and requests for help to each session
- trust their own experience, skills and intuition.

Mentoring support and supervision should be provided.

Mentor development and support

Cashmore and Sweeney (1998) found that the following processes were useful in mentor support in their scheme in Pearl:

- network of mentors
- four-monthly review
- regular workshops
- learning sets of mentors
- mentor pairs for mutual support
- mentor handbook
- mentor news sheet
- mentor website.

Networks, four-monthly reviews, workshops, learning sets, pairs, a handbook, news sheet and website can be developed for the MES scheme.

What the Papers Say: conclusions

The assumptions about what a mentoring relationship is are changing. As mentoring has become part of mainstream management practice, managers and academics are beginning to reflect upon mentoring as a process. The definitions, boundaries and rules of the mentoring relationship are now being challenged and re-written to cope with the increasing complexity of organisational life. These are having an impact across four main areas:

- organisational impact
- mentee role and behaviour
- mentor role and behaviour
- types of mentoring relationship.

Of course, these issues then carry with them implications for how a mentoring scheme should be set up. The main conclusions in terms of design are summarised below:

- Mentor and mentee training about the process is essential.
- Pairing of mentors and mentees needs to be based on a combination of similarity and difference.
- Mentors should ideally have supervision to help develop themselves further as mentors.
- As there are a diversity of forms and models of mentoring, some further empirical research needs to be done to determine the most appropriate scheme for CEO exporter mentoring in the South Yorkshire area.

Developing the scheme

Based on these conclusions, we engaged in a range of recruitment and selection activities, initially for mentors, followed by mentees. The aim of doing this was twofold - we needed, as suggested earlier - more data on what was appropriate for mentors and mentees as well as recruiting the participants themselves. As a result, we started to explore networks and forums through a range of contacts, including Business Link advisers, personal networks, university colleagues and local industry networks.

We held meetings with various people to explore the issues indicated in Table 13.1. We were advised by our Business Link colleagues that we should recruit not only MDs but also directors with responsibility for exports, both as mentors and mentees. We also explored the question of whether leaders of service companies as well as manufacturers would be potential mentees. In personal service companies in Sheffield, very often Leeds is considered an export opportunity! However, some service companies, such as training or consulting firms, can do a great deal of overseas activity. We explored whether companies had to be SMEs. It was felt that this is not necessarily the case, and certainly SME subsidiaries of large groups would

Table 13.1 Contacts and outcomes in mentor development

Contact	Outcome sought
Officer of local branch of Institute of Directors	To elicit IoD support and co-operation
Researcher, Enterprise Centre, Sheffield Hallam University	To see if the EC's profiling research would give the MES project data we could use for selecting, matching and/or evaluating
Change Management Forum, Sheffield Hallam University	To determine interest in being mentors and to seek views of the proposed scheme
Business Link Advisers	To crystallise proposed design, agree schedules and seek nominees as mentors and mentees
Local press	To publicise scheme and attract participants
Director of European Mentoring Centre, industrialist, ex-chair of Sheffield TEC and Chamber, and Master Cutler	To seek suggestions as to likely mentors and to explore with established contacts the possibility of service export interest

be welcome, so long as they have discretion over where they sell. We initially intended that this scheme would not be concerned with one person companies or small start-ups, in order to maximise its impact, although this was changed in practice in the recruitment of mentees.

Numbers of mentors and mentees

Our Business Link colleagues proposed that the scheme should include at least six pairs from their respective areas. If there are strong expressions of interest, it would be possible to increase this number somewhat, but it would be important not to increase it too much in order that individual attention could be given to supporting the pairs and that we can thoroughly research their experience.

Principles to be adhered to and pitfalls to be avoided

It was agreed by our Business Link colleagues that the quality of the mentors was a crucial part of the scheme. They both felt that the mentors should have credibility and be able to demonstrate the benefits of the process to people in their own organisations. One concern expressed was that there was sometimes a danger of overloading useful contacts due to their involvement in other schemes. It was therefore agreed that the Business Link advisers would use their knowledge of individual exporters to avoid this happening.

We all agreed that generating positive feedback was important as this often creates a critical mass of interest in and support for projects. In order to do this, we felt that it was important to manage the expectations of the participants by contacting them regularly and offering support, so as to ensure that they retain their enthusiasm for the project.

At our meeting with our Business Link colleagues, we agreed, at that time, that the initial meetings with mentors should be held separately from the meeting with mentees. Having said this, we held onto the importance of allowing maximum choice for both mentees and mentors in the matching process.

Mentor approach

We decided that that the success of the project would come from having a number of strong success stories to share. The quality of these stories was considered to be the most important factor for a pilot scheme, rather than generating a large number of pairings. The diversity of mentors and their styles was discussed with our Business Link colleagues. Although one of them made the point that he might feel obliged to intervene if he felt the mentor's advice was inaccurate or inappropriate, it was agreed that mentors (as well as mentees) are likely to differ in style and that meant that a diversity of styles was desirable in terms of generating appropriate matches. Our task with the mentors is to help them become the kind of mentor that they aspire to be, rather than to impose uniformity.

A key part of the discussions were focused upon the matching of mentors and mentees. Robin Bairstow (Rotherham Business Link) in particular made the point that the perceptions of director/owners were likely to differ according to the size, sector and location of the firms they represented. We made the point that it was important that the matches are well constructed, ensuring that those involved have sufficient things in common to make the relationship productive, but at the same time avoiding matches between firms that are too similar or that are close competitors. However, although it was important to try and make matches as effectively as possible, we felt that it was important to retain some element of choice for mentors and mentees about who they wished to be matched with.

There was some discussion about running matching events for mentors and mentees. Although we had initially felt that it was important to have all participants together, it was ultimately felt that it would be preferable to have meeting events for mentors and mentees separately. These forums will serve as vehicles for support and familiarisation with the scheme and its principles. They took place in September and October 2000, either as breakfast or early evening meetings, on the advice of our Business Link colleagues.

In summary, our initial discussions yielded the following conclusions:

- Workshop should be set up for mentors and mentees.
- Processes for workshops and matching needed to be devised.

MES in practice

The preceding analysis has focused on the preparatory work for the scheme. At the time, our conclusions and assumptions seemed reasonable and logical. However, as always with research, the practice of establishing and running the scheme has yielded several surprises, tensions and fascinating issues. We present these in roughly chronological order, drawing out the key lessons as before.

Initial discussions: starting the mentor recruitment process

Our study of the mentoring literature had suggested that mentoring schemes tend only to work when both mentor and mentee get something out of the scheme. As a result, we prepared a pack that articulated both mentor and mentee benefits and provided some suggestions of how to think through what each might want from the process. In our initial discussions with prospective mentors, however, we were heartened to find that many of our mentors 'just wanted to help people' using their experience of exporting. Herein, however, was also a potential obstacle to an effective mentoring process. Our research into mentoring suggested that the mentoring relationship was wider than simply providing information and offering experience (see Clutterbuck and Megginson 1999: 14, for a discussion of mentoring roles). Although we wished to allow mentors to develop their own style of mentoring, we were keen to differentiate mentoring from other types of helping e.g. coaching, teaching, counselling and consulting. Our initial discussion with prospective mentors was designed to enable a mutual exploration of ours and the mentor's personal agenda towards the scheme in general, and towards mentoring in particular. Another key finding from these discussions was that mentors were relatively open about who they wanted in terms of a mentee, although a minority did say they wanted to work with someone who operated in a different setting from themselves.

Mentor and mentee workshops

We had expected, following discussions with our Business Link colleagues, that the recruitment of mentees would be relatively unproblematic, though we intended to use a virtually identical process as for mentors. However, we found that our confident predictions regarding mentees did not materialise! With the help of our advisers we did manage to recruit enough companies but we had to run several extra mentee workshops for small numbers of mentees. In spite of our earlier intentions, some of the mentees were one-person companies or new start-ups.

In both mentor and mentee workshops (around two and a half hours), participants were first given space to introduce themselves to their peers and to identify what would be a 'big win' for them both from the session and from the scheme. Following this, initial concerns and questions were raised which we tried to address and discuss as a group - these concerns were generally focused on time commitments and the type of export help that each would want to offer/receive. In answering some of their questions we found it useful to draw upon a list of what a mentor does (Clutterbuck and Megginson 1999: 14- 15). For completeness, the role titles are reproduced here with a very brief summary:

- *Sounding Board:* someone independent and uninvolved who can give feedback on mentee's ideas in the light of their own experience.
- *Critical Friend:* someone able to provide challenge to a mentee that others in their own organisation are reluctant to do, due to embarrassment, fear or politeness.
- *Listener:* someone who just listens and gives help simply by giving the mentee space to speak uninterrupted.
- *Counsellor:* someone who listens but who also asks reflective or empathetic questions, acknowledging the emotional side of working life.
- *Career Adviser:* someone who helps the mentee to think through career options, plan personal development and learn lessons for their future.
- *Networker:* someone who 'knows a person who can', providing the mentee with access to important networks.
- *Coach:* someone who can provide the mentee with specific help on certain aspects of behavioural change.

Each of these roles was explained to the group and they were then invited to rank each in terms of which they preferred to give or receive (depending on whether they were a mentor or a mentee). In several of the workshops, there were sharp differences between participants in terms of their rankings. However, following discussion, there was a general agreement that a mentor should provide something more than just a listening ear on the one hand, or specific export advice on the other. In one session two mentors saw no relevance for the framework. However, the remaining participants found the framework useful. Also, we found their answers useful in terms of matching mentors and mentees in the next stage of the process.

Emergent findings from the workshops

In addition to the mentoring roles, two further useful processes emerged from early workshops which we used in later ones. The first of these was where we asked participants to decide how much of the entire space of a mentoring meeting should be taken up by a mentor and how much by a mentee. Again, the answers tended to vary a great deal; some felt 50- 50 per cent was reasonable whereas others felt that it should be 25 per cent mentor, 75 per cent mentee. Once more we found that the figures used enabled useful discussions to take place about what was meant by personal space, i.e. was it simply speaking or more generally, personal impact? Also questions emerged about how those figures might change as the mentoring relationship progressed.

The second emergent finding was that it can be useful to put prospective mentors and mentees together in the same workshop. Initially, this occurred due to pressure of time and the need to integrate new participants onto the scheme. We were concerned that this might provide some confusion for both parties in terms of each having different agendas. However, we found that approaching the role-ranking exercise from both perspectives gave each party fresh new insights into the process and appeared to help.

The gathering

Between two and three months after the initial workshops we held a gathering of both mentors and mentees to discuss their experience so far. The agenda was as follows:

1   Experience so far (plenary): good things, surprises, things gained.
2   Concerns (separate mentee/mentor groups): individual, scheme concerns.
3   Feedback issues (plenary): general issues discussed.
4   Summary.
5   Networking.
6   Close.

This was an extremely rich session, lasting about three hours. From these discussions a number of key issues and tensions emerged that are discussed here. These issues are preceded however, by a description and analysis of part of the mentors' discussion in Item 2 of the above agenda. This is included now as it seems to us to illustrate many of the learning points that we were able to draw from the meeting and, indeed, from the workshop sessions.

Mentor discussion

Mentors

A = Mentor 1, whose issue was the focus of this discussion
B = Mentor 2
C = Mentor 3
D = Mentor 4
E = Adviser from export agency and supporter of the MES scheme
F = Researcher

F: Would anyone like to start us off with a problem or issue that they are facing in their relationship?
A: I have a challenge rather than a problem - which is finding the right level of advice to be useful. For example, in practical terms, it's no use saying to my mentee 'Here's a classic marketing plan - read it and learn!' He'll say 'Push off'. In the workshops you [F] talked about helping mentees to work things out for themselves, but you have to be helpful enough to enable him to do something. Also, you've got to deal with the complexity of what he's got to do - in my mentee's case finding a market that he can sell to competitively and where his products are culturally acceptable.
B: Does he have expectations of what mentoring and exporting will do for the firm?
A: I think he wants to grow incrementally through exporting. He's got a bit of time to play with as MD of an established company, though he's on a steep learning curve as far as exporting's concerned.

D: Mine's the same, though it's in a smaller company. At our next meeting I'll get him to think about a business plan.

C: Is A's mentee's product exportable?

B: He doesn't know what he's selling - whether it is a locale, a service or one stop shopping.

E: It's a service.

C: It'll be the authorities in the countries he's exporting to that he needs to work on.

E: Yes, I talked to him about that before he went on the trade mission. I could get someone to do an export audit for him - free of charge.

A: What would that involve?

E: A half-day survey of the firm and its products.

A: Send me the details and put it through me. I was thinking of creating models for him to work around - to help him think through the critical factors that he has to consider.

C: I'm interested in his motivation. I'm not sure he's committed! Why isn't he here tonight?

B: I think A has said things to indicate that he is committed. My experience is that in the early stage of a relationship - you've got to be totally honest - like when you first go out with a girl, or you get yourself into a lot of trouble.

A: As a result of the information you gave us, F, I said to my mentee, 'I'm not here to tell you what to do - let's see how it goes!'

C: Has he looked into exporting a lot? Is he frightened of it?

A: His current idea seems to be to sell to what you might call 'the expatriate market' in Hong Kong, South Africa, Australia. I'm saying to him, 'Think more widely - that may not be the right route'.

C: I've dealt with educational suppliers: the Irish buy from Britain by the boat load.

D: Your mentee could link with integrated exporters, I knew of an example where one exporter was given a contract to totally equip six schools in Ethiopia.

C: But success will come through gaining access to the authorities in the country of his choice.

In this extract our analysis suggests that A is dealing with conscious choice about how to mentor, and is opening himself up to the spectrum of solutions versus questions. He is being helped in this process by B, who is modelling both sharing his experience and asking open-ended questions. Both C and D are, in this context, keen to offer concrete, pragmatic advice, grounded in their experience. This raises two questions for further inquiry. First, does the behaviour of the mentors in this co-mentoring situation carry over to their relationship with their mentee? If so, what is the impact of this style on the success of the relationship as perceived by the parties involved? We consider these issues in our further follow-up with the protagonists.

A number of other points arise from this rich extract. First, there was a strong temptation for two of the mentors to make inferences about the motivation of A's mentee. C saw the mentee's commitment as suspect; B thought that A had provided evidence that the mentee was committed. One of the findings of the literature is that mentees value having a relationship without judgement where they can just be (and that this creates an opportunity for entering and using personal reflective space (Clutterbuck and Megginson 1999: 8- 10). Does making inferences about levels of commitment of the mentee run the risk of making the mentoring relationship judgemental?

Second, the extract offers an example of a possible difference between the experience offered by mentors and those offered by other helpers within the export service. E (a professional helper) indicated that he had already encouraged A's mentee into going on a trade mission, although the view of many mentors on the scheme was that missions were usefully seen as a late intervention in export development. One mentor on the scheme was reported by his mentee as saying, 'Don't jump on a plane; do your desk research here first. Don't go abroad till you have lots of contacts fixed up'. In the mentor discussion quoted earlier, E (the adviser) also adds that he has another product - the export audit - that is on offer. E is an intelligent and thoughtful adviser committed to developing his own skill as a mentor, so what is going on here? One of the pressures that E, and those in similar roles, experience is a requirement for delivering a target number of volunteers for each of the centrally determined initiatives. This narrow conception of performativity for advisers ('bums on seats') conflicts sharply with the reflexive approach that mentors can adopt ('let's work your issues').

Finally, the extract confirms the usefulness of having meetings of mentors with open, problem-solving agendas, in the manner of action learning (Pedler 1996). F was able to use the meeting to feed back to the parties concerned what he had observed of their interaction and the inferences he had drawn from them. The participants took from the meeting questions and ideas for their own mentoring practice. Other issues, drawn from our experience of the meeting as a whole, are analysed thematically in the following sections.

Dependence, independence, interdependence

An issue faced by Mentor A in the discussions also arose in the parallel mentee discussions. This was how to manage the issues of dependence, independence and interdependence. Clearly, Mentor A was keen to avoid alienating his mentee on the one hand, by suggesting he needed to be given a marketing plan, while providing sufficient challenge and advice on the other that would encourage the mentee clarify his thinking. Mentor A does not feel that his mentee has sufficiently developed his marketing plan to become a successful independent exporter on the one hand but must avoid patronising him and implying that he is incompetent on the other. This is was also reflected in discussions with the mentees, one of whom felt that his key challenge was to develop a way of 'extracting' what he wanted from his mentor so as to enable him to identify new markets effectively *on his own*. Another mentee was in a situation where his mentor was not an exporter himself but was an exporting service specialist. The challenge for this mentee was also to extract what he wanted from his mentor, largely by relying on networking. Hence this mentee was developing an appreciation for the value of networking, thus becoming part of an interdependent network with his mentor. He realised that, despite his initial reservations, which were based on wanting 'direct guidance on US markets' he found another model of helping which was proving to be equally useful.

Following Ibarra (2000), this meeting therefore provided evidence that mentees were selecting aspects of mentor behaviour which they might use in their own context. This was well illustrated by one of our mentees who referred to his mentor as 'a bossy headmaster'. However, this mentee was relatively unruffled by such an approach, perhaps because he was accustomed to working with his father in business!

Solutions versus questions

Another aspect of mentoring behaviour which seemed to be well illustrated by the mentoring discussion was Reg Revans' dictum that Learning = Programmed Knowledge + Questioning Insight (Pedler 1996). In other words, Mentors C and D were suggesting markets and offering solutions that related to their programmed knowledge about export whereas A and B were exploring issues which pertained to their preference for learning through questioning insight. From our perspective, both approaches seem relevant and in fact complementary - a mentee may well need access to programmed knowledge as well as questioning insight. However, as many of our group commented, there needs to be a balance between the two. This also sounded a cautionary note to us; being interested in mentoring and its reflective, questioning side may blind us to the fact that solutions are as important as insight for our participants.

Timing

On a more pragmatic note, the issue of timing in mentoring relationships was clearly an important one. This was true on several levels. First, several of our pairs had been unable to attend the gathering as they were abroad - this had also got in the way of several of our pairs arranging initial meetings. Some of them were moving into their busiest times of year and were unable to arrange meetings until after Christmas.

Timing was also important in the sense of a mentee being ready to export. Mentor A's mentee was the MD of a successful UK business but a serious export drive still lay in the future. However, another of the mentees felt that 'this was the perfect time as I'm starting to get orders and need some guidance'. Yet another mentee said, 'I have an opportunity to act for a manufacturer in overseas markets, so this could not have come at a better time'. Similarly, Mentor B was also keen to be involved as he was wanting to introduce a mentoring scheme into his own business. However, he also raised another issue about mentees' needs changing. His view was that what a mentee wanted from their mentor would change over time and that this might involve the relationship shifting in some way as time went on. This resonated with our own views on stages in the mentoring relationship (Megginson and Clutterbuck 1995: 30- 4).

Pairs and networks

Finally, one of the most interesting findings from the experience was the relationship between individual pairs and their links to the network of pairs on the scheme. Mentor B's comment that 'it's the whole thing' seemed pertinent here. He was referring to the fact that, as a result of our workshops and other networking opportunities, participants are simultaneously engaged in co-mentoring relationships with each other, passing on useful tips, knowledge and insights via complex interactions. One of the mentees at the gathering said that he had followed up what was, in effect, a peer mentoring relationship started at one of the initial workshops, where he had helped another mentee with a lead. He had met the other mentee subsequently and had helped him further with this issue. Our aim is to look into networking further as the scheme progresses, using electronic discussions groups, one-to-one discussion between researcher and participant, three cornered discussion between pairs and researcher, and other workshops.

Conclusion

In summary, our research via MES has raised some interesting questions for us in terms of the mentoring relationship. The issues of dependence/interdependence/ independence; solutions versus questions; timing and pairs versus networks are live for members of the scheme we are researching. They are also clearly of relevance for other export advice agencies seeking to set up a similar scheme. They may have relevance for others involved in mentoring in different contexts. However, the scheme is only in its infancy in terms of developing significant outcomes for mentees. We hope and expect there to be many more opportunities to enhance our understanding of the theory and practice of mentoring for export in particular and mentoring processes in general.

Acknowledgements

We would like to express our thanks to the funding bodies that supported this research, Yorkshire Forward and Rotherham Chamber of Commerce, Training and Education. We are grateful to the advisers who have supported this work in Yorkshire, East Midland and the Headquarters of Trade Partners UK. Above all, we thank the volunteer mentors and mentees, who gave their time freely and enthusiastically to both the scheme and to our exploration of their processes.

Bibliography

Allen, T., Joyce, E., Russell, J. and Maetzke, B. (1997) 'Formal peer mentoring: factors related to protege's satisfaction and willingness to mentor others', *Group and Organization Management*, 22, 4: 488- 507.
Alvermann, D. and Hruby, G. (2000) 'Mentoring and reporting research: a concern for aesthetics', *Reading Research Quarterly*, 35, 1: 46- 54.

Arnold, J. and Johnson, K. (1997) 'Mentoring in early career', *Human Resource Management Journal*, 7, 4: 61- 70.

Borredon, L. (1998) 'Getting to authentic conversation and dialogue', *Proceedings of the 5th European Mentoring Conference*, Sheffield: EMC/SBS.

Carter, S. and Lewis, G. (1994) 'The four bases of mentoring', *Proceedings of the 1st European Mentoring Conference*, Sheffield: EMC/SBS.

Cashmore, A. and Sweeney, J. (1998) 'Cascading mentoring at Pearl', *Proceedings of the 5th European Mentoring Conference*, Sheffield: EMC/SBS.

Christians, I. (1999) 'Wings: a business mentor pilot programme', *Proceedings of the 6th European Mentoring Conference*, Sheffield: EMC/SBS.

Clutterbuck, D. and Megginson, D. (1999) *Mentoring Executives and Directors*, Oxford: Butterworth-Heinemann.

Covaleski, M., Dirsmith, M., Heian, J. and Samuel, S. (1998) 'The calculated and the avowed: techniques of discipline and struggles over identity in Big Six public accounting firms', *Administrative Science Quarterly*, 43, 2: 293- 327.

Cox, E. (1999) 'The call to mentor', *Proceedings of the 6th European Mentoring Conference*, Sheffield: EMC/SBS.

Garvey, B. (1997) 'What's in it for me?', *The Learning Organization*, 4, 1: 3- 9.

Gibb, S. and Megginson, D. (1993) 'Inside corporate mentoring schemes: a new agenda of concerns', *Personnel Review*, 22, 1: 40- 54.

Green, M. (1995) 'Exploring the psychological boundaries between the individual and the organisation in the mentoring relationship', *Proceedings of the 2nd European Mentoring Conference*, Sheffield: EMC/SBS.

Holbeche, L. (1995) 'Peer mentoring: the challenges and opportunities', *Proceedings of the 2nd European Mentoring Conference,* Sheffield. EMC/SBS.

Hunt, D. and Michael, C. (1983) 'Mentorship: a career training and development tool', *Academy of Management Review*, 8, 3: 475- 86.

Ibarra, H. (2000) 'Making partner: a mentor's guide to the psychological journey', *Harvard Business Review*, 78, 2: 146- 55.

Kram, K. (1983) 'Phases of the mentoring relationship', *Academy of Management Journal*, 26: 608- 25.

Mead, G., Campbell, J. and Millan, M. (1999) 'Mentor and Athene: supervising professional coaches and mentors', *Career Development International*, 4, 5: 283- 90.

Megginson, D. (1988) 'Instructor, coach, mentor: three ways of helping for managers', *Management Education and Development*, 19, 1: 33- 46.

Megginson, D. (2000) 'Current issues in mentoring', *Career Development International*, 5, 4/5: 256- 60.

Megginson, D. and Boydell, T. (1979) *A Manager's Guide to Coaching*, London: BACIE.

Megginson, D. and Clutterbuck, D. (1995) *Mentoring in Action*, London: Kogan Page.

Palmer, C. (1995) 'How directors use mentors', *Proceedings of the 2nd European Mentoring Conference*, Sheffield: EMC/SBS.

Pedler, M. (1996) *Action Learning for Managers*, London: Lemos & Crane.

Ragins, B. R. and Cotton, J. (1999) 'Mentor functions and outcomes: a comparison of men and women in formal and informal mentoring relationships', *Journal of Applied Psychology*, 84, 4: 529- 50.

Sweeney, J. and Bloch, S. (1994) 'Organisational perspectives on mentoring', *Proceedings of the 1st European Mentoring Conference*, Sheffield: EMC/SBS.

Townley, B. (1994) *Reframing Human Resource Management: Power, ethics and the subject at work*, London: Sage.

Tranfield, D. (1994) 'Salesman, dreamer and son-of-a-bitch: QED for managers', *Proceedings of the 1st European Mentoring Conference*, Sheffield: EMC/SBS.

Viator, R. E. (1999) 'An analysis of formal mentoring programmes and perceived barriers to obtaining a mentor at large public accounting firms', *Accounting Horizons*, 13, 1: 37-53.

Walter, J. (1997) 'Mentoring - an untapped opportunity', *Practical Office*, 4, 10: 1-3.

14 Management development in micro and small firms in Ireland

Linking management development practices to firm size, strategic type, HRM orientation and owner-manager espoused values

Thomas N. Garavan, Alma McCarthy, Juliet McMahon and Claire Gubbins

Objectives

This chapter considers the influence of firm size, the generic business strategy of the firm, the firm's human resource management (HRM) orientation and the espoused values of owner-managers, on management development activities in micro and small firms in Ireland. It is based on the results of a cross-sectional survey of firms that are members of the Small Firms Association of Ireland. It is well established that, since the early 1980s, significant growth of micro and small firms has occurred, in both Ireland and the United Kingdom. In Ireland, the statistics reveal an increase in the birth rate of new small firms; small firms, in particular, are a significant source of employment creation in the Irish economy. Evidence presented by the Irish government reveals that small and micro firms are an important component of the economy, in both economic growth and employment terms. Many reasons are identified to explain this increased significance. They include major technological changes, the contracting out of activities by large firms, downsizing by major multinationals and the emergence of the service economy (Shutt and Whittington 1987; Tung-Chun 2001).

A less positive picture also emerges in the small firms' literature. The research evidence reveals that many small firms are lacking in dynamism, suffer from very high death rates and most significantly of all, invest proportionately less than their large firm competitors in management training and development (Marshall *et al.* 1995). It is well established that the quality of the owner-manager and the management team represent a vital component of micro and small firm success. Studies conducted by Wynarczyk *et al.* (1993) and Smith and Whittaker (1998) reveal that the quality of the management team will impact the development of the firm itself, its overall profitability and its longevity.

The small firm sector, both internationally and domestically, presents a number of challenges for management development. Investment in management development is important in achieving business success; senior management competence is closely related to firm success (Jennings and Beaver 1997; Cromie *et al.* 1995). Research undertaken in the United Kingdom reveals that successful small to medium sized enterprises provide more training and management development than average (Sadler-Smith *et al.* 1998); however, other evidence indicates that investment in formal training and management development is not a high investment priority for many small firms. Research conducted by Hill and Stewart (2000) and Westhead and Storey (1996) for example, reveals that where management training and development activities occur, they are likely to be informal, unplanned and reactive. The general view emanating from the literature is that management training and development is perceived as an unaffordable luxury for many small firms (Blackburn and Hankinson 1989; Vickerstaffe and Parker 1995).

In the Irish context, the work of Hitchens and O'Farrell (1990) and O'Farrell and Hitchens (1989) is of particular significance. In a number of their ongoing studies comparing small Irish firms with their counterparts in Scotland, Northern Ireland and England, they invariably found that Irish small firms were less competitive in terms of price, labour and quality. Skill quality problems at all levels, coupled with inadequate managerial training, were identified as major proximate causes of this lack of competitiveness. To increase the competitiveness of Irish small firms, a number of commentators have emphasised the need for investment in training and management development (Tansey 1998).

The development of managers within small firms is therefore viewed as a significant component of the need to develop the business itself. Research conducted on small enterprise owners' managerial skills (Jennings and Beaver 1997; Murphy and Young 1995) highlight a number of key findings that are relevant in the context of this chapter.

- Owner-managers do not invest in their skill development. They show a limited concern to professionalise their management skills and style and are poor on both delegation and control issues. They often espouse negative attitudes about the value of management development.
- Owner-managers often recognise shortcomings in their abilities as managers but are reluctant to relinquish personal control and delegate. These characteristics often explain their unwillingness to invest in management development for other managers within the small firm.
- There is evidence of a significantly higher level of investment in management development where the founding owner-manager is no longer part of the management structure of the small firm (Loan-Clarke *et al.* 1999).
- Owner-managers, particularly those with technical backgrounds, tend to place more emphasis on the acquisition of technical rather than managerial skills. This is based on the belief that it is important to participate in every job in the organisation (Martin *et al.* 1998; Loan-Clarke *et al.* 1999).
- Small firms face a double cost when investment in management development is

considered. Westhead and Storey (1996) highlight that the real cost of investment in management development is higher for small firms. This is due to the opportunity cost of management time off the job to participate on management development activities. Another reason for the higher cost is the need to source or design a more differentiated management development product. Blackburn and Hankinson (1989), for example, found that low participation in formal management development is attributable to both its expense and perceived inappropriateness by owner-managers.

- Where management development is undertaken, it tends to be ad hoc, accidental, relies upon informal interactions with clients and other contacts and is most likely not based upon a specific identification of learning needs. Murphy and Young (1995), for example, reveal that there is little reflection upon learning events. An Irish study by Tansey *et al.* (2001) reveals that managers devoted roughly one-seventh of their working time to training and development.

- There is limited evidence to date of research demonstrating relationships between investment in management development and the strategic focus and HRD orientation of the small firm. Henderson (2001), for example, reveals that the generic strategic direction of the small firm is a significant factor in explaining the extent and formality of management development, but is not significant in explaining the specifics of the management development policy or practice within the small firm. It also appears that the approach the firm adopts to managing its human resources is also significant.

This chapter focuses on four important dimensions of investment in management development by small firms in Ireland: the relationship between the strategic direction of the firm, its HRM orientation, the types of attitudes espoused by owner-managers and the nature and extent of management development undertaken.

Understanding management development, HRM orientation, strategic type and the types of attitudes espoused by owner-managers in small firms

The literature highlights two broad approaches to studying management development processes in organisations - internal and external. Dolan and Schuler (1994) argue that an internal approach focuses on understanding the elements that go into the design of management development activities. An external approach is concerned with the shape of management development activities, considered in conjunction with the firm's strategic focus and its HRM philosophy. This more contingent approach considers the types of factors that drive management development.

The management development literature generally utilises an internal approach; however, very little is known of the relationships between management development, HRM orientation, small firm strategic direction and the influence of owner-manager attitudes to management development. A number of scholars argue that management development as a discipline has placed too much emphasis on state of the art delivery at the expense of the critical connection between management development and firm strategy and profitability.

Two theoretical issues are of relevance in the context of this chapter: the centrality of managerial human capital and the identification of the relationships between investment in management development and the contingency factors referred to earlier.

Managerial human capital is a critical resource in most firms and of very particular significance to the micro and small firm. Five particular findings emerge from the extant research:

- Intangible resources are more likely than tangible resources to create competitive advantage (Spender 1996; Grant 1996). Intangible firm-specific resources such as knowledge and learning allow small firms to add value to incoming factors of production.
- Specific human capital attributes of owner-managers affect firm outcomes. Those of most significance are experience, education and skills (Huselid 1995; Pennings *et al.* 1998). Firm performance is enhanced by the way in which firms utilise managerial resources in the development and implementation of strategies (Robins and Weirsema 1995; Markides and Williamson 1996).
- The extent of investment in managerial human capital in small firms is impacted by the culture of the firm, its HRM orientation and specifically the attitudes of owner-managers. Owner-managers' perceptions of the value of management development and their perceptions of its nature and content, impact on the extent of investment by the small firm in management development (Merkx 1995).
- Competence-based management development approaches are considered to have enhanced potential to align management development with business needs (Strebler 1995; Whittaker *et al.* 1997). They possess the potential to upgrade the managerial human resource in line with the specific strategic needs of the small firm and additionally, they take into account individual manager objectives in respect of career and employability.
- Overall investment in management development for the small firm is considered fundamental, since it strengthens the development of the firm's managerial human resource into a valuable and unique resource that is difficult to imitate or substitute. This gives the small firm a potential source of internal competitive advantage.

There is some theoretical support for the proposition that the strategic direction of the small firm and its HRM orientation influences and explains the extent of investment in management development. Five theoretical contributions are relevant in the context of this chapter. Woolfe (1993) defines strategic alignment as a state in which the goals of the organisation are in harmony with its systems. These systems may include managerial processes, management development and other HRM activities. Semler (2000) proposes a model identifying eight components of alignment and he identifies training as one such variable that should be aligned with strategy. Wognum (2000) focuses specifically on three dimensions of human resource development and three levels of organisational problems. She found moderate evidence of alignment.

There is a considerable body of evidence to show that the personal preferences of owner-managers can have a strong influence on decisions about strategy, structure and HR processes (Waller *et al.* 1995). There is also a body of knowledge that suggests that the prior experience, preferences, ideologies and values of owner-manager actually influence the way they think about and perceive the environment and as a result their attempts to align strategies and HR processes to their perceptions (Weirsema and Bantel 1992). Weick (1979) makes the argument that owner-managers 'perceive' environments rather than see the totality of what is actually there. Weick (1979) calls this the enacted environment and this is the important component because it determines the way owner-managers will respond in terms of both human resource and non-human resource strategies.

Miles and Snow (1978) have developed this idea further and they specifically look at how enacted environments produce predictable patterns of strategy, structure and managerial behaviours. Their arguments are central to this chapter because one of the variables of interest is the relationship between strategic type and management development practices. They postulate four distinctive patterns of strategy-structural linkages. Owner-managers who pursue defender strategies have a relatively restricted field of products and markets. The owner-manager is concerned to secure a stable niche, focus on protecting that niche through high quality products or lower price. It is further postulated that the owner-manager will not be innovative in their HR management development processes and will concentrate on internal efficiency in order to do a quality job within a limited field. There will be a strong reliance on rules and procedures and on compliance behaviours for managers. They will most likely be low investors in management development.

Owner-managers who pursue prospector strategies are innovative and want to be the first into the marketplace. They are conscious of changes in the external environment and they read it effectively. They will make whatever changes are necessary and more likely to invest in management development if it facilitates innovation and change management. They are more likely to use project-based management development strategies, be concerned with empowerment and de-centralised decision making. It follows that they are more likely to develop lower level managers.

Owner-managers who pursue analyser strategies are concerned with having a limited product line combined with a need to innovate and copy what is already there. They are moderate on innovation and they monitor what other firms do. They will be concerned with flexibility because of the need to produce and be innovative; therefore the management development menu may be different components of the organisation. They strive to have an ambidextrous organisation.

Owner-managers who pursue a reactor strategy are inconsistent in their approach. They are unsure of their strategic direction and are seldom successful. They are unlikely to invest in management development. A significant issue emerging form the research is the notion of strategic disposition (Miles 1982). This is defined as a mindset, which the owner-manager develops about what is appropriate given the perception of the environment. This finding is of great significance because it argues that once the owner-manager makes choices it inhibits the adoption of other strategic approaches and it may also determine the extent to which other strategies are viable. This would suggest, in the context of management development, that where owner-managers do not consider it to be of value, they are unlikely to adopt it in the future without a significant change of mindset.

Two studies have investigated the relationship between Miles and Snow's (1978) strategic type typology and training and management development practices in organisations. Henderson (2001) investigated the relationship between the firm's strategic type and management development. This study highlights a number of significant findings:

- Few of the Scottish firms studied had formal management development policies or activities. They tended to implement more conventional management development approaches.
- The size of the firm was significant in explaining management development activities. The sample of firms studied was generally small to medium and they tended to adapt a conservative approach to management development.
- Strategic type (in the form of Miles and Snow's (1978) typology) was found to explain the extent and formality of management development activities.

Valle et al. (2000) found some support for the hypothesis that firms adopting a particular training and management development approach also adopted a specific generic business strategy type. They found, for example, that defender type firms adopt a more undefined training strategy, whereas both prospector and analyser type firms adopt a more systematic management development strategy. They found, however, that over time firms with either prospector, analyser or defender type strategies follow a similar type of management development strategy. In contrast, Henderson (2001) found that strategic type was significant in explaining management development strategy. Both studies have relatively restricted sample sizes, however they do identify a potential avenue for investigation utilising a sample of small firms in Ireland. The Valle et al. (2000) study had the advantage of longevity in its research design. A consistent finding from the research on management development is the need for strong top management support (Beer 1984; Yeung and Berman 1997). This variable is particularly significant in the micro and small firms where there is usually one key decision-maker. It follows that the attitudes and values espoused by the owner-manager in respect of management development will have a significant influence on whether management development takes place at all. There is a strong body of evidence to support this proposition. Hendry et al. (1991) and Jennings et al. (1996) argue that there is wide acceptance that owner-managers determine the ethos and strategic direction of the firm and the appropriateness of development. Stanworth et al. (1992) suggest that owner-manager commitment to management development is often little more than 'a motherhood' statement. Some owner-managers espouse the view that management development is an operational expense rather than an investment (Finegold and Soskice 1988) and that it is unnecessary to train beyond the immediate job. The challenge of convincing owner-managers of the benefits of management development is a difficult one due to the spread of micro and small firms (Kerr and McDougall 1999).

Research questions and methodology

The study set out to answer these research questions:

- What are the characteristics of management development strategies, policies and practices in small and micro firms in Ireland?
- What are the strategic and human resource management orientations of small and micro firms in Ireland?
- What is the relationship between the strategic orientation of small firms in Ireland, their HRM orientation, the perceptions of owner-managers of the value of management development and the nature of management development strategies, policies and practices implemented?

This study utilised survey research methodology. The population for study consisted of 250 small and micro firms derived from a list supplied by the Irish Small Firms Association. For the propose of the study, a small firm is defined as that employing fifty or fewer employees and a micro firm is defined as employing ten or fewer employees. The sample chosen was random.

The study replicated the questionnaire instrument designed by Henderson (2001). Some significant amendments were made to the wording of the questionnaire to suit the Irish context and to enable certain forms of analysis to be undertaken. The questions were formulated so that the variables were interval or ratio in nature. Owner-managers, utilising a telephone survey, responded to the questionnaire. The questionnaire consists of three sections: data on the firms' strategic type, data on the HRM orientation of the firm and data on the firms' approach to management development, including strategies, practices, policies and processes.

The variables investigated were:

- the perceived strategic orientation of the firm
- the perceived HRM orientation of the organisation
- the perceptions of the owner-managers about management development
- the nature and extent of management development within the firm.

A number of scale items were included in the questionnaire.

- *Human resource management orientation:* This scale consisted of seven items utilising Likert scales devised by Henderson (2001). The scale items measured the owner-managers' perceptions of attention to immediate/short-term personnel problems versus long-term personnel policy planning; perceptions of employees' compliance versus commitment to organisational values; the extent to which employees have scope to define jobs and work roles; the extent of individual or collective employee relationships; the extent to which day-to-day HR matters are dealt with by the owner-manager or line managers, rather than by a specialist; the relative importance of controlling employee costs versus the overall development of the firm's human resources. Henderson (2001) reported a Cronbach Alpha of 0.54. In this study it was 0.62.

- *Measures of Strategic Direction:* the study utilised a scale developed by Conant *et al.* (1990) which operationalised the Miles and Snow (1978) typology. This consists of an eleven-item scale for measuring a firm's strategic type as perceived by the owner-managers. Each item comprised four statements and the owner-manager was asked to select the statement most appropriate to his/her firm. Each statement measured one of the Miles and Snow's strategic types. It was not discernible to the respondent which one applied. The overall strategic type of the firm was established on the basis of the owner-managers' choices from the set of eleven items. The Cronbach Alpha for this study was 0.75.

- *Firm-level management development policies and practices:* A set of survey questions were used to gather owner-manager perceptions of the value of management development, evidence of specific management development practices and factual information on investment measures of management development such as number of days formal training and expenditure levels. The questions included are well supported by the management development literature and measured in addition; the firm's commitment to management development; reasons for not investing in management development; the owner-manager's perceptions of the nature of managerial work practices; the methods used to identify management development needs; the characteristics of the internal labour market of the small firm; the way in which management development is delivered and the extent of evaluation of management development activities.

The survey was conducted during the months of December 2001 to February 2002. Firms were selected by means of random numbers from a standard table and there was stratification on the basis of size. Initial contact was made with the owner-manager via telephone, to discuss the nature of the survey. A time was arranged to conduct the telephone survey.

Completed questionnaires were secured from 135 of the 250 firms contacted, giving a response rate of 54 per cent. There was a low level of item non-response because the researchers ensured that each question was completed. Owner-managers who responded to the survey were generally motivated and provided the data required. The most significant item of non-response, concerned details related to management development budgets, expenditure on management development in the previous year and expenditure on specific management development activities. The literature indicates that these details are notoriously difficult to secure with any degree of accuracy from small firm owner-managers.

Characteristics of management development in micro and small firms

Investment in management development

We divided the sample into micro firms and small firms, for the purposes of analysis; 44 per cent of micro firms and 71 per cent of small firm owner-managers indicated that their respective firms invested in management development; only 22 per cent of micro firms and 33 per cent of small firms indicated that they had a specific budget for management development. The mean budget size for micro firms was £3,000 (3,809 euro) and £5,700 (7,237 euro) for small firms. The majority of this budget, in both micro and small firms, is spent on training owner-managers and middle managers. The size of the budget allocation for management development has not changed significantly, for micro firms, from the previous year; 35 per cent of small firms indicated that it had increased over the previous year. This statistic supports the general findings that small and micro firms are significantly less likely to have a training budget for management development than is the case with larger firms. Table 14.1 summarises the main data on investment in management development by small and micro firms in Ireland. We must, however, interpret this data with some caution given that it is perhaps the most unreliable data collected during this study for the reasons explained earlier.

Extent and nature of management development practices/policies

The locus of responsibility for management development is the same for both micro and small firms. The owner-manager is the person who most frequently holds

Table 14.1 Investment in management development by micro and small firms ($N = 135$)

Dimensions of management development		Micro firms ($N = 45$)		Small firms ($N = 90$)	
		No.	*%*	*No.*	*%*
Firm invests in	Yes	20	44	65	71
management development	No	25	66	25	28
Specific budget for	Yes	10	22	34	33
management development	No	35	78	56	67
Budget size in previous	> 1,000	4	40	8	24
financial year	1,000≤5,000	6	60	6	18
	5,000≤7,500	-	-	14	40
	7,500+	-	-	6	18
% allocation of budget to	Owner-mgr	-	60	-	30
management categories	Middle mgr	-	40	-	60
	Junior mgr	-	-	-	10
Changes in budgetary	More than last				
allocation from previous	financial year	2	20	12	35
year	Same	7	70	18	53
	Less than last financial year	1	10	4	12

responsibility for management development. In smaller firms, this responsibility may also be part of another senior manager's role.

Written policies on management development are relatively rare in both micro and small firms; 31 per cent of small firms indicated that they had formal written policies whereas a very significant percentage (50 per cent of micro firms and 44 per cent of small firms) indicated that they had no formal policy at all. Another significant percentage indicated that they had an unwritten policy (50 per cent of micro firms and 25 per cent of small firms). Where a written policy does exist, the owner-manager prepares it. In small firms, other managers may have some involvement in formulating the policy. The majority of micro firms did not implement succession-planning processes for any category of manager. In small firms, succession planning is more frequently practiced for middle and junior managers. A small proportion of owner-managers plan for their own succession; they are the exception.

Perceived relationship between management development, firm objectives and strategic/business planning

Owner-managers have particular perceptions of the contribution of management development to the small firms. The general perception is that the purpose of management development is primarily to improve job performance. Small firms' owner-managers perceive that management development can contribute to profits; however, micro firms' owner-managers perceive such a link to be less strong. Micro firm owner-managers perceive that management development does not contribute to developing the firms' culture and it is not appropriate to utilise management development in this context. They do not perceive that management development can be used as a financial reward strategy or to facilitate career development and prepare managers for future firm growth. Both micro and small firm owner-managers do believe that they need to grow their own managers, rather than hire them from the external labour market. Paradoxically they do not perceive succession planning to be a significant component of the management development process.

Owner-managers do not perceive a strong link been investment in management development and the strategic planning activities of the firm. They perceive management development to be a reactive rather than proactive strategy or set of activities implemented in response to specific operational problems. The more sophisticated models of management development proposed in the literature, that it is an input to corporate strategy formulation, are not espoused by small and micro firm owner-managers. Table 14.2 summarises the main findings of the study on the extent of management development attitudes, policies and practices.

Nature of management development activities undertaken

Owner-managers and other managers within micro and small firms participate in relatively little management development; 70 per cent of micro firm owner-managers and 30 per cent of small firm owner-managers had participated in management

Table 14.2 Extent and nature of management development attitudes/policies/practices
(N = 135)

Management development policy issue	Micro firm		Small firm	
	Mean extent of responsibility		Mean extent of responsibility	
Responsibility for implementing management development				
Owner-manager	4.75		4.45	
Other member of senior team	1.25		3.45	
HR specialist	1.25		2.25	
Another manager	2.13		2.55	
Nature of policy on management development	*No.*	%	*No.*	%
Formal written policy	-	-	20	31
Policy not written but it is known and understood	5	50	16	25
No formal policy	5	50	29	44
Involvement in formulating management development policy	Mean extent of involvement		Mean extent of involvement	
Owner-manager	4.45		4.65	
HR specialist	1		2.65	
Other manager	2.15		3.15	
Perceptions of relationship between management development (MD) and firm objectives	Mean		Mean	
Purpose of MD is to improve present job performance	4.46		4.76	
Primary purpose of MD is to improve firm profit	3.15		4.65	
We need to grow our own managers	3.75		4.35	
We need to ensure that our managers have skills and knowledge for the future	1.65		3.15	
Management development ensures that firm culture is understood by employees	1.25		1.85	
Management development is part of a manager's overall financial reward	1.15		1.75	
The purpose of management development is to assist the manager's career	2.25		2.85	
Succession planning is the most important component of MD	1.25		2.65	
A managers expertise and development should always be linked	1.55		2.65	
Perception of relationship between management development and strategic/business planning in the firm	Mean		Mean	
Management development is carried out in response to specific problems rather than being pre-planned	4.25		3.95	
There is a management development programme not related to firm strategy	4.65		3.75	
The firm's management development is an input into firm strategy but is not a major influence	1.15		2.95	
Management development has a major input into corporate strategy	1		2.15	
Extent of succession planning	*No.*	%	*No.*	%
Owner-manager Yes	-	-	10	11
No	-	-	80	89
Middle manager Yes	10	22	29	32
No	35	78	61	68
Junior manager Yes	5	11	31	34
No	40	89	59	66

development activities in the previous three years. Middle and junior managers participate in significantly less management development. The mean days management development for micro firm owner-managers is 3.25 compared to 3.75 for small firm owner-managers. The nature of management development activities undertaken tend to focus on general management issues and the development of specific management competencies. Junior managers are significantly less likely to receive management development and where it is provided, it tends to focus on functional or specialist skills.

The most common mode of delivery for both micro and small firms is on the job or experiential type management development. There is limited use of customised formal in-firm management development activities; however, this mode is more likely to be used by small firms. Both micro and small firms indicated the use of external management development programmes; however, they are frequently used in small firms.

The data reveal relatively limited sophistication in the use of management development methods. Self-development/experience and mentoring/coaching processes are more frequently used in both micro and small firms. Micro firms utilise a very narrow range of management development methods, with a strong reliance on job instruction for the development of middle and junior managers. There is very limited evidence indicating the use of case studies, action learning, project-based management development activities or activities that involve teams of managers working together on a developmental experience within the firm.

The data suggest that small rather than micro firms practise identification of training needs more frequently; 60 per cent of micro firms do not undertake an assessment of management development needs. The owner-manager is the most likely individual to conduct the needs analysis and in small firms, a training or personnel specialist may undertake this activity.

Very little evaluation of management development takes place. Small firms are more likely than micro firms to evaluate management development, however 58 per cent of small firms that invest in management development make no attempt to evaluate its return. Where evaluation is conducted, it is most likely performed by the manager rather than by a specialist. Table 14.3 provides a summary of the results on the nature of management development activities undertaken by micro and small firms.

Firm strategic orientation, internal labour market and HRM characteristics

The majority of owner-managers in micro and small firms characterise the strategic orientation of their firm as either reactor or defender. These defender types concentrate on protecting a particular core model and are generally not entrepreneurial. Reactors have no specific stance on strategy. A number of small firms pursue an analyser or prospector strategy. These are more entrepreneurial in their strategic approach and are more likely to continually seek new product or market opportunities.

Owner-managers perceive flexibility, stamina and persistence, self-confidence,

Table 14.3 Nature of management development activities undertaken by micro and small firms ($N = 135$)

Management development activity			Micro firms			Small firms		
Percentage of managers who participated in management development			Mean %			Mean %		
Owner-managers			70			30		
Middle managers			20			45		
Junior managers			10			15		
Mean days management development			Mean			Mean		
Owner-managers			3.25			3.75		
Middle managers			1.75			2.15		
Junior managers			-			1.75		
Assessment of management development needs			No. %			No. %		
By individual manager			40			60		
By external agency			0			10		
By personnel/training specialist			0			35		
No assessment carried out			60			30		
Type of management development	OM	MM	JM	OM	MM	JM		
General management	2.75	1.25	-	3.15	1.75	2.15		
Human relations	-	-	-	-	-	-		
Self-awareness activities	-	-	-	-	-	-		
Managerial competencies	3.25	4.25	-	3.45	4.15	2.75		
Functional or firm specific skills	1.75	2.25	3.75	2.35	1.25	3.35		
Mode of delivery	OM	MM	JM	OM	MM	JM		
External consultant/institution	2.55	1.75	-	3.35	2.95	2.45		
Formal in-firm training	1.75	1.25	-	3.75	3.15	3.05		
On-the-job training	3.25	4.25	4.75	4.75	3.75	4.45		
Method of management development utilised	OM	MM	JM	OM	MM	JM		
Job instruction	-	3.35	3.85	-	2.75	3.15		
Case studies	-	-	-	2.15	1.65	1.25		
Action learning	-	-	-	-	-	-		
Outdoor training	-	-	-	-	2.15	-		
Self-development/experience	4.75	4.35	2.15	4.65	4.25	2.75		
Mentoring/coaching processes	3.15	3.25	2.25	4.05	2.95	3.75		
Job secondment	-	-	-	-	-	-		
Project work	-	-	-	2.65	3.15	2.15		
Distant learning programmes	-	-	-	-	1.85	1.25		
External academic courses	-	1.75	-	1.85	2.35	2.43		
Evaluation of management development			No.	%		No.	%	
Assessment by training specialist			-	-		4	6	
By owner-manager			6	30		20	31	
By line manager			-	-		10	15	
By an external agency			-	-		5	8	
Management development not evaluated			14	70		38	58	

Note
OM = owner-manager; MM = middle manager; JM = junior manager.

political skills and an ability to control people to be the most important managerial competencies necessary to be successful within the firm. Owner-managers place less emphasis on learned competencies such as the skills to develop people, analytical and problem solving skills and communication skills. These data would appear to indicate that owner-managers perceive a limited role for formalised or structured management development interventions, simply because the competencies that they consider important relate to the personal traits and characteristics of the manager.

There is relatively little sophistication in the way HRM is practised. The HRM orientation of micro and small firms is characterised in the following way: a strong attention to immediate personnel problems in preference to personnel planning, an emphasis on compliance to managerial instructions and managerial prerogative, limited use of formal job descriptions, a concern with the control of employee costs rather than the development of human resources and the delivery of personnel management through line managers. Micro firm owner-managers espouse a stronger control and cost focused HRM orientation than is the case for small firm owner-managers.

There is evidence of limited use of human resource management activities that have the potential to support management development. Performance appraisal processes for managers are virtually non-existent in micro firms and are more frequently used for junior and middle managers in small firms. Small firm owner-managers are preoccupied with the retention of staff, followed by recruitment and development of human resources. Micro firm owner-managers are concerned with retrenchment to a greater degree than small firm owner-managers.

Management positions are more likely to be filled from the internal labor pool in both micro and small firms. Small firms may also hire from outside the firm for some managerial appointments. The majority of current senior managers in the respondent firms were promoted to their current positions from within the firm.

Reasons for not investing in management development

Owner-managers reported a multiplicity of reasons for not investing in management development. Micro firms tend to report different reasons from those of small firms. Micro firm owner-managers focus on cost and time issues. The three highest ranked reasons reported: managers cannot spare the time ($M = 4.95$), the firm cannot spare the managers' time ($M = 4.75$) and the firm cannot afford it ($M = 4.35$). Small firm owner-managers also reported the lack of time as the most significant reason; however, they were less likely to report cost related issues as a primary reason for not investing in management development. Both micro and small firm owner-managers perceive that on-the-job experience is the most valuable form of management development; they also perceive that current managers are already sufficiently qualified. Table 14.4 provides a summary of the results of the strategic orientation and the internal labour market characteristics.

Table 14.4 Firm strategic orientation and internal labour market characteristics ($N = 135$)

	OM	MM	JM	OM	MM	JM
Managerial competencies	*Mean importance*			*Mean importance*		
Flexibility	4.75	4.65	4.45	4.65	3.85	3.45
Self-confidence	4.75	4.35	4.25	4.85	4.25	4.25
Political skills	4.75	2.65	2.15	4.65	3.15	3.25
Stamina/resistance	4.85	4.45	3.85	4.75	4.45	4.15
Communication skills	4.35	3.75	3.25	4.45	4.00	4.25
Ability to control other people	4.65	2.25	2.15	4.75	2.85	2.25
Efficiency	3.75	4.35	4.65	4.15	4.25	4.35
Developing other people	3.25	2.45	2.45	2.75	3.15	3.25
Analytical ability	2.75	2.95	3.15	2.95	3.45	3.65
Compliance	2.96	4.25	4.65	4.45	2.85	3.15

HRM orientation of firm			*Mean agreement*		*Mean agreement*	
Collective employee relations more important than individual manager- employee relations			1.15		1.44	
Attention to immediate personnel problems takes precedence over personnel policy planning			4.85		4.25	
Employee compliance to managerial instructions is more important than commitment to organisational values			4.95		4.25	
Shop floor/service operations are defined by management rather than employees			4.85		4.45	
Use of detailed job descriptions giving clearly defined work roles			1.25		2.35	
Day-to-day personnel matters dealt with by specialist staff rather than line managers			1.15		2.35	
Control of employee costs is more important than the development of human resources			4.45		3.15	

Strategic orientation of firm		*No.*	*%*		*No.*	*%*
Analyser		3	65		15	17
Prospector		2	55		17	18
Reactor		25	55		44	49
Defender		15	33		14	16

Use of performance appraisal for managers			*No.*	*%*			*No.*	*%*
Owner-manager	Yes		-	-	Yes		-	-
	No		45	100	No		90	100
Middle manager	Yes		2	5	Yes		22	25
	No		43	99.5	No		68	75
Junior manager	Yes		6	13	Yes		24	27
	No		39	87	No		66	13

Importance of personnel/human resource management activities	*Mean importance*	*Mean importance*
Retrenchment	2.85	2.25
Recruitment	3.75	3.95
Retention	4.14	4.35
Development	3.35	3.65

Table 14.4 Continued

Promotion/hiring practices		*No*	%		*No*	%
Management jobs filled from	Yes	26	58	Yes	67	74
internal labour pool	No	19	42	No	23	26
Firm at least as likely to hire from	Yes	14	31	Yes	41	46
outside for managerial appointments	No	31	69	No	49	54
% of senior managers promoted to current position from within company	*% Yes*			*% Yes*		
80% or more	84			63		
50% or more	10			29		
20% or more	6			8		
Less than 20%	-			-		
None	-			-		
Reasons for not investing in management development			*Mean*			*Mean*
We cannot afford it			4.35			3.15
The expense involved is not worth it			3.95			2.85
We cannot spare the managers' time			4.75			4.35
Managers cannot spare the time			4.95			4.15
Our managers are already sufficiently well qualified			3.25			3.35
We only employ sufficiently qualified managers			2.25			2.65
On-the-job experience is all our managers need			4.15			3.75
There are no suitable management development programmes			3.15			3.35
We do not know if suitable management programmes exist			4.15			3.15

Contingency factors relevant to management development

We specifically explored the impact of four factors in explaining the existence of formal and informal management development activities within micro and small firms. These factors are size; the HRM orientation of the firm; the influence of the generic business strategy of the firm and the perceptions and values of the owner-managers in relation to management development. We utilised ANOVA and predictive discriminant analysis to explore these issues. Table 14.5 presents the results of the ANOVA. We were interested in exploring significant main and interaction effects. We present the significant relationships here (i.e. $p<0.05$).

Firm size predicts the existence of formal management development, expenditure on management development, the perceptions of the owner-manager and the existence of a range of management development related HRM processes such as succession planning and performance management. The larger the small firm the more likely these dimensions of management development exist.

The HRM orientation of the firm influences four indicators: the existence of both formal and informal management development activities, the amount of managerial development activity and the performance management process. The level of significance is less than for firm size. Strategic type influences the existence of formal management development and expenditure on management development. The perceptions of owner-managers influence the existence of formal management

Table 14.5 Relationship between contingency variables and indicators of management development activity (ANOVA)

Predictor	Formal management development	Expenditure on management development	Informal management development	Succession planning	Performance management	Amount of management development activity
Firm size	$p < 0.001$	$p < 0.01$		$p < 0.01$	$p < 0.01$	$p < 0.001$
HRM orientation	$p < 0.05$		$p < 0.05$		$p < 0.05$	$p < 0.01$
Strategic type	$p < 0.01$	$p < 0.01$				$p < 0.01$
Firm size Owner-manager perceptions	$p < 0.001$	$p < 0.001$		$p < 0.05$		$p < 0.01$
Firm size HRM orientation			$p < 0.01$		$p < 0.05$	$p < 0.01$
Firm size Strategic type	$p < 0.01$	$p < 0.01$			$p < 0.01$	$p < 0.05$
Firm size owner-manager perceptions	$p < 0.001$	$p < 0.001$		$p < 0.01$		$p < 0.001$
HRM orientation Strategic type	$p < 0.01$	$p < 0.05$		$p < 0.05$	$p < 0.05$	
HRM orientation Owner-manager perceptions	$p < 0.01$	$p < 0.01$	$p < 0.05$			$p < 0.01$
Owner-manager perceptions Strategic type		$p < 0.05$		$p < 0.05$		

development, the amount of management development activity and the existence of succession planning processes.

We utilised predictive discriminant analysis to further explore the relationship between strategic type, HRM orientation and firm size and management development in the firm. This analysis revealed that strategic type was found to be a significant predictor ($p \le 0.01$). Analysis indicated that firms, classified by owner-managers, as analysers and prospectors, predicted the existence of formal management development; succession management; performance management activities and the amount of management development. Firms that were classified as defenders or reactors did not show any association. The analysis revealed that HRM orientation was a significant predictor ($p \le 0.05$) and indicated that firms that were classified as having a developmental HRM philosophy predicted the existence of formal management development, performance management and succession planning processes. The analysis revealed that firm size was a very significant predictor ($p \le 0.001$). Firm size predicted a formalised management development approach in addition to all of the other HR practices measured in the study. Based on the data derived form the study it is clear that micro firms invest significantly less in formal management development, therefore this finding is not unexpected.

The analysis of variance (ANOVA) reveals significant two-way interactions.

Firm size and perceptions of the owner-manager revealed the most significant interactions. These two factors interacting influence the existence of formal management development; expenditure on management development; succession management processes; the level of management development activity; firm size and strategic type influences. All of the factors interacted with each other to influence management development outcomes.

The status of management development in micro and small firms

Management processes, in the micro and small firm, are characterised by significant levels of adaptation, these adaptation activities include manipulating a limited pool of resources; a concern with the short term and a focus on controlling and adapting quickly to changing circumstances in the external environment. Owner-managers and other senior managers, where they exist, are presented with the challenge of developing tactics to mitigate and manage external influences and as such are often involved in the operational dimensions of the small firm. Owner-managers face a dilemma: they need to stay away from operational activities yet failure to attend to these in this context may impinge on the performance of the small firm.

These managerial characteristics and their associated dilemmas highlight the need to develop managerial competencies. Enhanced managerial competencies have the potential to improve the growth of the firm, however, many scholars and researchers highlight that limited levels of management development take place. A host of attitudinal, psychological and resource barriers inhibit the development of managerial competence, some of which are revealed in this study. There is a strong connection and intimate identification between the owner-manager and his or her business. The development of owner-managers' managerial competencies is closely linked to the development of the small business; it follows that the development of the small firm itself will almost certainly require the development of the owner-manager. There is strong support in the literature (Hendry *et al.* 1991) for the view that different stages of the life cycle of the small firm require specific competencies and behaviours of the owner-manager.

The results of this study of small and micro firms in Ireland reveal some incidences of formal management development. A significant proportion of micro firms invest very limited resources in management development and as a result, undertake very little formal management development activity. The findings reveal very limited sophistication in the use of management development strategies. The typical scenario is one where management development is likely to be informal and incidental in character and utilise a limited range of management development methods.

Where small and micro firms do invest in formal management development, a number of characteristics exist. There is an attempt to integrate management development with succession planning and performance appraisal. The HRM orientation of the firm is more likely to emphasise development and retention rather than focus on the containment of costs and the control of employees. Where management development does occur in micro firms it is more or less ad hoc in character. There is limited evidence of concern to identify management-training needs, devise learning objectives, implement systematic management development activities or evaluate the results of management development. There is little or no integration or alignment with other HRM practices such as succession management or performance management.

The study reveals a number of factors that are important in explaining the exist-ence of management development activities. Based on the data analysis, we can make a number of tentative conclusions. We are conscious, however, of the limitations of the study and the need to explore the issues studied with a larger more stratified sample of micro and small firms.

Firm size is a very significant variable in explaining management development activity (see Table 14.6). It appears to be important in explaining the existence of formal management development, the size of the budget for management develop-ment, the amount of management development activity, the utilisation of perform-ance management and the succession planning processes. Firm size interacts with HRM orientation and strategic type and most significantly with the perceptions of the owner-manager, in explaining the existence of a number of management development and related HR activities.

The data provide some support for the finding that strategic type influences the existence of management development. The least significant interaction effect is for strategic type and perceptions of the owner-manager.

Prospector and analyser firms adopt more structured and formal management development activities. This finding is in line with our proposition made earlier and would indicate that these firms use management development to enhance innova-tion and facilitate change. They are also more likely to put formal management development in place for lower level managers. Defender small firms are more likely to adopt informal management development approaches and reactor firms give little emphasis to management development. The cross-sectional nature of the study is important in interpreting this finding because it was a snapshot at one point in time. A more robust design combining elements of longitudinal analysis may reveal a different set of relationships. Research, for example, conducted by Valle *et al.* (2000) would indicate that the dimension of time is very important in explaining the strategic type management development relationship. They found that over time firms irrespective of strategic type had similar types of training and management development approaches. This suggests that the contingency approach, as advocated by Miles and Snow (1978), in respect of strategy, must be understood in a dynamic rather than a static way. The HRM orientation of the firm is significantly related to a number of management development activities. Firms that espouse a developmental rather than a cost containment HR philosophy are more likely to implement formal management development processes, in addition to the use of HR activities. The perceptions of the owner-manager interacting with firm size are particularly significant in explaining management development in the small firm.

Table 14.6 provides a summary of the key trends to emerge from the study. The findings indicate a relatively negative scenario in respect of management develop-ment in small and micro firms. Management development presents a single dimension of a complex set of factors that may have an impact on the growth of the

Table 14.6 Characteristics of small and micro firms and implications for management
development activities - summary of findings

Global characteristics of the micro/small firm	*Characteristics manifested and implications for management development*
Size of firm	*Characteristics* • Strong preoccupation with controlling costs • Emphasis on the operational realities of the firm • Very limited strategy formulation and focus on short-term results • Owner-manager will usually perform multiple roles *Implications for management development* • Owner-manager may have little time to participate in managerial development • Other managers may have little time for management development activities • Limited or scare financial resources available for managerial development • Reactive rather than proactive approaches to managerial development
Values and attitudes of owner-manager	*Characteristics* • Very personalised and informal management style • Very little focus or concern with planning for a successor • Strong focus on the present • Very limited strategic focus or big picture thinking • An unwillingness or lack of motivation to delegate work • A fear of creating a potential successor *Implications for management development* • A lower level of commitment to developing self or other managers • Narrow perceptions of the purpose of management development • Perception that management development is not related to firm strategy • Strong reliance on the view that the best development is achieved through experience
HRM orientation of the firm	*Characteristics* • A strong emphasis on individual employment relationships • A concern with operational rather than strategic HR issues • Little or no integration of HR activities • A concern with controlling employment costs rather than development of human resources • Reactive approaches to the management of human resources • Compliance is more valued than commitment to organisational values • Top-down approaches to the management of human resources • Lack of procedures or clearly defined job roles • Lack of specialist HR input *Implications for management development* • Relatively lower priority given to human resource development as an activity • Very little focus on developing junior managers

Table 14.6 Continued

Global characteristics of the micro/small firm	Characteristics manifested and implications for management development
	• Limited or no alignment of management development with other HRM strategies • Little focus on enhancing employability or career development • Little management development to build firm for future growth • Tendency to use management development as a strategy to deal with individual deficiencies
Strategic orientation of the firm	*Characteristics* • Limited or no strategic planning • Too much focus on short-term results • Strong defender or reactor strategy orientation • Limited focus on prospector or analyser strategic directions • Strategy formulation rests with the owner-manager • Owner-manager may lack a strategic orientation *Implications for management development* • Lack of perceptual link between strategic focus and role of management development • Management development activities reflect the dominant reactive strategic orientation of the firm • Lack of value attached to management tool as a mechanism to achieve firm strategies • Limited understanding of the role of human resources in achieving competitive advantage.

small firm. It is however, as revealed in this study, not generally perceived to be important by owner-managers. There would appear to be a low acceptance by owner-managers of management development initiatives and the related idea that the enhancement of managerial human capital is of importance to the overall growth of the firm. This suggests a need to develop a culture of learning within small and micro firms, where management development is espoused by owner-managers to be of value to the firm for growth purposes.

Delivery of management development

The study findings raise the question: what management development strategies are most effective and are guaranteed to get the involvement and participation of owner-managers and other managers in management development? This is a complex question because the study findings indicate that; there is an intimate and close relationship between the owner-manager and the small firm and owner-managers adopt pragmatic and action-oriented approaches to their development. They are likely to have negative or neutral attitudes in respect of management development. They are unlikely to have an interest in management development programmes that do not reflect firm concerns and are unrealistic given the context within which the firm operates. The literature and professional practice highlights a number of strategies that may be appropriate. We consider two dimensions of the strategies here; the extent to which they are individualised or group oriented and whether they focus on general or sector specific competencies. Figure 14.1 presents a menu of options.

We will comment on a number of these strategies in the light of the research findings discussed in this chapter.

Individual owner-manager targeted management development strategies

The research evidence indicates that individual owner-manager strategies represent the standard response and usually consists of short programmes focused on creating awareness, attitude change and addressing cognitive-type learning objectives. They are usually held external to the small firm and focus on opportunities for owner-managers to exchange experiences and develop general management and specific functional competencies. They may be offered at a convenient time for owner-managers. These programmes usually adopt a practical focus and are application-oriented rather than theoretical. The research evidence indicates that they are usually prescriptive and deal with contrived rather than real-life problems. The content and delivery modes may not be flexible and adaptable to the specific needs of the owner-managers. The evidence reveals that owner-managers may have little time to participate on such programmes.

Combined training and consultancy

This type of strategy is more firm specific but yet individualised in that it addresses the needs of the individual owner-manager. The mode usually involves some combination of short training sessions in conjunction with work related activities

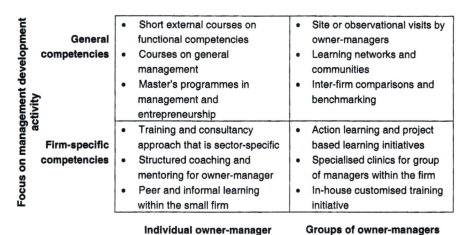

		Individual owner-manager	Groups of owner-managers
Focus on management development activity	**General competencies**	• Short external courses on functional competencies • Courses on general management • Master's programmes in management and entrepreneurship	• Site or observational visits by owner-managers • Learning networks and communities • Inter-firm comparisons and benchmarking
	Firm-specific competencies	• Training and consultancy approach that is sector-specific • Structured coaching and mentoring for owner-manager • Peer and informal learning within the small firm	• Action learning and project based learning initiatives • Specialised clinics for group of managers within the firm • In-house customised training initiative

Target of management development strategy

Figure 14.1 A typology of management development strategies for small and micro firms.

that are undertaken by the owner-manager, under the guidance of a consultant. This cycle may be repeated on several occasions and attempts to address the specific needs of the firm. It is usually a more long-term strategy.

Mentoring and coaching processes

This is a firm-specific strategy and focuses on the provision of mentoring and coaching processes for owner-managers. This strategy is generally directed to the specific needs of the owner-manager and the mentor or coach will usually be external to the small firm. The results of this study reveal some use of mentoring or coaching processes and they represent an appropriate option to deal with the time constraints and the negative perceptions by owner-managers of the value of management development.

Team-oriented management development strategies

The literature provides some support for the view that owner-managers may value interaction with peers, clients, customers and suppliers. Management development interventions that focus on bringing owner-managers in similar firms together are potentially effective where they share a common problem and where there is sufficient motivation to work together. It requires that owner-managers have a high level of confidence in the process and be willing to share experiences. Examples of team-based interventions include site visits and focus on inter-firm comparisons and benchmarking activities. It may also consist of business clinics for groups of owner-managers.

Action learning strategies

This management development strategy focuses on real-life problem-solving within a specific firm. It may not be a viable option for micro firms where there is a limited pool of managers to work as an action learning team. Managers are required to work on solving real problems that are unique to the specific firm. This strategy focuses on problem identification and on the implementation of actions to address the problem. The action learning strategy is more appropriate in the relatively larger small firm, where a pool of managers who have an interest in the problem exists and they are concerned that the problem is solved. It has the potential to change perceptions of the value of management development.

Learning networks and communities

Learning networks and communities are defined as strategies where the owner-manager learns through interaction with a range of network contacts. Based on the experience, information gathered, feedback and results derived from these interactions, the owner-manager can make changes to the operational and strategic activities of the firm. This strategy does potentially provide owner-managers, in similar or related businesses, with opportunities to learn from each other, provided that there is sufficient trust and confidence to participate in and sustain the learning network or community.

Conclusions

The study findings do provide support for the external or contingency approach to management development. The study found support for four factors operating individually, or in interaction, that have a significant impact on management development in the micro and small firm. Firm size and the perceptions of the owner-manager appear to be most significant, both individually and in interaction with each other. The finding raises important implications for the selection of management development strategies and highlights the need to raise awareness among owner-managers of the importance of developing their human capital as owner-managers and also of the need to develop other managers within the firm. However, we are conscious of the problem of mind-sets and how these may lock the owner-manager into a particular way of thinking about the value of management development. If they have negative mindsets it will be difficult to convince them of the value of management development and to use management development strategies within the micro and small firm to achieve strategic goals.

The study reveals evidence of limited formal management development in micro firms. This lack of investment in management development in micro firms is attributable to a number of very practical reasons; the inability to afford management development; the difficulty in allowing managers to participate in management development activities due to time constraints; the perception that on-the-job or informal and accidental management development is sufficient and a lack of knowledge about the existence of management development resources. This set of findings suggests that a particular set of interventions may be necessary to address the problems of the micro firm. They appear to be at a significantly earlier stage of the management development life cycle. Management development in small firms is fragmented, discontinuous and where it is provided, it is problem focused. Small firms are more likely to have more formalised management development activities.

A particular feature of the study findings is the reliance on more traditional development strategies. These management development strategies have the following characteristics; they focus on individual owner-managers; they are isolated and contrived learning events; they emphasise hypothetical rather than real problems; they emphasise generic rather than sector-specific competencies and there is limited emphasis on networking or team learning type strategies. The paradox, however, is that they represent the types of management development activities that owner-managers and other managers within the small firm find difficult to attend. Policy-makers and those institutions charged with responsibility for encouraging the growth of micro and small firms need to examine more creative ways of increasing awareness and developing positive attitudes among owner-managers of the value of management development. They also need to facilitate the design of learning events that are firm specific, real life and foster a culture of teamwork and learning within the firm. Action learning interventions and team mentoring and coaching processes present some potential in this respect.

Management development in the micro and small firm must be considered in the context of both the overall HRM philosophy or orientation of the firm and the types of HRM strategies that are implemented to support management development. The study findings indicate that the majority of micro and small firms pursue an individualised employment relationship combined with a focus on cost control, ad-hoc or low proceduralisation, a focus on the short term and a strong focus on compliance. These characteristics are not conducive to the practice of management development. There is limited evidence of both succession planning and performance management. This finding indicates that a fundamental antecedent to management development is the requirement to pursue a different type of HRM philosophy. This suggests that the degree of attitude change required of owner-managers is much deeper; they need to focus on the very assumptions they make about the nature of human resources, how human resources should be managed and the types of cultural conditions in which well developed human resources can flourish.

Bibliography

Beer, M. (1984) *Managing Human Assets*, New York: Free Press.

Blackburn, R. and Hankinson, A. (1989) 'Training in the smaller business: industrial and commercial training', 21, 2: 27- 9.

Conant, J. S., Mokwa, M. P. and Varadarajan, P. R. (1990) 'Strategic types, distinctive marketing competencies and organizational performance: a multiple measures-based study', *Strategic Management Journal*, 11, 5: 365- 83.

Cromie, S., Stephenson, B. and Monteith, D. (1995) 'The management of family firms: an empirical investigation', *International Small Business Journal*, 13: 11- 34.

Dolan, S. L. and Schuler, R. S. (1994) *Human Resource Management: The Canadian dynamic*, Scarborough, Ont: Nelson Canada.

Finegold, D. and Soskice, D. (1988) 'The failure of training in Britain: analysis and prescription', *Review of Economic Policy*, 4, 3: 21- 53.

Fox, R. (1996) 'Company training in Ireland', *Labour Market Review*, 5, 2: 26- 48.

Grant, R. M. (1996) 'Towards a knowledge-based theory of the firm', *Strategic Management Journal*, 17 (special issue): 107- 22.

Henderson, I. (2001) 'Strategic type HRM and management development in Scottish firms', in J. N. Streumer (ed.) *Perspectives on Learning at the Workplace*, Proceedings of 2nd Conference on HRD Research and Practice across Europe, University of Twente, Enschede, The Netherlands, January.

Hendry, C., Jones, A., Arthur, M. and Pettigrew, A. (1991) *Human Resource Development in Small to Medium Sized Enterprises*, Employment Department Research Paper 88, Sheffield: Employment Department.

Hill, R. and Stewart, J. (2000) 'Human resource development in small organisations', *Journal of European Industrial Training*, 24, 2/3/4: 105- 17.

Hitchens, D. and O'Farrell, P. (1988) 'Comparative performance of small manufacturing firms located in the Mid West and Northern Ireland', *Economic and Social Review*, 19, 3: 177- 98.

Hitchens, D. and O'Farrell, P. (1990) 'Comparative performance of small manufacturing firms located in the Mid West and East region of Ireland', *Irish Business and Administration Research*, 11: 24- 39.

Huselid, M. A. (1995) 'The impact of human resource management practices on turnover, productivity and corporate financial performance', *Academy of Management Journal*, 38: 635- 72.

Jennings, P. and Beaver, G. (1997) 'The performance and competitive advantage of small firms: a management perspective', *International Small Business Journal*, 15, 2: 63- 76.

Jennings, P., Banfield, P. and Beaver, G. (1996) 'Human resource development in small firms: a competency base approach', *Strategic Change*, 5: 89- 105.

Kerr, A. and McDougall, M. (1999) 'The small business of developing people', *International Small Business Journal*, 17, 2: 65- 75.

Loan-Clarke, J., Boocock, G., Smith, A. and Whittaker, J. (1999) 'Investment in management training and development by small businesses', *Employee Relations*, 21, 3: 296- 310.

Markides, C. C. and Williamson, P. J. (1996) 'Corporate diversification and organisational structure: a resource-based view', *Academy of Management Journal*, 39, 2: 340- 67.

Marshall, J. N., Alderman, N., Wong, C. and Thwaites, A. (1995) 'The impact of management training and development on small and medium sized enterprises', *International Small Business Journal*, 13, 4: 73- 90.

Martin, C., Beaumont, P. and Staines, H. (1998) 'Determinants of early and late adoption of management development practices: evidence from Scotland', *International Journal of Organisational Analysis*, 6, 2: 132- 45.

Merkx, S. (1995) 'Developing managing directors', *Management Development Review*, 8, 3: 13- 19.

Miles, R. E. (1982) *Coffin Nails and Corporate Strategies*, Englewood Cliffs, NJ: Prentice Hall.

Miles, R. E. and Snow, C. C. (1978) *Organizational Strategy, Structure and Process*, New York: McGraw-Hill.

Murphy, T. and Young, J. (1995) 'Management development and small business: exploring emergent issues', *Management Learning*, 26, 3: 319- 30.

O'Farrell, P. and Hitchens, D. (1989) *Small Firm Competitiveness and Performance*, Dublin: Gill and MacMillan.

Pennings, J. M., Lee, K. and Van Witteloostuijn, A. (1998) 'Human capital, social capital and firm dissolution', *Academy of Management Journal*, 41, 4: 425- 40.

Robins, J. and Weirsema, M. F. (1995) 'A resource-based approach to a multi-business firm: empirical analysis of portfolio interrelationships and corporate financial performance', *Strategic Management Journal*, 16, 277- 99.

Sadler-Smith, E., Sergeant A. and Dawson, A. (1998) 'Higher level skills training and SMEs', *International Small Business Journal*, 16, 2: 84- 94.

Semler, S. W. (2000) 'Exploring alignment: a comparative case study of alignment in two organisations', paper presented at the Annual Conference of the Academy of Human Resource Development, Raleigh-Durham, NC.

Shutt, J. and Whittington, R. (1987) 'Fragmentation strategies and the rise of small units: cases from North West', *Regional Studies*, 21: 13- 23.

Smith, A. and Whittaker, J. (1998) 'Management development in SMEs: what needs to be done?', *Journal of Small Business and Enterprise Development*, 5, 2: 176- 85.

Spender, J. C. (1996) 'Making knowledge the basis of a dynamic theory of the firm', *Strategic Management Journal*, 17 (special issue): 45- 62.

Stanworth, J., Purdy, D. and Kirby, D. (1992) *The Management of Success in 'Growth Corridors' Small Firms*, Small Business Research Trust, Milton Keynes: The Open University.

Strebler, M. (1995) 'Developing a competency based management development programme', *Management Development Review*, 8, 3: 32- 5.

Tansey, P. (1998) *Ireland at Work – Economic Growth and the Labour Market 1987 – 1997*, Dublin: Oak Tree Press.

Tansey, Webster, Stewart and Company (2001) 'Developing a model for SME training in Ireland: Irish and international SME training compared', prepared for the Skillnets Project, Dublin, Ireland.

Tung-Chun, H. (2001) 'The relation of training practices and organisational performance in small and medium sized companies', *Education + Training*, 43, 8/9: 437- 44.

Valle, R., Martin, F., Romero, P. M. and Dolan, S. L. (2000) 'Business strategy, work processes and human resource training: are they congruent?', *Journal of Organisational Behavior*, 21: 283- 97.

Vickerstaffe, S. and Parker, K. (1995) 'Helping small firms: the contribution of TECs and LECs', *International Small Business Journal*, 13, 4: 56- 72.

Waller, M. J., Huber, G. P. and Glick, W. H. (1995) 'Functional background as a determinant of executives' selective perceptions', *Academy of Management Journal*, 38, 4: 943- 74.

Weick, K. (1979) *The Social Psychology of Organising*, 2nd edn, Reading, MA: Addison-Wesley.

Weirsema, M. F. and Bantel, A. (1992) 'Top management team demography and corporate strategic change', *Academy of Management Journal*, 35, 1: 91- 121.

Westhead, P. and Storey, D. (1996) 'Management training and small firm performance: why is the link so weak?', *International Small Business Journal*, 14, 4: 13- 24.

Whittaker, J., Smith, A., Boocock, G. and Loan-Clarke, J. (1997) 'Management NVQWs and small and medium sized enterprises', project report for MCI and DfEE, March.

Wognum, A. M. (2000) 'Vertical integration of HRD policy within companies', paper presented at the Annual Conference of the Academy of Human Resource Development, Raleigh-Durham, NC.

Woolfe, R. (1993) 'The path to strategic alignment information strategy', *The Executive's Journal*, 9, 2: 12- 23.

Wynarczyk, P., Watson, R., Storey, D., Short, H. and Keasey, K. (1993) *Managerial Labour Markets in Small and Medium Sized Enterprises*, London: Routledge.

Yeung, A. K. and Berman, B. (1997) 'Adding value through human resources: re-orienting human resource measurement to drive business performance', *Human Resource Management*, 36, 3: 321- 35.

Index